PRECEDENCE

Social Differentiation in the Austronesian World

PRECEDENCE

Social Differentiation in the Austronesian World

edited by MICHAEL P. VISCHER

ANU

THE AUSTRALIAN NATIONAL UNIVERSITY

E PRESS

ANU E PRESS

Published by ANU E Press
The Australian National University
Canberra ACT 0200, Australia
Email: anuepress@anu.edu.au
This title is also available online at: http://epress.anu.edu.au/precedence_citation.html

National Library of Australia
Cataloguing-in-Publication entry

Title:	Precedence : social differentiation in the Austronesian world / editor: Michael P. Vischer.
ISBN:	9781921536465 (pbk.) 9781921536472 (pdf)
Series:	Comparative Austronesian series.
Notes:	Bibliography.
Subjects:	Differentiation (Sociology)
	Social control.
	Social structure.
	Precedence.
Other Authors/Contributors:	
	Vischer, Michael P.
Dewey Number:	303.33

Cover design by ANU E Press

Table of Contents

Acknowledgements

This volume has gone through a long gestation. Many of the papers in the final version of this volume were originally presented at a conference on Precedence held in Leiden, in 1996. That conference was sponsored by the International Institute for Asian Studies (IIAS) in Leiden and was organized by Dr Michael Vischer during his period as Research Fellow. Appropriate thanks are due to Professor Wim Stokhof, the then Director of IIAS, and to his staff Drs Ilse Laarschuit, Mrs Kitty Yant, and particularly Drs Marijke ter Booij for their help in organizing the conference.

Initial paper editing was done in Canberra by the late Mrs Norma Chin, who unexpectedly passed away in 1999. Those who had the opportunity to work with Norma Chin appreciated her dedication and meticulous work as an exceptional collaborator. Mrs Ria van de Zandt, formerly of the Department of Anthropology in the Research School of Pacific and Asian Studies, thereafter took up work on the volume. She and Dr Barbara Holloway edited the first set of papers and as more papers were added and earlier papers revised and updated, Ria van de Zandt carried on this work to the completion of the volume. Her task has been a formidable one and her efforts are enormously appreciated.

Ms Fatima Basic of the Cartography Unit of the School of Anthropology, Geography and Environmental Studies at the University of Melbourne prepared a number of figures and maps contained in this volume; these were corrected and finalized by Karina Pelling and Miska Talent of the Cartography Unit in the Research School of Pacific and Asian Studies at The Australian National University. Special thanks should go to Duncan Beard of the ANU E Press who has skillfully carried this volume through to publication.

The cloth on the cover of this volume is a *nae romo* cloth from the island of Palu'é; the photograph shows the brother and sister pair, Sundu and Mia Poké, with offerings made during the performance of the sacrificing cycle of the domain of Ko'a on Palu'é in 1994. These ceremonies are discussed in the paper by Michael Vischer in this volume which is intended to be read as a companion text to the film: "Contestations: Dynamics of Precedence in an Eastern Indonesian Domain" (edited by Patsy Asch, co-produced by The Australian National University and The International Institute for Asian Studies, Leiden).

1. Precedence in perspective

James J. Fox

The use of precedence in Austronesian ethnography

The concept of precedence defines a relative relationship. It is significant not in its focus on this single relationship but rather in the possibility it offers for a concatenation of relationships, thus producing an 'order of precedence' in which relations are recursively arrayed asymmetrically one to another. As such, precedence involves the conjunction of two analytic categories: recursive complementarity and categorical asymmetry (Fox 1994). A complementary category consisting of two elements – one of which is considered as 'anterior' or 'superior' to the other, such 'elder' > 'younger', 'first-born' > 'last-born' or 'trunk' > 'tip' – is applied in recursive, or repeated fashion, to produce an ordered series. This series is an 'order of precedence'.

Importantly, an 'order of precedence' can operate at various levels, differentiating relations within families, within larger social groups or throughout an entire society. The bases for the construction of precedence at different social levels may vary and, significantly, may be contested, reversed and reordered. This volume is taken up with the discussion of all of these possibilities. Each of the papers that comprise this volume explores the concept of precedence in the analysis of particular Austronesian-speaking societies.

The notion of precedence is hardly new to anthropology, particularly in the study of the Austronesians of the Pacific Islands. In *Kings and Councillors*, for example, A. M. Hocart refers to an 'order of precedence' in his discussion of the foundations of social differentiation (1970: 37). [1] Similarly, Irving Goldman, in his examination of contending principles of status in his study, *Ancient Polynesian Society*, argues that aristocratic rank rested upon 'a base of orderly precedence' but 'alternations in orders of precedence' were subject to 'changing estimations of chiefly power' and 'changing balances of power among contending parties' (1970:16). Marshall Sahlins in his *Social Stratification in Polynesia*, adopts a more specific focus in his use of the notion of precedence. He distinguishes two types of social organization in the Pacific: the one a 'ramified' and the other a 'descent-line' system. Although precedence, as discussed in the volume, might equally be applied to both types of organization, Sahlins associates precedence with status differentiation in 'descent-line' systems. Thus he writes that titles in such systems 'are arranged in a traditional order of precedence symbolized by seating position in administrative councils (*fonos*) and in the order of kava serving at the meetings of such bodies and other ceremonial occasions' (1958: 194). The societies he is referring to in this context are Futuna, Uvea and Samoa and his discussion reflects the use of precedence in the ethnographies he relies upon. For example, Sahlins quotes Edwin Burrows' comment on high title figures on Uvea: 'The order of precedence among Ministers governs seniority among lineages, rather than being governed by it' (1958: 191). To cite yet another pertinent example from the Pacific, Francis Grimble in his study of the Gilbert Islands, *Tungaru Traditions* edited by H.E. Maude, devotes an entire chapter, 'Precedence and Privileges of the Clans in the Maneaba' (1989 219-230), to an examination of the subtle distinctions, particularly ceremonial, that differentiate other clans in relation to the preeminent clan, *Karonga n Uea*. [2]

Similarly, Derek Freeman, in his London School of Economics thesis, *The Social Structure of a Samoan Village Community* — originally submitted in 1948 but only published posthumously in 2006 — makes a thoroughgoing use of the precedence in its social analysis of Samoan status. Although unavailable to Sahlins in his study and equally unknown, until its publication, to those involved in the Comparative Austronesian Project, Freeman provides a detailed examination of genealogies and lineage relations within a single village, that of Sa'anapu on the southern coast of the Samoan island of Upolu. In an attempt to provide a comprehensive understanding of titles and status in the village, he focuses considerable attention on relations within Sa'anapu's formal assembly *(fono)*: its strict seating pattern, the differentiation of rights among different title holders *(matai)* and the expression of honorifics *(fa'alupega)* required at all such gatherings. [3] It is to these relations he applies the concept of precedence: 'All of the *fa'alupega* of a village community are arranged in a strict order of precedence corresponding exactly to the seating order of its *fono* … For example, when a lineage *matai* enters the village *fono* all conversation is broken off until he takes his appointed place. As soon as he is seated, all the other *matai* present chant his *fa'alupega* in unison. It then falls to the newcomer to reciprocate this courtesy by reciting, in strict order of precedence, the *fa'alupega* of all the lineages (other than his own) represented at the *fono*' (2006:91).

Although certainly wide-spread in the study of Pacific ethnography, the use of the notion of precedence has not been confined to this region of the Austronesian world. Among Canberra-based anthropologists, precedence has been the subject of continuing discussion, especially in relation to Austronesian conceptions of origin (see Fox 1988, 1994, 1995). E. Douglas Lewis, first in his thesis, *Tana Wai Brama* (1983) and then in the publication of *People of the Source: The Social and Ceremonial Order of Tana Wai Brama on Flores* (1988), was the first to apply the concept of precedence in a systematic fashion to a specific ethnographic community, the Ata Tana Ai of central east Flores. Lewis used precedence to trace relations from clan, Ipir, as the 'source' of the domain of Wai Brama to other clans as well as to trace the ordering of houses within the clans of their founding mothers. Both usages of precedence were marshalled to explicate the Tana Ai idea of *oda* as 'sequence'.

Following on Lewis' initial study, a succession of doctoral theses produced in the Research School of Pacific and Asian Studies in Canberra resulted in a series of publications, all of which utilized the concept of precedence in the analysis of a specific society in eastern Indonesia. In an order based on the date of their submission as theses rather than eventual publication date, these studies include: 1) Andrew McWilliam, *Paths of Origin, Gates of Life: A Study of Place and Precedence in Southwest Timor* (2002), 2) Andrea Molnar, *Grandchildren of the Ga'e Ancestors: Social Organization and Cosmology among the Hoga Sara of Flores* (2000), 3) Tom Therik, *Wehali, The Female Land: Traditions of a Timorese Ritual Centre* (2004), 4) Thomas Reuter, *Custodians of the Sacred Mountains: Culture and Society in the Highlands of Bali* (2002a) and *The House of our Ancestors: Precedence and Dualism in the Highlands of Bali* (2002b), and 5) Philipus Tule, *Longing for the House of God, Dwelling in the House of the Ancestors: Local Belief, Christianity and Islam among the Kéo of Central Flores* (2004). A number of theses that make use of the concept of precedence still remain to be published. [4] Their authors have, however, written valuable papers, for the most part in various volumes of the Comparative Austronesian Project, that provide a clear idea of the direction of their research: Penelope Graham (1996), Michael Vischer (1996), Barbara Grimes (1996, 1997), Christine Boulan-Smit (2006) Minako Sakai (1997) and Philip Winn (2006). Others have also written on the use of precedence: Reuter has used precedence in a comparative analysis of various societies in Sumatra (1993); Lewis has compared precedence in the neighbouring societies of Tana 'Ai and Sikka (1996); while Fox has examined patterns of precedence in a number of societies of the Timor area and Flores (1996) and also specifically in relation to settlement formation among the Atoni Pah Meto of West Timor (1999). More recently, anthropologists have made use of the concepts of origin and precedence in the analysis of Austronesian societies elsewhere: Michael Scott in relation to the Arosi in the Solomon Islands (2007, 2008) and Harri Siikala in relation to Samoa and other Polynesian societies (2008).

Papers in this volume

The papers in this volume contribute to this widening discussion of precedence, both extending its scope and deepening the examination of specific aspects of it. This is the first volume of its kind to focus entirely on precedence and to provide an ethnographic articulation of an array of its uses among societies, many of which are closely related to one another. The comparative value of these papers is thus particularly pertinent.

Each of the 10 papers that comprise this volume offers a distinctive approach to its examination of precedence. Yet the papers relate closely to one another and are able to provide a variety of comparative reflections. The briefest of summaries gives some idea of the variety of these papers as well as their comparative significance.

The first paper by Reuter deals with one of the most complex social articulations of precedence in Indonesia, that of the Bali Aga or 'Mountain Balinese'. Reuter provides a masterful examination of the Austronesian categorical bases by which these Hindu Balinese construct inter-village and intra-council relations within a ritual domain (*banua*) centred on temples, some of which are among the most ancient on Bali. The spatial organization for the expression of precedence in the seating of the 'council of elders' in a Bali Aga village offers immediate comparisons with similar seating arrangements elsewhere in the Austronesian-speaking world, such as those in a Samoan *fono*.

Greg Acciaioli's paper shifts focus to South Sulawesi. Like many of the papers in the volume — those by Reuter, Lewis, Forth, Smedal and Kaartineen — Acciaioli's concern is to distinguish between hierarchy and precedence. His starting point is Dumont's notion of hierarchy but he carries forward from this starting point to examine different articulations of precedence. He focuses in particular on systems of 'apical demotion' or 'sinking status,' all of which involve the loss of status in the process of separation from a prestigious point of origin. Such systems place their emphasis on differentiation from a source rather than integration with that source. Geertz has convincingly described such a system for lowland Bali (1980); Fox, in his paper, describes a similar system for Termanu on the island of Rote; and, a similar dynamic underlies Sahlin's classification (1958) of so-called 'ramage' systems, such as on Tonga and Samoa in the Pacific (see H. Siikala 2008). The societies of South Sulawesi combine similar processes of status dilution based on an idiom of the loss of 'white blood' that has produced a complex intermeshing of status resulting from intermarriage among status levels.

The paper by Fox is concerned with precedence as a form of discourse and in particular with some of the more common categories, such as elder/younger or first-born/last-born, used by Austronesian-speakers to establish precedence distinctions. It is also concerned with the possibilities of categorical reversal as, for example, when the younger or last-born replaces the elder or first-born in a line of succession or when precedence by origin is overturned by the installation of the 'outsider' or 'stranger-king' (see Fox 2008). The focus in this case is the domain of Termanu on the island of Rote for which there exists a rich oral history that is intended to explain, even as it bolsters, precedence among clans.

Andrew McWilliam's paper continues the discussion of precedence as discourse, focusing on the use of the botanic idiom of 'trunk' and 'tip' in West Timor. The metaphor of the tree, in its many guises, is probably the most wide-spread source of imagery for conceptualizing the dynamics of growth, development, continuity and differentiation in Austronesian-speaking societies. McWilliam describes marriage relations among the Atoni Pah Meto as the 'tree of alliance' that provides a host of rich metaphors in which wife-givers are 'trunk fathers', the bride is 'the flower of the trunk' and groom is the 'twig' of another 'tree of origin'.

Each of the next four papers in this volume examines precedence in different social settings on the island of Flores. The first two papers — E. Douglas Lewis's comparison of the domains of Tana Wai Brama and Sikka and David Butterworth's examination of the Krowé region — deal with distinct social formations within a single language area — an area that Lewis, in his paper, calls an 'ethnological laboratory in miniature'.

This region of Flores is in fact named Sikka after the village (*Sikka Natar*) on the south coast that provided the ruling house of the colonial period. As such, the Rajadom of Sikka was a polity of places (*tana*). Each of its incorporated domains — large and small — acknowledged the authority and pre-eminence of the Raja of Sikka. As Lewis convincingly shows by reference to the histories of Sikka, the involvement of the Portuguese and then the Dutch transformed this arrangement, which was based on a form of precedence, into a hierarchy of social classes. This hierarchy had the House of the Raja at its pinnacle, a separate noble class that, in Dutch times, was assigned positions of rule in different areas, a large commoner class that embraced most of the population and an indentured class whose origins had been obliterated.

By contrast, Tana Wai Brama is a ceremonially ordered aggregation of five major clans, one among the many *tana* that comprise the Sikka region. As Lewis has shown (1988), its ritual dynamics are based on precedence among houses as well as precedence among its constituent clans. Butterworth's analysis is critical here. As he clearly notes, the 'structure of precedence of clans only operates within domains, not between domains'. Butterworth groups all the various local Krowé idioms into three analytic groups: first//subsequent, genitor//progeny and source//product and shows how they are used differentially in social life but come together in Krowé cosmology.

As in the case of Tana Wai Brama, precedence among the Krowé involves a profound cosmological conception in which the deity is the initial source and genitor of life. The clan acknowledged to have settled first in an area provides the *tana pu'an* or 'source of the domain' who must maintain the special link to the deity. This points to the radical political reordering achieved by the rulers of Sikka. Their precedence was not based on having arrived 'first'. Rather their histories insist, as Lewis explains, that they came on the 'second ship'. Hence the basis of Sikkanese rulers' claims to pre-eminence are those of a 'stranger-king' or, possibly more appropriately, those who mediated between the outside and the inside.

Like Lewis in his discussion of Sikka, Gregory Forth in his paper on Keo and Olaf Smedal in his paper on the Ngadha are both concerned with questions of the relationship between precedence and hierarchy. Both papers are focused on a region of central Flores, whose languages show linkages to one another (Fox 1998).

In his exquisitely detailed historical analysis of the structuring of a dual Keo village, Forth relies on analytic categories similar to those used by Butterworth. In the Keo case, these specific categories are 1) trunk/tip, 2) elder/younger and 3) mother/child. Although the mother/child category set have a temporal dimension, Forth views this particular binary set as constituting a 'whole/part' relationship. As such, he defines them as hierarchical 'wherein a greater part subsumes a lesser'. Thus he is able to argue that 'hierarchy and precedence, rather than denoting distinct or theoretically contrary principles of order, can define different aspects of one and the same order'.

Smedal's paper is both wide-ranging and salient. His ethnographic analysis focuses on the houses in Ngadha as 'simultaneously dwellings, corporate estates, ancestral abodes, ritual centres and repositories of heirloom sacra'. These Ngadha houses, including the land and persons they subsume, are classified in spatial terms as belonging to either a 'trunk side' or a 'tip side' and each house 'relates to any other of its side in an order of precedence'. Smedal goes on to consider the notion of values in relation to Ngadha nobles and what he calls the 'reproduction of ranked persons'. He also makes the relevant observation that contesting precedence does not represent a challenge to the system *per se* but is rather a competition among individuals or groups over the interpretation of particularities within it.

Kaartinen's paper encapsulates critical themes discussed throughout the volume. He is concerned with the idea 'localized origin' and, how in Kei society, various discourses are articulated on the basis of particular narratives of origin known as *tum*. He focuses much of his discussion on the relations between those who claim immigrant origins and those who maintain local or autochthonous origins. He also points to the ways that the concepts of precedence, on the one hand, and hierarchy, on the other hand, in the sense defined by Barraud in her own research on Kei (1990) resemble each other. 'Both involve asymmetric and complementary symbolic oppositions which are applied to social and cosmic relationships.' Barraud's understanding of hierarchy, however, implies a classification that embraces the whole of society, whereas precedence does not 'presuppose the existence of society as a whole' that focuses on metaphoric expressions that suggest processes of coming into existence.

Underpinning Kaartinen's analysis is a feature, both demographic and cultural, of all of the societies considered in this volume – one that is perhaps a feature of most Austronesian societies – namely the past historical mobility of populations. The Austronesians were and continue to be predominately mobile and their construction of society reflects a culture of mobility. Thus conceptions of the past, at whatever level they are enunciated, recount the movement and involvement of different ancestors and ancestral groups, resulting in narratives of multiple origins and the amalgamation of these groups in shaping present societies.

The final paper in this volume by Michael Vischer examines the use of precedence by means of an event-based analysis of the opening phase of a ceremonial cycle of sacrifices in one domain, Ko'a, on the tiny island of Palué off the north coast of Flores. The paper provides the setting for these ceremonial events and follows in meticulous detail the actions of its various participants in the negotiations and contestations over the performance of the ritual. The whole of this careful analysis is accompanied by a film, attached for viewing as part of this volume. Based on many years of research on Palué, Vischer's approach is altogether remarkable in its scope and, in many ways, unique in its perspicacious background understanding of the key actors involved in the ritual. The paper provides another distinctive presentation of the way in which the concept of precedence can be marshalled for social analysis.

Unlike some of the previous volumes in the Comparative Austronesian series that generally included a selection of papers from across a range of societies in different regions of the Austronesian-speaking world, this collection of papers focuses on one particularly diverse region – that of eastern Indonesia. It is hoped that a demonstration of the value of the use of the concept of precedence within this region will prompt a wider consideration of its use in other regions and in other contexts.

Bibliography

Barraud, Cécile

1990 'Wife-givers as ancestors and ultimate values in the Kei Islands' in *Bijdragen tot de Taal-, Land en Volkenkunde* 190 (2-3): 193-225.

Boulan-Smit, Christine

2006 'Traditional Territorial Categories and Constituent Institutions in West Seram: The Nili Ela of 'WELE Telu Batai and the Alune Hena of Ma'saman Uwei' in in Reuter, Thomas (ed), *Sharing the Earth, Dividing the Land: Land and Territory in the Austronesian World*, pp. 157-177. Canberra: ANU E Press.

Dumont, Louis

1980 *Homo Hierarchicus: the Caste System and Its Implications*. Chicago: University of Chicago Press.

Fox, James J.

'Origin, Descent and Precedence in the Study of Austronesian Societies'. Public Lecture in connection with De Wisselleerstoel Indonesische Studien given on the 17th of March 1988. Leiden University.

1994 'Reflections on "Hierarchy" and "Precedence"' in Jolly, M. and Mosko, M.(eds), *Transformations of Hierarchy: Structure, History and Horizon in the Austronesian World*, Special Issue of *History and Anthropology* 7 (1-4):87-108.

1995 'Origin Structures and Systems of Precedence in the Comparative Study of Austronesian Societies' in P. J. K. Li, Cheng-hwa Tsang, Ying-kuei Huang, Dah-an Ho and Chiu-yu Tseng (eds), *Austronesian Studies Relating to Taiwan*, pp 27-57. Taipei: Symposium Series of the Institute of History & Philology: Academia Sinica 3.

1996 'The Transformation of Progenitor Lines of Origin: Patterns of Precedence in Eastern Indonesia', in Fox, James J. and Clifford. Sather (eds), *Origin, Ancestry and Alliance: Explorations in Austronesian Ethnography*, pp.130-153.Canberra, Anthropology, Research School of Pacific and Asian Studies.

1998 'Foreword: The Linguistic Context of Florenese Culture' in *Antropologi Indonesia*, No. 56, pp. 1-12.

'Precedence in Practice among the Atoni Pah Meto of Timor' in Aragon, L.V. and Russell, S. (eds), *Structuralism's Transformations: Order and Revisions in Indonesia and Malaysia*. Tucson, AZ: Arizona State University, Program for Southeast Asian Studies, Monograph Series Press, 1999: 3-36.

2008 *'Installing the 'outsider' inside: the exploration of an epistemic Austronesian cultural theme and its social significance in Indonesian and the Malay World*,Vol 36, No 105: 201-218.

Freeman, Derek

2006 *The Social Structure of a Samoan Village Community*. Canberra: Target Oceania, Division of Pacific and Asian History Research School of Pacific and Asian Studies, The Australian National University

Geertz, Clifford

1980 *Negara: The Theatre State in Nineteenth Century Bali*. Princeton: Princeton University Press.

Goldman, Irving

1970 *Ancient Polynesian Society*. Chicago: The University of Chicago Press.

Graham, Penelope

1996 'Enacting Sovereignty: Sacrifice and the Power of Outsiders in Lewolama, Flores' in Howell, Signe (ed), *For the Sake of our Future: Sacrificing in Eastern Indonesia*, pp.148 – 175. Leiden: Research School of CNWS

Grimble, Francis

1989 *Tungaru Traditions: Writings on the Atoll Culture of the Gilbert Islands.* (Edited by H. E. Maude). Pacific Islands Monograph Series, No 7. Honolulu: University of Hawaii Press.

Grimes, Barbara

1996 'The Founding of the House and the Source of Life:Two Complementary Origin Structures in Buru Society' in Fox, James J. and Clifford. Sather (eds), *Origin, Ancestry and Alliance: Explorations in Austronesian Ethnography*, pp.199-215.Canberra, Anthropology, Research School of Pacific and Asian Studies.

1997 'Knowing your Place: Representing Relations of Precedence and Origin on the Buru Landscape' in Fox, James J. (ed), *The Poetic Power of Place: Comparative Perspectives on Austronesian Ideas of Locality*, pp.116-131. Canberra: Anthropology, Research School of Pacific and Asian Studies.

Henry, Teuira

1928 *Ancient Tahiti.* Bernice P. Bishop Museum Bulletin 48. Honolulu: Bishop Museum Press. (Kraus Reprint, N.Y: 1971)

Hocart, A. M.

1970 *Kings and Councillors: An Essay in the Comparative Anatomy of Human Society.* Chicago: The University of Chicago Press.

Lewis, E. Douglas

1988 *People of the Source: The Social and Ceremonial Order of Tana Wai Brama on Flores.* Verhandelingen van het Koninklijk Instituut voor Taal-, Land-en Volkenkunde No 135. Dordrecht: Foris.

1996 'Origin Structures and Precedence in the Social Orders of Tana 'Ai and Sikka' in Society' in Fox, James J. and Clifford. Sather (eds), *Origin, Ancestry and Alliance: Explorations in Austronesian Ethnography*, pp.154-174.Canberra, Anthropology, Research School of Pacific and Asian Studies.

1998 'Don Alésu's Quest: The Mythohistorical Foundation of the Rajadom of Sikka'. *History and Anthropology*, Volume 11 (1): 39 – 74.

2006 'From Domains to Rajadom: Notes on the History of Territorial Categories and Institutions in the Rajadom of Sikka'. in Thomas A. Reuter (ed.), *Sharing the Earth, Dividing the Land: Land and Territory in the Austronesian World*, pp 179-210. Canberra: Australian National University E Press.

McWilliam, Andrew

2002 *Paths of Origin, Gates of Life: A Study of Place and Precedence in Southwest Timor*. Leiden: KITLV Press.

Mead, Margaret

1930 *Social Organization of Manu'a*. Bernice P. Bishop Museum Bulletin 76. Honolulu: Bishop Museum Press. (Reprint: 1969)

Molnar, Andrea Katalin

2000 *Grandchildren of the Ga'e Ancestors: Social Organization and Cosmology among the Hoga Sara of Flores*. Leiden: KITLV Press.

Reuter, Thomas

1993 'Precedence in Sumatra: An Analysis of the Construction of Status in Affinal Relations and Origin Groups' in *Bijdragen tot de Taal-, Land en Volkenkunde* 148: 489-520.

2002a *Custodians of the Sacred Mountains: Culture and Society in the Highlands of Bali*. Honolulu: University of Hawaii Press.

2002b *The House of our Ancestors: Precedence and Dualism in the Highlands of Bali*. Leiden: KITLV Press.

Sahlins, Marshall D.

1958 *Social Stratification in Polynesia*. Seattle: University of Washington Press.

Sakai, Minako

1997 'Remembering Origins: Ancestors and Places in the Gumai Society of South Sumatra' in Fox, James. J. (ed), *The Poetic Power of Place: Comparative Perspectives on Austronesian Ideas of Locality*, pp.42-62. Canberra: Anthropology, Research School of Pacific and Asian Studies.

Scott, Michael W.

2007 *The Severed Snake: Matrilineages, Making Place, and a Melanesian Christianity in Southeast Solomon Islands*. Durham, N.C: Carolina Academic Press.

2008 'Proto-People and Precedence: Encompassing Euroamericans through Narratives of 'First Contact' in Solomon Islands' in Stewart, Pamela J. and Andrew Strathern (eds), *Exchange and Sacrifice*, pp. 141-176. Durham, N.C.: Carolina Academic Press.

Siikala, Harri

2008 'The House and the Canoe: Mobility and Rootedness in Polynesia' in Sather, Clifford and Timo Kaartinen (eds), *Beyond the Horizon: Essays on Myth, History, Travel and Society*, pp. 101-122. Helsinki: Finnish Literature Society.

Therik Tom

2004 *Wehali, The Female Land: Traditions of a Timorese Ritual Centre*. Canberra: Anthropology, Research School of Pacific and Asian Studies, The Australian National University

Tule, Philipus

2004 *Longing for the House of God, Dwelling in the House of the Ancestors: Local Belief, Christianity and Islam among the Kéo of Central Flores*. Studia Instituti Anthropos No. 50. Fribourg: Academic Press.

Vischer, Michael P.

1996 'Precedence among the Three Hearth Stones: Contestation of an Order of Precedence in the Ko'a Ceremonial Cycle (Palu'e Island, Eastern Indonesia) in Fox, James J. and Clifford. Sather (eds), *Origin, Ancestry and Alliance: Explorations in Austronesian Ethnography*, pp.175-198.Canberra, Anthropology, Research School of Pacific and Asian Studies.

Winn, Philip

2006 'Tanah Berkat (Blessed Land): The Source of the Local in the Banda, Central Maluku' in Reuter, Thomas (ed), *Sharing the Earth, Dividing the Land: Land and Territory in the Austronesian World*, pp.113-133. Canberra: ANU E Press.

ENDNOTES

[1] Even Louis Dumont refers to 'an order of precedence' in a crucial discussion of his notion of hierarchy in *Homo Hierarchicus* (see Fox 1994 for a discussion of Dumont's ideas in relation to the idea of precedence).

[2] Teuira Henry, in her classic study, *Ancient Tahiti*, does not use the phrase, 'order of precedence', but instead felicitiously writes of an 'order of prestige' uniting Tahiti, Moorea and the Tuamotus (1928:113)

[3] Interestingly, Margaret Mead does not make use of the term precedence in analyzing Samoan social status in her monograph, *Social Organization of Manu'a*, except briefly in relation to ceremonies in the *fono*: 'Seating arrangements, precedence in speaking, the serving of kava, are all performed meticulously …'(1930: 62).

[4] These theses include two theses on Flores: 1)Penelope Graham, *To Follow the Blood: The Path of Life in a Domain of Eastern Flores* (1991) and 2) Michael Vischer, *Children of the Black Patola Stone: Origin Structures in a Domain on Palu'e Island*, Eastern Indonesia (1992); three theses on islands in Maluku: 3) Barbara D. Grimes, *The Pursuit of Prosperity and Blessing: Social Life and Symbolic Action on Buru Island, Eastern Indonesia* (1993); 4) Christine Boulan-Smit, *We of the Banyan Tree: The Traditions of Origin of the Alune of West Seram* (1998) and 5) Phillip Winn, *Banda: The Blessed Land: Local Identification and Morality in a Maluku Muslim Community* (2002) plus a thesis that examines a society in Sumatra: 6) Minako Sakai, *The Nut Can Not Forget Its Shell: Origin Rituals of the Gumai of South Sumatra* (1999).

2. Origin and Precedence: The construction and distribution of status in the highlands of Bali

Thomas A. Reuter

What are the prospects for a universal theory of status? There is one major obstacle to all generalization attempts in the social sciences: the classes of phenomena they propose to exist and whose existence they seek to explain often show a very limited degree of cross-cultural validity. General theories of 'status' are no exception. The etymology of the word suggests something at a standstill, an image that is difficult to reconcile with the immense variability of status systems across different societies and in the same societies during different historical periods. Obviously, it is the most universal theories of status that also experience the greatest difficulty in accounting for the apparent lack of a universal status distribution pattern or a universal logical principle of status reckoning. However, it does not further the cause of social science simply to avoid the dilemma of generalization. Treating each individual status system as an utterly unique phenomenon is tacitly implying that it cannot be profitably compared to those of other societies. An explicit argument conceived in this spirit, however, would encounter the opposite problem: the status systems of widely separated societies in fact often show remarkable similarity.

This paper adopts an intermediate position. It is proposed that generalizations about status systems (and other social phenomena) across different societies are possible and profitable so long as we are able to offer a reasonable, explicit and testable explanation for the similarities that unite and the differences that distinguish them. A possible explanation for differences and similarities alike is to say that status or 'symbolic capital' is socially constructed by competing individual agents, but not randomly or at their complete liberty. Status is necessarily also constructed in a regulated or co-operative fashion, in accordance with culturally shared principles of classification, communication and social interaction. People who regularly interact thus tend to disagree and agree about one another's status at the same time. In order to explain similarities in cultural principles of status reckoning and distribution *across* different societies we need not assume the existence of a hypothetical universal structure in the individual mind either. Status systems and the cultures to which they belong are historical and 'fuzzy' systems of communicative and strategic action rather than permanent and easily separable metaphysical entities. Not many societies are clearly bounded or isolated from their neighbours today, and few ever were. In addition, different societies with a common historical origin and cultural heritage — though they no longer form a single or tightly cohesive social universe today — may still have many principles of status reckoning and distribution in common.

Indonesian societies, and indeed societies in the Austronesian-speaking world, appear to be related in this way (Fox 1993; Bellwood, Fox and Tryon 1995; Fox and Sather 1996). On the basis of rich historical, linguistic and ethnographic evidence it is thus reasonable to propose that a single theory may suffice to explain many common features and variations in their different status systems. This paper explores how status is constructed and distributed in one of these societies; namely, among the central highland people of Bali.

My results from more than a decade of ethnographic research indicate that it may be profitable to reconsider Balinese society, and its symbolic economy, from the wider perspective of a comparative ethnology of Indonesian and Austronesian societies.[1] Previous accounts of Hindu Balinese society have tended to stress its uniqueness in a predominantly Islamic Indonesia. These studies focused on the courtly culture of coastal Balinese polities whose rulers trace their origin to the Hindu Javanese kingdom of Majapahit. The more obviously 'Austronesian' heritage of the indigenous 'Mountain Balinese' or Bali Aga people had not been examined in sufficient depth. For the study of a Balinese status system this has meant that the importance of Indic elements (such as the concept of *varna*) could be overestimated and Austronesian elements ignored or discounted as an anomaly. Hindu Balinese society thus still tends to be attributed with a 'hierarchical' status structure in the Dumontian sense of the word (for example, Guermonprez 1990).

The analysis of their symbolic economies has been a perennial and contentious issue in the comparative ethnology of Austronesian societies. Two major approaches to the study of status in this region may be distinguished. One has been inspired by Louis Dumont's theory of 'hierarchy', a presumably universal model of status relations in pre-modern societies based on his case study of the Indian 'caste system' (Dumont 1980, 1986). Concerns about the predictive validity and portability of his theory to societies other than India have prompted ethnographers working in Austronesian societies to develop an alternative. A new theory has been promoted by a number of researchers associated with the Comparative Austronesian Project at the Australian National University (Fox 1988, 1989; Graham 1991; Lewis 1988; McWilliam 1989; Reuter 1993; Vischer 1992; and others). The aim was to do justice to the rather different principles of status construction and distribution found to be characteristic of Austronesian societies. Their alternative theory of status relations revolves around the two key concepts of 'precedence' and 'origin'. A consensus on the formal definition of these key concepts is beginning to take shape among the proponents of this approach, especially with the publication of this volume. Allow me briefly to define my particular usage of the two terms in this paper and in relation to my research in Bali before moving to a contrasting discussion of 'precedence' and 'hierarchy'.

In the present case, the terms 'precedence' and 'origin' have approximate equivalents in the Balinese terms *maluan* (from *malu*, 'earlier', 'preceding') and *kamulan* ('origin', 'beginning'). However, these and other expressions that emphasize the flow of time as the distinguishing feature of the 'quotidian world' (*sekala*, from *kala*, 'time') are not the most central terms in discussions about social status among the Bali Aga. Like many of their neighbours, they more often evoke an all-important order of time by narrative reference to a historical migration of people through space, or by a metaphorical comparison between social history and processes of organic growth (for example, *kawitan*, from *wit*, 'tree [trunk]'; also means 'origin'). In this paper, therefore, the terms 'precedence' and 'origin' are not merely translations of local terms but are used also as descriptive and analytical constructs which seek to unpack the meaning of key metaphors in the local culture.

A social order of precedence is herein defined as a system where the status or symbolic capital of a person or group is conceptualized by reference to a temporal sequence of culturally pertinent and recursive events, such as births, marriages, migrations, or the foundation of houses and settlements. The status of specific (classes of) persons is constituted upon such a temporal sequence by their association to one of its elements. In a temporal vision of the world, the 'earlier' element is distinguished from the one which 'follows' in the stream of time and life (a, b, c, …). This principle of division becomes value-laden because greater prominence is attributed to the preceding element and persons associated with it than to either immediate or more distant successors (a>b>c…). The valency and transitivity of the asymmetric relationships between the elements in an order of precedence thus rests upon a greater concern for the beginning of time; that is, for the 'source' or 'origin' of society and life in a sacred ancestral past.[2] Where there are two distinct points of origin, two lines of precedence may be traced in parallel, each relating to a different domain of social life or different social groups within a local society.

The notion of origin is conceptually central to the construction of an order of precedence, but it does not posit an absolute value or truth. In the highlands of Bali, a person who occupies a position of proximity to a sacred origin point may enjoy a higher status than others, but life and history are continuous processes and thus the position of an individual always remains changeable. First, as new elements are added to a sequence, all earlier elements move relatively closer to the point of origin with respect to the sequence as a whole. Second, while the value-concept of origin posits the past as a sacred beginning, the historical past does not determine in any simple way how the past is actually viewed in the present. Origin is usually interpreted divergently within different and competing narrative histories, each of which may locate points of origin and even define the rules of reckoning precedence in different ways. Thirdly, people may actually agree that two (or more) points of origin (for example, indigenous and immigrant) are both equally relevant to complementary social status claims within different contexts. Finally, even when a single point of origin is accepted by all concerned, the value or origin naturally posits a counter value, attached to the opposite and emergent pole of the temporal sequence rather than to its beginning. The growing extremity in an event sequence is open to new opportunities, subject to contingency, and frequently associated with 'the tip (of a plant)', 'fertility', 'the new', 'the foreign' or 'the powerful stranger'. This idea of life as a self-regenerating continuity thus imposes a general limit upon the value of origin, which represents the sacred source and unity of all life. In short, concepts of origin and precedence do not dictate current social relationships by reference to a fixed, incontestable and singular past. In Bali and beyond, precedence simply assumes temporal sequence as the basic principle of people's vision and division of their society in relation to status reckoning. Given that the vision is essentially religious, Balinese are primarily concerned with the work of maintaining the sacred unity of society or of a particular group through its rituals and temples. This effort toward maintaining unity is in perpetual tension with the work of status competition, which is based on a process of division.

Bali's position is at a theoretical cross road. The people of this island are close neighbours to eastern Indonesian societies, where precedence systems were first observed, and yet their society is also a bastion of Hindu religion and Indic culture, the Southasian variant of which provided the ethnographic case material which inspired the Dumontian model of 'hierarchy'. It may therefore be profitable to reflect briefly on the relationship between precedence and hierarchy (see also Fox 1990, 1994a; Platenkamp 1990) from a Balinese perspective.

The image evoked by the word hierarchy, following its Greek etymology, is of a divine rule or government; a sacred order (from *hieros*: 'holy, divine, sacred' and *arkhia*: 'rule, government') led by a priest-leader (*hierarkhes*) or other human representative of divine authority. *Hierarkhia* thus insinuates a relationship between 'the sacred' and '(the order of) society'. Emile Durkheim later expounded upon this ancient intuition in his now classic sociology of religion. He argued that the source of the very notion of the sacred, and of transcendental or universal values associated with the sacred, lies in the individual participant's experience of society as an objective and trans-individual reality. By arguing that the experience of the social transcends the boundaries of individual consciousness, Durkheim was moving firmly towards a sociology of knowledge. Social participation indeed calls for a cognitive process which Piaget later described as 'decentring', and it thus provides the supposedly self-enveloped *Ego cogito* of a Cartesian philosophy of consciousness with both an opportunity to transcend the limits of its own existence through communion with the whole and an opportunity to define itself as a separate part in relation to other parts. Durkheim's basic insight is that a notion of the sacred arises, necessarily, from the self-transcending experience of sociality, rather than being the product of a philosophical or theological imagination. In addition, the social experience of a 'participation mystique' must also be recognized as an enactment of the basic fact of the psychic unity of humanity, and ultimately the unity of all life, which — in my view — is a natural and physiological rather than a social phenomenon.

Symbolic economies nevertheless depend on 'social values', that is, values posited upon a human proclivity to socialize and be socialized. Values based on social co-operation, following Durkheim, are inextricably linked to a notion of 'the sacred' (in the wider sociological and not necessarily theistic sense). Even the values stipulated in modern moral philosophies, though they avoid references to the sacred (in the narrower religious sense), tend to appeal to a universal notion such as 'the common good'. They thus draw upon the same universal experiential ground of human sociality as their foundation. In this broadest sense, one could argue that society is by its very nature the experiential foundation of the sacred and of universal values. In short, society is a *hierarkhia* which reproduces itself by inculcating a specific value-orientation into the minds of its participants, against the penultimate background of the objective unity of life.

Cross-culturally, however, a universal 'sacred' experience of sociality may be interpreted in many specific and fundamentally different ways. The particular interpretation of 'the sacred' in Indonesian societies is reflected in the concept of origin and in an associated logic of precedence. Contemporary society is regarded as the product of a history of diversification. The contingencies of this diversification history and the contested nature of contemporary social orders are not denied. Rather, the enchanted vision of society as an undisturbed experience of sacred unity and harmonious collectivity is a vision projected into the past — the moment of origin. Unlike in the Western world, where the truly harmonious and sacred society has often been a utopian projection into the future, Indonesians have tended to focus on a collectively shared (and thus sacred) time of origin, the one root from which the many branches of society have grown.

It may be objected that the vision of the sacred for contemporary Indonesians is also prominently defined by one or another of the world's great religious traditions, in the Balinese case by Hinduism. However, while they may be required to profess publicly to one of the constitutionally-recognized world religions, many Indonesians simultaneously maintain an underlying concern for origins, in keeping with concepts and practices predating the arrival of Hindu-Buddhism, Islam and Christianity.

A common form of 'religious' (*agama*) or 'customary' (*adat*) practice in Indonesia is the 'worship' or rather 'acknowledgment' of deified ancestors associated with particular social groups and simultaneously with particular localities; with temples, cemeteries and other landmarks in a sacred topography. The names of these ancestors or places (or both) are often recorded in 'myths' or historical narratives that describe the creation of the world and the origin of society. The role of ancestry and topography in defining 'sacred origins' shall be discussed in detail later, using Balinese case material. For now, it is sufficient to note that this specific interpretation of the sacred generates a temporal and process-oriented system of social valorization. This stands in stark contrast to the substance-oriented notion of the sacred which has been reported in different studies of Indian society, and for which Dumont postulated 'purity' as the paramount value for the purpose of drawing status distinctions.

Although the notion of origin, as a specific interpretation of the sacred, is central to a specific form of *hierarkhia* in Indonesian societies, this does not necessarily imply that it constitutes a paramount value in the Dumontian sense. To begin with, Dumont's notion of hierarchy — as a social order based upon a single all-encompassing (religious) value — is a totalizing interpretation of Durkheim's notion of 'the sacred'. Durkheim's basic idea of the socio-genesis of the sacred and of social values may be correct. But although society generates and reproduces itself through an enchanting experience of sociality, it also generates the disenchanting experience of a multitude of separate individuals with often incommensurable positions and interests.[3] Social experience is characterised by *anarkhia* as well as *hierarkhia*.

Losing sight of specific historical and dialectic social processes, through which the order of a society is only ever enacted and reproduced in a partial and imperfect manner, Dumont focuses instead on an evolutionary social history following the trajectory of a universal Hegelian dialectic. His is a history leading from a pre-modern, unified and hierarchical to a modern, fragmented and egalitarian form of society. Adopting this evolutionary perspective, Dumont allows for a plurality of values only in the context of a modern society. His distinction between modern (individualistic) and pre-modern (collectivity-oriented) thinking also resonates with aspects of Max Weber's theory of modernity, who suggested that the singular value-orientation and sacred wholeness of hierarchical societies apparently became fragmented into a kaleidoscope of separate values and value spheres.[4] This argument denies in modern subjects the ability to experience sociality as an ontological ground from which universal values may be derived, as well as denying so-called pre-modern subjects the ability to acknowledge a plurality of social contexts and a diversity of positioned interests. Dumont's support for these unfortunate marriages, between modernity and value-fragmentation and between hierarchy and singular values, has earned him much criticism even on his home ground India.

The problem with a singular value theory of *hierarkhia*, of the relationship between the sacred totality of society and the values governing its status economy, is that the untold diversity of specific social categories in India (for example, *varna*, 'colours'), for example, cannot be logically predicted on the basis of a bland and colourless value such as 'purity'. Undifferentiated by its very nature, this concept is translated into a model of social differentiation by an interpretation of resemblances between a zero-state of 'purity' and the relative degree of pollution of different categories of persons or objects. A cultural system of hierarchization is thus always the result of a process of value exegesis, a struggle of representation driven by participants' experience of society as *anarkhia*. The transcendental unity of a single and featureless value, such as 'purity' or 'origin', must be shattered or 'fragmented' before it can provide a practical model for evaluating the social and natural world in all its complexity. The sacred as such is not yet a principle of social classification. It acquires relevance, in the conceptual and practical sense, through a collective labour of interpretation, no matter whether the sacred is conceived as 'origin', 'purity' or 'reason'. Only then can sacredness be attributed to persons and give rise to an order of precedence, a caste system, or a modern state bureaucracy. In my understanding of Indian ethnography, for example, the exegesis of the sacred as a state of purity relies upon a complex interpretive convention, a theory of substance and contagion, and on associated practices of segregation (cf. Marriott 1976). To describe Indian *hierarkhia* as the product of a single value is a tautology, in the sense that purity (a state of being without distinct properties) is as yet little more than a synonym for 'the sacred' (a society without individuals, individual interests or differences). Mistaking 'purity' as a full interpretation of the sacred is to ignore the enormous interpretive effort which separates the nameless 'purity' of the sacred, for example, from the purity of a substance such as clarified butter (*ghee*) or from the purity of a Brahmin.

The multiplicity and messiness of values 'in action' is less apparent when viewed across a temporal, cultural or presumed evolutionary distance than it is from the position of a local participant. It is all the more important that ethnographers approach the study of symbolic economies through intimate observation of local relationship practices and local discourses on human relatedness in all their complexity. It is easy to become enchanted by the simplicity of a transcendental value and its power to totally 'explain' a social order. However, it is not the task of social science to reproduce the totalizing attempts of local discourses at the level of analysis, let alone to create a totalizing vision of a state of affairs which the participants themselves recognize as a momentary state in a dynamic sequence of events. With these cautions in mind, let me proceed towards an ethnographic description of how status is constructed and distributed in the highlands of Bali.

The Economy of Status Among Mountain Balinese

From a Pan-Balinese perspective, the Bali Aga or 'Mountain Balinese' are recognized as a culturally distinct and indigenous ethnic minority. Most of their fellow Balinese in the southern lowlands hold them to be the island's original inhabitants. They are frequently associated with a distant past portrayed at once as a mythical time of sacred origin and as an uncivilized age. Other Balinese trace their origin to noble warriors from the Hindu Javanese kingdom of Majapahit; royal outsiders who presumably invaded the island in the fourteenth century and subsequently reconstructed Bali's (pre-colonial) socio-political order. From that time onward the Bali Aga lost all claims to political power, however, they managed to retain a number of important ritual privileges. Tens of thousands of pilgrims from the coastal regions continue to attend the annual festivals of Pura Pucak Penulisan, Balingkang and Batur and other ancient highland temples (*pura*) that remain firmly in Bali Aga hands. The ceremonies secure the fertility of the island's agricultural land as well as protecting and coordinating the life-giving flow of irrigation water (Lansing 1987, 1991). Even the heirs of the Majapahit invaders, the royal families of Bali's southern courts, will regularly attend these temple festivals.

In sum, the royal courts of southern Bali and their followers represent the political authority of Majapahit, a 'new' and external point of origin, while the Bali Aga, at least in some contexts, wield ritual authority as representatives of an ancient and internal point of origin; as the people whose ancestors first cleared and still protect the land. Political power and ritual authority in Bali are thus constructed upon distinct but complementary value scales, even though both of prominently evoke a notion of origin (external or internal). The institutionalized duality of 'newcomer' and 'indigenous' authority in Bali (Reuter 1999) is a variation upon a common cultural theme among Austronesian-speaking societies (see Fox 1994b).

Although the distinction between political and ritual authority may have become institutionalized in Bali, the distribution of symbolic resources between the two parties is the outcome of a specific political history, a complex and emergent arrangement that remains forever subject to contestation and change. That the Bali Aga have retained a significant stake in the symbolic economy of Bali over the course of this long historical struggle is not explainable by reference to a generic cultural theme, whereby the ritual precedence of indigenous people ought to respected by newcomers. Nor is it an accident. Research has shown that the Bali Aga are organized not simply in odd and inward-looking village communities, as was commonly believed, but in regional and inter-connected ritual alliance networks (Reuter 1998). These institution provided the social technology that has allowed them to resist cultural absorption. Regional research has also revealed that all Bali Aga villages share a common and typical pattern of local organization (Reuter 1996). Each community is governed by a complex rank order of elders.[5]

The two following ethnographic sections describe the ranking of villages within 'regional ritual domains' (*banua*) and the ranking of elders within the local 'councils' (*ulu apad*) of individual 'villages' (*desa*). It is argued that regional and local orders of precedence are both structured by a value orientation focused on a historical and process-oriented concept of sacredness, namely, on the idea of a sacred origin and a subsequent process of expansion.

Banua: Origin and Precedence in Regional Ritual Domains

In the highlands of Bali, a regional ritual alliance of villages is referred to as a *banua*. The meaning of this term is complex and variable. From a functional perspective *banua* may appear to be networks of ritual and political co-operation.[6] The participants themselves, however, prefer to phrase their relationships in terms of a shared ritual obligation towards a regional temple, a sacred place of origin and emblem of their sacred unity. The various relationships of member villages to the central temple, and to the origin village in which it is located, are defined by the historical order of their foundation. The history of the domain is commemorated by tracing the historical (or fictional) journey of the ancestors from the point of origin to the subsidiary member villages backwards, in a ritual journey of returning to the point of origin. Narrative origin histories and associated ritual enactments emphasize that each *banua* is a specific order of precedence, the unique product of a historical progression from an initial state of unity to a contemporary state of differentiation.

The most accurate and succinct way to convey the meaning of the concept *banua* is through the notion of a 'ritual domain'. The idea of a 'domain' captures the territorial connotations of *banua*, not only in Balinese but in many related languages. Reflexes of the Proto-Malayo-Polynesian reconstruction *banua* found in many contemporary languages of this language group are generally used to convey the idea of a 'land', 'territory', 'settlement' or 'village' (Fox 1993:12; Reuter 1998:68). For example, in Javanese, *wanua* or *wanwa* connotes a 'village territory' (Supomo 1995:295).

The various implications of 'participating in a *banua*' (*mabanua*) are expressed in Balinese by means of composite terms: *desa banua* — the oldest 'village' (*desa*) of a 'domain' heading a group of subsidiary settlements; *gebog banua* — 'a set' (*gebog*) of villages which recognize a common origin and ritual responsibility; *pura banua* — the principal 'temple' (*pura*) of a domain which marks its point of origin, or *keraman banua*, the congregation of the 'heads of households' (from *rama*, 'father') who finance and participate in the festivals of a *banua* temple. The terms '*banua*' and '*gebog*' carry similar meanings, except that *banua* is more suggestive of the domain as a space, whereas *gebog* refers to the inhabitants of a set of villages who are the foremost supporters of the domain's principal temple. Often the wider membership of a *banua* includes villages which are not part of this set of core supporters, but who still consider themselves entitled and obliged to participate in and contribute to the temple's ritual events on a regular basis.

Most informants portrayed their ritual participation in a *banua* as the fulfilment of their role as a specific part within an 'organic' whole. This idea of society as a 'body' finds expression in the symbolism of sacrifice, for the ritual order of a *banua* is also a sacrificial order. An animal victim, most often a buffalo, is sacrificed at every major festival of a *banua* temple. Its body symbolically represents the domain as a composite whole. The buffalo is slaughtered and dissected by ritual specialists. An assortment of specific bones and body parts is carved from the carcass in order to structurally reconstitute and symbolically 'resurrect' (*wangun urip*) the victim. The image of 'incorporation', of elements in a social whole or 'body' faithfully performing their specific part in the orchestra of collective ritual practices, does away with the conflicting symbolic interests that may create competition and sometimes even a permanent split among the different 'members' of a domain. Nevertheless, interviews with participants revealed that they are well aware of a disjuncture between this enchanted ideal of unity and the reality of status contestation within their domains.[7]

Occasional conflicts among the members villages of a *banua* tend to be focused on questions of ritual precedence. Most *banua* or, more precisely, their regional temples (*pura banua*) are controlled by only one of the participating communities. Most commonly, the village in whose territory the *banua* temple is located will claim a position of ritual precedence through explicit reference to the domain's origin history. The ritual specialists who conduct all ceremonies at a *banua* temple are recruited from among the priest-leaders of its origin village, though there is one case (Pura Indrakila) where priest-leaders from several communities rotate the status of 'ritual and organizational leader' (*pangamong* or *pangempon*).[8] These local terms are more suggestive of extraordinary duties than of superior rights. Nevertheless, questions of ritual precedence and relative status are of crucial importance in all *banua*. Narrative or ritually enacted status claims can be and frequently are subjected to contestation and refutation.

Their common designation '*banua*' is a reflection of the conceptual and organizational principles shared among the numerous ritual domains of the highlands (see Figure 1). Nevertheless, each one of them also forms a separate and historically unique symbolic economy. Of particular importance are variations in how asymmetric status relationships between older and newer villages in a *banua* are conceived and articulated. These variations shape the particular status narrative and distribution pattern within a domain, even though the basic principles of status construction and distribution always evoke notions of origin and precedence. Some examples of different types of *banua* may help to illustrate the range and scope of these variations.

The simplest type of *banua* is a small cluster of villages, one of which is regarded as the oldest and the origin of the others (*desa banua*). A mytho-historical relationship between the villages is enacted through reciprocal 'visits' during the festivals of village temples. The precedence status of the origin village is made obvious by distinguishing two types of 'visit'. For example, the village deity of the source village Bayung Gede is regarded as the parent of the deities of its branch villages. The parental gods sometimes 'go forth' (*lunga*) to visit their 'children', but more often the gods of the branch villages 'return home' (*mulih*) to visit their 'parent(s)'. Occasions for these ritual visits are the festivals of local temples such as a *Pura Bale Agung* ('temple of the great pavilion') or a *Pura Puseh* ('navel temple'). The 'going' and 'returning' of related ancestor deities and their human descendants combines the idioms of topography and ancestry. It conveys the idea of predecessors and successors ranked in a spatio-temporal order of precedence.

In a more human interpretation of history, the communities within small *banua* of this type regard themselves as linked by a series of ancestral emigrations. The idea of a common ancestry is conveyed through an idiom of place, given that there is no genealogical knowledge of sufficient depth to retrace the distant relationships between the founders of the participating villages. For example, many of the subsidiary villages of Bayung Gede are said to have grown from clusters of temporary dwellings (*pondok*) in garden plots too far removed from the source village for their occupants to return daily after completing their work. Penglipura is one of the downstream *pondokan* of the source village Bayung Gede which have evolved into separate village communities (*desa adat*) with their own sets of temples. The people of Penglipuran still pay ceremonial visits (*mabanua*) to the source village during major festivities, and are obliged to bring collective prestations as a village for the gods of Bayung Gede. 'Village-level prestations' (*atos desa*) constitute a key marker of a relationship between villages in a *banua* context.

Atos desa contributions are not explicitly recognized as exchanges between ranked status groups. They are exchanges in a rank order of divine beings in which humans participate as ritual facilitators. This displacement of human status relationships onto invisible agents successfully navigates some of the conflicts of interest among the partners in a regional ritual alliance.

Even recent immigrants within a branch village who have a separate ancestry must partake in rituals commemorating the deified founders of that village, and of the domain to which it belongs. In contrast to more exclusive notion of kin group affiliation by descent, a man's reliance on village land is sufficient grounds to demand his participation in village ritual. Most residents of branch villages, however, do claim that they are related to the source village by ties of common ancestry, particularly the village founder group. The visits to the source village serve in part as a mechanism to commemorate that the ancestry of the founder group is also the ancestry of the village, and to reinforce their privileged status or political power within the branch village. Nevertheless, *mabanua* is an activity involving villages (rather than descent groups) and generally strengthens their internal unity.[9]

There is another type of *banua* wherein the internal precedence ranking between villages is not as distinctly asymmetric. The common point of origin is no longer embodied and thus claimed by a living community, but is projected into the past. An example is the *banua* around Pura Tebenan, a forest temple located near the village of Manikliyu. The original village of Tebenan is said to have been destroyed in ancient times following a dispute and civil war. The survivors were scattered in the eight cardinal directions and founded eight new villages: Ulian, Gunung Bau, Bunutin, Langahan, Pausan, Bukhi, Bayung Cerik and Manikliyu, the one closest to the old Tebenan. Eventually the old temple of Tebenan was rebuilt following an initiative from Manikliyu. Ever since, the eight villages have gathered there for joint ceremonies to honour their common ancestors. The origin narrative establishes Manikliyu's role as honorary ritual leaders of the domain. However, in relation to the abandoned village of origin their status is merely that of *primes inter pares*. Note that Pura Tebenan no longer falls within the category of a village temple.

A third type of *banua* is based not on common ancestry but on patron-client relationships among villages with multiple ancestral origins. Most *banua* include newcomers as part of the population of their individual member villages. In these *banua*, however, the very founders of subsidiary villages within the domain of a large original village are believed to have been immigrants with no prior connection to the founders of the domain. The founder group in the original village claim that their ancestors were the first settlers who cleared the forest. They are the *wedan*, 'the people of the trunk' (from *tuwed* 'lower trunk, base or stump of a tree'). Other settlements were founded on vacant land within the territory of this large original village by later arrivals or *pendonan*, the 'people of the leaf' (from *don* 'leaf').[10] These newer settlements eventually developed into separate but dependent villages.

Selulung is the origin village of such a *banua*. The origin narratives of this domain describe how newcomers arrived, 'requested land' (*nunas tanah*) from the legendary 'Jero Pasek' of Selulung (still the title for the head of the founders' kin group), and established new settlements. Sometimes the relationship of land exchange was augmented by an affinal exchange, in which case the land was classified as a marriage gift (*tadtadan*, lit. 'things carried' or 'brought' by the bride). Uxorilocal newcomer grooms usually became founders of new branches to the local bride's paramount ancestral origin temple (*pura kawitan*, from *wit*, 'tree', 'origin'). However, all newcomer villages pay homage to the deified spirits of the ancestral founders of the domain at the main village-level temple of Selulung. The fact that some of them have immigrant clients or *pondokan* of their own, with secondary ritual obligations, creates a rank order of precedence within the domain.

Those who seek to be admitted into a status group are generally expected to conform to the behavioural norms and way of life of that group. A status group cannot be maintained without cultivating a sense of homogeneity, for it is the similarity displayed by its members which distinguishes it from others. In this type of *banua*, however, a sense of common tradition has to be maintained in the absence of a common ancestry and cultural heritage. This is achieved by stipulating that all client villages had to perform rituals (even in their local village temples) in conformity with the 'traditions' (*adat*) of the first settlers of the domain (that is, of the origin village) and abandon the traditions they may have had before their arrival.

At the same time, a degree of internal stratification can be maintained in a status group by restricting access to knowledge of more esoteric norms and symbolic capital to its core members. For example, informants in Selulung's client villages tended to have a sketchy knowledge of the domain's origin narratives and would frequently refer me to elders in the core village. Conformity to the same traditions may identify the members of this domain, but it does not identify them as equals in knowledge or status.

The client villages of Selulung have repeatedly attempted to gain ritual independence for themselves. In the absence of a shared ancestry, obligations to the founding ancestors of the core village are potentially contestable, provided that the clients are able to construct their own and separate origin as the beginning of 'relevant history'. Status distribution is problematic in all types of *banua*. There is usually sufficient 'historical uncertainty' to allow for a reinterpretation of the origin narratives and a reorganization of associated ritual practices.[11]

Finally, there are *banua* centred upon 'summit temples' (*pura pucak*) such as Pura Pucak Penulisan. These temples represent a more abstract idea of shared identity. At some time in Balinese history, possibly under the influence of early pre-Majapahit Hindu kingdoms, ritual alliances developed into institutions which transcended localized notions of origin. The larger *banua* temples have likewise transcended the character of a village temple. The status of these ritual centres is linked to narratives about distant historical and mythical events; about the first kingdoms that flourished in the highlands and about the time when paramount creator deities fashioned the world. Creation (*pangawit*) is believed to be an on-going process of growth rather than a *fait accompli*. A continuous and harmonious relationship among the natural, human and heavenly worlds needs to be actively maintained through a ritual process. Large *pura banua* are the sites of ritual for the revitalization of an entire realm and may have tens of thousands of supporters. In some contexts their deities may still be depicted as local ancestors, but in others they are portrayed as the creators and guardians of the entire island of Bali.

The festivals of large *pura banua* are of such a grand scale that they cannot be financed from the resources of one village alone. Instead of one village acting as the hosts who entertain and feed people from visiting villages, these festivals are organized, performed and paid for collectively by all core members of the (*gebog*) *banua*. Although all large *pura banua* are maintained by such a fluctuating core membership, this does not preclude additional villages or individual worshippers from presenting *atos desa* or personal offerings (*nyasah*).

The largest and most ancient domain of the highlands is that of Pura Pucak Penulisan, a temple located in the village of Sukawana. Like other domains of similar magnitude, the Penulisan network incorporates several smaller alliances such as the *banua* of Pura Tebenan. It is generally the case that large *banua* have major subsidiary lines of precedence beneath the supreme point of origin, embodied in an ultimate origin village. For example, Penulisan's core support group, figuratively referred to as 'the set of 800 [households]' (*gebog domas*), is divided into four 'sets of 200' (*gebog satak*). One of them is the above-mentioned group around the origin village Selulung.

The connections radiating from the centres of contemporary *banua* to their member villages, together with secondary links between the centres, create a pattern of staggering complexity (see Reuter 2002a for a more detailed description of these networks). The most important individual networks are represented in Figure 1. The diagram shows a pattern of ritual ties between villages which more or less adhere to 'Bali Aga traditions'. This is not to imply that the principles of regional ritual alliance which have been outlined above apply only to this part of Bali. Some southern Balinese temple networks employ similar concepts, narratives and ritual practices for their constitution and maintenance.[12]

Figure 1. Ritual networks in the highlands of Bali

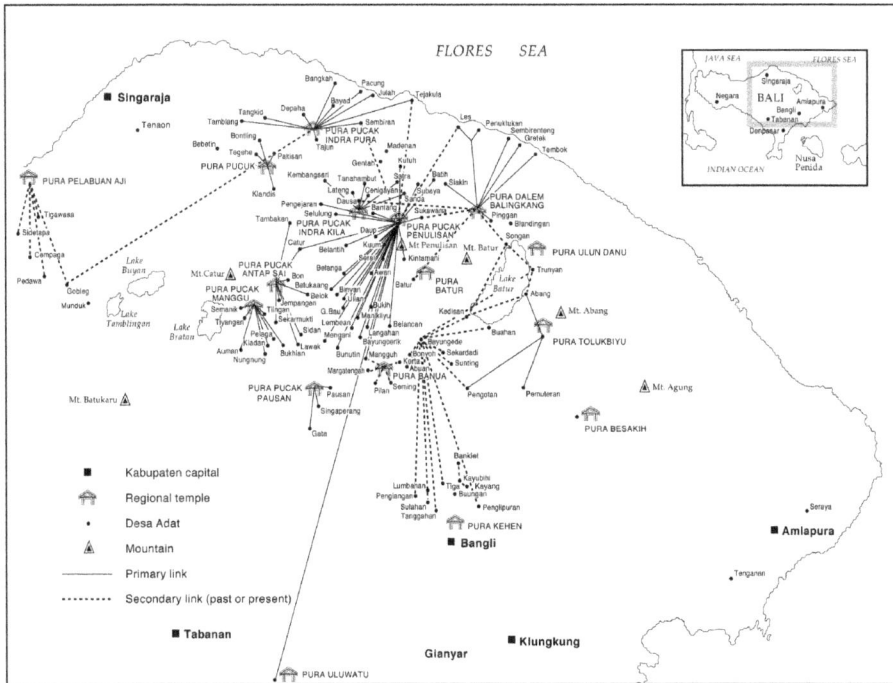

The general rationale of *banua* organization revolves around the two related key concepts of 'origin' (*kamulan*) and 'precedence' (*maluan*). The status of a village is indexed upon its time of foundation in relation to other foundation events. The temporal sequence of village foundations represents a chain of events tied to specific localities, and the emblems of these events are the temples which signal the birth of a new village. The relationship between villages closer to or further removed from the source is not one based upon a notion of logical encompassment or on a code of substance and purity. A local idiom of botanical metaphors describe a process of growth, a historical flow of life (*kauripan*) from the 'old trunk' to the 'new leaves', reciprocated by a flow of ritual prestations from the people of the present to their ancestors in the past, and extended forward through human procreation and the unfolding of history. The part-whole relationships in this model of society are not based on binary oppositions. Trunk and tip represent shifting polarities in a continuous expanding historical sequence resembling the growth process of a plant.

Desa Ulu Apad: A Ritual Community and its Ceremonial Assembly

It is paradigmatic of Balinese culture to find temples at the centre of various social networks. What distinguishes the *banua* temples of the highlands is that their members are *desa* (Sanskrit, 'village/place') whose inhabitants nearly always belong to several kin groups. *Banua* and *desa* are indeed closely connected and similarly conceived institutions. Both are ritual communities tied to a bounded territory in so far as they share a common obligation to the ancestral guardian deities of this land, and to their temples. The leaders of a *banua* have no mandate to interfere in the political or ritual affairs of member villages. The *desa–banua* relationship is best characterized as one of mutual support. A sense of unity is fostered among the internal factions of a *desa adat* ('customary village') by the fact that they must co-operate as a status group in relation to other villages in the domain. Interconnected highland domains also generate a regional sense of common Bali Aga identity in relation to the outside world. In turn, the *banua* relies for its very existence upon a voluntary co-operation among otherwise autonomous villages.

Desa Sukawana may serve herein as an exemplary case of how Bali Aga villages are organized. The highest ranking elders of Sukawana act as priest-leaders at Pura Penulisan on behalf of what is the largest *banua* in the highlands of Bali. By virtue of their status as custodians of this oldest and most significant ritual centre, Sukawana's traditions provide a local standard of authenticity.

Sukawana is a named village with a distinct territory, leadership and tradition. However, it is by no means a homogeneous community. A complex classificatory schema defines each person's status and role in relation to the village as a whole. A first criterion of status distinction is focused on a person's relationship to the land. The *desa adat* includes a considerable number of landless share-croppers, a group referred to as *desa giringan* ('aslant', that is, 'leaning onto the *desa adat* proper'). Share-croppers are classed as newcomers and their status is very marginal. However, given that they are permanent residents who partake in the produce of the land, they have a duty to contribute to the ritual life of the *desa adat*.[13] Share-croppers can be called upon for unpaid ritual labour services (*ngayah*) and must pay a quarter of a normal household share towards the 'ritual expenses' (*peturunan*) of the village. They are excluded from formal decision-making processes and rarely have the wealth to exert an indirect influence on village affairs.

The few newcomers who actually do own agricultural land in Sukawana must join the village assembly proper, the *desa ulu apad*. While newcomers thus are permitted to buy land, and are subsequently allowed and indeed required to join the *desa ulu apad*, they are barred from rising above the most basic level of rank therein (*saya tilem*, the group of junior members who serve the elders at new moon meetings). For this reason, separate membership lists must be kept; one for the descendants of Sukawana' founders (*wed desa*) and another for newcomers (*pendonan desa*). The small group of land-owning newcomers is referred to as *desa pamugbug* (from *bugbug*, a 'pile' or 'heap'), alluding to the fact that the ceremonial food portions for these unranked members of the *ulu apad* are piled up in an amorphous heap during temple feasts rather than laid out in order of rank.

The drawing of distinctions between share-croppers and land-owners, and between newcomers and locals, shows that a person's duties and rights in the ritual life of the *desa adat* are indexed upon their practical and historical involvement with the land. As a defined space, the *desa adat* is a highly inclusive category, so much so that even a person passing through its territory is for that time subject to its local customary laws. But in parallel to this power of inclusion a strategy of exclusion operates, whereby descendants of village founders enjoy ritual (and political) precedence over recent newcomers. Newcomers are prevented from taking control of the *desa adat* by denying them access to the higher ranks of the *ulu apad* or 'council of elders'. Some such form of stratification is found in most Bali Aga villages, though the specific distributions of rights and duties may vary. For example, in many other villages the core assembly members are also the people who have exclusive access to village-owned land (*tanah ayahan desa* or *AYDS*).[14]

At the time of research the village assembly (*desa ulu apad*) of Sukawana had 740 male members. Each male member of the assembly must be married. He thus represents a household (*kuren*, 'hearth') — the most basic social and corporate unit of Bali Aga society. A man becomes a member of the *desa ulu apad* after the third stage of the marriage ritual (*masakapan*) has been completed. The time of entry of a man's name into the village register permanently determines his relative rank in relation to others who joined earlier or later. The rank order in 'Bali Aga' villages thus is not, strictly speaking, a gerontocracy, though in general the time of marriage may correlate with chronological age. The basic principle is a ranking in order of precedence among households (married couples) rather than individuals. Nowadays the all-important register of members is kept in a notebook, which is awkward due to the constant changes in the ranks due to retirements. Formerly the rank order of members was recorded with a device consisting of a circular string to which many smaller and some larger bamboo tags were attached. The smaller tags carried the names of members and one was removed when the person retired. The larger tags were moveable, indicating who was due to fulfil a rotated duty at any given time.[15]

The rank-order of the assembly is expressed visually in the seating order of men during customary meetings (*sangkepan adat*) held in the ceremonial village 'longhouse' (*bale lantang*). Ceremonial longhouses are located in the Pura Bale Agung and in other village temples.[16] In Sukawana the elders (in smaller villages all assembly members) meet on each full and new moon (*purnama/tilem*) in order to discuss village matters and partake in a ritual meal. A formal seating order is observed (Figure 2). The food portions are laid out in a long double row and are taken in order of rank. The highest ranking members or 'elders' receive an honorific title and fulfil the most central ritual tasks. They sit at the upper end (*ulu*) of the *bale lantang*, which is pointing 'towards the mountain' (*kaja*) and the shrines of the village ancestors. Lower ranking members sit closer to the lower end (*teben*) pointing 'towards the sea' (*kelod*) and the realm of demonic spirits. In most villages, but not in Sukawana, the lowest ranking person also has a specific title (*pider/pamuit*) and function.

Figure 2. Rank order of elders in Sukawana (seating order during ritual gatherings at new moon)

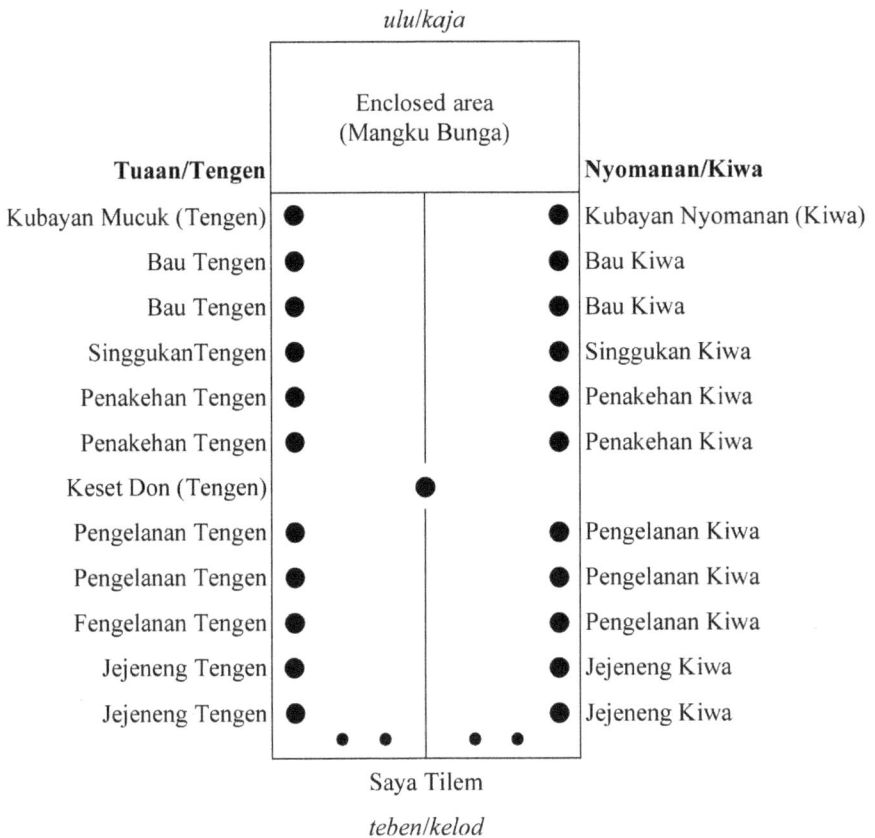

ulu/kaja

Enclosed area
(Mangku Bunga)

Tuaan/Tengen			Nyomanan/Kiwa
Kubayan Mucuk (Tengen) ●		●	Kubayan Nyomanan (Kiwa)
Bau Tengen ●		●	Bau Kiwa
Bau Tengen ●		●	Bau Kiwa
SinggukanTengen ●		●	Singgukan Kiwa
Penakehan Tengen ●		●	Penakehan Kiwa
Penakehan Tengen ●		●	Penakehan Kiwa
Keset Don (Tengen)	●		
Pengelanan Tengen ●		●	Pengelanan Kiwa
Pengelanan Tengen ●		●	Pengelanan Kiwa
Fengelanan Tengen ●		●	Pengelanan Kiwa
Jejeneng Tengen ●		●	Jejeneng Kiwa
Jejeneng Tengen ●		●	Jejeneng Kiwa

Saya Tilem

teben/kelod

The term *ulu apad* (or *dulu dapuh* in some villages) means 'the steps to the top [of the *bale lantang*]', from *ulu*, 'at the top/head'; and *apad*, 'the planks of wood between two posts which divide the longhouse into sections' or *dapuh*, 'the two long planks at the sides of the longhouse platform on which the elders sit'. It thereby refers to a process of ranking and succession common to all Bali Aga villages. A full member (*keraman*) may progress towards higher rank by gradually moving from the bottommost to the topmost position in the village assembly. He rises one step upwards each time a position higher than his own (on his side) is vacated by the death or retirement of a higher ranking member.

The membership of the *ulu apad* is further divided into two 'sides' (*sibak*) or ceremonial moieties of approximately equal size: those who sit on the left side (*sibak kiwa*) and those who sit on the right side (*sibak tengen*).[17] In Sukawana a man belongs to the same *sibak* as his father. The members of the right side are also referred to as *Tuaan* (from *tua*, 'old[er]') and those of the left as *Nyomanan* (from *nyom*, 'young[er]', or *nyoman*, 'third-born child'). By implication the *Tuaan* are symbolically 'male' (right), the *Nyomanan*, 'female' (left).[18] Because a Sukawana man belongs to the moiety and ancestral 'origin temple' (*sanggah kamulan*) of his father, this is not merely a symbolic but a social division of the village population into two groups. The relationship between the two *sibak* is a complicated matter to which I shall return later. However, there is no rule prescribing or prohibiting marriage between *sibak* (a slight statistical trend towards *sibak* endogamy in this case is merely coincidental to a preference for *sanggah* endogamy).

The top-ranking elders of the assembly form the *ulu apad* proper; that is, the leading body of the *desa ulu apad*. In the council of Sukawana there are 23 titled positions. Each named rank is associated with a specific ritual function, which is fulfilled by whoever holds that rank at a given time.[19] The required knowledge and skills are learned gradually. Each person observes and is instructed by those who precede him (*maluan*) and passes on their own knowledge to those who succeed him (*pungkuran*). The slow movement to positions of increasing responsibility involves such a thorough process of training that there is rarely any incompetence. The basic philosophy of the *ulu apad* system is that each person has a duty and a right to carry increasing responsibility and authority as they progress through a number of life stages. The responsibility and authority of elders in Sukawana is not confined to a ritual context. Though contentious community issues are discussed openly, the head elders have the final word in any decision.

A person's involvement with the *desa adat* does not begin with marriage. The status increase associated with having founded one's own household is as much the end as it is the beginning of a process. While marriage initiates a long upward progression towards greater ritual involvement as an adult, it also marks the end of a process of decline in ritual involvement, from childhood to puberty and marriage. In general, a person's ritual involvement in the *desa adat* is thus negatively correlated to their fluctuating involvement in worldly and sexual activity throughout their life.

During early childhood and until the awakening of a sexual awareness, children fulfil an essential role in the ritual life of Sukawana (and other Bali Aga villages). All children join organizations for boys (*sekaa teruna*) and girls (*sekaa daa*). The duties of *daa* relate to rituals of fertility. The arm movements in the *rejang daa* dance, for example, emulate the sowing of rice. The *teruna* are involved in activities displaying or requiring youthful vigour and a spirit of competitiveness, such as spear dances (*baris tumbag*). In addition, Sukawana has a special group of eight very young boys referred to as *mangku bunga* ('flower priests'). They are selected by the elders at an early age and are the only persons permitted to touch the sacred relics of Pura Penulisan. Surprising though it may seem in an apparent gerontocracy, they symbolically rank above the elders, and are accordingly seated in the top-most, boxed-in section of the ceremonial longhouse. Similar to initiated priest-leaders (the six top ranking elders), they may not cut their hair and must wear the traditional hand-woven black and white sarong (*kamben kotak geles*) and white head-cloth (*udeng putih*) which signify priesthood.

Membership in the *desa ulu apad* is limited to the duration of a person's married life, and relative rank is determined by the time of marriage. This focus on marriage as a marker of status within the *desa adat* is reflected in ritual practice. Marriage choice may be a matter in which the *desa adat* interferes only in so far as it does not sanction certain forms of marriage. However, a marriage is not valid unless it has been witnessed and confirmed by the elders. In most Bali Aga villages there is no exchange of bride-price between the families involved. And yet, taking Sukawana as an example, the husband must purchase and ritually offer two pigs to the *desa adat*, one for himself and one for his bride. This 'payment' to the village is called *tumbakan* (from *tumbak* 'spear') in Sukawana, and some say it used to be a payment for releasing a young man from military duty at the time of marriage.[20] In other villages the payment is called *bakatan* ('to obtain s.th.', 'to receive s.th. back') and is said to compensate the village and the ancestors for releasing a girl from her ritual duties as a 'village virgin' (*daa desa*).[21] This payment signals that the institution of the *desa* has to some degree appropriated 'marriage' from the domain of kinship and elevated it to a global principle of ranking. Among kin, the rank of households is signified by the position of their individual dwellings within an uphill-downhill oriented house row (or two parallel rows). This arrangement of the houses of kin in a houseyard already anticipates the structure of the *ulu apad* (see Reuter 2002b).

There are a number of special services and initiation rituals, the performance of which separates people at different rank levels in the *ulu apad*. The most extravagant ceremony (*mapurohita*) marks a person's transformation into a priest-leader (*Jero Bau*). Following that, there is one final rite which signifies the closure of the cycle of life. When a *Jero Bau* replaces a retiring *Kubayan*, he is installed as the new head elder in a ceremony called *mayah piteh*, 'to pay for turning around'. The candidate in this ritual turns around for the first time, from facing up-hill (*ulu*) like all other members of the assembly to facing *teben*. His former seat was on the tip (*muncuk*) of the long *dapuh* plank pointing *kaja*, to which he gradually advanced over the years of his membership, beginning at its base (*bongkol*). But from now on he will sit on the adjacent tip of the shorter *dapuh*, the tip of which points *kelod*.[22] He is now separated only by a thin wall from the *mangku bunga*, the emblem of the sacredness of youth. Both are in a liminal state at the boundary between life and afterlife, a boundary which for the old is death as for the young it is birth.

The architecture of Sukawana's *bale lantang* presents the partial image of a circle. Figure 3 illustrates how the transition to the highest rank is expressed in its design. Whenever a *bale lantang* is built, great care is taken to mark the tip-end and base-end of a pillar or plank as it is cut from a tree. Generally the tip-end (*muncuk*) of a piece of timber is fitted to a building so that it points to the sky (or uphill) as it did when it was still part of the tree. In this case, however, there are two notable inversions. First, the two upper-most pillars at the enclosure for the *mangku bunga* are placed with the tip pointing to the ground rather than the sky. Second, the upper, short *dapuh* on both sides have their tips pointing down-hill rather than up-hill (like the lower, long *dapuh*). This arrangement is said to emulate a circle (*windu*), the eternal cycle of life which unfolds in the visible world of living and time-bound beings (*sekala*, as opposed to *niskala*, 'sacred, time-less').

Retirement from the *desa adat* occurs at the end of a person's active married life. When a man's last-born child (*panak*) or first-born grandchild (*cucu*) — male or female — has married, he and his wife cease to be members of the *desa adat* (*baki*, 'to reach menopause'). Likewise, if either of the couple die, the survivor must also retire (*balu*, 'to be widowed'). The average age of retirement in Sukawana lies at about 50 years, while the approximate age at the time of becoming the lowest/highest-ranking elder lies around 45/60 years respectively. This means that while any member of the *desa adat* can become a ritual leader in principle, most people retire before reaching the rank of *Kubayan*. This system of retirement adds an element of chance or, as locals would say, 'divine providence' to what would otherwise be a predictable process of succession. The process of retirement can be and sometimes is manipulated. For example, an elder may hold on to his position by re-marrying, or by adopting another child.

Figure 3. Cosmology of the ceremonial longhouse (Sukawana)

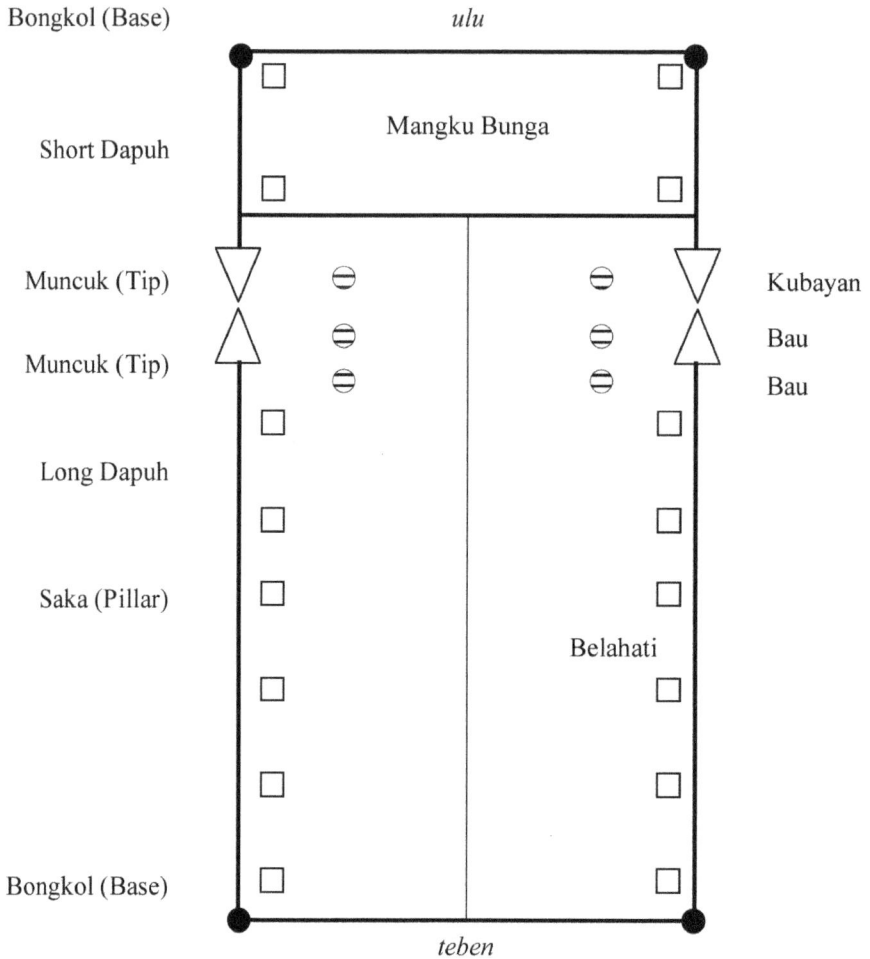

Bongkol (Base) *ulu*

Mangku Bunga

Short Dapuh

Muncuk (Tip) Kubayan

Muncuk (Tip) Bau

Bau

Long Dapuh

Saka (Pillar)

Belahati

Bongkol (Base)

teben

Origin and precedence: the vertical axis of the *ulu apad*

The case of Sukawana illustrates that access to status in the symbolic economies of Bali Aga villages is intimately connected with a person's relationship to the land, which is the primary resource of their material economies. Status may be distributed according to a rather equitable principle of precedence among those who are eligible to become full *ulu apad* members. However, a considerable proportion of the population is often excluded from the outset. A further tension arises because young men, though they may hope to rise to a position of authority in the future and are permitted to voice their opinion, must ultimately bow to the authority of older men.

Bali Aga village councils are an attempt to emulate and control the temporal flux of social history. A person's social experience is regulated by his passage through a number of categorical life stages. Each stage signifies a specific relationship between the person and the community as a whole. The historicity of an agent is not denied, as it is in societies where status is determined by their birth into a specific status group and conceived of as an essential and permanent quality of their being. Rather, the individual's life journey is regulated by imposing upon it an itinerary which reflects and retraces the itinerary of his historical predecessors. Every society requires cultural reproduction, and all too often societies pursue this task by promoting the idea that society is part of an immutable order of things. What is exceptional about the *ulu apad* is that it explicitly depicts society as a historical process, as an evolving rather than static system.

A person's relative rank within an *ulu apad* is permanently set by an event, a conjuncture in time, which signals his or her entry into the adult community. This event is 'marriage', which is synonymous with 'forming a household' (*makurenan*) in the Balinese language. Marriage indicates a conjuncture of female (*luh*) and male (*muani*) and thus signals the end of a formal gender segregation during childhood and/or adolescence into *sekaa daa* and *teruna*. What transforms this into a social event is the formal recognition of the new household as a legitimate productive and reproductive unit.[23]

If marriage can be described as a foundation event, as the historical origin of a new house, then particular marriages bear a temporal relationship to one another in the course of social history in general. Each such event has precedents and successions, reproduces and is reproduced. It is exceptional that all events which are classified as a 'marriage' and lead to the formation of a 'household' within the village are regarded as part of a single, overarching sequence. In other parts of Indonesia, it is only marriages causally related to one another in a biological sense that are socially recognized as an order of precedence. In these societies, the historical movements of out-marrying sisters and their daughters is regarded as a 'flow of life' between patrifocal origin groups (for example, Fox 1980, 1990; Reuter 1993).

Marriage among Bali Aga is constructed as an event that concerns the village as much or more than it concerns the two *sanggah* (ancestor houses) from which the couple originate. How then is the symbolic potential of marriage claimed by the institution of the *desa adat* rather than remaining within the boundaries of an ideology of 'ancestry' or 'alliance'? It is in this context that the practice of paying *bakatan* (or *tumbakan/kelaci*) to the village reveals its full significance. These payments are required before a marriage is socially validated, not only in Sukawana, but in nearly all villages with an *ulu apad*.

Once marriage has been constructed as a village affair, it can begin to serve as the basis of an index, the *ulu apad*, which relates each and every household in a specific way to the multitude of practices which make up the *desa adat*. The temporal sequence of marriages in a village establishes a rank order of precedence which is fixed in terms of the relative status of a member. The ancestors, as invisible members of the community, are the focus of a value orientation towards the past which renders the temporal ordering of households socially important. The value which permeates the organization of the *ulu apad* is that of 'origin'.

A second primary concern is to maintain an uninterrupted chain of links to the sacred 'source' which is represented by the elders and village ancestors. This desire to maintain a link with the original ancestors must be realized through the reproductive potential of their living successors. It is at this point where a status ambiguity arises between those whose seniority places them in the vicinity of the sacred origin of life, and those whose youthful potential of fertility places them in the vicinity of the sacred continuity of life. The constitutive events of this social order (marriages) are valued because they establish the conditions for the origin of new life in a procreational sense, a necessary material precondition for the perpetuation of the *ulu apad*. An unmarried man is unable to produce legitimate successors either for his kin group (*sanggah*) or for the village. The highly valued connection to ancestral origins is only 'alive' as long as it keeps on being reproduced from below, and hence each link in the sequence remains valid only so long as its representative remains productive (married and still nurturing dependents).[24] In the day-to-day running of village affairs, this interdependence between 'trunk' and 'tip' or between old and young must be denied in practice so as to uphold the authority of the elders. For this tension there can only be symbolic compensation in strictly limited ritual contexts. In neighbouring Desa Bantang, for example, there is a temple festival involving the ritual theft of the elders' rank-specific food portions by village youths, after which the thieves must run the gauntlet between two rows of other youths who will pelt them with chillie-laced palm wine.

The *ulu apad* is mapped upon a process of biological and cultural reproduction. This 'mapping' departs from a simple recognition of the biological facts of life. Firstly, even though the value of biological reproduction (fertility) is frequently asserted, the practical importance of the young and reproductively active adult members of the *ulu apad* itself is concealed by projecting this value instead upon unmarried children with a mere fertility potential (*daa teruna*). The former are thus disassociated from the potential counter-value of fertility, while the *daa* and *teruna* — no matter how important their ritual function may be — have no chance of challenging the authority of the elders. Secondly, the idea of 'cultural reproduction' is firmly attributed to a process of initiation. Rather than emphasizing the socialization of children by their parents, cultural reproduction is represented in the *desa adat* as a process of transferring ritual knowledge from village elders to their successors.

Complementarity and the lateral axis

In the preceding discussion of the *ulu apad* the focus has been on how a sequence of marriages or household foundations is used to construct a social order of precedence. The lateral axis within the *ulu apad* itself has been all but ignored until now, namely, the fact that it consists not of a single file of predecessors and successors but of two parallel lines, or put another way, of a sequence of paired ranks and titles.

The constitutive pairs of the village assembly as such are not married couples but pairs of symbolically 'male' and 'female' men. The gender conjuncture sanctioned by marriage heralds a couple's entry into adulthood and the rank-order of the *desa adat*, an event marked by the culinary incorporation of their marriage prestations into the 'body' (or bodies) of the assembly. However, the final rite of entry into the assembly (*menek makeraman*) symbolically transforms opposite-gender pairs into pairs of men. The male members are divided into 'right' and 'left' or 'male' and 'female' ceremonial moieties. Among the more than 50 village assemblies examined in the course of this research, only a few were found to lack a moiety division. This moiety system is hedged in with sanctions, such as a prohibition to cross the *belahati*, the narrow central plank that divides the platform of a *bale lantang* into two sides.

Where left or right is located depends on whether one is facing *kaja* or *kelod*. Given that the *Kubayan* usually faces in the opposite direction to the other elders, it is a matter of choice whose orientation becomes determinative. Nevertheless, this and similar pairs of spatial categories that are used to distinguish between moieties (for example, 'east-west', 'inside-outside') are all concerned with a lateral axis of orientation. They distinguish between two locations which are at the same physical elevation, or two elders who hold the same rank or 'social elevation'.

In Sukawana the moieties are referred to by birth-order terms, as *sibak tuaan* and *nyomanan* ('older' and 'younger' sibling). During formal gatherings the *Tuaan* always sits on that side of the *bale lantang* which is facing the inner courtyard, while the *Nyomanan* sits on the side facing the outer temple wall. Given that *bale lantang* are almost always situated at the right hand side of the temple court (as seen from the main entrance at the *kelod* end of the temple) an inside/outside distinction would be redundant were it not for the fact that in the Pura Puseh of Sukawana, the *bale lantang* is deliberately placed at the left side.

An explanation of this inversion and of how the two moieties are related in general is provided in one of Sukawana's origin narratives:

> Once the king of Java sent five brothers to bring a gift to the king of Bali who resided at Balingkang (*Dalem Balingkang*). The gift was a small basket (*sok*) with the finest onion and garlic. However, the brothers became lost in the forest (*wana*) and failed to find the king's palace. Meanwhile the onion and garlic began to sprout and they had no choice but to plant them there and then, and to establish a camp. They named the location after this mishap (*sok wana*, hence Sukawana). When the new crop was harvested, a huge basket was filled and brought to the palace at Balingkang which they had finally managed to locate. The king complimented them on the fine flavour of the onion and garlic but noticed that it differed from the Javanese variety. So they narrated the events of their journey, and the king ordered three of the brothers to return to Sokwana and continue planting these crops. Wayan (the eldest brother) settled with his wife in Banjar Kelod and Made (the second born) in Banjar Kauh. Nyoman, the third and youngest brother, was still unmarried (*teruna*) and lived by himself in Banjar Jero. One morning he heard a cock crow and went to investigate. He discovered smoke coming from a house which belonged to a young girl (*daa*). They fell in love and were married. The land which had belonged to the girl was henceforth called Banjar Tanah Daa, and the residence of Nyoman was called Banjar Jero. The many houses in the three hamlets (*banjar*) of the three brothers still belong to a single origin temple (Pura Kawitan Pasek Bendesa). The descendants of the two elder brothers are called Tuaan, while those of the youngest brother and of the local bride's relatives are called Nyomanan.

The origin group 'Pasek Bendesa' are thus outsiders, but were the first to settle in what is now Sukawana.[25] Like every mountain community, Sukawana's social order is modelled upon an underlying cosmic dualism, symbolically represented in the myth as *bawang*, red onion ('female') and *kesuna*, white garlic ('male'). These plants had to be put into the soil 'because they began to sprout', that is, the outsiders began to take roots in a new locality. The 'second crop', their offspring, 'took on a local flavour'. The newcomers, in this case, were installed on the inside. The youngest ('female') brother, Nyoman, facilitates this process by incorporating the indigenous population through marriage.

The *Tuaan* maintain a degree of dominance in several aspects of village life, as older brothers tend to have authority over their younger brothers. They provide the *Kubayan Mucuk*, the very highest authority in *adat* matters, and the *Jejeneng Tengen*, the worldly executive of the assembly. In most ritual matters (for example, buffalo sacrifices), however, the *Kubayan Nyomanan* will take the lead. One of the most pertinent expressions of this dual division is the association of the *Tuaan* with the Pura Bale Agung and the *Nyomanan* with the Pura Puseh. For example, during the great annual village festival (the *usaba gede*) each *Tuaan* household will offer one large rice cone (*pendek*) on the third day, in the Pura Bale Agung, while each *nyomanan* will offer a *pendek* on the fourth day, in the Pura Puseh. In general, the *Nyomanan* take precedence in organizing all rituals at the Pura Puseh, whereas the *Tuaan* have a greater part in the rituals of the Pura Bale Agung.[26] The Pura Puseh (or 'navel temple') is associated with the ultimate origin of the village, with its land and with harvest rituals.[27] The Pura Bale Agung is associated with government and official status; that is, with discussion and decision-making during the meetings of the council and with any ritual indicating a personal status change in relation to the *ulu apad*. In terms of ritual status, the Pura Puseh with its deities rank higher. For example, the offerings used on the fourth day of the *usaba* in the Pura Puseh will be re-used again on the fifth day in the Pura Bale Agung. This indicates that the deities of the latter can accept the left-overs (*lungsuran*) of the former while the reverse would be unthinkable.

In sum, the *Nyomanan* are associated with village origins and with the land while the *Tuaan* are outsiders from across the sea who established the order of the *ulu apad* and hold executive powers within it. Their seating position towards the temple court marks them as outsiders who have been installed on the inside.[28] The *Nyomanan* are considered to form the 'left' part of the assembly which carries a 'female' connotation, as does their association with the 'younger sibling'.[29] Likewise, the *bale lantang* in the Pura Puseh, associated with the *Nyomanan*, is on the left, which is the position of the women's longhouse (*bale pelokayu*) in the Pura Bale Agung.

Sukawana's origin narratives suggest that at some time in the past there was an influx of outsiders who were not only integrated into the local social organization but managed to gain political supremacy.[30] In many other villages where *sibak* affiliation is hereditary, the 'right' side of the assembly is associated with an origin group who hold political privileges similar to those of *Tuaan* in Sukawana, privileges which are attributed to their status as local representatives of foreign kings. Such claims to an outside origin and an associated political authority may not always be based on historical fact, though it is likely that particular local factions gained control of the management of village relations through their association with external political authorities.

Paired Categories	
Nyomanan	Tuaan
younger sibling	older sibling
left	right
'female'	'male'
base (*bongkol*)[31]	tip (*mucuk*)
insider (seated on the outside)	outsider (seated on the inside)
women's pavilion	men's pavilion
pavilion on the left (P. Puseh)	pavilion on the right (P.B. Agung)

This does not mean that the existence of ceremonial moieties can be explained entirely from an historical perspective of 'dual origins'. In this context it must be noted that in several other Bali Aga villages a man does not belong to his father's *sibak* because moiety affiliation is arbitrary and unrelated to ancestry (Figure 4). In the Sukawana type of village assembly, succession takes place in a bilinear fashion and there are separate rank lists for the two *sibak* (Type I). Each pair of elders is thus comprised of two men who have the same rank order number in their respective *sibak*. In a number of other villages (Kintamani, Pengejaran, Bayunggede, Bonyoh, Kayubihi, Batih, Lateng, Satra, Sanda, Cenigayan, Madenan and Sembiran) this is not the case. There, the division into *sibak* is purely symbolic, succession is unilinear, and only a single rank list is kept. As a man moves up through the ranks, he proceeds in a zig-zag pattern, alternating his symbolic *sibak* affiliation with every rise in rank (Type II). A man's entry into such an *ulu apad* always begins from the lowest position on the 'left'. The highest ranking *keraman*, the *Kubayan Mucuk*, always sits on the 'right' side.

Why is a lateral division into *sibak* considered so essential that it can be maintained independently of a notion of dual and separate ancestry? The insistence on paired elders or moieties in an *ulu apad* may derive from the Balinese cosmological principle of *rua bineda*; namely, that each living whole is necessarily composed of 'two [parts] which are different' and complementary in their function. The left-right division of village assemblies may be linked to observations of symmetry in nature, primarily in the human body, to which the structure of an *ulu apad* is said to correspond. This idiomatic focus on the lateral symmetry of the body does not take into account that 'bodies' can be male or female. The body symmetry of the *ulu apad* in effect substitutes body symmetry for gender bimorphism, thereby partially excluding women from what is meant to be a symbolic representation of the community as a whole. On a symbolic level, a 'male-female' couple is replaced with a pair of 'male' and 'female' men. Nevertheless, there is a residual awareness that such a pair, though it may suffice to form a symbolic whole, does not hold any potential for the biological reproduction of society. Marriage is thus the prerequisite for a man to become and remain a member of the assembly.[32]

Figure 4. Bilinear and unilinear succession in two types of *ulu apad*

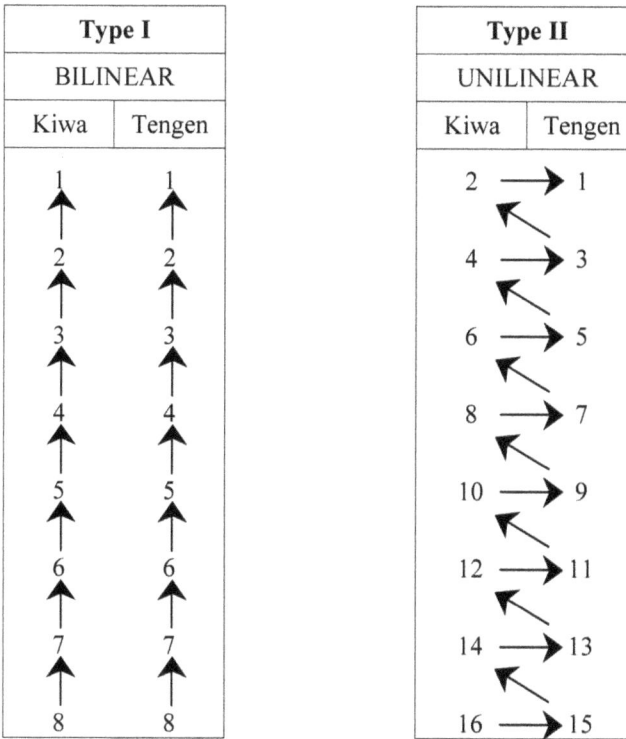

Type I		Type II	
BILINEAR		UNILINEAR	
Kiwa	Tengen	Kiwa	Tengen
1	1	2 → 1	
2	2	4 → 3	
3	3	6 → 5	
4	4	8 → 7	
5	5	10 → 9	
6	6	12 → 11	
7	7	14 → 13	
8	8	16 → 15	

Perhaps the most fundamental difference between the two types of *ulu apad* is that in Type II, the vertical dyads of 'predecessors and successors' (in terms of rank level) are reproduced on the lateral axis of paired elders. In a unilinear (zig-zag) pattern of succession, one of the two elders in each pair (for example, 'Kubayan') is always the predecessor of the other since their rank order number differs (in this case #1, #2). Consequently, an asymmetric relationship between the two elders and the respective *sibak* is already anticipated within the pattern. In a Type I arrangement, this is not the case since both elders in a pair hold the same rank order number in relation to their respective *sibak* (for example, both 'Kubayan' are #1). The notion of paired elders being 'equal in terms of precedence but different in kind' in Type I assemblies appears to be an innovation.

In sum, the *ulu apad* is characterized by a pairing of complementary categories on a lateral axis which intermeshes with a notion of temporal precedence in the vertical axis to produce a complex pattern of status distinctions. The logic of this pattern may be described as 'recursive dualism'. The pairing of male elders, as if they were couples, may in part be an ideological compensation for the virtual exclusion of women from positions of political and ritual leadership in Bali Aga society. But in many cases it is also a commentary on social and, most often, historical divisions between different origin groups within a village. As the example of Sukawana has illustrated, the relationship between powerful royal newcomers and ritually superior indigenous people in a village is like a miniature replica of the institutionalized relationship between Bali Aga and Bali Majapahit.

Conclusion

The preceding discussion of regional and local institutions has illustrated the paramount importance of 'origin' and 'precedence' as principles of vision and division within Bali Aga society. The value attached to these concepts is linked to an idea of the sacred as the domain of the deified ancestors and creator gods in whom human society has its ontological and historical origin. This orientation to a sacred origin is the basic criterion for ranking persons or person categories, distinguished as predecessors and successors within different social contexts and associated orders of precedence.

The value of origin is open to contestation both in its contextual definition and in its historical interpretation. Evidence of conflicting views and of associated status struggles are more clearly visible in regional and loosely structured domains than they are in the tightly organized *villages* of highland Bali. The membership and status of a village within a domain is ultimately voluntary and negotiable, but the negotiation takes place in an idiom of precedence. Even at the village level, there is at least some scope for contesting the rules of eligibility for joining a village council or for questioning the distribution of authority among its moieties by proposing different definitions or interpretations of origins.

These observations have important implications for deciding on the prospects of a cross-cultural or universal theory of status.

1) In view of the findings presented by other contributors to this volume it has become evident that the same logic of origin and precedence that informs the symbolic economy of Bali Aga society is also a fundamental principle of vision and division in other Austronesian societies. This confirms that a general theory of precedence can offer a high degree of cross-cultural validity as an analytical tool for the social analysis of many societies within this larger region. It was also noted that the time-based principle of precedence is very dissimilar to the substance-based principle of purity and pollution that informs the symbolic economy of the Indian caste system. In short, the predictive power of a cross-cultural theory of status tends to be directly proportional to the degree of cultural similarity among the symbolic economies it seeks to explain.

2) Origin is an 'absolute' value in its spiritual aspect (as a concept of the sacred), but it also encourages an interpretation and construction of 'the sacred'

(society) in terms of a relativistic temporal logic of status distribution. The social outcome are rank orders of precedence with a shifting but nonetheless unequal distribution of symbolic capital. This suggests that a universal theory of status may still be possible, though only insofar as we may assume that the core values of all societies reflect the same human desire for a vision of unity or wholeness as well as a proclivity for dividing the whole, and that every society is therefore to some degree a *hierarkhia*. Indeed, in one sense every society (or its privileged members) must evoke its own sacredness as a society (on the grounds of the self-transcending social experiences of individual agents) in order to legitimize and reproduce its particular pattern of symbolic capital distribution. An absolutely 'egalitarian' society would lack a symbolic economy, and such societies do not exist.[33]

3) The notion of origin in itself does not normally specify precisely who will precede whom in different contexts. Between the positing of the sacred or 'universal' and the creation of a specific status system lies an important step of interpretation. Interpreting agents have two stakes, one in their own particular symbolic interests and another in maintaining their social co-operation with others (to satisfy collective interests and to define the rules of the game that makes status competition possible in the first place). It may thus be argued that any symbolic economy exists in a state of tension; between stability and change, consensus and contestation, totalizing values and value fragmentation. For example, in order to retain a continuous chain of links to its sacred origins in the past, the social order must reproduce itself in the here and now. This evokes a residual counter value of human sexuality and worldly immanence as opposed to the disembodied transcendence of the deified ancestors. In short, there are no utterly non-egalitarian societies either. Labelling other societies as essentially 'hierarchical' comes at the risk of endorsing their local totalizing discourses (which may proclaim the dominance of one value or value sphere over all others), and of ignoring the presence of counter discourses and other forms of resistance.

4) In any symbolic economy some participants are disadvantaged. It is difficult but possible to ensure that they tolerate this fact or that it escapes their full recognition. Status differences in an order of precedence, for example, are relatively small, transient and easily tolerated. Nevertheless, it seems that the disadvantages that do exist are significant enough to create a need for a social technology of hierarchization, a technology for preventing the rise of widespread social discontent. A recognition of disadvantage may be prevented by the natural enchanting power of the sacred, the lived experience of partaking in a group or society. However, that this enchantment should permanently outweigh experiences of disenchantment and symbolic violence cannot be assumed to be a natural state of affairs. The form of *hierarkhia* that is characteristic of Bali Aga society evidently requires for its maintenance a tremendous investment of time, effort and material resources into producing heightened experiences of sociality

— in the context of joint ritual. These experiences of sacred socialityare apparently intense and formative enough to ameliorate people's lived experiences of a lack of social unity in every-day life, though they are insufficient to prevent conflict altogether.

References

Bellwood Peter, James J. Fox and Darrell Tryon (eds)

1995 *The Austronesians: historical & comparative perspectives.* Canberra: Department of Anthropology, Research School of Pacific and Asian Studies, The Australian National University. Comparative Austronesian Series, ANU E Press: http://epress.anu.edu.au/.

Dumont, L.

1980 *Homo hierarchicus: the caste system and its implications.* Revised English edition. Chicago: The University of Chicago Press.

1986 *Essays on individualism: modern ideology in anthropological perspective.* Chicago: The University of Chicago Press.

Fox, James J.

1980 Introduction. In James J. Fox (ed.), *The flow of life: essays on eastern Indonesia*, pp.1–18. Cambridge, MA: Harvard University Press.

1988 Origin, descent and precedence in the study of Austronesian societies. Public lecture in connection with De Wisselleerstoel Indonesische Studiën, 17 March 1988, Leiden.

1989 Category and complement: binary ideologies and the organization of dualism in eastern Indonesia. In David Maybury-Lewis and Uri Almagor (eds), *The attraction of opposites: thought and society in the dualistic mode*, pp.33–56. Ann Arbor: University of Michigan Press.

1990 Hierarchy and precedence. Working Paper No. 3, Comparative Austronesian Project. Canberra: The Australian National University.

1993 Comparative perspectives on Austronesian houses: an introductory essay. In James J. Fox (ed.), *Inside Austronesian houses: perspectives on domestic designs for living*, pp.1–29. Canberra: Department of Anthropology, Research School of Pacific and Asian Studies, The Australian National University. Comparative Austronesian Series, ANU E Press: http://epress.anu.edu.au/.

1994a Reflections on hierarchy and precedence. *History and Anthropology* 7(1–4):87–108.

1994b Installing the 'outsider' inside: an exploration of an Austronesian cultural theme and its social significance. First International Symposium on Austronesian Cultural Studies. Universitas Udayana, Bali: 14–16 August 1994.

Fox, James J. and Clifford Sather (eds)

1996 *Origins, ancestry and alliance: explorations in Austronesian ethnography*. Canberra: Department of Anthropology, Research School of Pacific and Asian Studies, The Australian National University. Comparative Austronesian Series, ANU E Press: http://epress.anu.edu.au/.

Graham, P.

1991 To follow the blood: the path of life in a domain of Eastern Flores. Unpublished PhD thesis. Canberra: Department of Anthropology, The Australian National University.

Guermonprez, J.-F.

1990 On the elusive Balinese village: hierarchy and values versus political models. *Review of Indonesian and Malaysian Affairs* 24:55–89.

Lansing, J.S.

1987 Balinese water temples and the management of irrigation. *American Anthropologist* 89(1):326–341.

1991 *Priests and programmers: technologies of power in the engineered landscape of Bali*. Princeton (NJ): Princeton University Press.

Lewis, E.D.

1988 *People of the source: the social and ceremonial order of Tana Wai Brama on Flores*. Verhandelingen van het Koninklijk Instituut voor Taal-, Land- en Volkenkunde 135. Dordrecht, Holland/Providence, USA: Foris Publications.

MacRae, G.

1995 Ubud: cultural networks and history. Paper presented at the Third International Bali Studies Conference at the University of Sydney, 3–7 July 1995.

Marriott, McKim

1976 Hindu transactions: diversity without dualism. In Bruce Kapferer (ed.), *Transaction and meaning: directions in the anthropology of exchange and symbolic behavior*, pp.109–142. Philadelphia: Institute for the Study of Human Issues.

McWilliam, A.R.

1989 Narrating the gate and the path: place and precedence in South West Timor. Unpublished PhD thesis. Canberra: Department of Anthropology, The Australian National University.

Platenkamp, J.D.M.

1990 Some notes on hierarchy in Eastern Indonesia: a comment on J.J. Fox's 'Hierarchy and precedence'. Paper presented at the Conference on Hierarchy, Ancestry and Alliance, The Research School of Asian and Pacific Studies, The Australian National University. Canberra: 25–30 January 1990.

Reuter, T.A.

1993 Precedence in Sumatra: an analysis of the construction of status in affinal relations and origin groups. *Bijdragen tot de Taal-, Land- en Volkenkunde* 148(3, 4):489–520.

1996 Custodians of the sacred mountains: the ritual domains of highland Bali. Unpublished PhD thesis. Canberra: Department of Anthropology, The Australian National University.

1998 The Banua of Pura Pucak Penulisan: a ritual domain in the highlands of Bali. *Review of Indonesian and Malaysian Affairs* 32 (1):55–109.

1999 People of the mountains — people of the sea: an Indonesian cultural theme and the negotiation of marginality in modern Bali. In L. Connor and R. Rubinstein (eds), *Staying local in the global village: Bali in the twentieth century*, pp.189–216. Honolulu: University of Hawaii Press.

2002a *Custodians of the Sacred Mountains: culture and society in the highlands of Bali*. Honolulu: Hawaii University Press.

2002b *The house of our ancestors: precedence and dualism in highland Balinese Society*. Koninklijk Instituut voor Taal-, Land- en Volkenkunde, Verhandelingen 198. Leiden: KITLV Press.

Supomo, S.

1995 Indic transformation: the Sanskritization of *Jawa* and the Javanization of the *Bharata*. In Peter Bellwood, James J. Fox and Darrell Tryon (eds), *The Austronesians: historical & comparative perspectives*, pp.291–313. Canberra: Department of Anthropology, Research School of Pacific and Asian Studies, The Australian National University. Comparative Austronesian Series, ANU E Press: http://epress.anu.edu.au/.

Vischer, M.P.

1992 Children of the black patola stone: origin structures in a domain on Palu'é Island, eastern Indonesia. Unpublished PhD thesis. Canberra: Department of Anthropology, The Australian National University.

Wurm, S.A. and B. Wilson

1975 *English finderlist of reconstructions in Austronesian languages (post Brandstetter)*. Pacific Linguistics, Series C, No. 33. Canberra: Department of Linguistics, Research School of Pacific Studies, The Australian National University.

ENDNOTES

[1] This paper is based on ethnographic field research carried out in 1993–94 (see Reuter 1996) and during several shorter visits until the present, funded predominantly by the Australian Research Council. Dr Reuter is currently a Senior Research Fellow in Anthropology within the School of Political and Social Inquiry at Monash University.

[2] The valency of the relationship may at times appear to suffer an inversion in the course of specific changes in the political history of a polity. In Bali, for example, the descendants of Majapahit immigrants enjoy a higher status than the Bali Aga in most social contexts, even though the latter are presumed to be a remnant of Bali's original settlers. The newcomers successfully proposed a 'new' and external origin for Bali, on the assumption that its civilization was not merely added to but created by Majapahit. The Bali Aga, of course, hold different views on the matter.

[3] Purity, according to Dumont the singular and all-encompassing value of Indian social hierarchy, is a pertinent example, for does it not conjure up an entity or state without attribute, colour, taste or otherwise differentiated substance? Purity is a vacuum, a silent emptiness at the eye of a storm of social ambitions. It is for Indian society almost what the Indian concept of zero is for mathematics. In this sense Dumont's claim that the value of purity is all-encompassing cannot be debated. However, this does not rule out the existence of alternative Indian values, or of rival interpretations of what purity means in relation to the status of particular human beings.

[4] Durkheim's own theory of modernity also tends to discount the importance of 'the sacred' (the experience of the social) in modern societies. He suggests that the individual subject's capacity for introspective moral judgement has eclipsed society as the fountain of sacred or universal normative standards. For Durkheim, this normative weakness of modern society was merely the symptom of a transition state from mechanical to organic solidarity, but until now history has led to such a transition.

[5] Further regional similarities were observed at the level of kinship and affinal relations.

[6] A clear distinction between the religious and political domains of life is not easily drawn in relation to Bali Aga society. In Bali generally, political protests are frequently phrased in a religious idiom. Open opposition to the national government was not tolerated until after the fall of the Suharto regime in 1998.

[7] The complex process of dissecting and reconstructing a sacrificial body in Bali Aga ritual, which is the main focus of ritual labour, presents an image of society as a 'body' that is not just received as a given and 'natural' order but created and constantly re-created. The wholeness of the sacrificial body may be a sacred given, but what counts is how it is carved up, and in the end, who receives which part of (and status within) this body during a subsequent communal ritual meal.

[8] *Pangamong* is derived from *among*, 'to take care of/stand guard' or *ameng*, 'to hold or wield a weapon'. *Pangempon* is derived from *empon*, 'to take care of a task'/'to organize an event' or *empu*, 'to nurse or look after [a child]'.

[9] Some exceptional cases were observed where only one faction within a village joined a *banua* temple in another village. In all of these cases, this was indicative of an acute power struggle in the branch village.

[10] Several subcategories of reconstructions of the Proto-Austronesian word for 'leaf' (*da'un*, whereby 'au' is blended into 'o' in Balinese *don*), feature an initial 'n' or 'en'; for example in Proto-Oceanic *ndaun

(Wurm and Wilson 1975:118). This may explain the derivation of the Balinese verb *endon* ('to come, arrive'), which is commonly regarded as the free morpheme in *pendonan*.

[11] For example, if the core group of 'founders' within a client village loses political and ritual control to their own immigrant clients, the latter may decide to detach the entire village from the cult of the *banua* temple in the origin village. In general, such a separation is implemented by conveniently 'forgetting' an earlier obligation. Open confrontation would only reduce the status of both parties.

[12] For comparison I refer to the research of Graeme MacRae (1995) concerning ritual connections between the temples in Wos valley communities and Pura Gunung Lebah in Ubud, and to Lansing's (1987) work on ritual networks relating to irrigation in Bali.

[13] Crops are normally divided equally between land-owner and share-cropper.

[14] Sukawana does not have land classified as AYDS, but in other Bali Aga communities it can amount to more than two thirds of all arable land. The *desa* is thus not merely a site for negotiating a local status distribution. It is often just as relevant to the control of material resources.

[15] This device is called *pangeling-ngeling desa* (lit. 'circling or rotating of the village'), and I thank the *Kepala Desa* of Dausa for allowing me to study one of the few remaining specimens.

[16] The term '*Pura Bale Agung*' ('temple of the great pavilion') is a common designation of a type of temple which is found in nearly all Balinese villages. In the highlands the temple is popularly known as *Pura Desa*. '*Pura Bale Agung*' is somewhat of a misnomer in that there are also ceremonial longhouses (*bale agung* or *bale lantang*) in the Pura Puseh and Pura Dalem of many mountain villages.

[17] Note that both in ritual and every-day speech contexts, it is always 'left and right' rather than 'right and left'. Likewise, people always say *luh-muani* (female and male) and *daa-teruna* (girls and boys).

[18] A male-female sibling pair in mythology usually incorporates an older brother and younger sister, thus equating 'younger sibling' with 'female'. A couple before they are married will address one another as *kaka* (older sibling, female addressing male) and *adi* (younger sibling, male addressing female). Also, young men are often accused of going to the temple only 'to worship Dewa Nyoman and Dewa Ketut (third and fourth born)', which means that they only attend to perve at the young girls in their tight sarongs. Younger brothers are symbolically equated with females in that they — like the sisters — tend to receive less of the paternal inheritance than their older brothers and are somewhat subservient to them until they are married.

[19] Only a detailed discussion of ritual processes would suffice to provide the contextual information necessary in order properly to appreciate the ritual and social responsibilities of elders in accordance with their rank. However, it is worth pointing out that one context from which the titles of Sukawana elders are symbolically derived is the division of sacrificial animals; namely, the victim's forelegs. Specific parts of the forelegs at first become part of the *wangun urip*, an offering consisting of selected bones which are rearranged as if the animal were 'brought to life again'. After the *urip* has been offered to the gods these bones are divided among elders according to rank. The term *Bayan* refers to the centre of the body (*bayan* 'heart') and the *Jero Kubayan*'s portion is the tip of the shoulder blade, closest to the heart or spine. The *Jero Bau* (*bau* 'shoulder') receives the remainder of the shoulder blade along with the shoulder joint (*tulang tambah*). The *Jero Singgukan* (*singguk* '[to nudge with] the elbow'), in turn, receives the elbow joint (*siku*). The tip of the foreleg, including the hoof (*kuku*) is shared equally among the top thirteen elders. The right and left forelegs belong to the elders of the *Tuaan* (right) and *Nyomanan* (left) respectively. Possibly, the title *Pengelanan* is derived from this schema as well (*pagelangan* 'wrist').

[20] Such service was expected of unmarried men (*teruna*). Until today their ritual duties include the performance of a spear dance (*baris tumbak teruna*).

[21] It is also possible that the word *bakatan* derives from *bokat*, 'a short spear'.

[22] These paired terms, *muncuk* and *bongkol*, also imply a distinction of male and female in that they also carry the meaning of 'penis' and 'vagina' respectively. Since the *sibak tuaan* is symbolically 'male', the *Kubayan Tuaan* is also referred to as '*Kubayan Mucuk*'. The title *mucuk* is a contraction of the word *muncuk* ('tip [of a plant]' or 'penis'), or may be the transitive form of *pucuk* or *pucak*, both of which indicate a 'tip, pinnacle, or peak [of a mountain]'.

[23] This interpretation can be supported by reference to situations which depart from the ideal script. Sexual liaisons before marriage are generally discouraged, but are by no means uncommon. If such liaisons become continuous and public knowledge, parents or village leaders will strongly urge or even force the couple to marry.

[24] Just as the upward end of an *ulu apad* points beyond, towards disembodied and deified predecessors, so is its lower end directed at unborn future successors with similar qualities. In some villages the *daa* and *teruna* (one sibling pair from each household) are ranked by seniority and led by a *Kubayan Teruna*

(for example, Kintamani), which suggests that brother-sister pairs form a symbolic extension of the *ulu apad* at its lower end. In Bali Aga mythology, such brother-sister pairs are of great importance, for example, in the tale 'I Barak-Ni Petak' ('red [brother] and white [sister]') from the Lake Batur area. Generally, red represents 'female' (blood) and white represents 'male' (semen). In this myth, however, the B-Z pair of twins eventually become a H-W pair. After their marriage they are called Ni Barak and I Petak (red female-white male).

[25] Sukawana is first mentioned in *prasasti* Kintamani C (ca. AD 970) as Kintamani's northern boundary. According to one legend, old Sukawana (Kuta Dalem) was one *desa adat* with Kintamani until newcomers established the main settlement on the northern slope (contemporary 'Sukawana') and shifted the Pura Bale Agung and Pura Puseh.

[26] For example, the *Kubayan Kiwa* dedicates the offerings and only the *Mangku Bunga Kiwa* may carry the sacred objects during the festival of the Pura Puseh. All offerings are prepared by the women of the *Nyomanan (kiwa)*. By contrast, the festival of the Pura Bale Agung coincides with that of the Bendesa clan temple controlled by the *Tuaan*.

[27] In Desa Julah, for example, the deity of the Pura Puseh is called *Ratu Maduwe Karang*, 'the deity who owns the land'.

[28] Placing the 'outside' at the 'tip', and the 'inside' at the base, is a variant of this arrangement transposed to a vertical axis of orientation. During post-mortuary ritual, a temporary pavilion in the house yard is decorated with two specific cloths. At the upper end or 'tip' a Chinese gold-embroidered cloth (*kain lelintangan*, 'cloth brought from far away') is placed, symbolizing the newly imported from the outside world. At the lower end or 'base' a Balinese double-*ikat* cloth from Tenganan (*kain geringsing*, 'cloth of no illness') is placed, symbolizing the ancient and indigenous.

[29] The sister in Bali Aga mythology is almost always a younger sibling (*adi*), and men often address their lovers or wives as 'younger sibling'.

[30] A conceptual distinction between 'locals' and 'newcomers' need not be based on an actual historical migration, although in this case it probably did occur.

[31] The head elder of the right is always called *Mucuk* ('tip', also 'penis'), and thus corresponds to the upper end of the vertical axis. The symbolic correspondence between the left side of the lateral axis and the lower end of the vertical axis (both 'female') is expressed very openly in Desa Les, where the *sibak tengen* all face *ulu*, whereas the *sibak kiwa* face *teben* during formal meetings.

[32] he importance of women is also acknowledged in temple design. Many Bali Aga villages have a women's as well as a men's pavilion. While men and women may both gather in their respective 'longhouses' on a full moon (in some villages), only men are allowed to attend the new moon meetings in which all important community matters are decided.

[33] In modern consumer societies the importance of the symbolic economy may have been eclipsed with an increasing public focus on the material economy, whereby wealth acquires ascendency even as a status indicator. Such restricted symbolic economies are not necessarily more egalitarian, even though the stakes of the game of status competition may be reduced because status becomes an adjunct to wealth. Status also endures as an end in itself in many sectors of modern society, not the least in the academic world. In some post-modern religious systems we can observe that status and sacredness are becoming divorced from the numinous experience of the social (which many people now lack) and are referenced more directly to people's numinous experience of objective reality. Balinese too recognise this possibility within their esoteric religious systems, wherein the 'status' of a person is defined by their capacity to enter into personal communion with sacred as an objective reality (the spirit world or *niskala*) rather than by their formal position within society or their role in relation to public ritual.

3. Distinguishing Hierarchy and Precedence: Comparing status distinctions in South Asia and the Austronesian world, with special reference to South Sulawesi

Greg Acciaioli

Introduction

The importance of differential status in the societies of archipelagic Southeast Asia and the greater Austronesian world is conspicuous; the proper terms for analysis of this social phenomenon remain, however, problematic. In this paper I wish to explore some of the ways in which questions of differential status have been addressed. Specifically, I want to examine the notion of hierarchy, as it has been elaborated from the work of Louis Dumont (1980). In this treatment I suggest that his use of hierarchy in the analysis of South Asian caste has been somewhat misconstrued (largely due to misleading comments by Dumont himself) and propose a different generalized understanding of hierarchy based on the analysis of caste. This reframed understanding of hierarchy may then be contrasted with the notion of precedence that James J. Fox (1994) and several of his students have argued (convincingly) is appropriate to the study of many Austronesian societies. By suggesting more explicit notions of hierarchy and precedence, I hope to disentangle some of the confusing ways in which differential status has been discussed for societies of this region and suggest some more restricted ways in which these concepts might be employed more powerfully and less ambiguously. I use the example of Bugis and Makasar domains of South Sulawesi as a context in which to deploy these understandings, arguing that their peculiar intermeshing of hierarchy and precedence distinguishes them from societies also informed by precedence elsewhere in the archipelago, especially in eastern Indonesia.

The Logic of Hierarcy: Value and Exclusion in Caste

In his overview of stratification in Asia, Evans (1993:212) uses the term 'hierarchy' as a generic, indeed self-evident, term for the cultural ordering principles underlying stratified social systems. Specifically, in regard to South Asian caste, he equates hierarchy with the principles by which culturally discrete groups are ordered with respect to one another. When used in this general sense, the term hierarchy may be used for most any stratified society. However, those analysts more orientated to interpreting the particular logics, the underlying structural principles, of local cultural systems have tended to adopt Dumont's (1980) more specific characterization of hierarchy in his culturalist analysis of the South Asian caste system.

Other scholars' invocations of Dumontian notions of hierarchy as the basis of caste and other analogous examples of status ranking have demonstrated a curious tendency. Rather than examining the way in which Dumont has utilized the notion of hierarchy in his substantive analysis of caste, they (for example, Fox 1994; Allen 1985) have derived much of their basic sense of the Dumontian characterization of hierarchy from the 'Postface: Toward a Theory of Hierarchy', which Dumont (1980:237–240) added to the revised edition of *Homo hierarchicus* (first edition published in French in 1966). Dumont has explicitly acknowledged that the underlying conceptualization of this postface was based upon his study of a section of Apthorpe's unpublished D Phil thesis at Oxford 'subsequent' (Dumont 1980:239) to writing the original manuscript of *Homo hierarchicus*. In the version put forth in the 'Postface' he posits the basic principle of hierarchy as the encompassing/encompassed relation or, somewhat differently stated, the encompassing of the contrary in asymmetric opposition (Dumont 1980:241). This relationship is demonstrated by a box contained within a larger box as opposed to the simple relation of complementarity in which two adjacent boxes make up a unity (Figure 1). As Dumont puts it:

I think the clearest formulation is gained by separating and combining two levels. At the superior level there is unity; at the inferior level there is distinction, there is, as in the first case, complementariness or contradiction. Hierarchy consists in the combination of these two propositions concerning different levels. In hierarchy thus defined, complementariness or contradiction is contained in a unity of a superior order (1980:242).

As Fox (1994:90) has noted, this relationship corresponds with what others, most notably Jakobson and Greenberg[1] in linguistics, have identified as marking or markedness theory. In linguistic terms, this means that one member of an opposition (usually binary) may also stand for the opposition as a whole. For example, until the emergence of gender-neutral English, the personal pronoun 'he' could stand for agents of either gender at one level of contrast, though at a lower level of contrast 'he' was explicitly contrasted to 'she' as male to female. Fox (1994:91) has ingeniously exemplified how a term like 'man' may operate recursively as an unmarked form, encompassing an opposition of which it is itself one term, on a number of levels.[2]

However, I suggest that despite Dumont himself overtly labelling this postface as an extension of his own approach to caste in South Asia into a general theory of hierarchy, this conceptualization in terms of marking theory really does not capture the thrust of his own analysis of hierarchy in caste in the preceding chapters of his work *Homo hierarchicus*. In short, his afterword is more of an afterthought than a generalization. To support this characterization, I wish to traverse some of the major characteristics of Dumont's analysis of caste, a task to which I cannot fully do justice in the short compass allotted here. Hopefully, however, this traversal will highlight some aspects of caste that can enable a clearer contrast later with the notion of precedence. Dumont himself tended to use the term 'precedence' almost as a synonym of hierarchy: 'Nowadays hierarchy, or rather the existence of an order of precedence, a status ranking, usually compels recognition ...' (Dumont 1980:75). But I hope to show from the terms of Dumont's own analysis that some fruitful distinctions can be made, although such a revised conceptualization requires going beyond some of Dumont's own terms. Later, I will illustrate the applicability and articulation of these distinctions with some examples from the operation of status among the Bugis and Makasar of South Sulawesi.

Figure 1. *Homo hierarchicus* (after Dumont 1980:242)

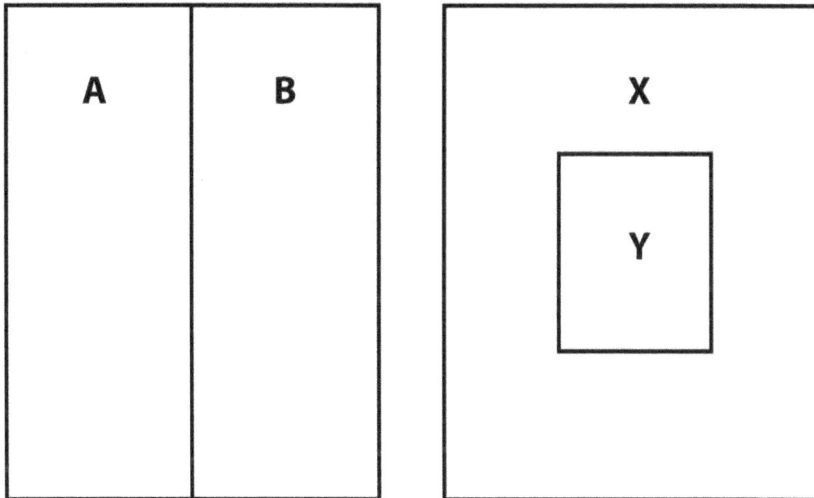

The Logic of Hierarchy

In many ways the fundamental structural logic of the caste system may be expressed as the recursive application of the asymmetric opposition of the pure and the impure. Dumont makes this basic point in chapter II of *Homo hierarchicus* (1980:43) after having devoted his first chapter to an overview of some past approaches to caste in the history of ideas. This opposition pure/impure is properly characterized as asymmetric, as one term of the opposition is valued more highly than the other. However, an asymmetric opposition is not necessarily a marked opposition; that is, it may not be the case that one of the terms serves to label the whole opposition, as well as contrasting with the other term (although all marked oppositions are, by definition, also asymmetric). In the case of caste, I would argue that this opposition is indeed not one of markedness, for in the recursive application of this opposition to form a hierarchy of castes, there is no identity of nodes across the levels of the hierarchy.

This property is most evident in the generation of the basic categorial division of South Asian society into *varna*, the 'colours' or 'estates' serving as the all-encompassing framework by which to render distinct caste hierarchies of various regions comparable. This division operates by the recursive application of the pure/impure (or, if one wishes to capture the relative nature of the contrast, purer/less pure) opposition, the subject of Dumont's third chapter.[3] As I discuss these levels, the first term I will mention occupies the position of [+pure term], while the second that of the [-pure term]. As Figure 2 shows, the first opposition is that of the *varna* system as a whole against the category of those who are outside the *varna* system, i.e. the Untouchables. Within the *varna* system itself, the operation of the pure/impure opposition at the next level divides the *triwangsa* ('twice-born') from the Shudras,[4] who are only once-born. Within the twice-born, the subsequent operation of the pure/impure opposition divides off those who can exercise dominion from those who cannot, that is, the Vaishyas. Among those who can exercise dominion, the Brahmans are finally distinguished from the Kshatriyas as those who are allowed to perform sacrifice due to their greater purity. Thus, the recursive operation of the asymmetric pure/impure opposition has generated the four *varna* of South Asian society, along with the structural residue of those too impure to be within the *varna* system itself.

It may be argued that, in one sense, the recursive operation of the opposition may be seen as one in which the pure always encompasses the impure, since it is successive degrees of purity that are distinguished. Each succeeding node going down the layers could be labelled [+pure]. But it is important to note that one could not label each node as Brahman in ever more restricted senses until one arrives at the most restricted sense of Brahman in the final level of contrast. A Kshatriya is not a type of Brahman at the next higher level (nor vice versa), in the way that a woman is a type of man, when man is used as an unmarked category to encompass the man/woman opposition. According to Dumezil, whom Dumont explicitly cites as the inspiration for his own analysis of caste as a recursive succession of dichotomies (Dumont 1980:67–68), the Brahmans and Kshatriyas together compose the 'two forces' (*ubhe virye*), while the 'two forces' along with the Vaishyas compose the 'twice-born', and the 'twice-born' plus the Shudras compose the *varna* as whole. So to label the levels of the system is simply to work up the levels (from greater to lesser purity) which I worked down (from lesser to greater purity) in generating the system. The labels at each level once more illustrate that no intermediate node is the same as one of the two nodes into which it is divided by the subsequent application of the pure/impure opposition. The figure thus resembles more closely a key (Fowler

1977:225-226) or tree (Tyler 1969:10-11) rather than a taxonomy; the nodes label underlying semantic features rather than categories, although in this case, unlike most keys or trees, it is the same feature operating at each node, thus exemplifying recursiveness.

Figure 2. Hierarchy in Hindu *varna* system

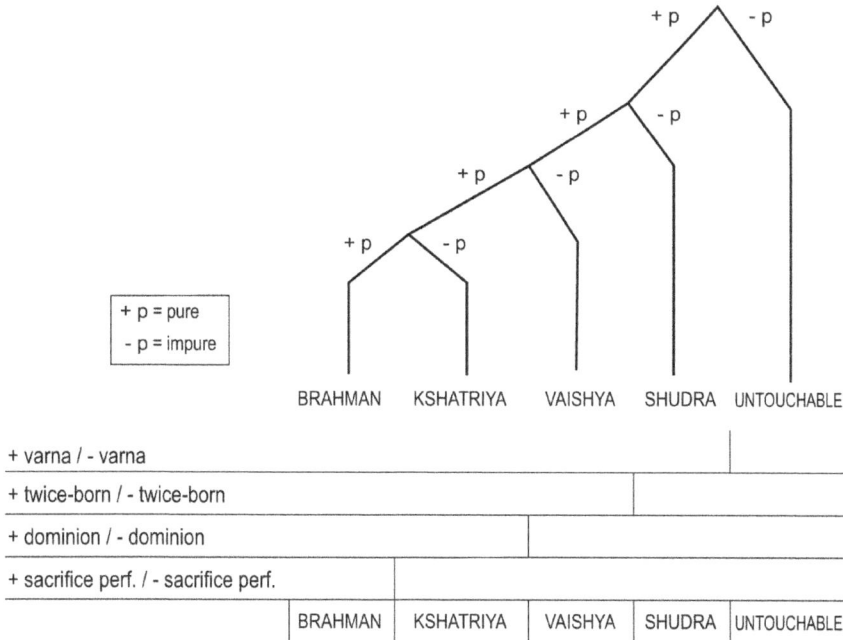

The division of South Asian society into the actual castes (*jati*) of specific regions can be conceptualized in much the same way. As shown by Figure 3, it is once again the successive operation of the pure/impure distinction that separates clumps of castes from each other. However, moving from the *varna* model of Indian society to the level of actual castes complicates the homogeneity of the analysis. As Dumont himself notes:

> The caste, unified from the outside, is divided within. More generally, a particular caste is a complex group, a successive inclusion of groups of diverse orders or levels, in which different functions (profession, endogamy, etc.) are attached to different levels (1980:34).

Basically, the division into castes in a region may be analysed structurally by regarding the asymmetric pure/impure relationship as a meta-opposition, which is realized in specific oppositions as a number of different criteria. For example, with reference to Figure 3, representing a hypothetical case, the criterion of members eating meat may divide one set of groups (A,B,C,D), those who do not eat meat, as relatively pure, as opposed to the relatively impure groups who do eat meat (E,F,G,H). However, another criterion will divide the whole set of groups into two different subsets. Groups A, B, and C are distinguished from all those below (D, E, F, G, and H) by their refusal to accept food from meat-eaters, a characteristic that ranks them as relatively purer than those latter groups that do accept meat. Simply by using these two criteria, group D has been isolated as occupying a unique niche in the middle of the set, for it is the only group that does not eat meat, but will accept other kinds of food from members of meat-eating groups. This manner of using criteria differentially to isolate terms, which are thus defined by unique strings of components, the values of the intersecting criteria, thus corresponds to distinguishing terms according to a paradigm rather than a taxonomy or key (Fowler 1977:223-225; Tyler 1969:9-10). As Figure 3 shows, by successively applying a number of such oppositions that isolate subsets of groups at different points along the spectrum, with those on the left of the line of distinction always judged as purer than those on the right, eventually each of the groups is distinguished by a unique set of restrictions. For example, members of group A do not eat meat, do not accept other kinds of food from meat-eaters, do not allow widows of their group to remarry, do arrange infant marriage, do not eat beef (a redundant feature for this group, since its members do not eat any kind of meat), and do not tan leather. Members of group B observe all the same restrictions, except for arranging infant marriages for their children, thus being ranked as somewhat lower than group A's members in regard to purity due to nonobservance of that one criterion.

Although admittedly hypothetical in its specific clustering of oppositions, this example does, however, reveal how a large number of groups can be distinguished simply by the iterative application of the pure/impure meta-opposition with regard to a number of criteria. Some of these criteria are distinct, while others may be related by entailment and hence redundant for some groups. For example, for those who do not eat meat, the question of eating other specific types of meat, beef vs. nonbeef or domestic vs. wild, simply does not arise. But these latter distinctions are significant in determining the ranking of those castes whose members do eat meat. Examination of the structural logic of this case makes even clearer why the characterization of hierarchy as the encompassment of the contrary does not quite capture the dynamics of caste hierarchy. As the figure reveals, there is no single path of application of the pure/impure distinction, and the series of terminal nodes of the diagram, that is, the specific castes that are separated into distinct categories with a unique constellation of observances and prohibitions, does not contain any single category that can represent higher nodes or groupings of the castes at intermediate levels.

Figure 3. Logic of inclusion/exclusion in Hindu caste hierarchy

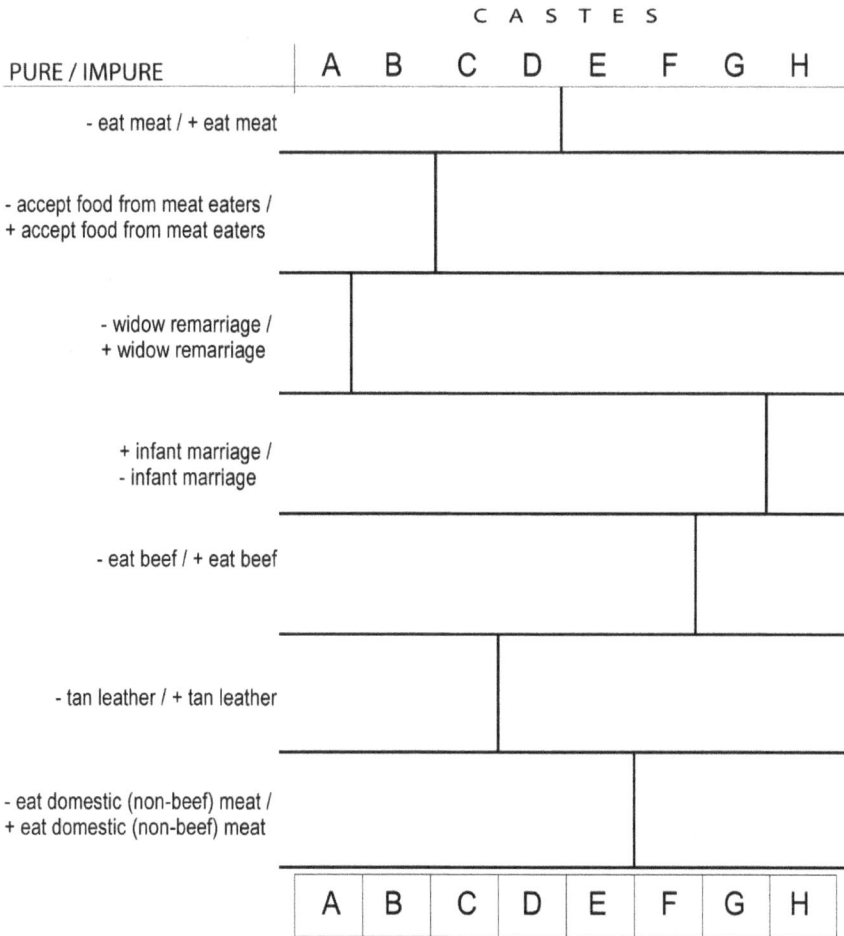

C A S T E S

PURE / IMPURE   A   B   C   D   E   F   G   H

- eat meat / + eat meat

- accept food from meat eaters /
+ accept food from meat eaters

- widow remarriage /
+ widow remarriage

+ infant marriage /
- infant marriage

- eat beef / + eat beef

- tan leather / + tan leather

- eat domestic (non-beef) meat /
+ eat domestic (non-beef) meat

A   B   C   D   E   F   G   H

Two characteristics, however, do stand out as underlying this structural logic, and it is these, I argue, that distinguish hierarchy as a particular type of status ranking procedure. First is the issue of *unitary value*. In his postface Dumont himself emphasizes the importance of value, defined as the according of superior and inferior poles to the oppositional relation, to the construction of hierarchy (Dumont 1980:244). What strikes me is that it is not so much the attribution of value (that is, asymmetry) that is distinctive of hierarchy, but the constitution by unitary value. That is, the hierarchical system can be generated by the recursive application of a *single* differentiation in value, in this case that of pure vs. impure. Fox (1994:95, 106) too has noted that this single opposition is the 'basis of all hierarchy' for Dumont. Although the criterion of separation may be different for the specific opposition applied at each level, the terms defined by each criterion may be judged in terms of the value defined by the meta-opposition 'pure/impure'. Indeed, that is the rationale of all the specific oppositions.

Secondly, the system does not operate as a mechanism for successive encompassment, which is by definition a type of inclusion. Rather, the point of the whole system is *successive or graduated exclusion*. Those who can be characterized as occupying the pure pole on the greatest number of criteria are classed as at the top. As noted by Pocock (1957), in the very paper which Apthorpe cited as inspiring his own elaboration of hierarchy, the end which those at the top attempt to attain is the exclusion of those aspiring to their own status. This goal local actors strive to achieve by various strategies of endogamy (Pocock 1957:28), which may lead to the construction of endogamous marriage circles that may congeal, in time, into subcastes or even castes (Pocock 1957:22). Of course, this tendency is also countered by those from lower groups who seek to be identified with members of the higher groups by a countervailing process of inclusion which is realized in various hypergamic strategies. But the overall thrust of the recursive application of the single valued opposition is to emphasise the dynamics of exclusion as an end to the system. Indeed, our understanding of caste as a unique social formation depends heavily on the exclusive character of its strata, with caste endogamy seen as more definitive of the cultural system than hypergamy despite the empirical incidence of the latter.

The Logic of Precedence

I have emphasized these two characteristics of hierarchy — unitary value and exclusion as an aim — precisely in order to distinguish it from the notion of precedence. In one of his most explicit theoretical treatments of this latter concept, Fox (1994) notes that there is no absolute distinction between precedence and hierarchy, although each exhibits different potentials given the development of each in association with analyses of a particular ethnographic context, that of South Asia in the case of hierarchy and that of the Austronesian world, particularly eastern Indonesia, in the case of precedence. Both systems of status discrimination are based on a notion of opposition, and indeed of asymmetric, but also complementary opposition. Fox (1994:87) has 'argued that an "hierarchical" use of dual categories involves the conjunction of two analytic features: categorical asymmetry and recursive complementarity'. As his own examples later in the same article attest, the same two features characterize the operation of systems of precedence as well.

What Fox does emphasize as distinctive of precedence is the complex operation of a number of valent oppositions, rather than simply the continued operation of one privileged (meta-)opposition. This *multiplicity or diversity* of relevant oppositions facilitates the possiblity of categorical reversals of valency of any categorical asymmetry. Precedence is thus subject to greater possibilities of social contention or contestation than hierarchy (Fox 1994:96–98). It is easier to move from a position as wife-taker to wife-giver in a system of asymmetric connubium organized by precedence than for a Shudra to leapfrog up to Kshatriya or even move simply to Vaishya status. Fox also emphasizes one other characteristic, which I feel is perhaps one of the most crucial hallmarks of prececedence: the necessity for *an initial term or inception point* (Fox 1994:98 [my italics]). In the Austronesian case, Fox argues that this leads to a concern with 'origins' or 'sources', whether expressed spatially or temporally (and often in both modes). Precedence systems are generated on the basis of measuring social distance from some origin line or point. Most often, such systems in the Austronesian world are articulated by basic metaphors (Fox 1980b) that oppose branches to trunks or bases; the term that literally means 'trunk' or 'root' tends to be used metaphorically in these Austronesian languages to mean 'source' or 'origin'. Precedence is based on a movement from trunk to tip through a profusion of branches. Such a movement may be taken as a hallmark of precedence conceptually rather than just areally. And in certain respects the other characteristics that distinguish precedence systems may be seen to follow from this characteristic. Perhaps a couple of examples will best illustrate the operation of precedence systems.

The Operation of Precedence in Eastern Indonesia

Fox (1994:99–106) has already elegantly summarized the operation of precedence in the asymmetric connubium of the Timorese Atoin Pah Meto, the Javanese kinship terminology, and the dynastic politics of Termanu in Roti. Rather than recapitulating those examples, let me first simply highlight a major characteristic of the Timorese case before proceeding to two other examples. There the system of precedence works by the notion of degrees of proximity to the origin, an order of precedence enshrined in myth by temporal precedence and sustained in contemporary social relations by wife-giver/wife-taker relations in a fixed order. What is significant is how this system does not depend upon a system of exclusion and separation in terms of some common underlying notion, like degrees of purity. It is a system for assimilating or incorporating groups and building larger structures, precisely the function accorded to generalized exchange structures by Lévi-Strauss (1969). Although newer groups may be first incorporated at lower levels of the structure, the potential for reversing wife-giver/wife-taker relations provides the basis for leapfrogging in the system that allows the specific status order to be reconfigured, although the basic asymmetric opposition and warrant of the system — wife-givers are of higher status than wife-takers — remains stable.

The Ata Tana 'Ai of central Flores demonstrate how a different set of overt social manifestations — earlier social theory would have labelled the Ata Tani Ai as matrilineal as opposed to attributing patrilineality to the Atoin Pah Meto — may realize the same logic of precedence. For the Ata Tana 'Ai, the term *oda* signifies the succession or order of events, the sequencing that makes up history (Lewis 1988:81). *Oda* is also the term used to label orders of social precedence among the Ata Tana 'Ai. For example, there is the order of precedence *among* clans in a domain, which depends, as in the Atoni Pah Meto example, on the order in which ancestors of the clans first came to the domain in the origin myths. This order of precedence determines the ranking of responsibility for the rituals that are deemed necessary for the continuity of the domain, as overall responsibility for the most important rituals rests with the origin clan, and ultimately with the 'Source of the Domain, the center, source, trunk, and foundation of the domain' (Lewis 1988:76), a functionary whose epithets clearly resonate with the trunk-tip metaphors of precedence elsewhere among Austronesian societies.

But *oda* is also relevant *within* the clans to set up a system of precedence operating, as in the Atoin Pah Meto case, through the dynamics of marriage exchange. In every clan there is one descent line considered as the *pu'an*, the source or origin, whose members claim descent from the first ancestor of the clan to arrive in Tana 'Ai. The descendants of these source ancestors make up a house (what previous kinship theorists would have labelled a lineage) within the clan; other houses within the clan are conceptualized as following behind the source house. This 'following behind' depends on a system of marriage in which the bestowal of men outside the clan (see Figure 4) should be reciprocated in the next generation by the return of a woman to marry a member of the original husband-bestowing clan, a usage labelled 'returning the father's forelock' (Lewis 1988:205ff.). The descendants of the woman bestowed then become a segment or a house of the now expanded clan into which she has returned through (father's forelock) marriage. Thus, within the clan the order of precedence is determined by the succession of returning a woman, the father's forelock, back to the house from which a man had been received in marriage. Here is Lewis's explanation of this figure:

> In the first instance, a man of house A1 marries a woman of clan B. One of his daughters is returned to clan A by means of the transfer of father's forelock. The daughter enters her father's clan, marries her father's sister's son, and founds within clan A the house A2. In the next generation, another man of house A1 marries a woman of clan C, and a man of A2 marries a woman of clan D. Daughters of these men are subsequently returned to clan A, marry their fathers' sisters sons, and found houses A3 and A4, respectively. House A5 is founded in the sixth generation as the result of the marriage of a man of house A4 to a woman of clan E. The oda ranking, that is, the order of precedence of the houses, is established by the order in which their founding mothers enter the clan (1988:230).

Figure 4. The organization of houses within the clan Ata Tana 'Ai (Lewis 1988:230)

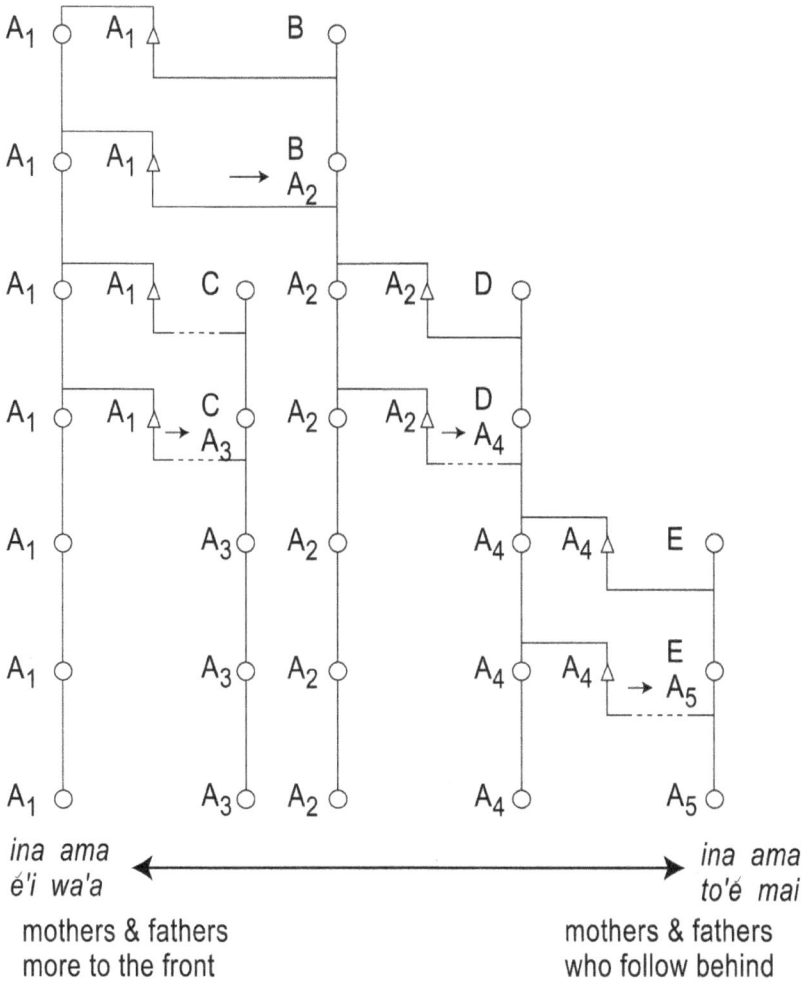

ina ama
é'i wa'a

mothers & fathers
more to the front

ina ama
to'é mai

mothers & fathers
who follow behind

(after Lewis 1988: 230)

So, considered as houses within the clan, A1 is ranked higher than A2, while A2 is ranked higher than A3 and A4, which rank higher than A5, and so on in an order of precedence, according to the succession of marriage exchanges involving the father's forelock. The house to which one's own clan gives a woman as father's forelock is regarded as ahead in the order of precedence and labelled as *ini ama e'i wa'a* 'mothers and fathers who are more to the front', while those to whom one bestows a man and subsequently receives a woman are *ini ama to'e mai* 'mother and fathers who follow behind'. The order of precedence is thus established by the order in which founding mothers enter the clan. This movement of other clans into the source clan as houses leads to a movement of women from the periphery to the centre of the clan, as men are spun off to more peripheral groups, resulting in greater consolidation of maternal descent groups in the centre: the central and older houses become relatively more powerful because they are wealthiest in term of the number of women. As Lewis describes the point of the whole system:

> In Tana Wai Brama, daughters are wealth. The larger the number of women in a house, the greater is the productive capacity of the house and the larger the surplus from gardens that can be converted into ceremonial goods (*to'o balik*). A clan's reserves of ceremonial goods thus tend to be concentrated in the source house and those houses of the clan which are *e'i wa'a*, closer to the source, who wield corresponding power in the clan by virture of being able to decide how that wealth is used in securing (through father's forelock exchanges) women from other clans (1988:232; italics in original).

In contrast to the precedential ordering of social segments according to marriage exchanges among the Atoin Pah Meto and Ata Tana 'Ai, both largely interior swidden horticultural societies of eastern Indonesia, precedence also operates in other societies of different scale and social composition within the region by invoking other mechanisms. Status ranking in coastal Balinese rajahdoms or *negara*, to take one example of a society often regarded as more complex in regard to the multiplicity of groups and ways of assessing status,[5] can also be analysed, at least in part, as organized by precedence. For example, as delineated by Geertz (1980), the ranking of royal houses depends upon a notion of distance from an origin line, as well as from an origin point. As Figure 5 reveals, the ruling line of Gelgel is seen as continually 'sinking' in status as it falls away through the generations from its origin in the god Batara, through the semi-divine *mpu* spirits, a term that like Tana 'Ai *pu'an* refers to source or origin. The royal line becomes that of the Dangiang Brahmana, who begets a line of Ksatriya rajahs, the *Kresna kepakisan*. Seven generations down the line, the ruler can only assume the lower title of Dewa Agung, while in the next generation, when the domain of Gelgel disintegrates and is replaced by Klungkung, the ruler suffers yet another drop in title status, as the process of 'sinking' continues off the diagram to the end of that dynasty. Fox (1995:224-225) has noted how this Balinese system of 'sinking status' is but one variant of the formal structure of 'apical demotion' that is characteristic of societies found on smaller islands in the Austronesian world whose elites, preoccupied with status, have developed this device to maintain their exclusivity (*cf.* Fox on Termanu, this volume).

Figure 5. Sinking status of royal lines in Bali (schematized from Geertz 1980)

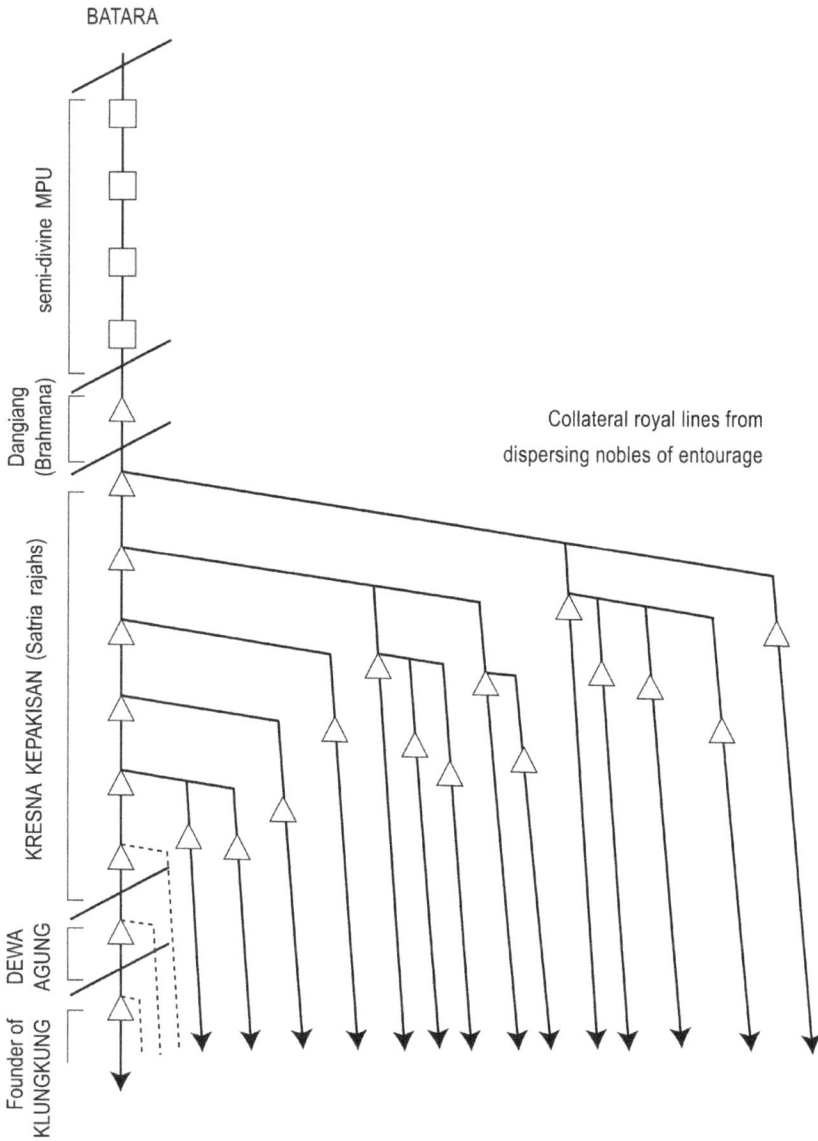

BATARA

semi-divine MPU

Dangiang (Brahmana)

KRESNA KEPAKISAN (Satria rajahs)

DEWA AGUNG

Founder of KLUNGKUNG

Collateral royal lines from
dispersing nobles of entourage

This line of the diagram demonstrates the operation of 'sinking status' (Geertz 1980:16ff.) with respect to the divine origin ancestor. But there is also a lateral movement, with noble members of the rajah's entourage breaking off to found their own domains away from the central palace.[6] And these new royal lines are ranked too, with those that have diverged in earlier generations ranked as lower than those that break off closer to the reigning rajah of the origin line. Such an attribution is consistent with that of the origin line itself, since over the generations these diverging lines are conceptualized as moving further from the origin line by the principle of sinking status. Those local royal lines shown closer to the origin line in Figure 5, which means those that have broken away most recently, are higher in rank and those further away, those who have broken away earlier, some of which will have their own breakaway offshoots, are lower. Proximity to an origin point and to an origin line thus determines ranking in this system.

This same precedential logic based on a calculus of generational distance from an origin point and an origin line informs other levels of Balinese socio-political structure. The Balinese also have a patrilineal descent group organization, based on a unit called the *dadia*, which like the Tana 'Ai clan is composed of houses. Sinking status articulates the relations of houses within a *dadia*, as illustrated by Figure 6. The earlier a line breaks away to form a house within a royal *dadia*, the lower its rank: noble house A is lower in status than noble house B, which is lower than C, which is lower than D, and so on. The same principle of sinking status that orders royal lines among themselves also distinguishes the houses within a *dadia*. Status distinction in these aspects of Balinese sociopolitical structure depends upon notions of proximity to an origin line.

Figure 6. Gentry descent: the principle of sinking status

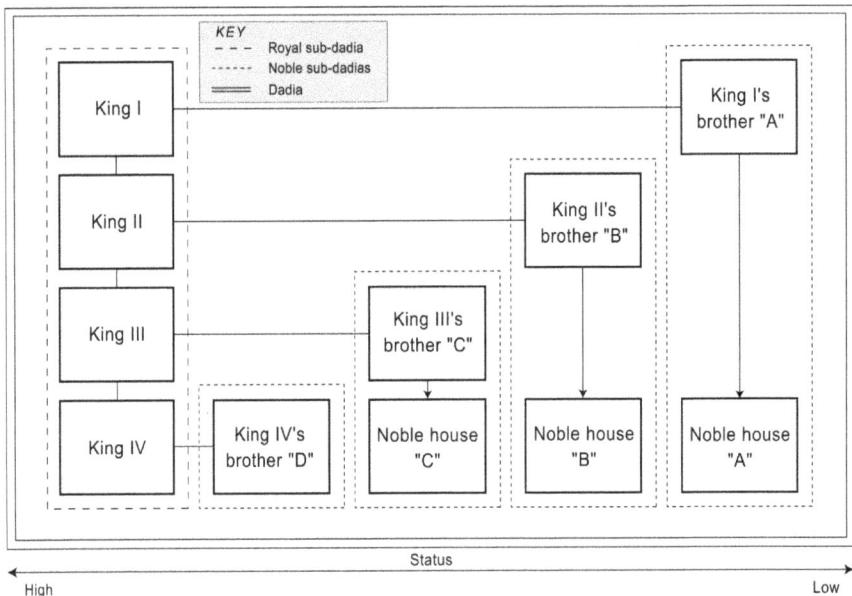

Interestingly, the Balinese of these *negara* reverse the value of the Ata Tana 'Ai order of precedence of houses of the clan. Among the Ata Tana 'Ai, those houses incorporated first through father's forelock marriage exchanges rank higher in the precedence system. In Bali those houses that diverge first from the main line within the *dadia* rank lower. Such a difference highlights two of the functions of precedential ordering. As in the case of Timorese marriages, precedence among the Ata Tana 'Ai operates to incorporate or include lines within a house, whereas with the Balinese *dadia* precedence operates to differentiate lines within the descent group. Such a difference is to be expected, as in the former cases precedence operates through an order of marriage exchanges, while in the latter it operates through an ordering of filiation and descent lines. Both functions, however, exemplify different operations of precedential logic. And in both cases there is still the option of manipulating the system through strategies involving categorical reversal. Precisely that potential is what differentiates the operation of these systems from hierarchical systems orientated primarily to exclusion rather than incorporation and differentiation.

The Bugis and Makasar in South Sulawesi: Intermeshing Hierarchy and Precedence

The analysis of the societies of the Bugis and Makasar peoples of South Sulawesi provides an interesting opportunity to examine the applicability of notions of hierarchy and precedence to a particularly problematic archipelagic Southeast Asian context. Errington (1989) has labelled the societies of South Sulawesi as more representative of hierarchical, centre-oriented Indic states than of eastern Indonesian systems organized by complementarity and exchange. Indeed, she classifies the polity of Luwu' in South Sulawesi and the other Bugis and Makasar realms of the southwestern peninsula as belonging to the 'Centrist Archipelago', encompassing (from the northern point proceeding clockwise) the Philippines, Halmahera, Buru, Sulawesi, Bali, Java, Kalimantan, and the Malay peninsula (Errington 1989, pt. III:207ff., map on p.208; reiterated in Errington 1990:39ff., map on p.xvii). Errington explicitly contrasts this Centrist Archipelago with eastern Indonesia in her earlier version (Errington 1989:209) and then with the 'Exchange Archipelago' in her later rendition (Errington 1990:39).[7] Many of those working outside the Centrist Archipelago (for example, Forth 1992) have sharply criticized Errington's account for her failure to note the continuities that cut across her two archipelagoes, many of which are expressions of the precedence structures that occur as well in Sulawesi. Indeed, my own inclusion of the operation of precedence structures in Bali (see above) may be taken as yet another example of such continuities across her apparently contrasting units. Errington has also been taken to task by other reviewers for assuming that the polities of Sulawesi, Luwu' in particular, may be analysed as Indic states based on the *mandala* model of political power (for example, Babcock 1991; Caldwell 1991).

With these critiques I am in accord. One need only compare the way in which bamboo clumps are used to model the relations of social groups among the Bugis nobility of Luwu' and, to take but one example from eastern Indonesia, among the Ata Tana 'Ai, to realize the depth of continuities across the boundary Errington posits (Errington 1989:33, 215; Lewis 1988:75).[8] However, when reading the accounts of ritual and social organization in eastern Indonesia, and even more forcefully when watching filmic accounts of the enactment of precedence in eastern Indonesian ritual, I cannot help but feel that there is a very different cast to the enactment of status difference in Bugis and Makasar rituals, most notably weddings (Millar 1983, 1989), in South Sulawesi (and coastal Central and Southeast Sulawesi as well) compared to their expression in eastern Indonesia. Errington may have somewhat misconstrued this difference by reducing the complexity of precedence, a term she does not herself use in a specific sense, in eastern Indonesian societies to the modelling of the relations of constituents upon elder/younger oppositions, both 'older brother'/'younger brother' [sic][9] and older generation/younger generation (Errington 1989:206ff.) Her assertion that 'in the more hierarchical societies of island Southeast Asia, the generational layers are overlaid, but not displaced, by institutionalized structures of inheritable prestige' (Errington 1989:206) also leads to some further misconstruals, such as her subsequent assertion that it is (primarily) in these latter societies of the Centrist Archipelago that terms of respect tend to implicate ancestors or the 'source' (Errington 1989:206). However, Errington's phrasing of differences does lead one to posit a possible divergence in the way that precedence and hierarchy are intertwined in these societies. In the paragraphs that follow I hope to explore this difference by arguing for a different elaboration of hierarchy among these peoples of South Sulawesi, while noting the continued operation of precedence structures in arenas of status recognition and assertion.

Such an approach is not really novel. Accounts of Bugis and Makasar society have tended to emphasize the interplay of various features of status discrimination. On the one hand, the society has been described as articulated by a pervasive sense of hierarchy (for example, Pelras 1971, 1996:110). Nobles have the warrant to rule by virtue of prerogatives derived from their inherent qualities, whether conceptualized as the greater whiteness of their blood (Matthes 1875:4) or their greater concentration of potency (Errington 1983a). Commoners and slaves in this view 'naturally' carry out the commands of their betters with all due deference in recognition of their leaders' greater worth. Contrasting with this 'highly formalised class structure'[10] (Chabot 1967:191), which pervasively influences the conduct of everyday life, is a complementary emphasis upon enterprise, the individualistic achievement of status through success in economic endeavours, political office, or educational achievement. On the one hand, a person's position is seemingly set by birth, an inherent status fixed unalterably by the positions of one's father and mother in the rank system. On the other hand, status is also the outcome of how well one competes in the arena of social life, the fortune that one creates for oneself and one's family through work (*jama* [B][11]) (Acciaioli 2004). The system of ranks is at once inalterably fixed by custom (*ade'* [B] or *adat* [I]) and yet also fluid, for individuals can gain social recognition for a different ranking for themselves and for their families by manifest success in economic endeavours, masterful negotiation in political affairs, and scholarly accomplishments in education. Social hierarchy and economic enterprise, pervasive rank and competitive mobility, traditionalism and opportunism — such oppositions have been put forth as constituting the distinctive dynamic of Bugis and Makasar society. What I hope to do is to reformulate some of these contradictions more elaborately by invoking more specified senses of hierarchy and precedence.

However contradictory these poles might appear, they are united in their orientation to certain cultural foci of the Bugis and Makasar. The assertion of status, both its maintenance and its achievement, is a primary concern, perhaps even an obsession in local culture. In her study of weddings in the Bugis domain of Soppéng, Millar has labelled this absorption a preoccupation with 'social location', of negotiating for ever higher positions (and making sure that one falls no lower) in variously defined status continua:

> Social relations among the Bugis are fluid, equivocal, and competitive, yet strongly hierarchical. Within this society individuals simultaneously compete for higher achieved status, on the one hand, and jealously guard their privileges based upon ascriptive status on the other. Consequently, for the Bugis, the question of the social location of individuals is a matter of continuous tension; it is always important yet seldom certain (Millar 1989:1).

Rephrased in Bugis terms, it is a concern for defining one's place in relation to all others in the society, as Errington (1983b:197, 200ff.) has rightly noted.

The Bugis term *onro*, which is most often glossed as 'place', is marked by both geographical and social connotations. The definition in Said's dictionary of spoken Bugis stresses both physical location (*tempat* [I]) and social status or rank (*derajat* [I], literally 'degree', and *pangkat* [I], social position). Matthes's dictionary, highlighting more the literary form of Bugis used in *lontara'* manuscripts in Boné and elsewhere, begins its entry for *onro* (Matthes 1874:836) with a number of derived verbal forms that emphasize keeping one's whereabouts constant or a general physical stasis. For example, *monroi daranna* [B], literally 'her blood remains', signifies that a woman is not menstruating, thus implying that she is pregnant. However, the signification of the term relating to social status also emerges in such forms as *to mangonrong*, a debt slave. Thus, like the term *empo* used by the neighbouring Makasar people (Cense with Abdoerahim 1979:204), Bugis *onro* locates objects and individuals in a space that is both physical and social.

Such dual significance — one not unfamiliar to us in our own usages such as 'knowing one's place' — accords well with the functioning of Bugis society, especially the organization of social occasions. Social status is negotiated and validated precisely in such contexts as the organization of seating arrangements at a wedding feast or other ceremony. As Millar (1989) has shown, in such settings, physical place indexes relative rank. Ladies of higher rank sit on the upper platform at the front of the kitchen partaking of cakes, as lower status 'co-workers' toil at the pots beneath them. Hosts agonize over where to seat their guests, endeavouring always to reserve the front-row seats for the guests of highest rank. Traditionally, in the Bugis-Makasar area nobody could ever be seated on a level with the ruler. Physical placement thus signifies social location.

The rank that is signified by such placements is in theory articulated in the Bugis system of *wari'*, the structure of status levels given as one of the five foundations of Bugis-Makasar society in the *latoa* and other *lontara'* manuscripts.[12] According to Matthes (1874:641), the term *wari'* is related to the Makasar and Bugis term *barrisi*, meaning line or stroke, row or series (*streep* [D] *rij* [D]). The term is thus cognate with *baris* [I], which is the Indonesian gloss Said (1977:221) gives for the term *wari'* in his dictionary. Said also provides the gloss *tuturkan* [I], 'to relate, narrate, tell about'. *Wari'* thus has the sense of prescribing an unfolding narrative in a proper series. This indigenous theory posits a rigid system of status levels or ranks elaborating upon the three basic levels found throughout Sulawesi and elsewhere in the archipelago (not just the Centrist Archipelago!). A basic trichotomy of nobles, commoners and slaves provides the fundamental structure upon which is built a refined latticework of 'intermediate ranks' (*tusschenstanden* [D], as they are called in older Dutch works).

What I want to argue is that the *wari'* system of assessing rank operates as both a system of hierarchy and one of precedence. Its characterization in terms of the former construct derives from its recursive usage of a single idiom of differentiation — the possession or absence of white blood — and from its tendency to emphasize exclusion rather than incorporation or differentiation for the reproduction of the privileged centre of the system, or, to use Errington's problematic phrase, as 'a vast device, backed by (unstable) force for restricting access to potency' (Errington 1989:10).[13] However, as the account below reveals, the system also has its foundations in a myth of origin, and in many ways the logic of differential nobility is based on increasing divergence from an origin point of deities of pure white blood, a movement that is reminiscent of the 'sinking status' of the Balinese. However, these deities are not regarded as the progenitors of humankind as a whole, but only of the nobility, regarded as a late emergent upon the social scene, rather than an origin that establishes a logic of precedence for the society as a whole.[14]

The *wari'* system operates to generate intermediate ranks between nobles and slaves as a result of intermarriages of white-blooded nobles with red-blooded commoners and slaves. Although various domains differ in the names accorded these lower nobles and the number of intermediate ranks recognized, the basic logic of their genesis is constant. A fundamental dichotomy is posited between nobles on the one hand and commoners and slaves on the other. Pure nobles, those theoretically most eligible for succession to the rulership of a domain, constitute a different order of being. Unlike mere mortals, they are the descendants of the *tomanurung* (Matthes 1875; Friedericy 1933; Pelras 1996:32), heavenly beings who descended to the land in order to establish order on a chaotic social landscape.[15] Their pure descendants are entrusted with the task of continuing this order on earth; hence to them is reserved the theoretical right to rule. However, many of these descendants have intermarried with commoners and slaves. Their descendants are of less noble rank, a condition given symbolic expression as the dilution of their otherworldly 'white blood' with the red blood of mere worldlings.[16] The idiom of white blood thus serves as a counter that exactly places all individuals on a scale of nobility in a manner *theoretically* determined only by marriage and descent. The marriage of a pure noble with a commoner or slave[17] produces an intermediate rank of descendants with diluted white blood. Subsequent marriage of pure nobles with members of this intermediate rank produces yet another intercalated rank for descendants. These descendants are higher in rank than the progeny of nobles intermarried with pure commoners, but still of inferior or diluted status compared to the offspring of spouses who are both of pure heavenly (that is, white-blooded) descent. The members of this intercalated rank may then marry with pure nobles to produce yet another intermediate level for their descendants. This process may continue across the generations until eventually the rank of descendants produced is considered a scarcely distinguishable subcategory of the purest nobility. In the opposite direction, descendants of the intercalated noble ranks can marry downward with commoners or slaves to produce more intermediate levels of descendants that move toward the commoner end of the spectrum of rank. Eventually, the offspring of a marriage between a member of a sufficiently low intermediate rank and a spouse of the commoner level are considered as nonnoble, though perhaps commoners of a slightly elevated status (that is, *tau décéng*, literally 'the good people'), those who can claim a measure of aristocratic descent, but whose blood is sufficiently diluted so that they cannot exactly trace the original connections to noble forebears.

The process of intercalating ranks, which moves both in the direction of the purest nobility and toward simple commoner status, can logically proceed without limit. Figure 7 presents a simplified, generalized model of this theory of intermediate rank generation, omitting a variety of possible marriages among the members of the intermediate ranks themselves. In fact, the number of recognized and labelled intermediate ranks determined by such marriages among members of different ranks constitutes one of the primary contrasts between the status systems of different domains in South Sulawesi. Figure 8 illustrates how the rank system of Wajo' as reported by van Rhijn and presented in Friedericy (1933:458–459) resembles to a great degree the logical model of Figure 7.[18] However, the divergence of representations, as formalized from the same source (Friedericy 1933), of the rank systems of Mandar (Figure 9) and Goa (Figure 10), the latter the most powerful domain of the Makasar, also suggests that other factors militate against the potential for infinite gradation of ranks. As these diagrams illustrate, not only the number of intercalated ranks and the types of marriages that are asserted to generate them, but also the boundaries at which the major categories are delimited vary across domains. Whereas in Mandar and Goa only subdivisions of the nobility are created by these means, in Wajo' distinct status levels that are intermediate between pure nobility and commoners are generated. By such means the entire system is open to more variant interpretations, as the exact boundaries where nobility has become so diluted as no longer to warrant the title are rendered more obscure. As divisions multiply in systems like that of Wajo', the boundaries between gradations are blurred. The possibility of status mobility is thereby entrenched more firmly in the entire system.

So set out, the *wari'* system constitutes an attempt to define a single all-embracing hierarchy based on a single valent (that is, asymmetric) idiom (white blood/red blood). This opposition has been the basic principle regulating not only possible marriages, but a whole set of sumptuary laws, judicatory arrangements, restrictions on land tenure, and ways of extracting labour and payments from the populace. The scale of white blood can serve as a counter, a comprehensive measure of worth upon which various gradations of nobility could be placed. Absence of white blood demarcates the status of simple commoner. The idiom of blood thus operates very differently from those eastern Indonesian societies in which the transmission of (a homogeneously conceived) blood symbolically functions as the metaphoric channel of the 'flow of life' (Fox 1980a, 1980b) for all members. In such systems, blood is coupled with semen in order to produce the human person. The redness of blood is thus in a complementary opposition with the whiteness of semen, with the latter term sometimes transmuted into the whiteness of bone in the newly formed child, where both are necessary for the continuity of life along lines of whatever rank.[19] However, the complementary duality in eastern Indonesia of red and white, blood and semen/bone, with both necessary for procreation, is usurped for purposes of status reckoning in the South Sulawesi context by the idiom of the dilution of white blood through marriage. White and red are differentiated within the metaphorical substance of blood itself, as the asymmetric opposition of white blood/red blood functions like the asymmetric opposition of purity/impurity in South Asia to divide the society hierarchically into ranks.

Figure 7. Abstract schema of Bugis status levels

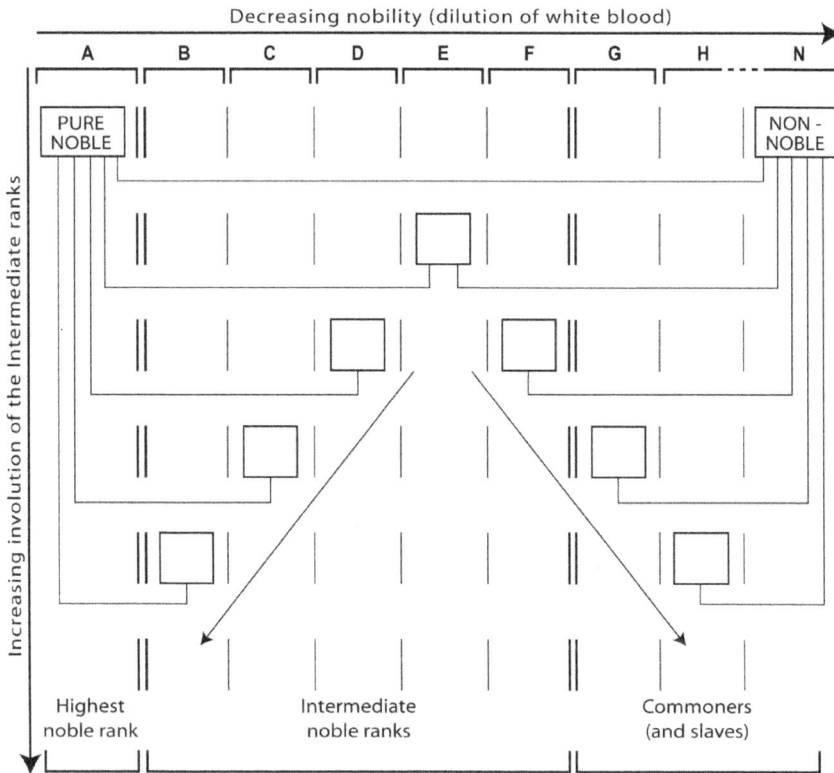

Figure 8. Schema of status levels in Wajo'

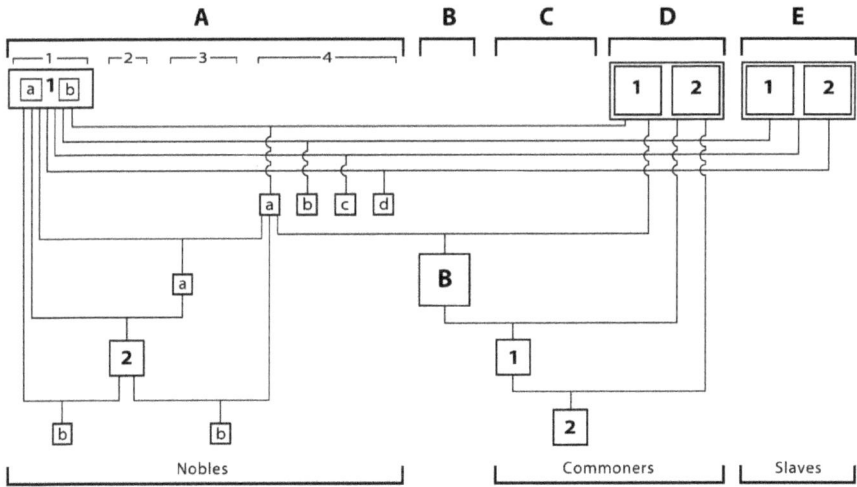

Nobles   Commoners   Slaves

Key

A		**ANA'-MATOLA** *(Princely nobility)*
	A1	Ana'-Matola
	A1a	Ana'-Matola
	A1b	Ana'-Matola
	A2	Ana'-Sangaji *(Princely children)*
	A3	Ana'-Rajeng
	A3a	Ana'-Rajeng-Lebbi
	A3b	Ana'-Rajeng
	A4	Ana'-Cera'
	A4a	Ana'-Cera' Sawi
	A4b	Ana'-Cera' Pua
	A4c	Ana'-Cera' Ampulajeng
	A4d	Ana'-Cera' Iyatang Dapureng
B		**ANAKKARUNG** *(Children of the Rajah)*
C		*(No label given)*
	C1	Tau Déceng
	C2	Tau Tongeng-Karaja
D		**TAU MARADÉKA**
	D1	Tau-Maradéka-Mannennungeng
	D2	Tau-Maradéka-ri-Sampengi
E		**ATA** *(Slaves)*
	D1	Ata-Mana
	D2	Ata-Mabuang

NOBLES   COMMONERS   SLAVES

Figure 9. Schema of status levels in Mandar

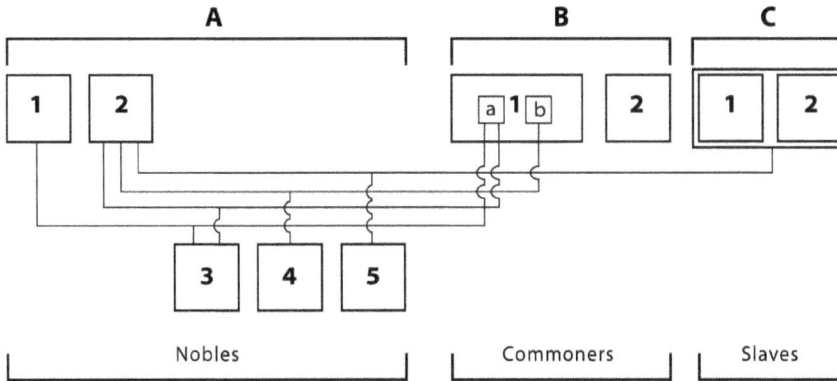

Figure 10. Schema of status levels in Goa

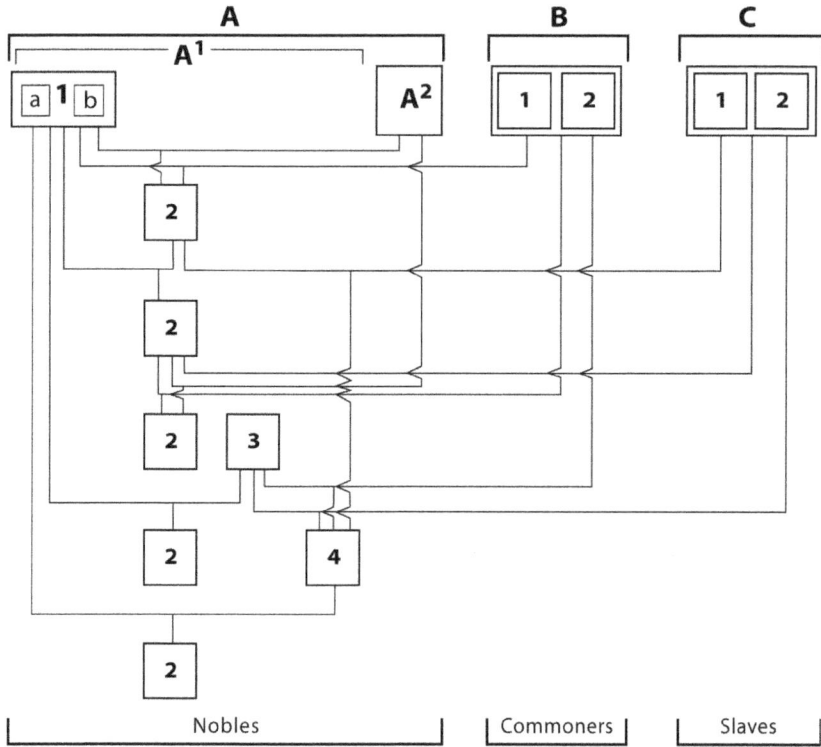

Key

A

A1		Ana'-Karaéng-ri-goa *(Children of the ruler of Goa)*
	$A^1$1	Ana'-Tino' (Ripe or cooked children)
	$A^1$1a	Ana'-Patola
	$A^1$1b	Ana'-Manrapi
	$A^1$2	Ana'-Sipué (Half children)
	$A^1$3	Ana'-Céra (Blood children)
	$A^1$4	Ana'-karaéng-sala ('Wrong' children of the ruler)
A2		*Other* Ana'-karaéng

B TU-MARADÉKA *('Free people')*
  B1 Tu-Baji' (Gentry)
  B2 Tu-Samara (Commoners)

C ATA (Slaves)
  C1 Ata-sossorang *(Hereditary slaves)*
  C2 Ata-Nibuang *(Those thrown away)*

Yet, in its image of continual dilution of white blood, the *wari'* system also presents a dynamic that resonates with the movement from trunk to tip, with the image of 'sinking status' by which noble rulers in the Balinese *negara* have descended from deity to mere humanity across the generations. Even Errington herself has noted how terms for the nobility tend to implicate not only the ancestors, but also the source. In most languages of the South Sulawesi stock (Mills 1975), the usual term of reference for the highest nobles is *puang*, a term presumably derived from the Autronesian reflex for trunk or source, while the term of address used in Bugis realms for such high nobles, *petta*, is an abbreviated form of *puang* + *ta* ('our lord'). Here rather than the genealogical model of consanguines moving away from the trunk or origin line, it is a movement away from the reference line of purest white blood effected by marriage. And so it is to an examination of Bugis marriage strategies, especially among nobles possessed of white blood, that we must turn for further elucidation of the dynamics of hierarchy and precedence.

Like other societies of the archipelago, the Bugis acknowledge a distinction between younger and elder members of a particular category, as do the Makasar. For example, among siblings of the same status, the eldest is sometimes said to be expected to succeed to a parent's political office, although this expectation does not constitute a right,[20] and is often overridden by considerations of personal ability and political expediency. Precisely because such considerations of strategic practice have obtruded so frequently in the choice of an actual successor, Bugis political order cannot simply be mapped out either according to either the logic of a Malay 'status lineage' (Gullick 1958), a Balinese model of 'sinking status' (Geertz 1980), a Rotinese dynastic genealogy, (Fox 1971) or a general Austronesian model of 'apical demotion' (Fox 1995), although all these notions do have their parallels in structural models that partially inform Bugis and Makasar practices of status reckoning. Younger siblings in succeeding generations do not become the branching points of groups of successively greater distance — and hence lower status — from the line of primogenitural descent from a source ancestor.

In fact, although the Bugis sibling terms *kaka'* and *anri'* (Lineton n.d.:228) encode the same differentiation of elder and younger found throughout Austronesian systems, the differential valuing of these terms reverses the tendencies found in many other systems of reckoning. Elder siblings (*kaka'*) are due a certain amount of respect due to their age, but it is the term for the younger sibling that has become generalized as the most common title for members of the nobility, for the noble status title *Andi'* often inserted before the personal names of nobles is but a variant form of *anri'* (younger sibling). It is the younger or youngest sibling who is most to be cherished, deserving of the nourishing care lavished on nobles. Though not without parallel elsewhere in Indonesia (see Fox (1994:105) for a parallel valuing of the younger over the elder in the domain of Termanu), the younger sibling is the one accorded the value of greater honour, however ambivalently evaluated this deference is (Acciaioli 2004:74-76).

In part, this tendency may be traced to the marriage strategies of Bugis nobles. These strategies contrast overtly with those of Malay rulers and nobles. According to Gullick (1958:55ff.), a sultan in one of the indigenous Malay polities usually married a woman of royal descent as his first wife and royal consort, only subsequently taking wives of inferior status. In most cases, then, the eldest children would be born of this first wife of highest rank. Sons, especially the eldest from this union with a mother of royal descent, were known in Malay as *anak gahara* or *waris beneh dan tanah* ('heirs by the seed and soil'), while the sons from subsequent wives of lower status, who would in most cases also be younger, were known as *anak gundek* (children of a secondary wife). It is evident then that the Malay status lineage, with younger sons diverging from the origin line sustained by their elder siblings of royal status, derives from this precedence in the order of wives.

In contrast, high-noble leaders of Luwu', in accordance with a pattern shared elsewhere in South Sulawesi (Errington 1989:262ff.), traditionally tended to marry their wives of lower status first,[21] before obtaining a wife of the same status. Thus, the marriage system, like the Malay system, included aspects of both hypergamy and endogamy, but in a temporal succession reversing the Malay order of precedence among wives. In the case of Luwu', and in other domains of South Sulawesi as well,[22] marriages with wives of lower status enact a 'centrifugal' strategy aimed at producing followers of lower status (that is, diluted white blood) for the noble and his descendants of the same status. These latter children and grandchildren, offspring of a mother of the same status as their father, would continue the line of highest descent, that preserving as undiluted the purest line of white blood, a centripetal effort at conserving status. Since these latter offspring were likely to be the younger children of later noble wives, it is thus fitting that the term for younger sibling has been generalized as a status term for the nobility.

Marital strategies among Bugis and Makasar nobles in South Sulawesi, in their centrifugal and centripetal movement, present an intermeshing of precedence and hierarchy. Whereas the basic opposition of older sibling/younger sibling (*kaka'/anr[d]i'*) echoes such distinctions of precedence as are found in the Javanese kinship terminology (Fox 1994:102–104), the appropriation of the younger sibling term for the stratum of nobles of the higher degrees of white blood operates to reinforce a pattern of ultimate marital choice that exhibits the exclusiveness characteristic of hierarchy. It is these status-endogamous marriages that have created alliances across the highest levels of nobility among the polities of South Sulawesi, so much so that the nobility has sometimes been characterized as a peninsula-wide stratum crossing all the polities. That is, the highest nobles across all the Bugis and Makasar domains constituted a restricted 'marriage circle', very much like that described by Pocock for subsections of high castes in India (Pocock 1957:28): 'The higher levels exclude the lower by refusing to give them their daughters in marriage and in this way preserve their distinctiveness without effecting a rupture in the caste'. In both cases, it is the women who are prohibited from marrying a husband of a lower rank, serving as the symbolic conservators of high rank (Chabot 1996). As in the case of caste itself, this process of exclusion is balanced by a process of inclusion in the South Sulawesi rank system, as noble men, especially the lower nobles who are the offspring of the lower noble and commoner wives whom their father has married first, engage in marriages with women of lower *wari'* rank in order to gain followers for themselves, on a smaller scale, and for their higher ranking father, on a larger scale (one might in this respect even say a more encompassing scale).

The two movements, exclusive and inclusive, or centripetal and centrifugal in Errington's terms, define the marriage system as a whole:

> Thus a dual movement is required by marriage for high nobles. The one, outward and dispersing, dilutes white blood. The other, inward and conservative, preserves and perpetuates white blood. The two contradictory movements are both necessary. They are effected by the unitary high-core center when it divides itself into two aspects, one conserving, one dispersing. Another name for these two aspects is 'sister' and 'brother' (Errington 1989:260).

Of course, even a glance at the Ata Tana 'Ai system of 'father's forelock marriage' sketched above reveals that the same tendency to send brothers/sons centrifugally, and bring in daughters/sisters centripetally is operative in eastern Indonesia. The symbolic weight of the two poles is markedly similar, undermining the contrast Errington wishes to make between the salience of the brother-sister bond in the hierarchical societies of the Centrist Archipelago and of the conjugal bond in both the 'level' societies of the Centrist Archipelago and in eastern Indonesia (Errington 1989:237). But there is indeed a difference. In Luwu' and indeed perhaps most all the domains of the Bugis and Makasar in South Sulawesi, it is the exclusionary, endogamic marriage circle of the highest nobles that knits together the domains in exchanges among those of the same status. The integrity of this stratum depends upon marrying isogamically, to use Errington's term for same-status marriages (Errington 1989:259). In contrast, the anisogamic marriages do not follow a finely gradated series in which there are particular lines of marriage to be followed with specific provisioners of partners of only the next lowest level in the precedential ranking of clans or similar groups. In short, these marriages do not follow a strict line of precedence. Although there was a tendency to 'rope' local followers back into the followerships (*kapolo*) of high nobles by making sure that marriages were arranged for sons with distant cousins of lower status whose families were losing contact with the centre, these never formalized into enduring alliance structures with recognized houses of lower status along an order of precedence in Luwu' or elsewhere in South Sulawesi.

In this regard, Errington has captured a significant difference between these societies. The contrast is not nearly as stark as she would have it, but inheres in how the hierarchic aspect of the *wari'* system has been able to tilt the inclination of the system towards conservation of a widespread (i.e. cross-polity) centre by exclusionary endogamy and expanding of a local periphery by opportunistic marriages of ever receding kin and other followers. Imagistically, it is the difference between a profusion of casting nets with mesh of ever fluctuating extent, each linked to a common weighted centre, of purest white to be sure, for the societies of South Sulawesi on the one hand, and a series of chains forged by links of descending rank circumference, each with its origin link, all of which may themselves be linked to secure the linear chains to each other in the eastern Indonesian case on the other. The images are similar, and the construction of the meshed nets and linked chains are forged of the same metaphors of centre and periphery, trunk and tip, but the ways the mesh and links articulate with each other in their respective nets and chains do contrast.

Conclusions

As Fox (1994:88) has noted:

> The concept of precedence, I would argue, is applicable to Indian society
> and its use is, I believe, detectable in Dumont's own analysis. Similarly,
> a concept of hierarchy is of great pertinence to Austronesian societies.

Perhaps it may lead to greater conceptual clarification if the term 'hierarchy' is restricted to only certain classification systems within a society, such as the *varna/jati* system in South Asia or the *wari'* system in South Sulawesi. Then, it would not be correct to assert, for example, that South Asian society is hierarchical. Rather, a system of hierarchy may be said to inform (or, more forcefully phrased, partially constitute) South Asian society, but other social mechanisms (regional affiliation, Sanskritization, *jajmani* labour exchanges, rural/urban contrasts, emergent class differences with capitalist penetration, and so on) inform it as well. These distinctions all operate in complex ways to reinforce or mitigate the effects of caste depending upon regional and historical vicissitudes. Similarly, precedence structures, polyvalently operating with characteristic metaphors to incorporate and differentiate constituent groups, inform Austronesian societies, but they do not exhaust the ways of assessing and asserting status in those societies, nor are they necessarily pre-eminent as a status-reckoning mechanism. In many of these societies, univalent hierarchical systems also operate to form exclusionary circles, hence also informing the procedures of discriminating status. Surely, it is not simply the societies of the 'Centrist Archipelago' that are structured by both hierarchy and precedence, as I am sure other East Indonesianist contributors to this volume will affirm. The analytical task then becomes one of assessing how these systems of status discrimination interact in particular contexts, and indeed reinterpret and inflect each other in ever shifting ways. If I may be forgiven the pun, the South Sulawesi case exemplifies how precedence structures may be recast(e) along hierarchical lines.

To take another case from Errington's Centrist Archipelago, perhaps (and I offer this with trepidation as a very tentative interpretation) the Balinese case demonstrates how hierarchy may be reoriented along the lines of precedence. As the example of the sinking status of the royal line of Gelgel in Bali had indicated, there was a relative ranking of Brahman and Kshatriya. Of course, these terms are part and parcel of the caste system, part of the very fabric of the Hinduism which the Balinese practise. However, as Evans, basing himself on Howe (1987), has argued:

> Bali is the main bastion of Hinduism outside India and it has a caste system of sorts ... whether one decides a caste system exists or not in Bali depends on whether one is interested in religion or social stratification or some other aspect of Balinese culture. From the point of view of religious ritual ... there clearly is. But this has few ramifications in other social institutions or in inter-personal interaction as it does in India. Furthermore, the Balinese bilateral kinship system does not lend itself to endogamy and self-contained corporate groups, and caste is largely articulated through membership in caste temples. But one can decide to belong to such temples, or to belong to several of them which, as Lansing points out, 'simply translates into supporting more temple festivals and rituals and having more "kinsmen"' ([Lansing] 1983:110), or to change ones [sic] 'caste' several times in a lifetime (Evans 1993:218).

Obviously, the caste system has not retained its exclusively univalent ('encompassing' if one wishes) character in Bali. As Vickers (1989:50) notes, the priestly function is not monopolized by Brahmans in Bali, upsetting the final level of the operation of the pure/impure opposition in Dumont's model of caste. Indeed, Vickers (1989:50) argues that caste was merely an image of social order used to preserve a rank system which existed in looser fashion before the sixteenth century. The principle of sinking status allows even those of the lowest caste to claim descent across numerous generations from kings or priests of the highest castes (Vickers 1989:51).

Geertz (1980:16) has also argued that caste functions as only one title system among many and that its operation diverges from the South Asian model. In South Asia one witnesses the operation of successive differentiations that progressively isolate the Untouchables outside the *varna* system, the Shudras outside the *triwangsa* ('twice born') category, the Vaishyas outside the dominion system, and finally the Kshatriyas outside the circle of those allowed to make sacrifices to the deities, the task left exclusively to the Brahman at the top of the purity scale. In contrast, in Bali there is a system that seems to have some of the foundations, but the Untouchables are, however, not to be found, and the Sudra are outside the Balinese variant of the *triwangsa*. In fact, the members of the *triwangsa* are referred to as *wong jero* ('insiders'), while the Sudra are termed *wong jaba* ('outsiders') (Geertz 1980:26). Here the oppositions centre/periphery and inside/outside, which structure the metaphors of precedence, are apparent in the Balinese idioms of caste hierarchy. Additionally, when considering the entitlement to power and the exercise of domination, the Brahmana largely drop away from the possibility of actual command, while the Sudra emerge as able to play a considerable role in supravillage politics. Finally,

> Only the Satrias and Wesias were possessed of the one and could acquire the other so as to attain genuine authority, substantial legitimacy, and become the pivot upon which the entire system — priests, commoners, and less successful gentry — turned (Geertz 1980:27).

Geertz's use of the term 'pivot' here not only recalls the titles of Central Javanese rulers, but also suggests that the insider/outsider opposition is complemented by another opposition of the centre/periphery type, in which the Satria and Wesia realize the positively valenced term of legitimate (central) authority, while the Brahmana and Sudra occupy the negatively valenced peripheral term of debarment or 'exclusion' from such authority (Figure 11). The caste system has thus been transformed in the Balinese context into a different sort of structure, one still retaining some of the idioms of hierarchy (for example, exclusion), but also increasingly characterized by multivalent oppositions suggesting the operation of precedence.

As analysis of the cases of South Sulawesi and Bali have exemplified, and, doubtless, examination of further cases throughout the Austronesian world would also reveal (one cannot help but think of the highly articulated rank systems of Polynesia), the analytical task is not one of typifying a society as exclusively or even predominantly hierarchical or precedential, but of trying to make sense of how these modes of status discrimination interact in the everyday and ritual practices of the members of these societies. Whether precedence can be said to encompass hierarchy or hierarchy to encompass precedence is not really the issue. Neither is *a priori* more encompassing. I would thus disagree with the suggestion that 'the totality of contexts in which these different systems of precedence operate (or conflict with one another) is what may constitute hierarchy' (Fox 1994:99), for so to construe the situation is to assert hierarchy as more encompassing than precedence. Nor should precedence be said to encompass hierarchy precisely because in precedence there is no one privileged opposition, but rather a complex interaction of valent oppositions (Fox 1994:98). Rather, these models of status ranking are analytically distinguishable by hierarchy's emphasis on a single underlying asymmetric (that is, valent) opposition operating to construct exclusion and precedence's emphasis upon multiple valent oppositions linked to origin operating to differentiate and incorporate groups. But in actual societies these principles meet and intermesh, differentially invoked in strategies for maintaining and achieving status, setting together in unique solutions and mixtures the parameters of members' 'rivalrous delight in the "celebration of spiritual differentiation"' (Fox 1994:106).

Figure 11. Balinese title system (an adaptation of Hindu caste)

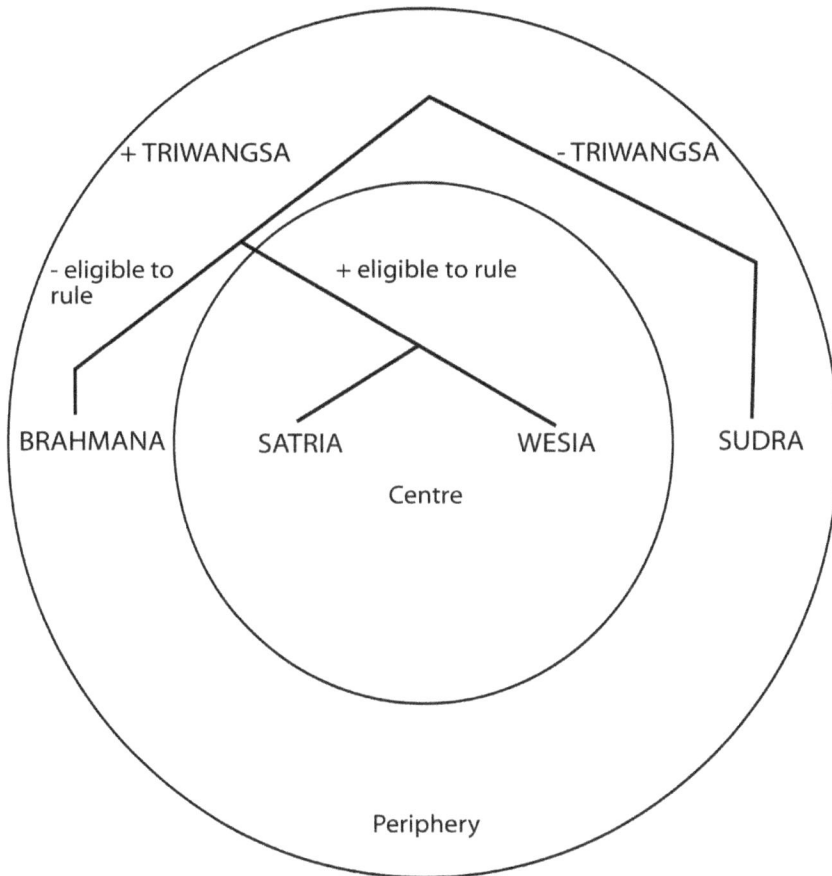

References

Acciaioli, G.

1989 Obituary: Taroh Goh (1958–1988). *Canberra Anthropology* 9(1):136–138.

1990 How to win followers and influence spirits: propitiation and participation in a multi-ethnic community of Central Sulawesi, Indonesia. *Anthropological Forum* 6(2):207–235.

.2000 Kinship and debt: the social organization of Bugis migration and fish marketing at Lake Lindu, Central Sulawesi. *Bijdragen tot de Taal-, Land- en Volkenkunde* 156(3):588–617.

2004 From economic actor to moral agent: knowledge, fate and hierarchy among the Bugis of Sulawesi. *Indonesia* 78:147-179,.

n.d. Exposing invulnerability: knowledge, competition, and hierarchy among the Bugis of South Sulawesi, Indonesia. Unpublished manuscript.

Allen, N.J.

1985 Hierarchical oppositions and some other types of relation. In R.H. Barnes, Daniel de Coppet and R.J. Parkin (eds), *Contexts and levels: anthropological essays on hierarchy* (JASO Occasional Papers No. 4), pp.21–32. Oxford: *JASO* (*Journal of the Anthropological Society of Oxford*).

Andaya, L.Y.

1981 The heritage of Arung Palakka: a history of South Sulawesi (Celebes) in the seventeenth century. Verhandelingen van het Koninklijk Instituut voor Taal-, Land- en Volkenkunde 91. The Hague: Martinus Nijhoff.

Babcock, T.

1991 Review of Errington, *Meaning and power in a Southeast Asian realm*. *Pacific Affairs* 64:135–136.

Blok, R.

1817[1759] *History of the island of Celebes by Mr. R. Blok, governor of Maccassar.* Transl. Captain J. Von Stubenvoll. (Including a Memoir by Governor Blok, Report on the Slave Trade of Maccassar by a Dutch Committee, and Trial and Sentence of Col. Filz who surrendered Fort Victory to Captain Edward Tucker) 4 vols. Calcutta: Calcutta Gazette Press.

Brooke, J.

1848 *Narrative of events in Borneo and Celebes down to the occupation of Labuan* (2nd edn), 2 vols. London: John Murray.

Caldwell, I.

1991 The myth of the exemplary centre: Shelly Errington's *Meaning and power in a Southeast Asian realm. Journal of Southeast Asian Studies* 22(1):109–118.

Cense, A.A. with Abdoerahim

1979 *Makassaars-Nederlands woordenboek met Nederlands-Makassaars register.* 's-Gravenhage: Martinus Nijhoff. (Voor het Koninklijk Instituut voor Taal-, Land- en Volkenkunde.)

Chabot, H.Th.

1967 Bontoramba: a village of Goa, South Sulawesi. In Koentjaraningrat (ed.), *Villages in Indonesia*, pp.189–209. Ithaca, NY: Cornell University Press.

1996 *Kinship, status, and gender in South Celebes.* Koninklijk Instituut voor Taal-, Land- en Volkenkunde, Translation Series 25. Leiden: KITLV Press.

Dumont, L.

1980 *Homo hierarchicus: the caste system and its implications.* Completely revised English edition. Transl. Mark Sainsbury, Louis Dumont, and Basia Gulati. Chicago and London: The University of Chicago Press.

Errington, S.

1983a Embodied Sumange' in Luwu. *Journal of Asian Studies* 42(3):547–570.

1983b The place of regalia in Luwu. In L. Gesick (ed.), *Centers, symbols, and hierarchies: essays on the classical states of Southeast Asia* (Monograph Series No. 26), pp.194–241. Foreword by C. Geertz. New Haven: Yale University Southeast Asia Studies.

1989 *Meaning and power in a Southeast Asian realm.* Princeton NJ: Princeton University Press.

1990 Recasting sex, gender, and power: a theoretical and regional overview. In J.M. Atkinson and S. Errington (eds), *Power and difference: gender in island Southeast Asia*, pp.1–58. Stanford: Stanford University Press.

Evans, G.

1993 Hierarchy and dominance: class, status and caste. In G, Evans (ed.), *Asia's cultural mosaic: an anthropological introduction*, pp.205–233. New York: Prentice-Hall.

Forth, G.

1992 Conjecture, comparison and the coaxing of souls. *Bijdragen tot de Taal-, Land- en Volkenkunde* 148:125–128.

Fowler, C.

1977 Ethnoecology. In D. Hardesty (ed.), *Ecological Anthropology.*, pp. 215-243. New York: John Wiley and Sons.

Fox, J. J.

1971 A Rotinese dynastic genealogy: structure and event. In T.O. Beidelman (ed.), *The translation of culture*, pp.37–77. London: Tavistock.

1980a Introduction. In J.J. Fox (ed.), *The flow of life: essays on eastern Indonesia*, pp.1–18. Cambridge, MA: Harvard University Press.

1980b Models and metaphors: comparative research in eastern Indonesia. In J.J. Fox (ed.), *The flow of life: essays on eastern Indonesia*, pp.327–333. Cambridge, MA: Harvard University Press.

1989 Category and complement: binary ideologies and the organization of dualism in eastern Indonesia. In D. Maybury-Lewis and U. Almagor (eds), *The attraction of opposites: thought and society in a dualistic mode*, pp.33-56. Ann Arbor: University of Michigan Press.

1994 Reflections on 'hierarchy' and 'precedence'. In M. Jolly and M. Mosko (eds), *Transformations of hierarchy: structure, history and horizon in the Austronesian world. History and Anthropology* (Special Issue) 7:87–108.

1995 Austronesian societies and their transformations. In P. Bellwood, J.J. Fox, and D. Tryon (eds), *The Austronesians: historical and comparative perspectives*, pp.214-228. Canberra: Department of Anthropology, as part of the Comparative Austronesian Project, Research School of Pacific and Asian Studies, The Australian National University.

Friedericy, H.J.

1933 De standen bij de Boegineezen en Makassaren. *Bijdragen tot de Taal-, Land- en Volkenkunde van Nederlandsch Indië* 90:447–602.

Geertz, C.

1980 *Negara: the theatre state in nineteenth-century Bali.* Princeton: Princeton University Press.

Goh, T.

1991 *Sumba bibliography* (Occasional Papers). With a foreword by James J. Fox. Canberra: Department of Anthropology, Research School of Pacific Studies, Australian National University.

1998 *Communal land tenure in nineteenth century Java: the formation of Western images of the eastern village community.* Canberra: Department of Anthropology, Research School of Pacific and Asian Studies, The Australian National University.

1977 *A new invitation to linguistics*. Garden City: Anchor Books.

Gullick, J.M.

1958 *Indigenous political systems of Western Malaya*. London: Athlone Press. (London School of Economics Monographs on Social Anthropology no. 17.)

Hamonic, G.

1987 *Le Langage des Dieux: Cultes et pouvoirs pré-islamiques en Pays bugis Cèlébes-Sud, Indonésie*. Paris : Editions du Centre National de la Recherche Scientifique.

Harvey, B.S.

1974 Tradition, Islam, and rebellion: South Sulawesi 1950–1965. Unpublished PhD thesis, Department of Government, Cornell University.

Howe, Leo

1987 Caste in Bali and India: levels of comparison. In L. Holy (ed.), *Comparative anthropology*, pp.135–152. Oxford: Basil Blackwell.

Kennedy, Raymond

1953 *Field notes on Indonesia: South Celebes, 1949–50*, ed. H.C. Conklin. (Behavior Science Monographs.) New Haven: Human Relations Area Files.

Kooreman, P.J.

1883 De feitelijke toestand in het gouvernementsgebied van Celebes en Onderhoorigheden. *De Indische Gids* 5(1):167–200, 358–384, 482–498, 637–655; 5(2):135–169.

Lansing, J.S.

1983 *The three worlds of Bali*. New York: Praeger Publishers.

Lévi-Strauss, C.

1969 *The elementary structures of kinship*. Revised ed. J. H. Bell and J. R. von Sturmer, trans. R. Needham, ed. Boston: Beacon Press.

Lewis, E.D.

1988 *People of the source: the social and ceremonial order of Tana Wai Brama on Flores*. Verhandelingen van het Koninklijk Instituut voor Taal-, Land- en Volkenkunde 135. Dordrecht: Foris.

In press *The Stranger kings of Sikka*. Verhandelingen van het Koninklijk Instituut voor Taal-, Land- en Volkenkunde. Leiden: KITLV Press.

Lineton, J.A.

1975 Pasompe' Ugi': Bugis migrants and wanderers. *Archipel* 10:173–201. (Special issue: Célèbes-Sud.)

n.d. An Indonesian society and its universe: a study of the Bugis of South Sulawesi (Celebes) and their role within a wider social and economic system. Unpublished PhD thesis. London: School of Oriental and African Studies (SOAS), University of London.

Matthes, B.F.

1874 *Boegineesch-Hollandsch woordenboek met Hollandsch-Boegineesche woordenlijst en verklaring van een tot opheldering bijgevoegden ethnographischen atlas.* 's-Gravenhage: M. Nijhoff (voor het Nederlandsch Gouvernement).

1875 *Bijdragen tot de ethnologie van Zuid-Celebes.* 's-Gravenhage: Gebroeders Belinfante.

Mattulada

1985 *Latoa: suatu lukisan analitis terhadap antropologi orang Bugis.* Yogyakarta: Gadjah Mada University Press.

Millar, S.

1983 On interpreting gender in Bugis society. *American Ethnologist* 10(3):477–493.

1989 *Bugis weddings: rituals of social location in modern Indonesia* (Monograph Series, no. 29). Berkeley: Center for South and Southeast Asian Studies, University of California.

Mills, R.F.

1975 Proto South Sulawesi and proto Austronesian phonology. Unpublished PhD thesis, Linguistics, The University of Michigan.

Pelras, Ch.

1971 Hiérarchie et pouvoir traditionel en pays Wadjo' (Célèbes). *Archipel* pt. 1, 1:169–194; pt. 2, 2:197–223.

1996 *The Bugis.* Oxford: Blackwell Publishers.

Pocock, D.F.

1957 Inclusion and exclusion: a process in the caste system of Gujerat. *Southwestern Journal of Anthropology* 13:19–31.

Raffles, T.S.

1830 *The history of Java* (2nd edn), 2 vols. London: John Murray.

Reuter, T.

1993 Precedence in Sumatra: an analysis of the construction of status in affinal relations and origin groups. *Bijdragen tot de Taal-, Land- en Volkenkunde* 148(3, 4):489–520.

2002 *The house of our ancestors: precedence and dualism in highland Balinese society.* Leiden: KITLV Press.

Sahlins, M.D.

1963 Poor man, rich man, big-man, chief: local types in Melanesia and Polynesia. *Comparative Studies in Society and History* 5:285–303.

Said, M.I.

1977 *Kamus Bahasa Bugis-Indonesia.* Jakarta: Pusat Pembinaan Dan Pengembangan Bahasa, Departemen Pendidikan Dan Kebudayaan.

Schmidt S.W., L. Guasti, C. Landé, and J.C. Scott (eds)

1977 *Friends, followers, and factions: a reader in political clientelism.* Berkeley: University of California Press.

Stavorinus, J.S.

1798 *Voyages to the East Indies.* Transl. Samuel Hull Wilcocke, 3 vols. London: G.G. and J. Robinson.

Thontowi, J.

2007 *Hukum, kekerasan & kearifan local: penyelesaian sengketa di Sulawesi Selatan.* Yogyakarta: Pustaka Fahima.

Tyler, S.A.

1969 Introduction. In S.A. Tyler (ed.), *Cognitive Anthropology*, pp. 1-23. New York: Holt, Rinehart and Winston.

Vickers, A.

1989 *Bali: a paradise created.* Ringwood, Vic: Penguin Australia.

Wolters, O.W.

1982 *History, culture, and region in southeast Asian perspectives.* Singapore: Institute of Southeast Asian Studies.

Zerner, C. and T. Volkman

1988 The tree of desire: a Toraja ritual poem. In J.J. Fox (ed.), *To speak in pairs: essays on the ritual languages of eastern Indonesia* (CambridgeStudies in Oral and Literate Culture, no. 15), pp.282–305. Cambridge, Melbourne: Cambridge University Press.

ENDNOTES

[1] Greenberg, more than any other linguist, has elaborated markedness relations into an entire theory of hierarchy in all levels of linguistic structure. For a brief glimpse of this achievement, see Greenberg (1977).

[2] I shall return to this principle of recursiveness below in the discussions of the logic of hierarchy and of precedence. Fox (1989, this volume) has identified recursiveness as one of the underlying features of precedence as well.

[3] I realize that even in this third chapter, Dumont characterizes hierarchy as 'a ladder of *command* in which the lower rungs are encompassed in the higher ones in regular succession' (Dumont 1980:65), but I hope to show that in his working out of his subsequent definition of hierarchy as 'the *principle by which the elements of whole are ranked in relation to the whole*' his notion of encompassment is not that of marking theory, but of the continued application of the same asymmetric opposition. Encompassment thus is largely synonymous with recursiveness or iteration.

[4] I adopt the conventions of the English translation of the revised edition of *Homo hierarchicus* (Dumont 1980) in regard to the spelling and pluralization of South Asian terms. I also maintain the use of the term 'Untouchables' from this translation rather than the contemporary term of choice, Dalits.

[5] Reuter (2002) has already elegantly demonstrated the centrality of precedence in the analysis of the highland communities of Bali, demonstrating significant continuities with societies elsewhere in eastern Indonesia.

[6] This aspect of the operation of 'sinking status' also parallels the logic of succession in the 'status lineage', as elucidated by Gullick (1958) for Malay society.

[7] The only difference between the earlier concept of eastern Indonesia and the later concept of the 'Exchange Archipelago' is the inclusion of Sumatra in the latter, a point she finessed in her earlier account. Reuter (1993) has insightfully illustrated the operation of precedence structures across Sumatra.

[8] See also Zerner and Volkman (1988) for the bamboo clump as a model for familial relations among the Toraja, the nearest neighbours to Luwu'.

[9] Elder/younger terminological oppositions in eastern Indonesian societies, indeed in the terminologies of most societies in the archipelago and Austronesian world, tend not to relate only to brothers, but to siblings whose gender is not specified. Analogously, 'houses' in eastern Indonesia need not be patrilineal, as the case of the Ata Tana 'Ai testifies. In both these assumptions Errington has failed to capture the range of differences in eastern Indonesia and failed to analyse the senior/junior categorical dynamic adequately.

[10] Unlike Chabot, I shall avoid the term 'class' in describing this status system, instead using such terms as 'status level' or 'rank'. Although in the past the various levels certainly corresponded more closely to classes that held differential positions with respect to the control of productive resources, this is less so in the modern context. Many commoners are members of an emergent capitalist middle class, while nobles are not infrequently impoverished. In addition, the primary means of ascribing status, the *wari'* system (see below), was not in the Bugis view based on such control, but conceptualized purely on the basis of marriage and descent. Having stated this, let me add that the accounts of the prerogatives of nobles in the *Adatrechbundels* for South Sulawesi, and especially the detailed account by Kooreman (1883) of payments due to nobles for the various types of land over which they had control, argue persuasively for identifying nobles, commoners and slaves as classes in past decades. Even in the modern context, such a rough correlation of rank with class persists in some areas. As Lineton states, 'the *anakkarung* [the highest rank currently recognized in Wajo, consisting of descendants of local rulers] of Anabanua are in general owners of sufficient land to be able to exist without the necessity of farming their own sawah, which is let out under sharecropping arrangements' (Lineton 1975:193). Lineton herself argues that the difference between ranks like the *tau décéng* and *tau sama*, high and ordinary commoners respectively, is ultimately based on wealth distinctions (Lineton n.d.:156). However true this may be for this particular division of commoners, it cannot account for the elaboration of distinctions among nobles given in Friedericy's analysis of *wari'* discussed below.

[11] Letters in [] following italicized terms indicate the language of the preceding term: [B] stands for Bugis, [D] for Dutch, [I] for Indonesian.

[12] The *latoa* genre deals with the political constitution and operation of the polity in the context of Bugis cosmology. See Mattulada (1985) for an example and analysis of this genre. Besides *wari'*, the other elements upon which the well-being of a land depends are: 1) *ade'* or *adat*, the ancient customs; 2) *undang*, the laws; 3) *bicara*, the system of jurisprudence; and, since the advent of Islam, 4) *sara'* or *syari'at*, Islamic law.

[13] I label this phrase problematic because I disagree with Errington's characterization of *sumange'* as a free-floating sort of soul substance (along animatistic lines) which can be differentially concentrated and dispersed in ways that accord mainly with the social ranks of various actors. Especially, among Bugis commoners *sumange'* is used to indicate individual souls (along animistic lines) attached to various sorts of bodies, both animate and inanimate. Further discussion of this divergence in interpretation, ultimately grounded in whether the animatism of R.R. Marett or the animism of E.B. Tylor is more applicable in interpreting the concept of *sumange'*, can be found in Acciaioli (1990, 2004, n.d.).

[14] Such tales thus are analogous to the pattern of 'the stranger-king' (Fox 1995:217-219, this volume; Lewis, In press). However, in the Bugis/Makasar case, there is less emphasis upon the complementary retention of an indigenous immobile authority, although the function of the *bissu* priests might possibly be interpreted along these lines (Hamonic 1987). There is a greater displacement of authority of all sorts into the hands of the newcomers, a usurpation that confounds the mobile/immobile distinction characteristic of the complementary conceptualization of power in societies more exclusively informed by precedence structures.

[15] Numerous students of Bugis society have interpreted the *tomanurung* [B] tales in the I La Galigo myth cycle as symbols of the origin of larger confederacies among smaller scale Bugis communities. Kooreman explicitly advanced the theory that originally independent small realms (*onafhankelijke rijkjes* [D]) controlled by elders were unified into larger domains (*regentschappen* [D]) by the ancestors of the contemporary regents. The earlier rulers were reduced to village headmen, with only their titles and sometimes their regalia (*gaukeng* in Bugis; *arajang* in Makasar) remaining as evidence of their prior independent authority (Kooreman 1883, (1):174). Stavorinus did remark, however, upon the vestigial independence of these 'inferior chiefs, whom they call galarangs, ... [who] ... live quietly under their own laws, and in the enjoyment of their own religion ... and perform the feudal services required' (Stavorinus v.2 1798:254) by their regents and the Company (i.e. VOC).

Modern historians, particularly those teaching or trained at Cornell, have traced a more elaborate evolution of individual *gaukeng* communities uniting in loose confederations to mediate their inter-community quarrels and to form defensive alliances (Andaya 1981:12ff.). The rulers of the kingdoms thus formed were simply overlords, big men, or 'men of prowess' (Wolters 1982:6), viewed as concentrating in themselves greater potency (Errington 1983a). Each of the sub-rulers they dominated possessed his own localized personal following and was accorded considerable autonomy outside the range of certain specified duties.

Such a theory has obviously been considerably influenced by anthropological models of local-level leadership emerging from accounts of New Guinea and Polynesia (Sahlins 1963) and by models of patron-client relations largely developed by political scientists working in Southeast Asia, the Mediterranean and other areas (Schmidt et al. 1977). However, it remains basically an updating of the analysis of traditional political organization in South Sulawesi as fundamentally feudal. This feudal model has been invoked from at least the eighteenth century (Stavorinus 1798; Blok 1817 [written 1759]) through the nineteenth century (Raffles 1830; Brooke 1848; Kooreman 1883) and on into the twentieth century. (Friedericy 1933; Kennedy 1953; Harvey 1974) However, I refrain here from addressing the question of the extent to which this model has facilitated or distorted apprehending interpolity relations in traditional South Sulawesi. Instead, my current concern is to address the variant ways in which status is claimed and assessed among the Bugis and Makasar.

[16] The white blood of the *tomanurung* and their descendants is compared to the white sap of the *takku* tree, which like the mythical heavenly figure *Batara-guru* and his consort from the underworld *Ue Njili-timo*, mediates the opposition of the upper and lower realms by growing upward from the ground to the sky in this world (Matthes 1875:4).

[17] In all cases marrying downward is a possibility only acknowledged for male members of a particular rank. Marriage with a status inferior on the part of a noble woman was a heinous crime among the Bugis and Makasar (Friedericy 1933:557), resulting in the execution of the offending man (and, in most cases, the woman as well). Even among commoners, such a marriage would result at least in the exile of the couple from the local community. Friedericy states that the original ideal was status-level endogamy, but over time hypergamous marriages came to be accepted. In fact, the possibility of polygyny among the nobility required permitting such marriages. Even in the contemporay context, marriages of daughters with husbands of lower status are rejected by many parents, often leading to the scenario of elopement (*silariang*) and subsequent retribution carried out by the woman's brothers, father or other near relative against the offending man and often against the offending sister/daughter/niece as well (Thontowi 2007).

[18] Lineton presents a somewhat simplified set of Bugis status levels traditionally recognized in Wajo' as a whole: 1) *ana' matola*, pure-blooded royalty as represented by the ruler and highest officers in the state; 2) *arung*, chiefs of the petty princedoms in a state; 3) *tau décéng*, wealthy and respected commoners who could trace an admixture of noble blood; 4) *tau maradéka*, free commoners; and 5) *ata*, slaves (Lineton 1975:191). Presumably, the same sort of specification of these status levels in terms of marriages could be made if more data were supplied concerning reckoning in the system. In fact, based on her fieldwork in the Wajo' village of Ana'banua, Lineton reports that the local commoners usually recognized only three main status divisions or *tingka'*: 1) *arung*, descendants of the former *Arung Ana'banua* and of rulers of other *wanua* or villages; 2) *andi'*, lower nobles with no direct relationship to the former ruling family, a category often not distinguished from *tau décéng*, the upper level of commoners; and 3) *tau maradéka* or *tau sama*, ordinary commoners (Lineton n.d.: 98).

[19] Errington's phrasing of the (father's) semen/ (mother's) milk contrast may perhaps be interpreted along the lines of an asymmetric complementary opposition that serves some of the symbolic functions of the semen/blood contrast in eastern Indonesia: 'Although ToLuwu' regard themselves as related to both parents, and tend to see semen and mother's milk as parallel substances, still, semen creates, while mother's milk nourishes' (Errington 1989:261). The existence of such an opposition in Luwu' once again illustrates the permeability of the boundary between the Centrist Archipelago and the Exchange Archipelago.

[20] Friedericy hesitates to label primogeniture a norm of Bugis society, though he does note its incidence in Goa (Friedericy 1933:488).

[21] Modernist Islam, in the guise of Muhammadiyah and other Islamic educational and political organizations, has promulgated the limitation to four wives for all believers, thus limiting the extent to which nobles may engage in numerous marriages with commoner wives. This curbing has been heightened by Indonesian government regulations limiting civil servants to only one wife, since many nobles have now chosen political careers as a way of maintaining their power. Under these circumstances, the tendency toward status endogamy has been reinforced for those highest nobles who, if limited to only one spouse, now often prefer to seek a spouse of the same status.

[22] One of my own best informants among the Bugis migrants at Lindu in Central Sulawesi was a lower noble from Boné who was a son of one of the highest Boné nobles and his first wife, who was herself of commoner status. Seeing no opportunities for himself in his Boné homeland, he chose to become a migrant (*pasompe'*) (Acciaioli 2000:598-600; *cf.* Lineton 1975), unlike many of his younger siblings born to subsequently married but higher ranking wives of his father. Such an example illustrates how the Bugis fit the 'system of lateral expansion' that Fox asserts to be typical of those bilateral societies 'found on the relatively large islands of the Austronesian world, areas of potential expansion, where land and other resources are (or, in recent historical times, were once) readily available' (Fox 1995:222). In such systems relative age provides the principal axis of social differentiation, 'whereby the younger – or in a few cases, the elder – sibling simply moves away to found a new settlement' (Fox 1995:223). The latter alternative is often the case among the Bugis, in part because the first wives of Bugis nobles tended to be commoners, yielding their children as lower in rank than those of subsequent higher-status wives, as discussed in the text above. However, as has already been noted, the *wari'* system as a structure of status differentiation in Bugis and Makasar societies also operates similarly to the 'system of apical demotion' (Fox 1995: 223), a mode of 'ever-more-exclusive' status reckoning that Fox identifies as typical of the societies on smaller islands and on the coastal margins of larger islands where trading and raiding are major preoccupations. Indeed, Fox himself identifies the societies of 'the former Bugis and Makassarese' as among the examples of royal societies using apical demotion as a dynastic device of the elite (Fox 1995:223). The Bugis and Makasar societies thus bridge this posited opposition of societies using lateral expansion or apical demotion, illustrating both the possible co-existence of these modes of status reckoning within the same society and the permeability of yet another analytical dichotomy, though one very different, given its loose ecological and economic underpinnings, than the Centrist and Exchange Archipelago formulated by Errington.

4. The Discourse and Practice of Precedence

James J. Fox

Introduction

Precedence refers both to forms of discourse and of practice. In considering precedence as an analytical category, it is appropriate to distinguish aspects of discourse and practice. However, in social analysis based on the use of precedence, it is the fusion of these aspects that gives credibility to the concept.

In this paper, I wish to begin by considering precedence as discourse, focusing on the kinds of relational categories that, applied recursively, provide coherence to forms of precedence. From this vantage, I would like to consider briefly how such discourse relates to practice in a number of different Austronesian-speaking societies. My selection of examples is intended not to cover anywhere near the full range of possibilities but rather, for the purposes of this paper, to highlight a number of contrastive forms. In particular, I am concerned to examine the difference between claims to precedence and claims to pre-eminence and how they relate to one another. Finally, I would like to outline a specific system of precedence, the status order of the domain of Termanu on the island of Roti, with particular attention given to claims to precedence and to pre-eminence by rival factions within its ambit.

Precedence as Discourse

As an analytic category, precedence defines an asymmetric relationship that may be extended recursively. Elsewhere (Fox 1989:44–48), I have defined the underlying features of precedence as 1) categorical asymmetry, 2) recursive complementarity, and 3) (the possibility of) category reversal. I should also note that precedence as a focus of concern often derives from a study of identities based on the investigation of origin structures.

Linguistically, precedence may be defined by any of a large and diverse class of lexical categories posed in an oppositional arrangement. I have referred to all such oppositional terms as 'operators'. What distinguishes these oppositional terms as operators is the fact that in discourse, one term of the pair is accorded a 'value' over the other. It is this imposition of a culturally defined value that gives an asymmetry to any particular opposition and to the relationship to which it applies. Thus, to give an example — of relevance to the case I present in this paper — the relative age categories, elder/younger, often serve as a common operator to define precedence in eastern Indonesia. In perhaps a majority of cases, elder is defined as superior to younger. The relationship of elder is given precedence over younger. The asymmetry of this relationship may be represented as Elder < Younger. There is nothing necessarily inherent in this asymmetry and, as comparative Austronesian ethnography makes abundantly clear even in cultures where this valorization is regarded as the norm, there are situations where this relationship may be reversed: Younger > Elder. It is the possibility of such reversal that is critical to the discourse and practice of precedence. All lexical operators that are used to define precedence have this potential capacity and therefore may be said to function as 'lexical converses' (Cruse 1986:231–232).

Although a single relationship may be considered the limiting case, precedence may more generally be applied to an extended set of relationships. To define such relationships, it is essential that all operators, as complementary categories, have the capacity to be applied recursively to embrace an extended set of relationships. Thus, in the examples I have cited, the relative age categories, elder/younger, may indeed be applied recursively to include a wide number of individuals or groups.

For eighteenth century Maori society, for example, elder/younger categories were supposed to have included all members of a tribal group in a single all-embracing order (Metge 1967:21–24). This arrangement of precedence would be represented, in recursive notation, as follows: Elder > Younger/Elder > Younger... In this order of precedence, most individuals (or groups) are assumed to be involved in dual relationships that make them both younger to some and older to others. The claim to be first, foremost or pre-eminent in a line of precedence generally requires special 'grounding' and is invariably hedged with additional cultural explication.

In the study of precedence among Austronesian-speaking populations, it is rare to find an order of precedence that simply, unequivocally and undisputedly organizes a society. To the contrary, what occurs are a variety of categorical oppositions that pertain to different contexts, frequent contention over the application of competing oppositions, or over priority among multiple oppositions, and always the possibility of category reversal.

Complementary categories in the discourse of precedence

The distinction between elder and younger is a categorical opposition shared widely among Austronesian-speaking populations. As such it provides one of the most elementary 'operators' for the creation of precedence and is widely used in the assignment of status but it is not necessarily the most pertinent for social differentiation. The Paiwan in southern Taiwan, for example, are one society that lacks this categorical distinction. They have a single term, *kaka*, which applies to all siblings and cousins without distinction of age or gender. Lacking an elder/younger resource, the Paiwan stress the importance of the 'first born', either male or female. This person is known as the *vusam*, 'seed millet', and it is in relation to this *vusam* that a complex botanic idiom is elaborated. The first-born as 'seed millet' inherits the natal house and from this house 'gives seeds' (*qumusam*) to all younger siblings who are thus recognized as the 'seeds' (*qusam*) from that house. The house of the *vusam* is fixed in relation to other houses that derive from it. In the past, after the millet harvest, this botanic discourse was given explicit representation in the return of a bundle of millet to the *vusam* by each out-marrying, younger sibling. Thus a botanical discourse, an idea of derivation and a chain of succession among the Paiwan have the capacity to produce lines of precedence, which, over time, like lines of precedence in other societies, can become the subject of dispute, especially in claims to chiefdomship (see Matsuzawa 1989, Chiang 1993).

In a Paiwan village, all houses have names (*ngadan*) and are ordered in terms of (ritual) seniority. The chief of a Paiwan village can be regarded, in Chiang's words, as the '*vusam* written large in the extra-familial context' (Chiang 2007). In Paiwan origin narratives, an order of arrival or appearance is translated into a sibling birth order: the first to arrive (or the first egg to open) becomes the first-born. This order also distinguishes nobles from commoners. But this discourse can also be overturned. Chiang contrasts the founding narratives of the Kuvulj and Durong villages with those of Parilaiyan and Talavatsal villages in which an outsider is first incorporated within the village by founding autochthonous houses but then usurps their position to establish its rule as chief. In some instances, the outsider and autochthon share complementary privileges (Chiang 2007; see Fox 2008 for a variety of Austronesian narratives of 'outsiders installed inside'). Thus even where a categorical opposition predominates, it can be reversed to produce a new line of precedence. This reversal can be socially specific to particular groups, as Chiang has indicated, serving to establish the predominance of a chiefly house in some (but by no means all) Paiwan villages.

In analysing the deployment of claims to precedence in various Austronesian-speaking societies, it is critical to distinguish the concept of precedence from that of hierarchy (Fox 1994). Whereas much discussion of precedence has focused on hierarchical relations (where precedence may cohere with, or even underpin, hierarchy), it is notable the claims of precedence can occur as well in relatively egalitarian societies as in societies with more stratified social formations.

In traditional kindred-based Iban society, for example, all individuals were considered equal (*sebaka*) and free to compete for power, prestige and wealth. The oppositional categories of elder and younger (*aka/adi*) were a resource for possible differentiation but they were not determinative in accession to the *bilik*-household within a longhouse. Despite the emphasis on equality of relationships, there were clear notions of precedence among the Iban. As Freeman first noted (1981:31) and as Sather has described in greater detail (1996), much of the Iban discourse on precedence centred on the term, *pun*, whose literal meaning was 'trunk' or 'stem' but whose figurative meaning was that of 'source', 'basis', 'origin', or 'cause'. The term could be applied both to persons and to activities (see Fox 1995a for a discussion of the use of this 'trunk as origin' discourse in a variety of Austronesian-speaking societies; see also McWilliam in this volume).

According to Freeman, the root meaning of *pun* was 'that of stem, of a tree, from which the development of any activity springs' (Freeman 1981:31). Thus as Freeman explains, anyone could declare himself as an 'initiator' or 'leader' of a journey (*bejalai*) to gain wealth and recognition and if others chose to follow him, he would be considered the *pun bejalai* of the group. Similarly in other significant activities, such as launching of a raid or establishing a new longhouse, the initiator of the activity, if he managed to gather followers, would be considered that activity's *pun* and leader (*tuai*). The use of *pun* in such discourse focused on the formation of social followings, many of which were limited in time and scope but provided personal reknown. In Freeman's words, each 'individual had to be the source (*pun*) of his own achievements' (Freeman 1981: 350). For some, this offered a fleeting form of precedence but, for others, it became the basis of a continuing recognition.

The semantics of *pun* among the Iban also carries the implication of succession and continuity. Every longhouse community gave recognition to its founder who erected the first house pillar or 'trunk' (*pemun > pun*) and was known as its *pun rumah* or 'source'. Over time, there would be a succession of *pun rumah*, as indeed there was a succession of household source-figures (*pun bilik*) who assumed precedence in ritual and invariably had greater access to the longhouse as well as household land. The memory of their succession would figure in the main-line (*pun tusut*) of recited genealogies. Sather has noted the consequences of this discourse in Iban practice most clearly:

> Recognition of this double meaning of *pun*, as both initiator and locus of continuity, helps illuminate the historical dynamics of Iban leadership. Thus in times of outward expansion, the Iban were able to throw up an array of effective leaders, who, as initiators of action and organizers of collective projects, led migrations, pioneered new areas of settlement, defeated rivals and competitors in war, felled jungle, and founded new longhouses and *bilik*-families. Those who were successful in these undertakings were, and continue to be, remembered, and so form the principal founders and connecting links in the main-line genealogies by which Iban remember and celebrate their ancestral past (Sather 1996:82).

More interesting still, in the analysis of precedence, are those societies where claims to precedence are couched in a metaphoric idiom that utilizes a variety of 'operators' whose layers of meaning can give rise to varied assertions and permutations in local practice. The more such oppositions are given credible valency, the more complex the contentions that can be generated over precedence. Thus while any one 'operator' — such as the distinction between elder/younger, or that between 'seed' and 'seeded' or 'trunk' and 'tip/branch' — offers a relatively simple means of differentiation, the multiplication of such operators offers fertile grounds for subtle distinctions and nuanced contention.

A good example is that of the Tanimbarese of Fordata Island in the southern Moluccas, which is clearly hierarchical with a hereditary class of nobles, commoners and (former) slaves but whose internal relations are ordered by a complex system of precedence. The Tanimbarese discourse on precedence uses a variety of idioms encountered elsewhere in eastern Indonesia, yet results, in practice, in a distinctive set of social arrangements. This discourse focuses heavily on the relationship between wife-givers and wife-takers. This relationship can be taken as a primary 'operator' which embodies an enduring linkage between 'brother' and 'sister'. As elsewhere in eastern Indonesia, wife-givers are considered as 'male' (*brana*) and wife-takers as 'female' (*vata*). Since wife-givers are regarded as superior to wife-takers, in the semantics of this relationship, *brana* has valency over *vata*: *brana>vata*. These categories are applied to houses (*rahan*) rather than to individuals.

To this discourse is added a botanic idiom of sources that combines with ideas about the transmission of blood. The house of the 'brother' as wife-giver is the 'source' (*mata*) of a 'sister' whose 'blood' (*lara*) carries the potential of life for his sister's children. These progeny are the 'sprouts' (*mata/rubun*) from his house (see Fox 1996 for similar relational conceptions in the Timor area). As the Tanimbarese assert, the purpose of a house is to 'multiply its sprouts a thousandfold' (see McKinnon 1991:111).

Another idiom in this rich discourse is drawn from the practice of sailing. The house of the brother is an anchored place of origin that launches boats that carry sisters to the houses of their husbands. The stability of this source insures the success of the journey and the return of valuables to the place of origin. In this context, male fixity stands in contrast to female mobility.

This discourse is utilized in the practice of a directed, asymmetric exchange of women between houses. Houses, however are themselves differentiated on the basis of an opposition between elder and younger. 'Elder' houses bear names (*naran*) and possess long-enduring affinal relationships; these extended relationships form what are called 'rows' (*lolat*). These 'rows' (and one's house's position within them) determine precedence. They form lines of precedence and pathways for the differential exchange of male and female goods based on long-standing alliance relations. By contrast with elder houses, younger houses have no names and their affinal relations extend for only a few generations.

They are still in process of possible development. All marriages initiate a set of exchanges that continue for three generations and then conclude. If, however, marriage is renewed, this affinal line, known as a 'sister and aunt' pathway, takes on greater status and may 'feed' into a 'small row', thus establishing an initial position of precedence within the network.

'Rows' of affinally allied houses can be of varying length. Differentiation among 'rows' introduces the notion of relative size to this discourse on precedence. 'Small rows' (*lolat ko'u*) are said to 'feed' into 'big rows' (*lolat dawan*) and these 'big rows' can feed into the 'Great Row' (*lolat ila'a*) that 'anchors' the network of all exchange pathways. Strikingly, this 'Great Row', which links the four major houses of Fordata with the four major houses of the island of Sera, represents a reversal of the principle of asymmetric exchange on which all other 'rows' are predicated. Relations among the houses that comprise the 'Great Row' are symmetric — a double cycle of intermarriage in which all participating houses are considered of equal status. This 'Great Row' is considered to be a unity that transcends the opposition between brother and sister, male and female that underlies the other rows (see McKinnon 1991 and 1995 for a fuller account of this exceptionally rich social formation).[1]

While each of these sketches illustrates some of the basic possible workings of precedence, it is clear that the specifics of precedence in any one local social formation demand close, detailed examination. For this purpose, I examine one such case in more particular detail.

Precedence and Pre-Eminence in the Domain of Termanu

At this point, I would like to examine in detail a particular case of precedence based on reference to a set of oral narratives which claim to represent the establishment of precedence in one domain, Termanu, on the island of Roti in eastern Indonesia.

As a domain, Termanu (or Pada, as it is also known) represents itself as an assemblage of nine clans arrayed around a single noble 'origin' or 'trunk' group, known as Masa-Huk, that has grown and divided into two complementary but unequal clans, one male and one female. The male clan, which retains its designation as Masa-Huk, consists of a proliferation of ranked lineages surmounted by a royal lineage, Fola-Tein, that provides the ruling Male Lord (*Manek*) of the domain. The female clan, designated as Kota Deak, which means 'Outside the Fortification' retained its rights as lesser nobility but held only a minor political and ritual position.

Unlike other realms in eastern Indonesia (or even other domains on Roti where male and female clans preside over moiety groups), Termanu was, by long historical tradition, a markedly male-centred polity. Clans recognized by the

Male Lord held a seat at his court and performed their 'origin' rituals (*hus*) either in relation to, or as lesser participants at, the great origin ritual of Masa-Huk.

The oral traditions that endeavour to account for the complex relationships within the domain are a diverse collection of chants, narratives, commentaries and genealogies, all of which are socially embedded in the individual traditions of separate clans. These traditions recount the founding of the domain, its coalescence and expansion, internal disputes among clan ancestors over critical resources, the transference of rule and the organization of precedence within the domain. Throughout these narratives, there occurs continuing comment on the nature of rule and on the role of cunning and cleverness in the achievement of pre-eminence.

Each individual narrative within this tradition is recognized as a true 'standing' tale (*tutui-tete'ek*) by its reference to specific named places within the domain and by its identification of actors in relation to named figures in the genealogy of the trunk group, Masa-Huk. Masa-Huk thus provides the focal genealogy without which no historical narrative can establish its position or its authenticity as a narrative of the domain.

The collection of oral chants and narratives pertaining to the domain of Termanu that I have (so far) collected come to more than a hundred pages of translated text. In this paper, I wish to examine the genealogy of Masa-Huk in relation to the particular narratives that establish the organization of precedence in the domain. I also wish to comment on the claims to precedence and pre-eminence that are either asserted or implied by these narratives. I begin with the genealogy of Masa-Huk.[2]

All genealogies on Roti are a recitation of names, each name consisting of two separate terms. Succession in a genealogy is achieved by the retention of the first term of a name as the second term in the succeeding name. Thus, in the recitation of the genealogy of Masa-Huk, Bui Putu is succeeded by Kilo Bui who is, in turn, succeeded by Kai Kilo.

To be understood properly, the genealogy of Masa-Huk must be conceived of not just as a temporal succession of names but also as spatial emergence from an earthly base. The first fifteen names of the genealogy chart a progression through three realms: from the earth through the seas to the heavens. Although not all names are intelligible or translatable, the recurrence of terms for earth (*dae*), for the sea (*sain*) and finally the term for the moon (*bulan*) imply this emergent process. The occurrence of the terms for stalk (*putu*) and tree (*kai*) are similarly evocative of a botanical emergence. Thus the genealogy begins with the name, Paki Dae, which might be translated as 'Earth Fastener' followed by Hu Paki-Paki, 'Base of Fastening' and then Dae Hu, 'Earth Base' and proceeds through such names as Sain Paliko, 'Sea Paliko' and Nggeo-Nggeo Sain, 'Darkness of (or on) the Sea' to the name, Bula Kai, 'Moon Tree'.

It is important to note that Rotinese Christians who are concerned to reconcile this genealogy with the Biblical genealogy offer an exegesis on these names that identifies particular names as native equivalents of Old Testament names: hence Dae Hu is identified as Adam and Nggeo-Nggeo Sain as Noah. As a general point, it is essential to recognize the exegeses that accompany both narratives and genealogies. Even when there is agreement on the content of a genealogy or tale, there may be alternate interpretations of its meaning and significance and these varying interpretations can affect claims to precedence that may derive from it.

Figure 1. The first 15 names of the genealogy of Masa-Huk (represented as an 'upwards' progression from Paki Dae to Bula Kai. All genealogical recitations must begin with Paki Dae.

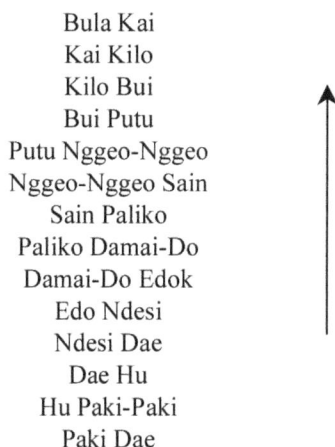

Bula Kai
Kai Kilo
Kilo Bui
Bui Putu
Putu Nggeo-Nggeo
Nggeo-Nggeo Sain
Sain Paliko
Paliko Damai-Do
Damai-Do Edok
Edo Ndesi
Ndesi Dae
Dae Hu
Hu Paki-Paki
Paki Dae

Only after these fifteen names, there occurs the first ancestral name, Ma Bulan, for whom there exists a full narrative. It is this narrative that provides the foundation of the domain.

This first narrative recounts the encounter of Ma Bulan with an 'autochthonous' figure named Pada Lalais. The names of both these ancestors are significant. Pada Lalais is represented as the first inhabitant of the island. He is intimately associated with the earth and is the ancestor of the clan that holds the ritual position of Head of the Earth (Dae Langak). Yet his name, which translates as 'Heavenly Pada', indicates a heavenly origin, which is asserted in the narrative.

As for Ma Bulan, although his name implies a heavenly origin, exegesis on this name interprets the term, Ma, as shortened form of Ana Ma(k), 'Orphan'. By this interpretation, Ma Bulan's name is 'Orphan Moon', thus suggesting some disjunction with a prior heavenly association. Ma Bulan is described as a wanderer, recently come from the sea, who encounters the settled Pada Lalais and immediately disputes his temporal priority and his rights to precedence. To determine precedence they agree to a contest.

> The first contest involves the planting of trees to see which tree flourishes. Pada Lalais plants a quick growing *damar* tree whereas Ma Bulan plants a slow-growing *bubuni* tree, but after the trees are planted, Ma Bulan comes back and switches the trees and thereby claims a victory. Since Pada Lalais does not accept this outcome, they agree to a further contest.

> This time, they vie with each other over who can command the sea to come. Since Ma Bulan knows the sea well since he is identified as a fisherman, whereas Pada Lalais only possesses a knowledge of the earth, Ma Bulan tells Pada Lalais to call the sea as the tide is going out. He calls but the tide recedes. Ma Bulan waits until the tide is about to come in; he then calls the sea and it comes to him, thus winning the second contest.

> Finally the two agree to have a third contest by examining each other's houses to see which is the older one. Ma Bulan immediately rethatches his house with eucalyptus leaves and then lights a fire which quickly turns the thatch soot black. When they inspect each other's houses, Pada Lalais' lontar leaf thatch is not as black as the eucalyptus thatch of Ma Bulan's house. Ma Bulan once more claims victory.

> In the end, Ma Bulan, who has demonstrated the cleverness required of a ruler offers the following solution to divide their functions. He says: 'It would be good if I became Lord and you became Head of the Earth for succeeding generations. When men have filled this domain, I will rule them and you may levy a tribute on the domain and take a portion of lontar syrup from each person who lives in the domain. And for all times, since you were the first to settle in this domain, this domain will be given the name Pada, in keeping with your name, Pada Lalais, and your grandchildren and descendants.'[3]

Thus the domain is founded on a critical differentiation. The trunk line of Masa-Huk, via Ma Bulan, becomes the ruling line that is characterized as knowledgeable (*malelak*) and cunning (*kekedi*) while the line that begins with Pada Lalais becomes the ritual overseer of the earth that is characterized as dumb (*nggoa*) and ignorant of worldly wiles.

In Termanu, this division is complete and undisputed and has come to be represented as complementary division. In the traditional structure of the domain, the Head of the Earth represented by the clan, Meno, was given a place at court and thus fully incorporated into the domain. Elsewhere, however, in some of the domains of Roti, where a similar division between Ruler and Head of the Earth occurs, the enmity inherent in this division is stressed and narratives recount the attempts by the Head of the Earth to exterminate the ruling line. In some domains, the Ruler and the Head of the Earth could not be present together at any function.

Thus in Termanu, the fundamental division between Ruler and Head of the Earth is a muted source of dispute over precedence. Later differentiation within the line of Masa-Huk provides more immediate sources of dispute over precedence.

The recitation of genealogical names continues from Ma Bulan through six generations to Tola Manu without further significant differentiation. These names are listed as follows:

Figure 2. The next seven names of the genealogy of Masa-Huk (recited 'upwards' from Ma Bulan to Tola Manu)

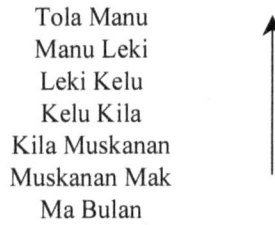

Tola Manu
Manu Leki
Leki Kelu
Kelu Kila
Kila Muskanan
Muskanan Mak
Ma Bulan

The richest part of the narrative history of Termanu pertains to the figure of Tola Manu who is represented as the warrior founder of the domain, which then assumes his name (Tola Manu = Termanu) as well as that of Pada. Most of the ancestors of clans are incorporated into the domain during the reign of Tola Manu, either by conquest or by an alliance with Tola Manu. Only after the death of Tola Manu is there further differentiation in lines of precedence within Masa-Huk.

The next bifurcation is between the sons of Tola Manu: Seni Tola and Lusi Tola. The narrative of these two sons introduces another theme in the telling of the history of the domain. Whereas precedence is supposed to be accorded to the elder in a line of succession from elder to younger, this principle is inverted in the case of succession to the lordship of Termanu. Thus, among two brothers, the younger succeeds to rule; among several brothers, the youngest succeeds — if not immediately, eventually. While for Masa-Huk as a whole, the principle is either Elder < Younger or First-Born < Last-Born; for the royal line, this principle is reversed: Elder > Younger or First-Born > Last-Born.

In the narrative of the sons of Tola Manu, Lusi Tola is identified as the elder; Seni Tola as the younger. In exegesis, Seni Tola's name is referred, by folk etymological association, as 'Sengi' which means 'to win, to conquer, or to overcome'. This name is said to signify his triumph over his elder brother. Seni

Tola's conquest follows the form of other narratives and thus involves a contest between the two brothers for which the 'Portuguese' serve as judges to determine the Ruler. The contest is to determine who is the heavier of the two brothers and thus the appropriate successor of Tola Manu. Seni Tola as the younger and lighter of the two brothers straps lead to a belt which is hidden by his sarong and is thus judged the heavier of the two. In Rotinese terms, he demonstrates that he is the more cunning of the two and therefore the more appropriate successor. His descendants continue the ruling line of Masa-Huk while those of Lusi Tola become the line of the Female Lord (Mane Feto or Fetor) and give rise to the clan, Kota Deak. The sign of the office of Male and Female Lord are staffs with either a gold or a silver capped-top. The Portuguese award the gold staff to Seni Tola and the silver staff to Lusi Tola.

The recitation of the genealogy of Masa-Huk continues. Just as the previous juncture produced a division between male and female clans, subsequent junctures in the genealogy produce the ranked lineages (*teik*) within the male clan, each of which forms a branch (*ndanak*) of the trunk, Masa-Huk. According to the genealogy and exegesis on it, Seni Tola had three sons. The youngest son, Kila Seni, succeeded to his father's position while the eldest son, Edo Seni, gave rise to the first of the noble clans of Masa-Huk, Hailiti-tein. (The second son, Bengu Seni, is said to have had no sons to succeed him.) In turn, Kila Seni is said to have had two sons, Pelo Kila and Sinlae Kila.

The genealogy of Lusi Tola within Kota Deak continues in parallel with that of the genealogy of Seni Tola in Masa-Huk. Lusi Tola is said to have had one son, Kiu Lusi, who in turn had two sons, Sadu Kiu and Ndoki Kiu. Following normal precedence, Sadu Kiu as the elder succeeded his father as the third Female Lord of Termanu.

The two parallel genealogies may be represented as follows:

Figure 3. The next three names in the genealogies of Masa-Huk and Kota Deak (recited 'upwards' from Tola Manu to Pelo Kila and Sadu Kiu)

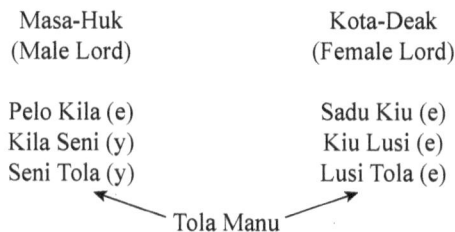

Masa-Huk   Kota-Deak
(Male Lord)   (Female Lord)

Pelo Kila (e)   Sadu Kiu (e)
Kila Seni (y)   Kiu Lusi (e)
Seni Tola (y)   Lusi Tola (e)

Tola Manu

At this juncture, according to the narratives, Pelo Kila, the elder of the two sons of Kila Seni, succeeded to the position of Ruler while at the same time, Sadu Kiu, the elder son of Kiu Lusi, mounted a challenge and attempted to displace Pelo Kila in the order of precedence within the domain.

Another contest ensued. In this contest, the 'Portuguese' were again called upon to test which of the two disputants' shit smelled sweetest. Sadu Kiu gave a feast to Pelo Kila who gorged himself while Sadu Kiu ate nothing but dilak fruit. As a consequence, Sadu Kiu's shit smelled sweeter and the gold-topped staff was given to Sadu Kiu and the silver-topped staff to Pelo Kila. But the narrative does not end with this reversal of fortune but continues to explain how 'cleverness conquers stupidity'.

In time, according to the narrative, Pelo Kila challenged Sadu Kiu on the grounds that he alone knew Malay and that he alone could deal with foreigners who came to Termanu. He accused Sadu Kiu of being a mere girl while he described himself as a 'real man' (*tou manek*, literally, 'a male man'). This play on words was intended to underline their true functions as Male and Female Lords of Termanu. Sadu Kiu relented and they exchanged staffs of office. The narrative ends with the comment that after a long reign Pelo Kila as elder brother surrendered his position to his younger brother, Sinlae Kila, who continued the ruling line of the domain. Pelo Kila established the branch lineage, Nelu-tein while Sinlae Kila continued the trunk line of Masa-Huk.

It is at this point that independent outside commentary based on Dutch archival sources can be brought to bear in a consideration of the oral narratives of Termanu. From the late 1670s, there are frequent references in these archives to Pelo Kila as 'regent' and Sadu Kiu as 'mede-regent' of Termanu. What is more, the *General Missiven* of the Dutch East India Company contain a short report that states that in 1679 the young regent Pelo Kila was taken to Kupang to learn Malay. By 1700, although Sadu Kiu continued as 'co-regent', Pelo Kila had been replaced by his brother, Sinlae Kila [in the Dutch records: Sinlay Kiera].

According to the genealogical narratives, a similar pattern was repeated in the following generation. Sinlae Kila had six sons: Ndaomanu Sinlae, Edo Sinlae, Kila Sinlae, Muloko Sinlae, Loe Sinlae and Fola Sinlae. Of these sons, the eldest, Ndaomanu Sinlae, (a figure of great prominence in Dutch archival records) was made Ruler but, after a disastrous attack on some Dutch officers, he was deposed and replaced by his youngest brother, Fola Sinlae. Each of the brothers, including Ndaomanu, became founders of separate lineages in Masa-Huk: Ndaomanu Sinlae established Ndaomanu-tein; Edo Sinlae, Edo-tein, Kila Sinlae, Kila-tein and Muloko Sinlae, Muloko-tein, and Loe Sinlae, Loe-tein.

In the next generation, Fola Sinlae was succeeded by his younger son, Muda Fola while his elder son, Muskanan Fola, became the founder of yet another lineage, that of Muskanan-tein.

As the genealogy of Masa-Huk proceeds, a process comes into play for which the Rotinese botanical image of a growing tree provides the most apt description. As the trunk continues to grow upward, branches formed at a lower level come to hold a lesser rank than branches formed at a later stage of development. This is the principle of apical demotion that underlines most Austronesian status lineage systems (see Fox 1995b:223ff). In Termanu, Pelo Kila is the ancestor of Nelu-tein. This lineage has a higher rank than Hailiti-tein which separated earlier from the main trunk of Masa-Huk. In turn, Nelu-tein has a lesser status than the lineages, such as Ndaomanu-tein or Kila-tein, formed in the next generation's branching. All these lineages in turn have lower status than that of Muskanan-tein of the next generation.

What is distinctive of Termanu is that elder lines are systematically demoted because the younger (or youngest) line in each generation represents the point of highest status. All of the lineages of Masa-Huk in the order of their separation form a line of precedence with its apex, the royal lineage of Fola-tein. This may be represented diagrammatically by the following figure:

Figure 4. An illustration of the principle of apical demotion in which the younger (or youngest) is accorded precedence

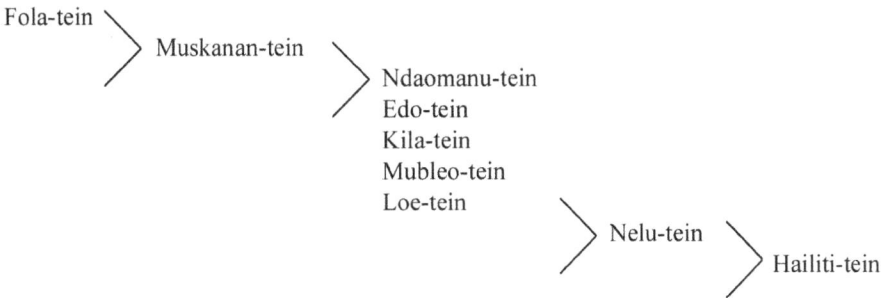

In the generation of Fola Sinlae, five branch lineages are said to derive from the trunk, Masa-Huk. Since this multiple branching process occurred in the same generation, among several brothers, the relative status of these lineages is a contentious subject. While the youngest brother's pre-eminent status is not disputed, the status of the other brothers is ambiguous. There is no clear ordering rule.

The normal status principle would assign precedence to the eldest but, in the noble traditions of Termanu, it is possible for the next 'youngest' — the brother closest to Fola Sinlae — to claim the next highest status. However, in Roti, only the position of first and last-born child are categorically distinguished. All other children occur in the 'middle'. Hence special claims among the 'middle' brothers are difficult to sustain. Other criteria are necessary to support claims to precedence, the most prominent of which is the claim to have continued to marry with the royal line.

Figure 5. Lines of precedence in Masa-Huk

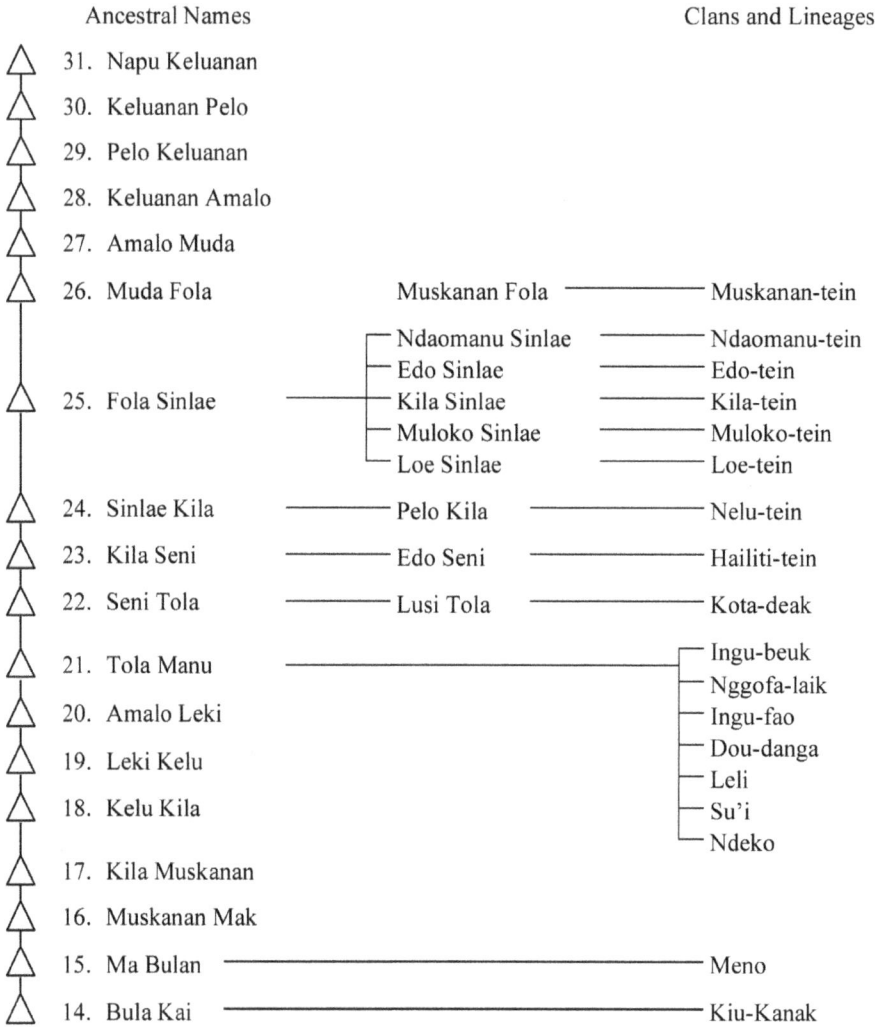

Ancestral Names   Clans and Lineages

31. Napu Keluanan

30. Keluanan Pelo

29. Pelo Keluanan

28. Keluanan Amalo

27. Amalo Muda

26. Muda Fola   Muskanan Fola ——————— Muskanan-tein

                         ┌ Ndaomanu Sinlae ——————— Ndaomanu-tein
                         ├ Edo Sinlae ——————— Edo-tein
25. Fola Sinlae ————————┼ Kila Sinlae ——————— Kila-tein
                         ├ Muloko Sinlae ——————— Muloko-tein
                         └ Loe Sinlae ——————— Loe-tein

24. Sinlae Kila ——————— Pelo Kila ——————— Nelu-tein

23. Kila Seni ——————— Edo Seni ——————— Hailiti-tein

22. Seni Tola ——————— Lusi Tola ——————— Kota-deak

                                                    ┌ Ingu-beuk
21. Tola Manu ——————————————————————————   ├ Nggofa-laik
                                                    ├ Ingu-fao
20. Amalo Leki   ├ Dou-danga
                                                    ├ Leli
19. Leki Kelu   ├ Su'i
                                                    └ Ndeko
18. Kelu Kila

17. Kila Muskanan

16. Muskanan Mak

15. Ma Bulan ——————————————————————————— Meno

14. Bula Kai ——————————————————————————— Kiu-Kanak

E. Douglas Lewis (1996:163–168) has devoted careful attention to the branching structures that create lines of precedence among the Tana 'Ai and he makes the fundamental observation that there is a difference between lines of precedence based on branches that bifurcate creating two new entities and those in which one line creates a bifurcation while the other maintains what is considered to be the main trunk line.

Termanu presents an interesting case in this regard. Fola-tein is recognized as a distinct lineage; at the same time, it is recognized as the pre-eminent continuer of Masa-Huk. It is my suspicion that as long as the rituals of Masa-Huk were performed, Fola-tein's position was emphatically that of the 'trunk' but with the abandonment of 'ceremonies of origin' (*hus*), Fola-tein's position, without its ritual underpinnings, has come to be regarded as the foremost branch lineage among a group of status lineages.

Relative derivation within Masa-Huk is not the only criterion of status. Marriage with Fola-tein (or with any lineage of higher derivation) is also a criterion and indeed evidence of the capacity to retain status. While relations of derivation are phrased in terms of elder/younger, relations based on marriage are phrased in terms of the gender categories, *mane/feto*, which translate both as male/female and brother/sister.

To maintain their position of pre-eminence, the rulers of Termanu have consistently married royal women of other domains. For all other lines within Fola-tein and within all the status lineages of Masa-Huk, past marriages have created a complex network of relationships on which to claim status. Only Muskanan-tein has succeeded in retaining its relative rank. For all the other lineages, the picture is less clear-cut and made even more complex by the rise to high status of a powerful client line within Fola-tein itself. Although it is impossible here to sketch this complexity, it is important to note that arguments over precedence generally focus more on marriage relations among the status lineages rather than on relations of derivation which are commonly agreed upon and thus tend not to be disputed.

Thus two different ways of reckoning precedence — one by derivation and the other by progenitor relations — provide the contentious basis for claims to status in Termanu.

Concluding Comment

It is appropriate here to emphasize that the application of the concept of precedence in the study of indigenous ideas of origin is still in its early stages. Although it clearly provides valuable insights, it also prompts further questions for consideration, which in turn may allow us to refine and develop the concept itself.

As illustration, I provide one example. In this paper, I have focused on the recursive application of certain asymmetric oppositions in the construction of precedence. It is also possible, it would appear, to construct relations of precedence on the basis of lexical triplets. Tom Therik in his study of Wehali on Timor notes a set of such relationships (Therik 2004). This set consists of the categories: Reclining > Sitting > Standing which are also given physical expression in ritual interactions. Thus, among the Wehali, the pre-eminent ritual figure is that of the Maromak Oan, who is defined as the 'reclining' lord.

While this set may be regarded as composed of dyadic sub-sets, the set as a whole is more than these oppositions. The set is asymmetric but instead of being recursive, it is fixed and stable. With this example in mind, it is reasonable to look for other ethnographic examples of such triplet sets and to compare the way they function in organizing relations of precedence.

It is also worth noting that the concept of precedence offers one mode of apprehending Austronesian societies. It is a means of apprehending and understanding formal relations in Austronesian societies. There are, however, many Austronesian societies where formal relations are themselves implicitly, and often explicitly, left undeveloped in favour of individuality and autonomy. Thus, among the Iban, as described by Sather (1996), relations of precedence may be individually imagined and even enacted at each *gawai* performance; such precedence is left to continuous individual reformulation.

The metaphor of the 'path' is a recurrent Austronesian trope. Often it is used to describe recognized lines of precedence within a society but just as often in other societies, it describes a trajectory toward the individual achievement of power, prestige, and renown. From a comparative perspective, those societies that place great emphasis on individual autonomy and independence are generally characterized by what I have elsewhere described as systems of lateral expansion (Fox 1995b:222–225). Such systems occur, or have tended to occur, in conditions, such as unrestricted horticulture, shifting cultivation or boat nomadism, that place few limitations on the formation of new groups. As restrictions begin to occur, patterns of precedence also begin to emerge. Such patterns take many forms. One such pattern, for example, which is to be found in eastern Indonesia is what might be called 'seasonal precedence' in which a period of the year is marked out for the performance of rituals that are organized according to rules of precedence, after which individuals disperse to scattered fields where relations of precedence rarely impinge on daily life. In such societies, precedence is concentrated within a temporal modality.

The concept of precedence may thus be called upon as an analytic category for ethnographic description but also as a comparative index of social transformations within the Austronesian-speaking world.

References

Chiang, Bien

1993 House and social hierarchy of the Paiwan. Unpublished PhD thesis. Philadelphia: University of Pennsylvania.

2007 Articulation of hierarchies: house, community and value among the Paiwan. Unpublished paper presented at a Taiwan seminar (29 October 2007) in the Department of Anthropology, Research School of Pacific and Asian Studies, The Australian National University, Canberra.

Cruse, D.A.

1986 *Lexical semantics.* Cambridge: Cambridge University Press.

Fox, James J.

1971 A Rotinese dynastic genealogy: structure and event. In T.O. Beidelman (ed.), *The translation of culture*, pp.37–77. London: Tavistock.

1989 Category and complement: binary ideologies and the organization of dualism in eastern Indonesia. In David Maybury-Lewis and Uri Almagor (eds), *The attraction of opposites: thought and society in a dualistic mode*, pp.33–56. Ann Arbor: University of Michigan Press.

1994 Reflections on 'hierarchy' and 'precedence'. In M. Jolly and M. Mosko (eds), *Transformations of hierarchy: structure, history and horizon in the Austronesian world. History and Anthropology* (Special Issue) 7:87–108.

1995a Origin structures and systems of precedence in the comparative study of Austronesian societies. In P.J.K. Li, Cheng-hwa Tsang, Ying-kuei Huang, Dah-an Ho and Chiu-yu Tseng (eds), *Austronesian studies relating to Taiwan*, pp.27–57. Taipei: Symposium Series of the Institute of History & Philology: Academia Sinica 3.

1995b Austronesian societies and their transformations. In Peter Bellwood, James J. Fox and Darrell Tryon (eds), *The Austronesians: historical & comparative perspectives*, pp.214–228. Canberra: Department of Anthropology, Research School of Pacific and Asian Studies, The Australian National University. Comparative Austronesian Series, ANU E Press: http://epress.anu.edu.au/.

1996 The transformation of progenitor lines of origin: patterns of precedence in eastern Indonesia. In James J. Fox and Clifford Sather (eds), *Origins, ancestry and alliance: explorations in Austronesian ethnography*, pp.130–153. Canberra: Department of Anthropology, Research School of Pacific and Asian Studies, The Australian National University. Comparative Austronesian Series, ANU E Press: http://epress.anu.edu.au/.

2008 Installing the 'outsider' inside: the exploration of an epistemic Austronesian cultural theme and its social significance, *Indonesia and the Malay World* 36(105): 201–218.

Freeman, Derek

1981 Some reflections on the nature of Iban society. Occasional Paper. Canberra: Department of Anthropology, Reseach School of Pacific and Asian Studies, The Australian National University.

Lewis, E.D.

1996 Origin structures and precedence in the social orders of Tana 'Ai and Sikka. In James J. Fox and Clifford Sather (eds), *Origins, ancestry and alliance: explorations in Austronesian ethnography*, pp.161–182. Canberra: Department of Anthropology, Research School of Pacific and Asian Studies, The Australian National University. Comparative Austronesian Series, ANU E Press: http://epress.anu.edu.au/.

Matsuzawa, Kazuko

1989 The social and ritual supremacy of the first-born: Paiwan kinship and chieftainship. Unpublished PhD thesis. Syracuse, New York: Syracuse University.

McKinnon, Susan

1991 *From a shattered sun: hierarchy, gender and alliance in the Tanimbar Islands.* Madison: The University of Wisconsin Press.

1995 Houses and hierarchy: a view from a South Moluccan society'. In Janet Carsten and Stephen Hugh-Jones (eds), *About the house: Lévi-Strauss and beyond*, pp. 170–188. Cambridge: Cambridge University Press.

Metge, Joan

1967 *The Maori of New Zealand*. London: Routledge and Kegan Paul.

Sather, Clifford

1996 All threads are white: Iban egalitarianism reconsidered. In James J. Fox and Clifford Sather (eds), *Origins, ancestry and alliance: explorations in Austronesian ethnography*, pp.72–115. Canberra: Department of Anthropology, Research School of Pacific and Asian Studies, The Australian National University. Comparative Austronesian Series, ANU E Press: http://epress.anu.edu.au/.

Therik, Tom

2004 *Wehali, the female land: traditions of a Timorese ritual centre.* Canberra: Department of Anthropology, Research School of Pacific and Asian Studies, The Australian National University in association with Pandanus Books.

ENDNOTES

[1] There are many features of this Tanimbarese marriage exchange network that call for further investigation. The relational terminology of the Tanimbarese of Fordata Island is one of symmetric, rather than asymmetric alliance; its institutions, at all but the highest level, operate to promote and extend asymmetric marriage. It would be most interesting, if this network could be formally modelled to better understand its inner dynamics.

[2] The full genealogy of Masa-Huk can be found in Fox 1971:51-52.

[3] The narrative ends with the final observation to explain why the domain is known both by the name, Pada, and the name, Termanu:

In the time of Lord Tolamanu Amalo, a descendant of Ma Bulan, the Company asked Tolamanu: 'What is the name of your domain?' So Tolamanu said: 'It is called Tolamanu in recognition of my name.' So it was called Termanu but the name Pada did not disappear. The domain is called by both names, Pada and Termanu, to the present time.

5. Trunk and Tip in West Timor: Precedence in a botanical idiom

Andrew McWilliam

Introduction

This paper brings together an appreciation of two related cultural themes from the island of Timor in eastern Indonesia. The first of these themes explores the expression of precedence in Timorese social contexts and its significance as an index of status differentiation. A second related concern, and one that arguably represents a key indigenous expression of precedence, is the enduring representation of social processes through botanical idioms and particularly the metaphor of the tree. In Timor, the botanical idiom of the tree is often expressed in binary metaphorical form as 'trunk and tip'. It is this particular encoded configuration of process and relation that informs and expresses aspects of temporal precedence.

The proliferation of references and writings on the issue of botanical metaphors in the literature of eastern Indonesia attests to the importance of this classificatory dualism and its variants throughout the region (e.g. Fox 1971, 1988, Aoki 1986, Traube 1986, 1989, Platenkamp 1988, Grimes 1993, McWilliam 2002 and Therik 2004). This ubiquity of botanical imagery in social forms is perhaps unsurprising given that people reliant upon agriculture for their welfare tend to find in the vegetative properties of nature a rich resource for comparable association.[1]

For the Meto speaking communities of west Timor,[2] the use and expression of botanical metaphors is broad and compelling. Meto express a wide variety of social relations in terms of botanical analogy. They draw on many contrastive and reproductive properties of creeping vines, herbaceous plants, and tended and wild plants to create cultural metaphors of social process. Formal marriage, for example, may be expressed as the union of betel nut ingredients in which the conceptually 'female' areca nut is combined with the 'male' fruit of the betel vine. Progeny of informal marriages, otherwise known as 'marriages in darkness' (*kaib mesokan)*, are referred to as the *koto ma boko* (beans and pumpkins). These agricultural products are grown in the more distant, less tended, forest gardens and grow in tangled indiscriminate ways. The Meto also describe the cyclical closure of certain marriage exchanges in botanical terms; namely, as the 'return of the young banana and young sugar cane' (*seb nafani uik ana ma teuf ana)*. The image here is one of a type of reaping or harvesting the fruits of marriage alliance planted by the original wife-giving house.[3] Such marriages are auspicious as they help to revitalize alliance relationships that may have grown slack with time.

In these and other ways the botanical idiom is a primary language of relationship and process among Meto speakers and it is within this idiom that I seek to focus upon the core image of the tree. With its extended cycle of woody growth, flowering and fruit, decay and renewal, the generic image of the tree parallels many of the central properties of social life. In its core representation as 'trunk and tip' (*uf ma tunaf*) the category asymmetry, I would argue, expresses an archetype of precedence. Trunk is superior to tip, but more than this, trunk comes before tip, both in a temporal sense and a spatial one. This self-evident relationship makes it an exemplary dichotomy for explorations of social precedence.[4]

Economic and Ritual Significance of Trees in Meto Society

For the Meto, who occupy the hinterland and mountainous interior of west Timor, the biological world of plant life and forest regrowth is not simply a tableau from which social significance is drawn and metaphorically adapted. Rather it belongs to the world of practical knowledge, the lived in world of everyday experience and engagement. In a real sense fallowed regrowth forests and the land on which they grow are fundamental to the reproduction of Meto agriculture and society. Trees are significant in Meto society both as economic commodities and ritualised living forms.

One tree species that has had profound consequences for the historical development of Meto society is white sandalwood (*Santalum album L*) also referred to as *hau meni*. Formerly this tree species grew in great abundance across Timor and sustained a thriving export trade that attracted a variety of foreign influences to the island including Chinese, Portuguese and Dutch trading interests. For local populations the control and sale of sandalwood stocks provided a rich resource for generating wealth and political influence.

In contemporary times, with the long-term decline of sandalwood stocks through over-exploitation and mismanagement, other tree species have emerged as important part-replacement market commodities for the now poor mountain farming communities of west Timor. These species include Tamarind (*Tamarindicus indica*: *hau kiu*) which produces a seasonal source of income through the sale of the fleshy seed pulp. Meto sometimes refer to the tamarind as their *hau loit*, their money tree, which grows without tending and does not hinder the planting of seasonal crops around its base. Large palms are also classified as trees in Meto taxonomy. The ubiquitous coconut (*Cocos nucifera* : *hau noah*) and the betel palm (*Areca catechu*: *hau puah*) provide sustenance and items of trade. The lontar (*Borassus flabillifer*: *hau tua*) and the gewang palm (*Corypha elata*: *hau tune*) have long been utilized for a diverse range of products.

Both palms are tapped for their juice that is fed to domestic pigs, fermented to produce an alcoholic beverage *(laru* or *lalu*), or boiled with cow fat to produce red sugar discs for sale. The trunks are split and used in building and the leaves and stalks of the palms are widely utilized as roof thatch and house cladding, or fashioned into buckets, woven mats and a range of plaited baskets. Even the pith of the gewang finds a use as a starchy foodstuff in times of scarcity.

Other species which contribute in varying ways to the domestic economy include the mango (*Mangifera indica*: *hau upun*), candle nut (*Aleuritis mollucana*: *hau fenu*), ficus species (*hau nunuh*) and the forage legumes, *Sesbania grandiflora* (*hau kane*), acacia species (*hau kabesa*) and *Leucaena leucacephola* (*pates*). These and many other non-cultivated tree species of the remnant forests supply all manner of local community needs, including medicines and dyes, firewood and fencing materials, foodstuffs and farming tools.

This central significance of trees to Meto social and economic life is exemplified by their focus within a series of important collective ritual activities. One of the descriptive terms for the former indigenous Meto religion is *hau le'u faut le'u*. The phrase may be glossed as the 'sacred tree and the sacred stone' and refers to a central feature of Meto sacrificial ritual comprising an upright post or tree to which is attached a flat altar stone. Ritual offerings to the dualistically conceived deity (*Uis Neno-Uis Pah*) and the ancestors (*nitu*) were conducted at these sites (McWilliam 1991). They included prayer offerings for the conduct of rainmaking and harvest rituals in the agricultural cycle, as well as more personal invocatory rituals to house ancestors and those of the wider name group (*kanaf*).

The motif of the tree is also evident in life cycle rituals within Meto communities. A good example in this respect is the 'birth tree' which, at least until the widespread conversion to Protestant Christianity during the 1960s, was maintained widely throughout Meto territories. As part of the post-partum rituals accompanying birth it was common practice to place the umbilical cord (*usan*) and placenta (*olin*)[5] of the newborn in a small plaited basket and to hang this in the branches of a designated tree. The practice is still maintained in some Catholic areas of west Timor. These trees, usually Chinese oaks (*Schleichera oleosa*: *hau usapi*), candle nut (*hau fenu*) or large banyan trees (*hau nunuh*), with their clusters of drying birth baskets, represented a graphic image of the related community's 'tree of life'.

A third example of the ceremonial significance of trees is evident in the former practices associated with the cult of headhunting and the incorporation of smoked and dried severed heads into the spirit collectivity of the victorious community. Headhunting and internecine warfare flourished in Timor until well into the twentieth century, and as part of the rituals of incorporation, many communities made use of large banyan (*Ficus virens*) or oak trees (*Schleichera oleosa*) as storage places for the skulls of slain enemies. These trees were usually located adjacent to the enmity cult houses (*uim le'u musu*) of the hamlet community. Festooned with yellowing skulls these 'head trees' (*hau nakaf*) or 'head banyan' (*nunuh nakaf*)/ 'head oak' (*usaip nakaf*) stood as vivid markers of the murderous success of the local cult (McWilliam 2002). Like the 'birth trees' of new life, these 'trees of death' also communicated ideas around life, death and its inter-relation.[6]

These examples of the use of trees in both the economic life of Meto communities and as a focus for ritual elaboration hint at the central importance of the representational qualities of trees in west Timorese culture. In the following section I seek to expand upon these qualities, focusing in particular on the significance of the binary properties of 'trunk and tip' as an idiomatic set.

Trunk and Tip as an Idiom of Precedence

The generic term for tree in the Meto language (*uab meto*) is *hau*. However, in its representation in ritual speech (*natoni*), the tree is abstracted as 'trunk and tip' (*uf ma tunaf*). Like other significant paired categories in Meto cultural schemata, the classification of 'trunk and tip' represents a complementary set of differentiated elements. Central to the relationship between the paired terms is a notion of asymmetry, whereby the status of one element is higher or greater than its complement. In this case it is the term *uf,* trunk, stem or origin, which is designated with a higher value in relation to its 'tip' (*tunaf*) complement.[7] I would argue that the particular application of this dualism in different social contexts provides a basis for Meto collective representations of precedence and the tendency to classify social and political relationships in differentiated or asymmetric terms. 'Trunk and tip' is a particularly instructive dichotomy because of its application across a variety of semantic domains within Meto cultural practice. The metaphor has a wide appeal in Meto society and carries with it a certain privileged valency as one of the primary ways that individuals and groups assert political and social seniority. This is not to say, that 'trunk and tip' represent an eastern Indonesian version of the hierarchical encompassment or unitary value of the Hindu pure/impure variety postulated by Dumont (1980). Rather, 'trunk and tip' needs to be viewed as only one of a number of equally central dual categories that serves to differentiate social relations and which are strongly dependent upon circumstance and context. Precedence in this context emphasizes the diversity of contrasting values which can be brought to bear on social contexts. Exclusion may be sought, but the extant plurality of relevant values in any social context remain dynamically contested and give rise to potential reversals and inversions of the logical categories (see Fox 1989, Platenkamp 1990, Vischer 1996).

Closely related to the formal metaphor of 'trunk and tip' are the associated dual categories of 'trunk and flower' (*uf ma sufan*) and 'trunk and twig' (*uf ma tlaef*). These metaphors express a synonymous kind of marked relationship, but their application is associated conventionally with slightly different social and ritual contexts. Each of these representations exhibits the same concern with a temporal distinction that also expresses a spatial difference. Trunk and tip and its variants express the existential Meto truth that human relations are inevitably asymmetric in character, relatively unequal yet complementary. In the conduct of social and political life these status differences are also defined and contested on the basis of assertions and acknowledgments to temporal precedence

The Trunk of Agnation

In exploring the relevance of the tree as a metaphor of social relationships, members of Meto communities recognize at least two types of what might be termed socio-cultural trees. In the following discussion I will describe these arboreal tropes as trees of agnation and trees of alliance. Generally speaking these distinctions are notional collectivities rather than interactive groupings. The distinction is also partial to some extent and involves a certain degree of overlap.[8] However, for heuristic purposes I would distinguish between people who are related through actual or classificatory agnation and others who are aligned through marriage and affinity.

In terms of agnation, all Meto individuals belong to one or another shared name collectivities or *kanaf*. Members of the same *kanaf* share the same name which is ideally perpetuated through the affiliation of children to their father's *kanaf* group.[9] Members of the same *kanaf* also share the same ritual observances and place of origin which, typically in Timor, is associated with one of the prominent limestone outcrops called *fatu*. In formal verse this 'rock and tree' (*fatu ma hau*) of origin constitutes the imputed ancestral beginnings of the *kanaf*.

Another characteristic feature of *kanaf* in west Timor is their dispersal over the Meto landscape. Segments of larger *kanaf* collectivities are found scattered throughout Meto domains usually in combination with other *kanaf* segments in co-resident hamlets. The complex pattern of *kanaf* settlement throughout the region is a consequence of politico-historical factors mediated by the enduring Meto orientation towards arable land for shifting cultivation. One result of this dispersal is that over time people and communities which share the same *kanaf* affiliation may have long since diverged and relinquished any continuing ritual or social ties with one another. In such cases these groups will often nevertheless acknowledge a shared origin by casting their relationship as one of *uf mese*, one trunk or one stem of origin (in Indonesian the equivalent is *satu rumpun*).

In this conception the founding/origin ancestor is considered the trunk (*uf*) and their progeny the twigs (*tlaef*), tips (*tunaf*) and flowers (*sufan*). The collective name group is therefore considered to be a tree (*hau uf mese*: one tree trunk) in which there is an unbroken and organic link to the ancestral 'trunk' father. The emphasis here is upon a male ideology. It is the image of the permanent tree with its spreading branches representing the divergent agnatic segments of the dispersed *kanaf* group which are linked organically, biologically, to their ancestral origins at the base or trunk.

A further cultural conception of the collective agnatic group is found in the phrase *sufaf ma kauf*. This expression refers to a gender distinction between types of flowers of a tree. *Sufan* (female flowers) and *kauf* (the male flower or part thereof) combine to produce fruit of the 'agnatic' tree. The cognate term *kaum* is often used to refer to the extended family tracing links to putative origin ancestors.

In stressing the importance of origins, this needn't necessarily mean privileging some ancient beginnings. Origin structures in Meto representations can be of relatively short duration and precedence invoked or asserted by proximity to a relatively recent trunk of agnatic origin. One characteristic distinction made in this respect is that between 'before' (*nahun*) and 'after' (*namuin*) in the reckoning of locally contextualized authority. People may speak disparagingly of another's claim to local knowledge or entitlement with the dismissive phrase, 'Ah ... he came later' (.. *in nem namuin*). Such a statement implies the idea of distance from a trunk or origin or the issue at stake, of only grasping the 'tip' and therefore lacking any authoritative claim.

Similarly, for co-resident *kanaf* segments within a defined region, status distinctions are typically cast in terms of 'younger/elder' (*olif tataf*) which designate birth-order of siblings and classificatory siblings. To be the elder sibling (*tataf*) is to be closer to the origin trunk (*uf*) and the authoritative place of the ancestors. As such there may be a claim to seniority or precedence in terms of *kanaf*, hamlet or domain authority. The precedence here is primarily a temporal one, an antecedence which confers seniority or status (see Schulte Nordholt 1971:395 who reiterates this finely articulated attention to status difference)

In such a conception of affiliation to the ancestral past it seems culturally inappropriate to speak of descent as the mode of agnation. Meto botanical models of agnation are perhaps more productively viewed as ascending systems which place cultural emphasis on temporal and spatial distance from the source of life (Fox 1988). In this regard I note the Meto classificatory kin term for grandchild, *upuf*, and thought this might well refer to an organic connection with or extension of an ancestral trunk. No-one I spoke to agreed with this suggestion, however, although everyone would acknowledge that the relationship between the alternate generations was a special one. Indigenous names (*kan meto*) for example, tend to be passed from the grandparent generation to the newborn and the *upuf* is thought to be inextricably tied to its ancestral trunk. However, linguistically the [f] in the term *upuf* functions as a suffix in generalized reference and is dropped in its spoken address form '*upu*'. It is therefore not cognate with the term, *uf*. Nevertheless, the point remains that one expression of the concept 'trunk and tip' in Meto classification is its application to the name group (*kanaf*) which conjoins generations of agnatically related men and women in an assemblage of shared rights and interests. The former practice of maintaining the hamlet 'birth tree' where the birth by-products of newborn members of the *kanaf* were stored is a visual representation of this metaphorical understanding.

What remains significant in this affirmation of shared *kanaf* origins is the moral authority of the ancestral trunk in relation to the present tip progeny. In an important sense all moral authority in Meto society derives from the ancestral past, or rather, via an appeal to the past conveyed in narrative form.

In speaking of a *kanaf* 'trunk of agnation', a tree of life so to speak, the image also expresses the historical trajectory of the ancestral name from its putative place of origin to the multiple de-centred scatter of contemporary membership. Meto speak of this process of *kanaf* expansion in terms of a continuing movement from the narrow confined lands (*pah malenat*) characterized by discord and dispute, to the broad and wide lands (*pah manuan*) of agricultural plenty and grazing space.[10] Oral records and collective memories of these travels and generational wanderings are maintained through the recitation of formal poetic narratives. These ancestral chants are expressed in a formal parallel speech known as *natoni* and recount the heroic and formative episodes of the particular *kanaf* history. A characteristic feature of this oral genre is its topogenic quality. In place of a genealogical recounting of sequentially named ancestors, these narratives typically trace the origins of the *kanaf* spatially as a journey of place names through a landscape (Fox 1995). Named places are markers of events, settlement and points of divergence along this ancestral path of the name (McWilliam 1997).

Another way people describe these narratives is in terms of 'trunk speech' (*uab uf*), 'narratives of origin' which recount the beginnings of the group and among other things, authorize the contemporary legitimacy of territorial claims. Traube (1986), speaking of the neighbouring Mambai people of east Timor, uses the term 'trunk of discourse' for describing a similar narrative concern with origins. It is a concern with carrying the words of the ancestors, the trunk speech (*uab uf*), which confers or at least asserts the legitimacy of place in the branching tips of the contemporary world.[11]

All *kanaf* maintain and reproduce their 'trunk speech', their discourse of origin. However, individual knowledge and capacity to narrate the origin journey of the *kanaf* is restricted. There are two main reasons for this. Within any particular region, certain *kanaf* hold an historically based politico-ritual seniority. These *kanaf* are the representatives of the former indigenous political and ritual leaders of Meto domains. Their privileged narrative perspectives on the past contribute to the prominence accorded one broadly shared narrative discourse into which lesser *kanaf* groups articulate their own positions.

More specifically at the level of individual ability to narrate origins, such skills and knowledge are thought to be bestowed upon select members (usually male, but I have met female chanters) of the *kanaf* as a kind of inspirational gift. The majority of people may only hold a schematic outline of the 'trunk speech' and would defer to more knowledgeable seniors. Moreover, the words of origins are considered to be an inheritance from the ancestors and therefore imbued with ancestral sanction. To speak the formal phrases incorrectly or without due regard is therefore potentially dangerous.

Among the diverse properties of this genre of narrative discourse on the past, trunk speech (*uab uf*) asserts a legitimacy of both origins in terms of place, and authority in terms of named *kanaf* groups. At the level of domain, certain canonical oral texts serve as political statements of claim to political leadership; forms of Malinowskian charter that legitimate contemporary political configurations. At more local levels, chanting one's origin may serve to define rights to contested lands. In either case the veracity of one's assertion rests upon the linking of precedence in terms of place and political alliance. This narrative linking can be seen in the following segment which, in total, addresses the political order of the former domain of Amanuban in central southern Timor. Here, I simply stress the opening stanza where the speaker begins this segment of the narrative by establishing both a place of origin and a named political ordering;

Neon apinat neon aklahat Shining day glowing day[12]

ma amakau ma enakau and (honouring) my father and my mother

nok neno afi neno ahunut together in those days, the origin days

fai ahunut ne the origin nights[13]

Koli na Toli na Ami na Nope the Lords — Koli, Toli, Ami, Nope

na Nuban na Toi Nuban and Toi

ambi Klabe Tainlasi in Klabe, Tainlasi

Maun nu Niki Nik ..... Maun nu Niki Niki .....[14]

In most areas of west Timor the existence of the 'trunk settlement' (*kua uf*) from which the contemporary *kanaf* segments have dispersed, represents an important focus for orientation in both the political and physical landscape. The 'old settlement, the old place' (*kuamnasi balemnasi*), although nowadays largely abandoned and uninhabited, remains the critical link to the ancestral trunk and the origins of Meto personal identity. This linkage is often given as a reason why in many areas, a few households of the contemporary community maintain relatively remote residences in the origin settlements of the group.

The Tree of Alliance

An alternative representation of trunk and tip is found in Meto notions of marriage and alliance between *kanaf*. As elsewhere in eastern Indonesia and as a recurrent theme in broader Austronesian social constructs, marriage exchange and the creation of affinal alliance relationships between groups has been characterized as a 'flow of life' (Fox 1980). The gifting in marriage of a member of one social group to another in exchange for certain prescribed or negotiated reciprocal gifts and services typically provides the basis for the social and culturally acceptable, biological reproduction of the *kanaf*. Among Meto communities of west Timor, ideally it is women, or rather daughters of the *kanaf* group, who move between agnatically constituted houses (*ume*) in marriage. Women are the source of life for their husband's group and the basis for the continuity of his *kanaf* over time. More particularly it is the inherent fertility of a new wife which is keenly sought as one component of marriage exchange. The movement of a woman to another *kanaf* group in marriage, and by extension the children she will bear, adds to the collective life of her husband's name group.[15] Conversely a woman's marriage also represents separation and a potential loss to her natal group. This is why in some Meto areas of west Timor, the first born child of the new marriage is returned to the woman's family in exchange for the life they relinquished.[16] Frequently too the cost of fulfilling bridewealth obligations may require extended periods of residence with the wife's natal group and the provision of labour and other 'bride' services to secure the formal incorporation of children of the marriage into the father's *kanaf*.

One way Meto characterize *kanaf* relationships between 'givers of life' and 'receivers of life', progenitors and progeny, is as male and female respectively.[17] The gender distinction emphasizes the status asymmetry of the exchange. Those houses which 'give life' are symbolically male (*atoin amonet*) and establish precedence vis-à-vis their categorically female affines (*atoin amafet*) who thereafter commit themselves to a lifelong series of obligations and formal respect. In this indigenous representation 'male' groups engender and procreate 'female' groups in negotiated orders of precedence.

The conduct of marriage exchange also engages what I term a Meto 'tree of alliance'. This is evident in the preparatory exchanges and meetings between the marrying groups which are cast in botanical idiom. In formally requested unions, those said to be conducted in the light of day (*neno pupu*), references are made to the bride as a ripening fruit, a green lemon (*hit leno, hit muke*). This image is developed and elaborated in the main formal exchanges which represent the public expression of the transfer of the bride to the husband's group. In this ceremonial exchange, termed 'the gifting of the old areca and old betel' (*fe puah mnasi manu mnasi*), two sets of prospective affines come together for feasting, ritual exchanges of goods and formal speeches (*natoni*). Typically, the formal meeting of the prospective affines is marked by a mock battle in which the two sides attempt to wrestle their respective gifts from one another. In this faux mêlée the bride is represented by an elaborate bamboo framework known as a *skiki,* decorated with sprouted coconuts or areca nuts, as well as various woven baskets and cloths (all conceptually female objects). The symbolism here is fairly transparent as is the objective of the 'wife-takers' in wrenching the *skiki* from the protection of the bride's mother's brothers (*atoin amaf*). In another example I witnessed, the *skiki* was fixed upon a pole that had been smeared with fat and oil and planted in the ground making it slippery and difficult to 'uproot'. The idea of the bride as the fruit of a tree was even more pronounced in this case.

From the perspective of the wife receivers,[18] the wife giving affines are constituted in terms of at least three significant groups who must be acknowledged and who represent the groups to whom they remain indebted during the life of the marriage. The actual number, in fact, will vary with circumstance, but each identified representative group should receive a formal gift which has been determined in consultation prior to the gathering.

These formal gifts represent an acknowledgment of an ordered series of life giving exchanges which have preceded the new union. The conceptual framework which links these prior exchanges to the present marriage is contained within a relationship of trunk and tip, or more specifically as one between a 'trunk father' group (*am uf*) an original wife-giver, and the 'flower of the trunk' (*uf in sufan*), namely the bride. In this perspective the groom, who becomes known as the *moen feuf* (the new man), is metaphorically said to be a *tlaef*, a small twig, attached to his own named 'tree of origin', or *kanaf*.

Between these markers of extended alliance lie two key affinal groupings. Firstly, the bride's mother's brother, the *atoin amaf* (father people) who is ritually responsible for his sister's children's development and who maintains significant rights in respect to their life cycle transitions.[19]

The second key affinal exchange group focuses upon the bride's father and his male siblings. They are referred to as the *am tunaf* and *ama nana* (inside fathers) respectively. Initially I assumed the term *am tunaf* to mean 'tip father' in distinction to the originating 'trunk fathers' and still feel that this is a consistent interpretation. However, most people with whom I discussed this issue stated that the term *'tunaf'* in this context refers to a stone hearth. Hence the meaning of the phrase is really that of 'hearth' father. This is consistent with the collective ritual phrase describing both the bride's parents as *oe maputu ai melala* (hot water burning flames), where the reference alludes to the process of the bride's birth and the role of the father in maintaining the smouldering fire under the 'roasting' platform (*hal se'it*) used in post-natal heating rituals (McWilliam 1994).

Notwithstanding this mixing of metaphors in the classification of marriage exchange the point remains that one primary indigenous representation of the creation of marriage alliance is the conjoining of trunk and tip/flower. In other words, the gifting of life in marriage is one that implies a kind of planting and prospective fertile growth. Marriage alliance is a kind of tree that must be fertilized in order to grow. That is why barren marriages are thought of as marriages with 'no stem, no growing tip' (*kama u kama tunaf*). They simply dry out and die off like their botanical counterparts.[20] An alternative phrase used is marriage 'without (female) flower and without (male) flower' (*kana suf ma kana kauf)* meaning in effect that there is no 'fruit' forthcoming from the union.

Figure 1. The tree of alliance

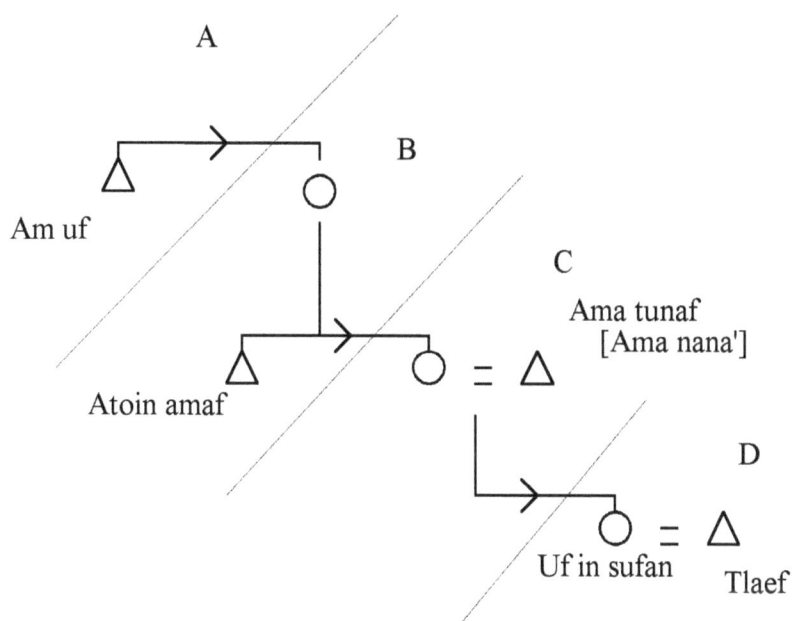

The 'tree of alliance' also engages an order of precedence which is reproduced through the conduct of mutual rights and responsibilities between respective alliance groupings. That a man's wife's relatives are socially superior is uncontested. Meto describe this relation in a variety of ways. In one sense they are perceived in terms synonymous with the ruler of the Meto domain. For the blessings of marriage one responds with *tolas* or *ut leot*, forms of harvest gifts offered to the ritual centre. Upon marriage, it is said that a man should not arrive at the house of his *atoin amaf* or *am tunaf* with 'empty shoulder or empty hand' (*kanemfa ben luman, kanemfa nim luman*). Young married men may genuinely fear their wife's father. To speak discourteously of one's wife's father, or wife's mother's brother, may result in sudden misfortune or illness. These sanctions and conventions all emphasize the main point that, in Meto terms, the movement of women between *kanaf* in marriage is a gift of life between houses, and for this gift, one paternal house is indebted to another.

An example of this botanical formulation of alliance can be seen in the following segment of ritual speech. These words were offered during the conduct of a formal marriage exchange between two previously allied groups in the mountains of south west Timor. Something of the stylized etiquette of formal speech which characterizes the public conduct of such occasions can also be read in this segment.

.....

he palmis lek leko with proper humility

ma baisenu lek leko and proper obeisance

neu au ena mahonit neknon to my cherished mother of life

ma ama mahonit neknon and revered father of life

uf tunaf trunk and tip

na kubiok nalalien have joined together

na peniok nalalien folded together

es au baisenu lek leko so that I beseech properly

ma lonaen lek leko and supplicate properly

ma toti manpenit and ask and obtain

mau nahe naufon nai that the woven mats be opened

ma benon nai and laid out

manbian haek nai [for] those who are assembled

namni nai and [those] in place

manbakus nhake nai and for the facilities assembled

namni nai and in place

henati sut ambi fufuk so that which is carried on the head

ma loit ambi benak and that carried on the shoulder[21]

nanebton ma nasaunton be taken down and put down

es na usikau on i for my lord in this way

tua kau on i..... my master in this way.....

The Grafting of Residence

If the symbolic gifting of women as brides in marriage creates the basis for affinal precedence between marrying groups, it is the relative residential location of the exchange groups which helps enact that precedence in local places.

Precedence is not an abstract quality or status but a binding claim on practical services and obligations. Its enactment in local contexts is the consequence of certain marriage outcomes mediated by place.

I have introduced this section with a botanical allusion of grafted residence. In fact the Meto have no traditional practices associated with grafting, nor do they use the metaphor to describe social process. Strictly speaking it is only in the relatively rare occasions of 'marrying-in' (*kaib natam*) when a man upon marriage is fully incorporated into his wife's *kanaf*, that a process akin to grafting might be said to occur. From my point of view, however, the notion well expresses the spirit of Meto hamlet development and dynamics. Here we need to understand the process of classification of households within Meto hamlets and something of the political strategies employed to secure precedence and status.

All Meto hamlets, or *kuan*, be they a small family cluster of closely related houses or larger settlements of several dozen houses, recognize three broad categories of people. The first category is a senior name group segment (*kanaf*) which represents simultaneously, the central political leadership of the hamlet, the senior land custodian and, typically, the contemporary senior agnates of the founding name group of the hamlet, that is the trunk (*uf*) of the place. Collectively this cluster of houses is referred to as the *kua tuaf* (hamlet boss or lord).

A second significant grouping is households of the hamlet that represent a union between daughters of the *kua tuaf* house, and in-marrying men, that is, men who reside in their immediate wife-giver's hamlet. These houses, affinal allies of the *kua tuaf*, are known as *atoin asaot* (marrying people). In return for placing themselves under the political authority of their wife-givers, these affinal houses gain access to arable land in the vicinity of the hamlet. They are said to 'eat' from the *kua tuaf* and in return offer political and ritual support.

A third notional category of resident is what is termed the *atoin anao amnemat* (lit., the people who come and go). These people are strangers to the extent that they have not yet secured an affinal alliance with settled residents of the hamlet. In this respect their social position is somewhat peripheral or marginal to the hamlet. Their right of access to land may become tenuous in the absence of any local marriage alliance. Significantly these people are also spoken of as having 'no stem, no tip' (*kama u kama tunaf*). Like 'barren' households they have no grounded fertility to enable them to prosper.[22]

In this threefold division of the community, which in terms of relative numbers can vary enormously between settlements, marriage exchange becomes one important strategy to secure and promote relative precedence vis-à-vis other households in the community. In this respect I would highlight two aspects of these relations.

Settlement endogamy is relatively common in Meto regions and for the majority of individuals the direction of marriage exchange between houses has little bearing on the structural precedence of community. Over time continuing exchange relations may result in alliance relationships being described as *feto mone* (female male), meaning they recognize a relative equality of status at a generalized level while still marking precedence at the level of individual exchange.

This is not the case for the senior *kua tuaf* group, or more specifically for the senior house of the senior *kanaf* in the settlement which represents the 'head of the settlement' (*kuan in a nakan*). In order for this house to maintain its position at the apex of a general order of precedence within the community, and as the trunk house of the settlement, it must seek wives from outside the settlement. This is because to marry within would place the senior house in a debt of life to one of its wife-receiving affines and political subordinates. Such outcomes are widely avoided for the ambiguity of authority they bring, but if unavoidable such outcomes can lead to bitter social divisions within the community.[23] My point, however, is that the position of *kua tuaf* at the local level, and by extension the political heads of indigenous Meto domains (*pah tuaf*), make use of the botanical idiom and image of trunk and tip in the construction and reproduction of precedence. To remain the trunk and source of authority requires conscious strategies of particular alignments and alliance.

Figure 2. Hamlet formation

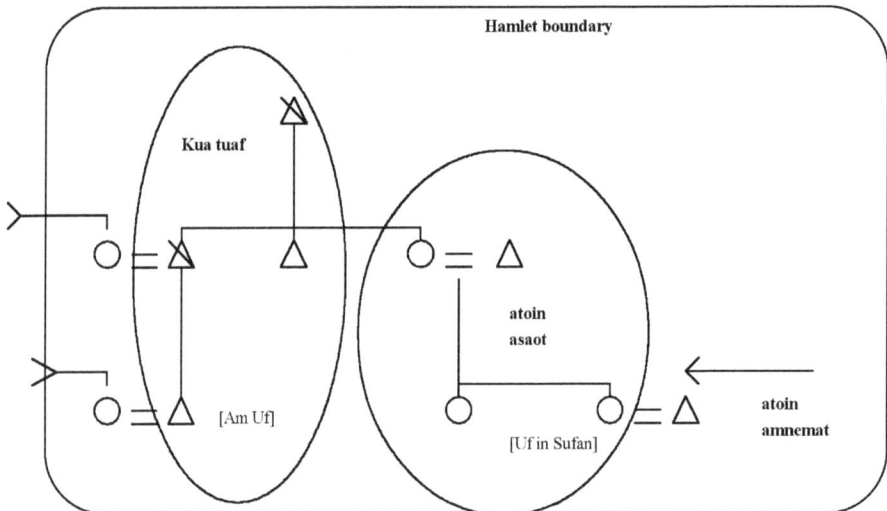

Newcomers and relatively recent arrivals over one or two generations are typically positioned at the periphery of these orders of precedence. To secure land access and the obligatory social networks of reciprocity these individuals need to marry into established *kanaf* groups of the settlement.

The idiom adopted is the tree of alliance with the *kua tuaf* often taking the role of the *am uf* (trunk father) or mother's mother's brother. As one man put it to me in the context of his house's political relationship with the *kua tuaf* of the settlement and simultaneously the senior political house of the domain (*pah tuaf*), 'We marry the flowers of the trunk, sir' (*haim kabin nok uf in sufan, pah tuan*). In doing so the central origin group of the settlement, like a large spreading tree, serves as a protective 'canopy and shade' (*aneot am ahafot*) for the subsidiary houses which shelter beneath.

Concluding Comments in Comparative Context

At the beginning of this paper I suggested that the inclination to cast social processes in botanical idioms is a pervasive and underlying orientation throughout eastern Indonesia. In this concluding section it may be instructive to make some comparative remarks on the general relationship between botanical ideas, notably trunk and tip or its variants, and orders of precedence as a strategic concern. I would add that this is not a comprehensive survey. It merely offers some exploratory comments on the scope and character of precedence in a botanical idiom.

Even a partial review of the ethnographic literature reaps a rich reward in terms of reported indigenous botanical imagery. An early example of work on indigenous metaphor is Fox's paper on Roti (1971) where the 'mother's brother of origin' grows the seed of his sister's children and provides a nurturing ritual supervision throughout their life. In a later reference, one Rotinese Dengka man remarked to Fox;

> We men here are like a tree with one trunk but three roots; the main root is our father of birth. The second root, our mother's brother of origin, the third root our mother's mother's brother of origin. As long as a person lives, these three roots cannot be done away with for they are our path of life (1980:118).

I have not heard Meto individuals speak specifically of origins in terms of roots (*ba'an*) but the sentiment expressed here is highly resonant with a Meto outlook on social life.

A somewhat different but equally compelling view has been recorded by Platenkamp in writing of Tobelo society in Halmahera. The Tobelo are a non-Austronesian language community with decidedly Austronesian cultural expressions. In his lengthy study which, in part, analyses an elaborate utilization of botanical imagery, we find a version of the familiar notion that 'the male children hold the stem, the fruit/flower they can give away' (Platenkamp 1988:62). Among the Tobelo, daughters of the agnatic *'fam'* are given out or rather, 'planted', in marriage as conceptual fruit/flowers. This process creates a new stem from the marriage fruit. Hence 'stems relate to other stems asymmetrically...one represents the giver of "life" and the other the [new] stem that has generated from that gift' (Platenkamp 1988:64). In this way an order of precedence between stems is created because the life giving stem gives existence to the life receiving fruit/stem.

A variation on the same theme can be read in Grimes (1993:169). Writing on the indigenous Austronesian communities of Buru island in Moluccas, she notes that 'prosperity and blessing are framed in terms of "roots" (*lahin*) and leaf tips (*luken*)' and that this metaphor 'labels a relation of cause and effect'. One of her conclusions in this study of Buru 'metaphors for living', is that 'precedence creates categories that are asymmetric in that superiority is placed on that which came "before" — elder is superior to younger, source (that is, root) is superior to tip' (1993:184).

For the Mambai of east Timor, the critical botanical categories are *fu* and *lau*, trunk and tip. In a detailed exposition Traube explores relations between Mambai notions of trunk and tip which are conceived of as both a product and a process. 'Trunks come before the branching tips they support, and the multiple usages of *fu* and *lau* work simultaneously to temporalize space and spatialize time' (1989:326).

Even in eastern Indonesian societies where alternative relational categories are more prominent in indigenous exegesis, botanical imagery is strongly evident. The Makassae community of eastern Timor have an ideology that represents the 'flow of life' primarily as an exchange of procreative fluids (Forman 1980). However, as Forman notes, a descent group (*sala fu*) is composed of a core of agnates who trace their connections to a founding ancestor who 'planted' the house. For Makassae, the progenitors are *oma rahe*, the house that spreads its branches like a shade tree for their progeny (*tufu mala* — little sisters or sister's child) (ibid.:156).

Similarly among the Lewotala communities of the Larantuka region, eastern Flores, the flow of procreative blood is the predominant idiom of alliance and affiliation, but notwithstanding this emphasis local communities value highly a marriage with the 'squash seed bean seedling' (*besi kulun ulan era*). This type of marriage represents the closure of an asymmetric cycle of marriage exchange in which the (female) affinal seed which was given out in marriage is returned to the progenitor source (*puken*).[24] As Graham puts it, 'So the seeds which stem from clan sisters are gathered, then germinate to reproduce life for the clan which is their source' (1991:139).[25]

Stated in general terms we might conclude on the basis of this brief review that the conduct and reproduction of social relations in eastern Indonesia is a form of gardening by another name. Life giving trees, by definition generations old and continuing, are the source of fertile seeds/fruits which are transplanted to others who reap a harvest of new life and ensure the development of their own ancestral trees. In this forest of social relations the transfer of life engages obligations and establishes recursive patterns of precedence which are reflected in differential status.

This is not to say that a botanical casting of precedence produces predictable or largely identical social forms and practice. On the contrary, precedence is dynamic process, context dependent and usually contested. Any integrative or ordering authority inherent in the principle of precedence typically rests upon a negotiated and temporary consensus. As Schulte Nordholt has commented on Meto classification but the point remains valid for the wider region, 'time and again people rely on a few basic relations but every time they do this they create new configurations if only by construing relationships in several ways' (1980:247). In other words the tree of precedence in eastern Indonesia might be thought of as a taxonomic family of trees within which speciation produces sometimes exotic varieties in different circumstances.

References

Aoki, E.

1986 The mother as the primeval stem, the father as the deep root: kinship ideology and its manipulation in central Flores. *Japanese Journal of Ethnology* 51(2):168–190.

Bloch, M.

1992 What goes without saying: the conceptualization of Zafimaniry society. In A. Kuper (ed.), *Conceptualizing society*, pp.127–146. London: Routledge.

Dumont, L.

1980 *Homo hierarchicus: the caste system and its implications.* Chicago: The University of Chicago Press.

Forman, S.

1980 Descent, alliance and exchange ideology among the Makassae of East Timor. In James J. Fox (ed.), *The flow of life: essays on eastern Indonesia*, pp.152–177. Cambridge, MA: Harvard University Press.

Fox, James J.

1971 Sister's child as plant: metaphors in an idiom of consanguinity. In R. Needham (ed.), *Rethinking kinship and marriage*, pp.219–252. London: Tavistock.

1980 Obligation and alliance: state structure and moiety organization in Thie, Roti. In James J. Fox (ed.), *The flow of life: essays on eastern Indonesia*, pp.98–133. Cambridge, MA: Harvard University Press.

1988 Origin, descent and precedence in the study of Austronesian societies. Public lecture in connection with De Wisselleerstoel Indonesische Studiën, 17 March 1988, Leiden.

1989 Category and complement: binary ideologies and the organization of dualism in eastern Indonesia. In David Maybury-Lewis and Uri Almagor (eds), *The attraction of opposites: thought and society in the dualistic mode*, pp.33–56. Ann Arbor: University of Michigan Press.

1995 Origin structures and systems of precedence in the comparative study of Austronesian societies. In P.J.K. Li, Cheng-hwa Tsang, Ying-kuei Huang, Dah-an Ho and Chiu-yu Tseng (eds), *Austronesian studies relating to Taiwan*, pp.27-57. Taipei: Symposium Series of the Institute of History & Philology: Academia Sinica 3.

Fox, James J. (ed.)

1980 *The flow of life: essays on eastern Indonesia*. Cambridge, MA: Harvard University Press.

Francillon, G.

1967 Some matriachic aspects of social structure of the Southern Tetun of Middle Timor. Unpublished PhD thesis. Canberra: Department of Anthropology, Research School of Pacific Studies, Australian National University.

Graham, P.

1991 To follow the blood: the path of life in a domain of Eastern Flores. Unpublished PhD thesis. Canberra: Department of Anthropology, The Australian National University.

Grimes, B.

1993 The pursuit of prosperity and blessing: social life and symbolic action on Buru Island, eastern Indonesia. Unpublished PhD thesis. Canberra: Department of Anthropology, Australian National University.

Lewis, E.D.

1988 *People of the source: the social and ceremonial order of Tana Wai Brama on Flores*. Verhandelingen van het Koninklijk Instituut voor Taal-, Land- en Volkenkunde 135. Dordrecht, Holland/Providence, USA: Foris Publications.

McWilliam, A.R.

1991 Prayers of the sacred stone and tree: aspects of invocation in west Timor. *Canberra Anthropology* 14(2):49–59.

1994 Case studies in dual classification as process: childbirth, headhunting and circumcision in west Timor'. *Oceania* Vol 65(1):59-74.

1997 Mapping with metaphor: cultural topographies in west Timor. In James J. Fox (ed.), *The poetic power of place: comparative perspectives on Austronesian ideas of locality*, pp.103–115. Canberra: Department of Anthropology, Research School of Pacific and Asian Studies, The Australian National University. Comparative Austronesian Series, ANU E Press: http://epress.anu.edu.au/.

2002 *Paths of origin, gates of life: a study of place and precedence in southwest Timor*. Verhandelingen van het Koninklijk Instituut voor Taal-, Land- en Volkenkunde 202. Leiden: KITLV Press.

Platenkamp, J.D.M.

1988 *Tobelo: ideas and values of a North Moluccan society*. Leiden: University of Leiden.

1990 The severence of origin: a ritual of the Tobelo of North Halmahera. In C. Barraud and J. Platenkamp (eds), *Rituals and socio-cosmic order in eastern Indonesian societies. Part II, Maluku. Bijdragen tot de Taal-, Land- en Volkenkunde* 146(1):74–92.

Rival, L.

1993 The growth of family trees: understanding Huaorani perceptions of the forest. *Man* (ns) 28(4):635–652.

Schulte Nordholt, H.G.

1971 *The political system of the Atoni of Timor*. The Hague: Martinus Nijhoff.

1980 The symbolic classification of the Atoni of Timor. In James J. Fox (ed.), *The flow of life: essays on eastern Indonesia*, pp.231–247. Cambridge, MA: Harvard University Press.

Therik, Tom

2004 *Wehali, the female land: traditions of a Timorese ritual centre.* Canberra: Department of Anthropology, Research School of Pacific and Asian Studies, The Australian National University in association with Pandanus Books.

Traube, E.G.

1986 *Cosmology and social life: ritual exchange among the Mambai of East Timor.* Chicago: The University of Chicago Press.

1989 Obligations to the source: complementarity and hierarchy in an eastern Indonesian society. In David Maybury-Lewis and Uri Almagor (eds), *The attraction of opposites: thought and society in a dualistic mode,* pp.321–344. Ann Arbor: University of Michigan Press.

Vischer, M.P.

1996 Precedence among the domains of the Three Hearth Stones: contestation of an order of precedence in the Ko'a ceremonial cycle (Palu'é Island, eastern Indonesia). In James J. Fox and Clifford Sather (eds), *Origins, ancestry and alliance: explorations in Austronesian ethnography,* pp.175–198. Canberra: Department of Anthropology, Research School of Pacific and Asian Studies, The Australian National University. Comparative Austronesian Series, ANU E Press: http://epress.anu.edu.au/.

ENDNOTES

[1] I am aware of the argument that natural objects do not function as metaphors for social processes because social relations are experienced as natural (Bloch 1992:130). My comment here is that the language of trunk and tip is that of the botanic and Meto do not confuse people with trees (see also Rival 1993).

[2] Also referred to in the literature as Atoni, Atoni pah meto, Dawan and Vaikeno (in the East Timor enclave, OeCussi-Ambeno). Meto comprise the predominant ethno-linguistic population in west Timor numbering around 750,000 people. The majority are smallholder farmers cultivating maize and secondary food crops. Domesticated livestock production forms an important component of rural economies, and seasonal off-farm labouring provides significant cash flow for many impoverished families.

[3] There is also an allusion here to the ceremonial gifts of banana and sugar cane which are presented to the groom's family at the completion of the central marriage rituals as an explicit gift of provision for the journey home with the new bride.

[4] I acknowledge the logical counterpoint here that in one sense 'trunk and tip' is a simultaneous relation, existing in a contemporaneous mode. One cannot have trunks without tips and vice versa. My point however, refers to the biologically derivative character of tips vis-à-vis trunks and the idea of proximity to an origin or starting point.

[5] The term *olin* means 'younger sibling' and represented the counterpart of the 'living' infant.

[6] Today these headhunting cult trees have been emptied of their skulls and stand as a mute testimony to the ceremonial violence of the past. According to older residents, many of the skulls were destroyed under Japanese orders during their occupation of Timor during World War Two.

[7] The term *uf* is a metathesized version of common Austronesian variants for trunk or origin such as *hu, fu, pu* (Fox 1995).

[8] An example of overlap is the instance of FZD MBS son marriage exchange which is permissible in terms of the symmetric kin terminology and is classified as a valued marriage path (*fe lanan, moen lanan*). Such marriages have the logical effect of marrying within the 'agnatic tree of relation' in my terms. They belong to the same 'tree trunk' (*hau uf mese*). This may be one reason why such marriage unions are not favoured in Meto ideals while MBD, FZS unions are sought. The latter represent a union of two distinct 'trees of affiliation'.

[9] Actual jural authority over children depends upon marriage outcomes and negotiation. Children may be affiliated with their mother's *kanaf* group in certain circumstances. The conventional ideal, however, privileges paternal affiliation.

[10] Choices for continued expansion to underpopulated and forested areas are fast declining on Timor. For many communities the reality is a downward spiral of soil depletion and low crop yields leading to increased exploitation of marginal country and poverty. Opportunities for transmigration beyond the island to West Papua and Sulawesi Tenggara have been pursued by Meto farmers during the late New Order period of government.

[11] An alternative term is *lais nu'un* or *lais nu'uf* which is used in a variety of ways to mean issues concerned with high rock outcrops, group origins and sacred/spirit places.

[12] An honorific which has the sense of extending respect.

[13] Fox (1995) has suggested that the word *nahun* may well represent a variation on the idea of 'trunk' (*uf*) with its connotation of origin /originator. Similarly the term *afi unu* is also cognate with a notion of trunk or origin time.

[14] The naming of a region by four points or places is a common feature of formal narrative discourse. The ritual centre mentioned here is better known simply as Niki Niki which was the residence of the former raja of Amanuban, the *kanaf* Nope.

[15] This is literally true in the sense that new lives are created, but also refers to the vitality or life force (*smanaf*) that the new wife brings to the collectivity of the husband's name group. In 'traditional' terms maintaining the collective '*smanaf*' of the name group, which included the ancestors, was a vital concern.

[16] Such return 'gifts of life' are based on voluntary agreements and not formalized arrangements as in other well documented areas of eastern Indonesia (see for example Graham 1991 for eastern Flores; and Francillon 1967 and Therik 2004 for the *mata musan* institution among the Tetun of central Timor). The decision is at times made reluctantly by parents.

[17] The classification of 'wife-takers' as female is also related to the understanding that children of the marriage are regarded as de facto 'female' (*feto*) members of the wife-giving group and constitute one of the highly favourable female marriage partners for sons of the original wife-giver's name group (that is, matrilateral cross-cousin marriage).

[18] I am conscious that this characterization of marriage as wife-giver/wife-receiver relations tends to obscure women's agency in the marriage process. Marriage is of course an emotionally charged process where choices, intentions and understandings among all participants is complexly variable. Here I simply seek to highlight a particular cultural representation of marriage that undoubtedly reflects a male bias.

[19] Not infrequently the *atoin amaf* takes the role of the 'trunk father' (*am uf*). In part this may be due to the difficulty of deciding upon the appropriate 'origin wife-giver'. Disputes over the correct representative can occur between competing claimants. Political considerations and questions of proximity may also play a part.

[20] In such cases the dissolution of the marriage would be possible without recrimination. Alternatively, as part of the explicit notion that marriage is a gifting of fertility and life, a man may justifiably seek to marry one of his wife's younger sisters in the hope of securing children.

[21] The speaker here is clearly referring to female and male guests. The verb *sut(ae)* is one conventionally used in reference to women carrying goods on their heads. Similarly it is men who carry goods and prestations on their shoulders.

[22] The phrase has a generic appeal and I have heard it used by women speaking disparagingly about the fortunes of their men-folk with money. Nothing tends to come of it.

[23] One exception to this is the case where households associated by *kanaf* with political leadership of the domain or wider territory find themselves in a subordinate political position vis-à-vis an existing *kua tuaf*. It is possible for this relationship to be reversed through marriage exchange to bring the local authority structure in line with the wider political order, but many factors may come into play in such circumstances.

[24] In local terms this relation is still described as 'following the blood'.

[25] See also Lewis (1988:215) writing on the Ata Tana Ai in adjacent Sikka Regency who speak of *mula puda* exchange as one of replanting the ancestral mother in the clan of origin.

6. Precedence in the Formation of the Domain of Wai Brama and the Rajadom of Sikka

E. D. Lewis

Introduction

The regency of Sikka in east central Flores is an ethnological laboratory in miniature for the study of differentiation in Austronesian societies. Except for an enclave of Lamaholot-speakers in north-eastern Sikka, a Lionese population in the district's west and small communities of immigrants from Sulawesi on the shore of Maumere Bay, all of the peoples of the regency of Sikka speak dialects of a single language, Sara Sikka, and possess a common cultural heritage. Nevertheless, the district's Sikkanese population includes communities whose patterns of social organization are quite distinctively different from one another. The most striking differences are those between the people of Tana 'Ai (most especially the ceremonial domain of Tana Wai Brama) in the mountainous eastern region of the district, the Ata Krowé of the regency's central and north coastal regions, and the Ata Sikka, the people of the south coast of the regency between Léla and Bola.[1]

The people of Tana Wai Brama are divided into five principal clans, each of which is made up of a number of houses. The people of Wai Brama reckon descent through women and each of the houses thus consists of people whose kinship is through consanguineally related women. Both the clans and houses of Tana Wai Brama are ranked in terms of the precedence of their founding ancestors and precedence informs activities in every realm of social life. Perhaps because of its relative remoteness, until the early 1990s and in contrast to the peoples of the central and coastal regions of Sikka, Tana Wai Brama and Tana 'Ai generally did not have intensive contact with outsiders. The people of Tana Wai Brama thus maintained their patterns of social order and exchange to a greater extent than other peoples of east central Flores.

By comparison, many communities of central Sikka have for centuries participated in trade and have been open to the movement in and out of the region of people of different cultures. Furthermore, until the decade following the end of World War Two, Krowé and Sikka were an indigenous rajadom under a ruling house in Sikka Natar, the south coast village of Sikka, one of many petty states found in eastern Indonesia. In historical times, the people of Sikka Natar were influenced by the Portuguese in the archipelago perhaps more than other communities of east central Flores. In the nineteenth century, the whole of Flores became subject to Dutch rule.

The interplay of their common cultural heritage and different histories produced social systems in Tana Wai Brama and the rajadom of Sikka that offer intriguing possibilities for studying social differentiation and, specifically, precedence and hierarchy, in closely related communities. But any attempt at comparison is confronted by certain challenges and difficulties. The challenges arise from the question of how the two societies diverged in the first place and whether or not, after they diverged, different historical processes were at work in the two societies. If there were, then the divergence of the two societies through time can be understood in terms of those processes and the principles of their common culture.

The difficulties arise from the requirement that there be sufficiently dependable historiographic and ethnographic material available to make such a comparison possible in the first place. Historiographic sources on Sikka are scarce and for Tana Wai Brama almost non-existent, unless we admit as evidence the oral and mytho-historical traditions of both peoples which are available from ethnographic research in the district. This is what I intend to do here.

The peoples of the domain of Tana Wai Brama in the mountains of Tana 'Ai and the village of Sikka Natar (the original seat of the Rajadom of Sikka) on the south coast of east central Flores both possess complex mythic histories that recount the origins of their societies in the coming together of groups of immigrants from many different places of origin. In Tana Wai Brama, the myths of origin are recounted orally on occasions of ritual. In Sikka, the histories are no longer told as a coherent body of myth on ritual occasions, but literary versions of the myths survive in manuscripts written by two Sikkanese authors between 1925 and 1960.[2] As the tales are told in the myths of the two societies, the Rajadom of Sikka and domain of Wai Brama evolved quite differently, but analysis of their mythic histories reveals themes and logics of history sufficiently similar to demonstrate an allopatric relation between the two. I will show how the Ata Tana 'Ai and the Ata Sikka use common themes and logics to account for the origins of quite different societies.

According to the mythic histories of its people, the domain of Wai Brama was formed from the sequential arrival of groups of immigrants. Each group was incorporated into the ceremonial system of the domain and the descendants of each group make up the clans that comprise the society today. The mythic history of Sikka Natar also recounts the arrival of groups of immigrants whose descendants make up the major groups of the contemporary society and to whom those groups trace their origins.

Sikka's myth of origin relates that two ships sailed from the west and landed, one after another, near the site of the contemporary village of Sikka. The crew of the first ship travelled inland, where they took up residence. A son of the captain of the second ship married an autochthonous woman and their descendants became the rajas of Sikka.[3] In contrast to Tana Wai Brama, after its formation, Sikka Natar became the centre of a rajadom, an expanding petty state over which the ruling house of Sikka exercised political dominion. The expansion of the Rajadom of Sikka involved the incorporation of subaltern *negeri* ('nations', that is, the villages of the region) in central Sikka into a single polity ruled by Lepo Geté, the 'Great House' of the rajas of Sikka. In contrast to Tana Wai Brama, the pattern of polity formation in Kerajaan Sikka (the Rajadom of Sikka) was thus one of the sequential incorporation of other communities by the geographical expansion of the polity.

Contrary to the sound advice of a respected mentor, I shall begin this essay with a disclaimer. I had intended this essay to defend a simple enough thesis, which is: whereas the society of the people of the domain of Wai Brama in Tana 'Ai is ordered by principles of precedence, that of the people of Sikka Natar and the rajadom through which their ancestors came to rule over most of the district of Sikka was ordered by hierarchy. In setting out the argument for this thesis I had thought, firstly, to add weight to arguments I have made elsewhere about the social organization of the Ata Tana 'Ai. Secondly, I wished further to develop observations I have made in print (Lewis 1996a) regarding the organization of authority in Kerajaan Sikka. Thirdly, I aimed to show that precedence, as a principle of social organization clearly at work in both Tana Wai Brama and Sikka, can manifest itself as hierarchy in certain circumstances, such as those in which the Rajadom of Sikka evolved. By showing that Tana Wai Brama is a society ordered by precedence in an historically uncomplicated form, whereas the Sikkanese rajadom, while founded in precedence, became a hierarchically ordered society, I intended to suggest that hierarchy does not accord in all societies with the general theory of hierarchy proposed by Dumont (1980), and that hierarchy can arise from sources other than the 'encompassment of the contrary'.

In pursuing these aims, I first encountered difficulties with the material available on the history of the Rajadom of Sikka. Then, in 1994, a corpus of more than 100 manuscripts composed by two Sikkanese writers came to light in Maumere. The large collection of papers greatly supplemented a single book length manuscript that had come into my possession in 1977. The information on Sikka's history and the myth of origin of the Sikkanese ruling dynasty contained in the manuscripts allows elements of precedence and hierarchy in the culture and society of the Sikkanese rajadom to be explored with the domain of Wai Brama as a comparable case. However, taking into account the literary evidence, the proposal that Wai Brama is a society ordered by precedence whereas Sikka was a society ordered by hierarchy is too simple to sustain.

Boer's and Kondi's *Hikayat Kerajaan Sikka*

Shortly after World War Two, Dominicus Dionitius Pareira Kondi, an Ata Sikka and an official in the government of the last raja of Sikka, completed an 86,000 word history of the rajadom. Somewhat earlier, his age-mate and fellow government official, Alexius Boer Pareira, completed exhaustive notes on the rajadom's myth of origin. Boer and Kondi began their careers as members of the small cohort of Sikka's first school teachers before raja Don Thomas da Silva drafted them into government service in the 1920s. Taken together, Boer's and Kondi's long manuscripts and some 100 additional documents in their handwriting comprise the *Hikayat Kerajaan Sikka*. The works were composed mainly in archipelagic Malay, the language of commerce and school tuition in Indonesia before the nation's independence, but include long transcriptions of Sikkanese ritual speech, the genre of Sara Sikka (the language of Sikka) in which Sikka's origin myths were once narrated orally.[4]

The first part of the *Hikayat* is a compendium of the mythic histories of Sikka and includes long narratives in the ritual language of Sikka. Boer and Kondi present the myths as a factual history of the origins of the rajadom. It is from the *Hikayat* and my own field notes from Sikka that I draw information for this essay.

The *Hikayat Kerajaan Sikka* is divided into four main parts. The first is a brief introduction in which Kondi identifies the 36 *suku bangsa* (BI 'tribes')[5] from which the people of Sikka originated and sets out their origins from places as diverse as other regions of Flores and 'Siam' and 'Hindia Belakang'.[6] The second part of the *Hikayat* is entitled 'Dewasa yang Pertama' ('The First Period') and is subtitled 'The history of the creation of the Rajadom of Sikka'. It is an account of a series of lineally related *mo'ang geté* (SS big men) who led the various communities of the Ata Sikka and who began extending their influence over other *negeri* by travelling about the region appointing *tana pu'ang* (SS 'sources of the earth') and establishing laws pertaining to religion in the period before the introduction of marriage, birth rituals, the settlement of disputes and Catholicism. This part of the work culminates with the dispossession of the people of Hokor and the seizure by the Sikkanese of their village, which became the contemporary Sikka Natar from which the rajadom expanded.

The third section of the *Hikayat* recounts the life of Don Alésu da Silva. Don Alésu journeyed to Malacca, where he met raja Worilla, the raja of Malacca, under whose sponsorship Alésu was educated in '*ilmu politik*' (BI 'political science', 'politics'), that is, government, and the precepts of the Catholic Church. Before he returned to Sikka, Alésu sent Augustinyu da Gama, a son of raja Worilla, to become the first teacher of religion in Sikka. The *Hikayat* details Don Alésu's consolidation of the various *negeri* of Sikka into a single polity, which occurred in conjunction with the conversion of all of the people of the rajadom to Catholicism.[7] Here the work tells how Alésu went about east central Flores creating alliances with leaders in the *negeri* of the region and, in many cases, raising up leaders in communities which had none before. With each alliance, Alésu established his own prior position by delegating authority over local matters to his new allies. The alliances were sealed by gifts of elephant tusks and other items of ceremonial wealth from Alésu to the leaders of each of the communities in turn. Augustinyu da Gama figures centrally in this part of the narrative. Da Gama's name is significant in itself, for it accords with the Sikkanese term for religion (that is, Catholicism), which is the Malay and Indonesian word *agama*, 'religion'. As a teacher of religion, da Gama brought Catholicism to Sikka. While recounting the creation of the Sikkanese polity in considerable detail, the *Hikayat* thus also charts the origins of the relationship between the rajadom and the Church in Sikka, and represents that relationship as one whereby the raja is prior and the Church of derivative or delegated precedence in the larger scheme of the rajadom (see Lewis 1998b).

The narratives of the 'Introduction', 'The First Period' and the early parts of 'The Second Period' have the character of myth and are undoubtedly written versions of the oral mythic histories of Sikka,[8] but Boer and Kondi refer to them as *sejarah* (M, BI 'history').

The bulk of Boer's notes concerns Sikka's mythic past while the fourth and last part of Kondi's manuscript consists of accounts of events in 'historical' times and deals with the period of the Dutch presence in the rajadom from the middle of the nineteenth century to World War Two. Here Kondi's manuscript includes simple chronologies of events and reproduces official documents of the period to which he had access as an official in the raja's government. This last section is unmistakably 'history' in the common sense of the term rather than myth. But the transition from the one to the other is gradual and is not signalled by Kondi himself in any way. There is simply a subtle shift in the narrative from a written down form of mythic history to a form of documentary history which deserves the most careful textual analysis.

The *Hikayat Kerajaan Sikka* is structured as a chronology of persons and events. These are undated in 'The First Period'. The dating of persons and events begins in 'The Second Period', in which some of the figures are, without question, historical persons while others may or may not have been. So, too, the events that Boer and Kondi recount. Those of the later period covered by the *Hikayat* were historical events and for some of them we can find corroborative evidence in documents such as the diaries (D *dagboeken*) written by the *controleuren* or *posthouders*, the Dutch colonial officials who lived in Maumere from the 1870s to 1942, when Maumere was occupied by the Japanese army.[9] Other events, such as Don Alésu's journey to Malacca, have the character of a mythic quest and whether or not there was a Sikkanese who travelled to Malacca and there met a raja named Worilla has proven resistant to verification by means of independent documentation.[10]

It is perhaps a logical necessity that all histories must start with persons and events and it is difficult to conceive of a history that does not in some way relate the one to the other. What is striking, but by no means unique (one can cite histories of European monarchies in which genealogy orders history and quarrels over succession are major events), about Kondi's history is that the main characters (excepting, of course, their antagonists) are persons who are related genealogically as ascendants and descendants to each other through time. Furthermore, there is an implicit assumption in Boer's and Kondi's writing that the events which chart the history of the creation of the Rajadom of Sikka are at least partly a consequence of the genealogical relatedness of the rajas, the protagonists in their narrative. In other words, it is not merely that the big men and rajas, whose tale the *Hikayat* is, are related, but that the fact of their relatedness lent extra force to the events by which the history is charted. Indeed, one view which can be taken of the *Hikayat* is that it is a document that justifies the claims of Lepo Geté, the Sikkanese royal house, to the authority to rule and its members' claims to status as rulers in terms of genealogy (see Lewis 1999). The individual persons of the tale are thus members of a central corporate group within which power is held and among whom political authority and rights to power are transmitted through time.

The royal genealogy of Sikka identifies 18 rajas who follow a succession of 11 big men, in all 29 persons who held authority in Sikka through 19 generations, according to one version of the genealogy.[11] These rajas were:

I. * Mo'ang Igor	X. * Mo'ang Mbako I Kikir Hiwa
II. * Baga Ngang	XI. Mo'ang Prispin
III. * Mo'ang Alésu	XII. * Don Luis
IV. Mo'ang Kapitang	XIII. * Mo'ang Mbo
V. Du'a Maria	XIV. * Mo'ang Andreas Jati
VI. Mo'ang Samao	XV. * Mo'ang Mbako II
VII. * Dona Ines	XVI. * Nong Méak
VIII. Mo'ang Sikukoru	XVII. * Mo'ang Thomas
IX. Mo'ang Juan Iku	XVIII. * Mo'ang Sentis

The asterisked names are those of persons whose careers and times Boer and Kondi treat at length or at least mention and it can be seen that six of Sikka's rajas are not dealt with in the *Hikayat*.

The persons whose lives and activities are the subjects of major chapters include, from 'The First Period', Mo'ang Bata Jawa. This paper consists mostly of a text in Sikkanese ritual language that recounts how Bata Jawa went about the district of Sikka designating *tana pu'ang* ('sources of the earth') who would thenceforth exercise ritual authority in each *negeri* of the region. Next comes Bata Jawa's son, Mo'ang Baga Ngang, a warrior whose power extended throughout much of central and eastern Sikka. Baga Ngang went around the district appointing secular leaders in each of the *negeri*.[12] Kondi recounts his activities in considerable detail. It was Baga Ngang who usurped the village of the Hokor people and made it the centre from which he exercised his power over the region, thereby setting the stage for the creation of the rajadom. The main figure in the early chapters of 'The Second Period' is Mo'ang Don Alésu, Mo'ang Baga Ngang's son. Don Alésu travelled to Malacca, returning to Sikka with a knowledge of government and the Catholic religion.

Several events, which Boer and Kondi clearly view as crucial to the shaping of the rajadom and the powers of its rajas, are recounted in some detail in the *Hikayat*. The first was a rebellion in north Sikka during the reign of raja Andreas Jati in the second half of the nineteenth century. The second was a rebellion led by a man named Teka and the raja's war against Teka and his followers which ensued. The third was a rebellion, led by a woman named Du'a Toru, by people in Tana 'Ai. The *Hikayat* ends with an account of events during the Japanese occupation, Sikka's role in the formation of the Republic of Eastern Indonesia, and the death of raja Don Thomas Ximenes da Silva in 1954.

The *Hikayat* is, in part, a chronology of events. Beyond that chronology, consideration of Boer's and Kondi's texts shows the ways in which the Sikkanese rulers represented their history and legitimated their authority. These they did not in terms of a logic of events ('historical' or otherwise), whereby event *A* gives rise to situation *X*, in which event *B* occurs, which results in situation *Y*..., but in terms of culturally given metaphors and a logic of myth. The metaphors and the logic by which they are articulated not only predated the clearly historical events recounted in the last chapters of the *Hikayat*, but can be seen at work in contemporary Sikka and neighbouring societies such as Tana 'Ai. Indeed, the metaphors and logic of the *Hikayat* are what bind the discrete events recounted in the text into a consistently coherent narrative. Causality as a linkage between events is notably absent from the structure of the narrative.

In the text we can see a construction and legitimation of social hierarchy through mytho-historical precedence. But, as Fox (this volume) points out, in addition to underpinning discourses of social order, precedence must do things, which is a way of saying that myth and history, to be meaningful, must have effect in the contemporary life of a community. In Tana Wai Brama, precedence, as a theory of the past, orders contemporary exchange between major social groups and the persons who act in ritual. In Sikka, precedence legitimates a political and social order, the core of which was Lepo Geté, the house of the rajas.

The Common Origin of the Ata Sikka and Ata Tana 'Ai

The *Hikayat* begins with accounts of the arrivals of two groups on the south coast of Flores, near the contemporary Sikka Natar. Both groups came by sea, from distant places to the west. The descendants of the first immigrants came to be known as Sikka's autochthons, while the descendants of the second ship would become Sikka's rajas. While the first group were immigrants, as the myth relates, they were predecessors of the second ship's company who also landed near Sikka Natar. By the logic of precedence, they were more autochthonous than the later newcomers and are represented as *orang asli* (BI original people) in the *Hikayat*. With respect to the arrival of the first newcomers, the *Hikayat* relates two couplets of ritual language, the language of myth in Sikka, followed by a brief comment:

Wawa Siam mai	[They] came from Siam
Siam sipa jong wutung	Skilfully sailing their ship from Siam
Sipa jong wutung	Skilfully sailing their ship
Léma Nidung Magé Gahar	They landed at Nidung Magé Gahar.

> It is evident they came from Siam by prau or ship and landed at Nidung Magé Gahar (between Sikka and Léla, between Ili Lewa and Napu Nao). They later moved to Mekeng Detung, to Iling Bekor, and then lived there. Because they were not healthy there, they then moved to Wolo Laru Poma Pihak Watu Daring in Mekeng Detung.[13]

Leaving aside the questions of how Kondi knew that the Sikkanese originated from 'Siam' (Boer's notebook has them arriving from 'Benggala' [Bengal]) and whether or not they did in fact, this passage from the *Hikayat* is nonetheless interesting on a number of points.

Firstly, the people who would become Sikka's autochthons were not autochthonous, but came from overseas. Secondly, they landed at a place on the south coast of Flores near Sikka Natar, which, in the later history of Sikka, would become the seat of the rajadom, but did not occupy the south coast. Instead, they moved inland to Mekeng Detung, a place near Ili Bekor, one of a range of mountain peaks in central Sikka.[14] Later in the *Hikayat*, Boer and Kondi recount the tale of how Mo'ang Baga Ngang captured the site of Sikka Natar from the people known as Hokor, who were then forced to flee eastward. The *ngeng ngérang*, the mythic histories of the people of Tana Wai Brama, name Mekeng Detung as the place of origin of Hading Dai Dor and Uher La'i Atan, the brothers who were the ancestors of Ipir Wai Brama, the 'source' (that is, founding) clan of the domain of Wai Brama. In the mythic histories of Wai Brama, Hading and Uher 'bubbled up' from a hole in the ground in Krowé, at Mekeng Detung, and from there set out on a search for uninhabited land which led them to Tana Wai

Brama (see Lewis 1988a:53ff., 1988b). Wai Brama's founders were thus of Sikka's autochthons. In the mythic histories of Tana Wai Brama, their origin is recounted as follows:

Bekor a'un wawa 'ia	My rising was over there (in the west),
Bubuk a'un wawa é	My bubbling forth was over there,
Wawa Krowé Kléga inan	(My) mother was there in Krowé Kléga,
Wawa Lépak Marin aman	(My) father was there at Lépak Marin,
Mekengdetung Woloarung [15]	At Mekeng Detung Woloarung
Popo Piak Watu Darin	At Popo Piak Watu Darin (Lewis 1988a:53).

Thus the mythic histories of both Sikka and Tana Wai Brama identify Mekeng Detung as important in the origins of these two peoples, for the one as the first place of settlement of newly-arrived off-shore immigrants and, for the other, the place of origin of founding ancestors who are said to have 'bubbled forth' from the earth at a place some distance from where they eventually established a new domain. If we juxtapose these two myths, it can be said that the origins of the Ata Tana 'Ai and the Ata Sikka are closely linked, if not common, a point readily made by contemporary Ata Sikka and Ata Tana 'Ai themselves.

Precedence in Tana Wai Brama

Much of my research in Tana Wai Brama has addressed questions about social and ceremonial hierarchies and the way that social organization and daily social life are informed by what some anthropologists working in eastern Indonesia have come to refer to as precedence. In the most general terms, precedence is the ordering of persons or a set of things in terms of a sequence of past events which brings those persons or things into ordered relationships. As the term has come to be used in analyses of social structure in eastern Indonesian societies, precedence is the ordering of social groups and the relationships of their members in terms of the temporal sequence in which those groups were (or are thought to have been) founded. In Wai Brama, the precedence of clans is encoded in the mythic histories of the founding of the domain, the main ceremonial and political domain in the mountains (see Lewis 1988a).

Tana Wai Brama is one of seven ceremonial domains into which Tana 'Ai, the mountainous eastern region of Kabupaten Sikka, is divided. The mythic histories of the domain recount the discovery of the forests and mountain valleys of Tana Wai Brama by two brothers, Hading Dai Dor (the elder) and Uher La'i Atan (the younger), who set out from Mekeng Detung in central Sikka to find empty land suitable for settlement. Hading and Uher became the founders of *sukun* (clan) Ipir Wai Brama, each the ancestor of one of the two branches into which clan Ipir is divided today. Ipir Wai Brama thus became the founding clan of Tana Wai Brama, which people today describe as the 'source' and 'central' clan of the domain. Over time, other people arrived in Tana Wai Brama. The discrete groups of newcomers were the ancestors of the people of clans Tapo, Mau, Magé and Liwu which, with clan Ipir, are today the five main clans of the domain.

As they arrived, each of the ancestors of the four subaltern clans of Tana Wai Brama received land for gardens from clan Ipir and were vouchsafed rituals to perform and a status in the *oda geté* (SS great precedence) of the domain. By virtue of these statuses and responsibilities in the ceremonial system of the domain, each clan is ranked in relation to the others in terms of the sequence in which the clans' founding ancestors arrived in Tana Wai Brama. Each clan thus has a position in the community which derives from the *oda* ('precedence') of clans in the domain. The *oda* of a clan informs the relationships of its members to people in other clans in the realms of ritual performance, alliance and exchange. I have elsewhere explored the internal organization of the domain of Wai Brama and the ways in which the conception of precedence orders relationships of clans, houses within clans and persons in ritual performance.[16]

For purposes of comparison with Sikka, I need only identify here in the most general terms the structure of the domain as it is represented in the mythic histories. That structure is one in which a ceremonial domain, which people conceive as a limited territory with undefined boundaries, has incorporated diverse immigrant groups who, over time, came together in one place and there formed a society whose internal organization is founded on a conception of the temporal precedence of the constituent groups. In essence and, as will be demonstrated here, in contrast to the rajadom of Sikka, the society of Tana Wai Brama resulted from the movement inward into the domain of origin groups from outside. The origins of Tana Wai Brama through time can be represented graphically as in Figure 1.

The sequence of the arrivals of the ancestors of these clans in Tana Wai Brama, the domain's *oda*, is elaborated in detail in the origin myths of the domain and the precedence of the members of the clans can be seen clearly today in the political, economic and, especially, ritual relations in the community. All such relations are ordered by the precedence relations of the clans which, all told, make up what James Fox (1995) has aptly described as an 'origin structure'. The phrase is apt because patterns of order in all realms of social life are legitimated by reference to their origins, which provide both corporate groups and individuals with identities and roles in the political and ceremonial order of the community. In particular, the precedence of the clans of the domain is maintained by the unique system of affinal alliance which is at the heart of exchange in the community and in the ordering of those large-scale ritual performances which involve persons from all of the domain's clans.

Figure 1. The evolution of Tana Wai Brama as a sequence of incorporations of immigrant groups with *sukun* Ipir Wai Brama as the *pu'an* ('source', 'central') founder group (time direction clockwise)

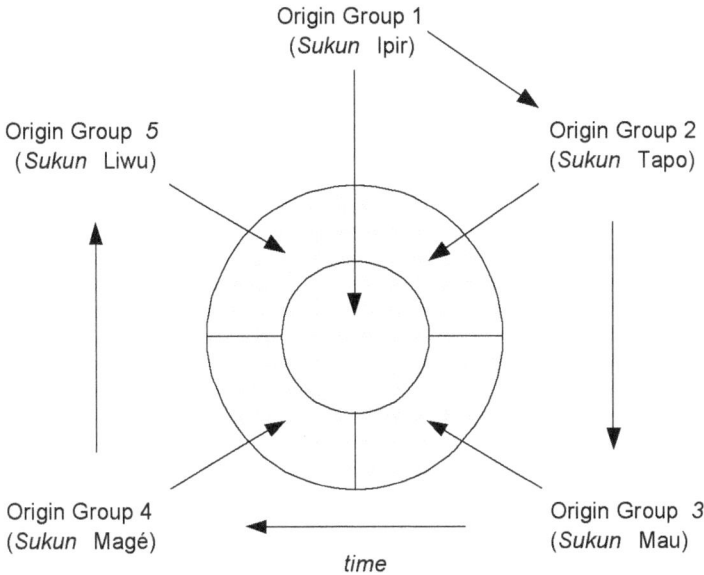

Representations of the Organization of Kerajaan Sikka: The Image of the Broken Plate

According to Sikka's *Hikayat*, the most important figures in the foundation of the rajadom were Mo'ang Bata Jawa, Mo'ang Baga Ngang and Sikka's first raja, Mo'ang Don Alésu. Bata Jawa was a law-giver who raised up ritual leaders in local communities throughout Sikka. Baga Ngang, Bata Jawa's son, captured the present-day site of Sikka Natar from the Hokor people. Baga Ngang's son, Don Alésu, is a figure of considerable stature in Sikka. Alésu completed the extension of the rajadom's power to the whole of the district of Sikka and was the first raja of Lepo Geté ('Great House'), the ruling house of the rajas, to use the Portuguese name da Silva, the name used since by all of Don Alésu's descendants and subsequent rajas.

The *Hikayat*'s account of the lives of these three figures includes a striking image representing the relationships of the various *negeri* ('nations') that the early rajas brought within the polity of the Rajadom of Sikka. I shall refer to that trope as 'the image of the broken plate'.

Porcelain plates found their way to Flores early in the history of trade in East and South-East Asia. Informants in Sikka remember tales of highly valued Chinese ceramics that predated the European presence in eastern Indonesia. Many porcelains from the Ming period (the fourteenth through the seventeenth centuries) were painted with cobalt oxide glaze, which yields a distinctive blue on white image. From the sixteenth century, potteries in Delft made fine, porcelain-like ceramics using tin glazes. The Dutch brought their Delftware to the Malayo-Indonesian archipelago, where it was widely dispersed through trade. In Tana Wai Brama, blue and white plates many of later Indonesian manufacture and not authentic Delftware are among the rarest and most highly valued clan heirlooms, which also include ivory tusks and silk Gujarati patola cloths.

The first reference to ceramic plates in the *Hikayat* is in the early chapter on 'The Life of Mo'ang Bata Jawa', which opens:

In his lifetime, Mo'ang Bata Jawa sailed here and there, obtaining on his journeys large plates which he then brought home to his country [Mekeng Detung]. After returning home, he visited all the inhabitants of his territory, telling them: 'We human beings must have a God, from whom we ask assistance. Thus there must be a place for making offerings. So the plates which I have brought I must divide [BI *membagi*] among all the nations [*negeri*] and designate in each a *tana pu'ang* (Source of the Earth).' So to those who had made villages first he said:

Tiat 'weli a'u nora pigang sisa, Dokang 'weli 'au nora luli lokang, Pigang sisa dena sisa mitang, Luli lokang dena lokang bura,	To them I confer offering plates, To them I give round drinking bowls, With the offering plates make black offerings, With the round drinking bowls make white pourings [of palm gin],
Sisa mitang wawa pu'a, Lokang bura réta wutu, Tena neni 'weli ihing, Tena prawi 'weli dolo,	Plates for black offerings down at the source [or trunk], Bowls for white pourings up at the tip [or crown of tree], With which to request crops, With which to beg for flowing lontar juice,
Ihing naha tama ronang Dolo naha tama téréng ...	Harvests which will fill the granaries, Flows of lontar juice which will fill large containers ...

Mo'ang Bata Jawa also distributed the plates to people called *pu'u*, 'those of the middle', to the west of Lio and other places.[17]

Later, Bata Jawa's son, Mo'ang Baga Ngang, went around the district pacifying and forming alliances with the leaders of various localities. As the *Hikayat* relates the tale, the *pigang sisa* (offering plates) make a second appearance in the narrative of Baga Ngang's career:

After setting things up in the same way as they had at Léku and the other places, [Baga Ngang and his entourage] proceeded to Wodong, to Kodé, to Ropé, and to Hubing, Weke, Wétak, Kangae, Nitung, to Habi Gahar and straight from there to Ili, Moro Piring, where there was a small village which they bypassed, and straight to Pogong Bola, Koker

Romanduru and the surrounding villages where they did as before, and then he returned to Natar Gahar safely and with gladness because he had accomplished the intention of his heart. ...

Then he made a journey to the west as far as Molé Kéli Samba [Lio] and then onward to Tonggo Keo and to Kasan Toring. Things he gave to a man who became *tana pu'ang* (*laki pu'u* [L central man]) there were kept [by the man's descendants] and included a plate called Pigang Sisa that was divided at that time, as well as a mug that was called Luli Lokang. ...[18]

Later in his career, Mo'ang Baga Ngang captured Sikka Natar, the village which would become the seat of the Rajadom of Sikka. Kondi recounts the ruse by which this was accomplished at some length and, in the following section of the *Hikayat*, entitled 'Mo'ang Baga Moves to Sikka (Old Hokor)', recapitulates the means by which the Sikkanese established their rajadom:

When Mo'ang Baga of Natar Gahar heard that the inhabitants of the village of Hokor had fled in disarray, the people who lived in his village dismantled their houses and set up households in the village of old Hokor, which was renamed Sikka, which means [in SS] 'to chase away'. After they had gotten themselves a good village they built houses that were as solid as palaces. ...

In that period, when we research the nation of Sikka, we find it was before the time of the Portuguese; when they arrived in the year 1559, indeed the people of Sikka were already established. ...

In a year which is not passed down in the history, Mo'ang Baga and Mo'ang Bata Jawa divided a plate as an offering by which they extended their power and came to be respected by all the inhabitants as far as the border of the territory to the east, at Egong and Natakoli Ulung Kowé [Krowé] Jawa; and to the west as far as Mole, Koli, and Samba, all the way to Eko, Leka, and Lambo, which borders Bima (Manggarai)'.[19]

To unravel the significance of the plates mentioned in the *Hikayat*, it is necessary to examine in some detail the actual language in which the *Hikayat* refers to them. In the first reference to the plates, in the early chapter on 'The Life of Mo'ang Bata Jawa', the *Hikayat* quotes Bata Jawa speaking in ritual language which employs the semantically paired phrases *pigang sisa // luli lokang* (see above).

Pigang is Sikkanese for 'plate', which can be a ceramic, metal or wooden plate. The word *sisa* is one of the wonderfully polysemous words in Sara Sikka that lend a certain sense of adventure to the translation of Sikkanese and Tana 'Ai ritual language. As a verb, *sisa* means 'to let go, to drop, to relinquish'. However, in the pleonastic phrase *sisa soba*, *sisa* means 'tribute, gift; a dedication', as in worship or ritual (Pareira and Lewis 1998). *Pigang sisa* thus has two meanings:

1. a plate which has been dropped, and thus shattered, and
2. a plate given as (or for giving) tribute or a gift, including such prestations made in dedication of something.

In the passage of ritual language cited by Kondi, *pigang sisa* is paired with *luli lokang*. In Sara Sikka and Sara Tana 'Ai, *luli* is a small bowl made from the fire-hardened shell of a coconut for, among other uses, drinking lontar gin, itself a ritual activity. *Luli* are referred to frequently in ritual language in both Tana 'Ai and Sikka, as in the phrases from Sikkanese ritual language:

luli wana luli wiri drinking bowls to the right and drinking bowls to the left

in reference to the ritual drinking of lontar gin to seal an agreement between two sides to a negotiation (as, for example, wife-givers and wife-takers who have reached agreement on bridewealth in anticipation of a marriage) and:

luli ra'in luli érin drinking bowls uphill (as in the upper course of a river or the upper part of a garden), drinking bowls downhill (as in the lower course of a river or the lower half of a garden).

It is noteworthy that in Tana 'Ai, certain rituals require participating ritualists to exchange *luli* of lontar gin and, in doing so, to pass one from downhill to uphill and the other from uphill to downhill. *Lokang* is a 'circle, a hoop, a disk'; it is also a circular race track, that is, a field of competition. The word also denotes the rapid clockwise, then anti-clockwise, rotation of a *luli* or a round basket containing slices of areca nut before drinking palm gin or chewing areca, a ritual gesture that is common in Tana 'Ai and may have been so in the past in Sikka.

The paired phrases in ritual language, *pigang sisa // luli lokang*, thus condense a thick web of reference to:

1. the breaking of plates and the sharing or distribution of the pieces;
2. the use of plates in rituals of offering and for the affirmation of alliances, contracts and agreements; and
3. the completeness and wholeness of a circle (which has neither a beginning nor an end) and is, nevertheless, a field of competition.

In normal speech, the precise meaning of utterances which draw upon these words is established by context. But ritual speech is syntactically elided and, in the technical terms of logic, intensionally ambiguous. It is frequently the case that in a phrase of ritual speech that employs a polysemous word, all of that word's meanings are implicated in the meaning of the phrase.

We are now in a position to register some of the echoes and evocations in Mo'ang Bata Jawa's account of the distribution of plates to his allies:

Tiat weli au mora pigang sisa	To them I distribute shattered plates OR plates for offerings OR plates as offerings
Dokang weli au mora luli lokang	To them I give circular drinking bowls OR bowls with neither beginnings nor ends
Pigang sisa dena sisa mitang	With the shattered OR offering plates make black gifts OR tribute
Luli lokang dena lokang bura	With the round drinking bowls make white circles OR circular motions
Sisa mitang wawa pu'a	Black plate sherds OR offerings down at the source
Lokang bura réta wutu	White circular motion OR round bowls up at the tip

To make matters more complicated, plurals are marked morphologically in neither Malay (the language in which Boer and Kondi composed their texts) nor in Sara Sikka. Thus, whether Bata Jawa distributed many whole plates or broke a single plate and distributed the sherds to his allies is also a point of ambiguity in the text of the *Hikayat*. In either case, the plate, as a symbol, connotes wholeness and completion and so the rajadom was completed by the incorporation of many *negeri*, to each of which Bata Jawa vouchsafed a plate from a stack of plates[20] or a sherd from a single, broken plate as a token of each *negeri*'s relationship to the rajadom.[21] The relationship of the sherds of a broken plate or each in a stack of plates to the other and to the basket in which they are transported is that of the parts to a whole, which is a relationship of complementarity rather than hierarchy. It is this image that Sikka's *Hikayat* iterates and reiterates in representing the relationship of Sikka and the rajas to the *negeri* of which the rajadom was composed. Thus, at the level of ideology, as encoded in speech and in a literary version of Sikka's history written by teachers who became officials in the raja's government, the relationship between raja and *negeri* was one of complementarity rather than hierarchy, as between ruler and ruled or superior and subaltern.

This image does not necessarily represent the actual political and social arrangements in the rajadom but, rather, a conception and representation of the relationship that is distinctly non-hierarchical. Indeed, the reality beyond the mythic history of the rajadom was somewhat different and certainly more complex than the depiction of Sikkanese society as sherds reforming themselves as a whole.

Precedence Relations in Sikka Natar and Hierarchy in the Foundation and Evolution of the Rajadom of Sikka

As told in the *Hikayat*, the history of Sikka unfolded in two principal stages. The first was the creation of Sikka Natar, a single village, and the second was the creation of the rajadom with Sikka Natar at its political centre. Sikka Natar grew by a process very similar to that which generated Tana Wai Brama. In both

Tana Wai Brama and Sikka Natar, a succession of groups of immigrants were incorporated into the community. In the second stage of Sikka Natar's history, in which it became the seat of a petty state, the community expanded its territory to subsume the whole of central Sikka by incorporating other communities into a single polity. The incorporation of newcomers in Wai Brama produced a society ordered by the precedence of its constituent groups while in Sikka, territorial expansion, a development that did not occur in Tana Wai Brama, produced a polity of allied groups among whom precedence was immanent and a differentiation of people into social classes of rulers and ruled ordered by hierarchy.

Fox (this volume) has noted that:

Precedence refers both to forms of discourse and of practice. In considering precedence as an analytical category, it is appropriate to distinguish aspects of discourse and practice. However, in social analysis based on the use of precedence, it is the fusion of these aspects that gives credibility to the concept.

The myth of the foundation of the Sikkanese rajadom, which is part of the expressive, representational and discursive repertoire of the Ata Sikka, includes an account of the evolution of Sikka Natar, which grew over time by the addition of groups of immigrants who, the *Hikayat* relates, originated from 36 different places. While neither Boer's and Kondi's version of the Sikkanese myth of origin nor those oral versions I have recorded in Sikka Natar emphasizes a precedence ordering of these groups, precedence can be detected in the relationships of their members, principally through the complex network of contemporary affinal alliance relationships in which their contemporary descendants are enmeshed. Thus, Sikka Natar can be seen as a precedence-based social order in which manifestations of precedence in social practice have been partially masked by the institutions of the rajadom while remaining a strong theme in myth and affinal exchange.

Whereas contemporary ethnographic data provide evidence for viewing Sikka Natar as a precedence-based social order, the history of the Rajadom of Sikka and the role of Sikka Natar in the evolution of the rajadom have eclipsed this aspect of representations of society. Instead, both the *Hikayat* and the testimony of my informants in Sikka emphasize a process of state formation that resulted in a polity and social order articulated by a hierarchy of social classes.

The people of Sikka Natar were distributed among four social classes: the class with the smallest number of members was Lepo Geté, the house of the rajas and their immediate kin. Clustered around the raja and Lepo Geté were a number of noble houses, from which came the *mo'ang pulu* (SS 'ten lords') and the *kapitang* (SS, from P, 'captain[s]'), such as Boer and Kondi, who were district officers in the raja's government. *Ata riwung* (SS 'thousands') or *ngasung riwung* (SS 'hundreds and thousands') were *rakyat* (BI 'society'), the free commoners of Sikka Natar and the rajadom. *Maha* (SS) were indentured retainers attached to the households of the nobles until the early post-war years. Many Sikkanese themselves have described their society as 'feudal', a description originating from the early missionaries of the Church.[22] The *Hikayat* affirms this view, but does not dwell on the social classes of Sikka Natar and the rajadom.

The royal house, according to genealogies compiled by Boer, traced its origin to Raé Raja and Rubang Sina, the captain of the ship carrying the second group of immigrants to land on Sikka's southern shore.[23] Their son, Mo'ang Sugi, married Du'a Sikka, who was *penduduk asli* (BI 'indigenous inhabitant'). The descendants of the union of autochthon and newcomer became the rulers of Sikka. The origins of the noble houses of Sikka, the *mo'ang pulu*, or 'ten lords', are not described in the *Hikayat*, nor have I much information on their origins in my field notes on Sikka. How some among the immigrants who came to Sikka came to be *mo'ang pulu* while others did not is another puzzle in the history of Sikka.

The *Hikayat* mentions the *mo'ang pulu* only three times. Firstly, in the account of 'The Life of Mo'ang Bako I Alias Mbako Kikir Hiwa' (Bako the First, known as 'Nine Fingered Bako'), the tenth raja of Sikka:

> So this was the era of the Portuguese government here in Flores, taxes were collected by their own king and they also organized their own government as is clear in the book of laws of the kingdom, that is *mo'ang pulu* alias the heads of every tribe in Sikka and every captain with his own tribe helped the king in his government and especially at the time they went down into the valley (times of war).[24]

Second is a brief mention of the death of the subaltern raja of Nita in 1891:

> On the 25th of November 1891 the corpse of the King of Nita was buried. Those who were present were only the King of Sikka with Commandant Joh Iking da Cunha from Maumere, Mo'ang Pulu from Sikka/Maumere and the chiefs [*kepala-kepala* BI heads] and the people from Nita.[25]

And, thirdly, in an account of a rebellion put down by the Sikkanese raja:

> The chiefs of Sikka (Mo'ang Pulu with five captains) intended to try and obtain compensation or reimbursement for their losses in the war or pay blood money [SS: *heka*] for all the deaths.[26]

Details of Sikka's social hierarchy remain, on the evidence, somewhat obscure, but it appears to have been founded on a conception of the proximity of a person or social group to the raja calculated in terms of the raja's origins and the origins of a related group. The raja was at the 'centre' of the rajadom while the nobles, commoners and retainers were increasingly 'distant' from the raja. The continuum formed by a periphery in relation to a centre, on which relations of precedence can be calculated, is a common dualistic metaphor in Tana Wai Brama. In Sikka Natar and the rajadom, the continuum of precedence was translated into a rank-ordering of social classes by the imposition of a schema of discrete categories onto the continuum (Figure 2).

Figure 2. Ranking of social classes in Sikka Natar and Kerajaan Sikka

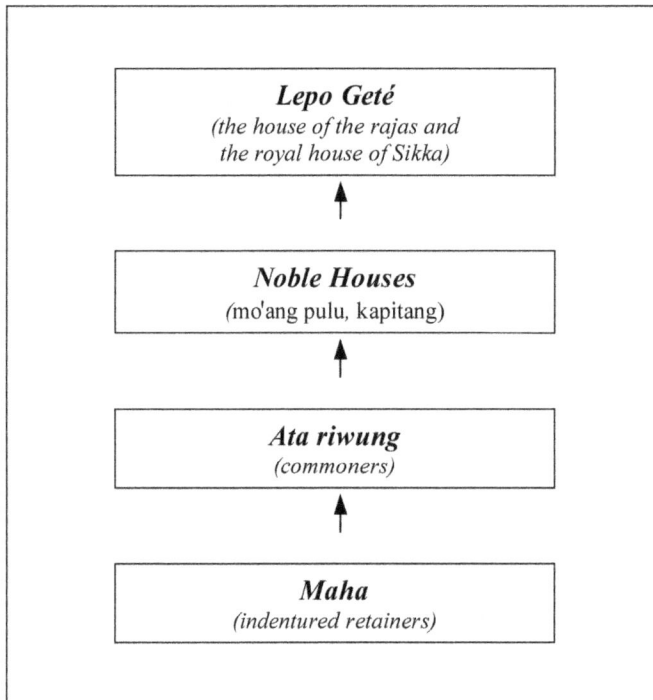

While reflecting an ideology of precedence, the *Hikayat* pays less attention to the internal organization of Sikka Natar and more to the hierarchical political structure of the rajadom. In short, the *Hikayat* is a charter of this hierarchy. Thus, the groups which make up the village community are linked by relationships founded in the precedence of their arrival in Sikka Natar, while the *kerajaan*, the confederation of *negeri* over which the rajas of Sikka ruled, is represented in the *Hikayat* as hierarchical in its structure. Even so, underlying the political organization of the rajadom as depicted in the *Hikayat* is the precedence of Don Alésu, as secular leader, over Augustinyu da Gama, the religious leader. In this respect, precedence underlies hierarchy in the evolution of the rajadom (Lewis 1996a).[27]

Four principal elements intertwined in the creation of the Rajadom of Sikka: an indigenous house which aspired to rule, the numerous independent and local *negeri* into which the Sikkanese-speaking peoples of Flores were divided, the introduction of Christianity, and the presence of Portuguese and, later, Dutch foreigners. The creation of the rajadom from these elements is the subject of much of the *Hikayat*. In synthesizing the principal elements of the rajadom into a narrative chronicle, Boer and Kondi construct a history of the rajadom in which an ordered sequence of incorporations of disparate communities into a polity is a major theme which is still of considerable force in the affairs of Sikka today. The persons who brought about these incorporations were related to one another in time and Kondi cites their genealogical relationships to legitimate their claims to authority and power in the rajadom thus created.

For almost a century from the second half of the 1800s, Sikka was a semi-independent *kerajaan*, one of a number of petty polities in eastern Indonesia recognized by the Dutch under the policy of *zelfbestuur* (D self-rule). The rajadom's semi-independence continued after Japanese troops entered Maumere in 1942, with the Japanese military government of the island levying taxes and corvée labour through the authority of the raja of Sikka, who was then Raja Don Thomas Ximenes da Silva. After the war, the rajas of Flores took the island into the briefly-lived independent Republic of Eastern Indonesia and, as head of the Dewan Raja-Raja Flores (the Council of the rajas of Flores), Raja Thomas played a central role in guiding both Sikka and the island through this fraught period in eastern Indonesia's history. Don Thomas died in Ende in 1954 and, although Don Sentis [Centis] da Silva, the *raja muda* (BI prince), assumed the title of raja, in all practical respects, the rajadom ended with Don Thomas's death.

As recounted in the *Hikayat*, Sikka expanded through a sequence of alliances contracted with independent *negeri* to the north, east and west of Sikka Natar. The practice of the rajas after Baga Ngang was as follows: the raja of Sikka contracted an alliance with a local leader by presenting to him items of ceremonial wealth, principally elephant tusks, but also *gai* (M *tongkat*), a staff of office. In return, the local leader pledged allegiance to the raja and accepted the raja's authority in matters outside of the immediate local concerns of the *negeri*. Later, with the rajas' appointments of *kapitang* as district heads, the rajadom came to exercise power within the *negeri* as well. The items of ceremonial wealth by which the alliance was secured were, with the exception of the *gai*, those used within Sikka Natar as bridewealth.

In bridewealth transactions, each party in a marriage makes prestations to the other. The goods exchanged are, however, of different kinds. Wife-takers, who are *mé pu* ('children and sisters' children'), give *ling wéling*, 'bridewealth',[28] to wife-givers. These gifts consist of ivory tusks, gold coins, horses and cash, goods classified as masculine. In return, wife-givers, who are *ina ama* (SS mothers and fathers), give to their wife-takers a counter-prestation called *'utang labu wawi paré* (SS [women's] cloths, blouses, pigs, rice), goods classified as feminine. While the Ata Sikka say that these reciprocal gifts are of equal value and balance each other, the prestations are laden with asymmetries of value: as parents are superior to children, so are wife-givers superior to wife-takers, and as masculine goods are conceived to be superior to feminine goods, thereby serving as proper tokens of exchange for the capability of providing the wife-taker's group with new life, so are wife-givers who receive masculine goods superior to wife-takers, who receive feminine goods.

The asymmetry of the wife-giver and wife-taker relationship rests, however, not on these relatively explicit evaluations of gifts, but on the unstated valuations of the *persons* exchanged. In strictly formal terms, in a Sikkanese marriage, an alien woman enters the house of her husband which, by the children she bears, she reproduces. Her own group loses her reproductive capacity and must seek women from yet other groups to perpetuate itself, a risky business in the Sikkanese conception.

The debt incurred by wife-takers when they receive the gift in marriage of a woman and her reproductive capacity is a debt that is never and cannot be fully discharged. For this reason, and with respect to 'the flow of life' between affinal allies, wife-givers are innately superior to wife-takers. The reason for this asymmetry of value is the greater power of women over men as reproducers of houses, regardless of the value (and valuation) of the prestations that serve as tokens of the exchange between houses and their alliance (and this among a well-educated people who have, nevertheless, not yet read Lévi-Strauss).

Thus, beneath the symmetry of gift-exchange (you give us ivory; we give you cloth), affinal alliance in Sikka is founded on a profound asymmetry of value in which the receiver of symbols of greater value (bride-wealth) is superior to the giver of those symbols (Figure 3). Bridewealth (*ling wéling*), which is classified as masculine, is of greater value than *'utang labu wawi paré*, the counter-prestation which is classified as feminine, precisely because women are more highly valued than men. The house that receives a woman thus also receives prestations of less ritual value than those which they give.

In the realm of the political alliances by which the Sikkanese created the Rajadom of Sikka, the value that was transacted was not the life-giving power of women, but political allegiance, authority, and power. Thus, while giving ceremonial wealth of a kind which, in the affinal alliance system, would be classified as masculine (thus implying that the recipients were the superior party), the raja received political allegiance and, in terms of the polity relationships, acquired political and hierarchical superiority over the *negeri*. Given that the unstated value transacted was power and authority, the formation of the political alliances upon which the rajadom was founded involved the same asymmetric relationship of giver and receiver of greater value that characterized (and still does today) the dynamics of affinal alliance within Sikka Natar. In political alliance it was the recipient of greater value (allegiance and the acknowledgment of the raja's power over the Sikkanese hinterland) who was superior to the giver. And as in affinal alliance, where the exchange of articulated value (*ling wéling* and *'utang labu wawi paré*) masks the transaction of a more fundamental value (life), so, too, in the political arena of the rajadom, the apparently symmetrical exchange of the articulated values of ceremonial goods for allegiance masked the asymmetric transaction of authority, a more fundamental value which was never redressed.

Figure 3. Affinal prestations in Sikka Natar

	Value of Person/ Goods Exchanged	Direction of Prestation
Woman:	+	**Wife-givers ← Wife-takers**
man:	−	**Wife-givers → Wife-takers**
Bridewealth (masculine):	+	**Wife-givers ← Wife-takers**
Counter-prestation (feminine):	−	**Wife-givers → Wife-takers**
Ritual superiority–inferiority:		**Wife-givers (as life-givers)** ↓ **Wife-takers (as life-takers)**

Thus, in political alliance, the raja gave the goods of bridewealth but received in return no material counter-prestation. Instead he received a pledge of the *negeri*'s allegiance to the rajadom. That pledge was vouchsafed in the person of the man who received the ivory from the raja's hand and who thereby acquired status in the rajadom for himself and his descendants. We might think, as Sikkanese from outside central Sikka have said to me, that this placed the *negeri* in a position superior to that of the raja as the *negeri*'s gift of allegiance made them 'wife-givers' to the raja by virtue of having received the superior symbol, the raja's bridewealth. But this was not the case from the rajas' point of view. The rajas had shifted the rules: what was transacted was not allegiance, per se, but power. The idiom of the transaction was that of bridewealth and the gift of bridewealth goods implied non-hierarchical, asymmetric, and cyclical exchange. But the fact was the establishment of a status system whose classes were related hierarchically rather than the simple elaboration of a system founded in the complementary asymmetries and precedence relations of affinal alliance.

It can thus be seen that the Sikkanese constructed their rajadom by drawing on principles of value and echange embedded in their culture and in the realm of domestic and affinal alliance within their home village, Sikka Natar, but with a peculiar play on the logic of exchange. The politics of exchange they invented were not merely a matter of the trappings of power and the ceremonial prestige which accrues to a ruler, but had material consequences. Among others, as the bearers of authority throughout their realm, the rajas recruited troops to aid the Portuguese in Timor and, later, reached accords with the Dutch whereby they taxed the people of their domain.

The same pattern can be seen in the mythic histories of Tana Wai Brama, in which the people of clan Ipir Wai Brama, by virtue of being the first to come to the domain, became the *tana pu'an*, the source of the domain. Each subsequent immigrant received land for gardens and positions in the ceremonial system of the domain, in return for which they recognized the authority of the source of the domain over the land and in relations with external powers such as (in later years), the Rajadom of Sikka. The difference between Tana Wai Brama and the Rajadom of Sikka was that the *tana pu'an* of Tana Wai Brama never acquired political power in the manner of the rajas but retained authority limited to the realm of ritual.

It is perhaps worth noting that the alliances between Lepo Geté and the *negeri* did not involve marriages of people of the *negeri* and the house of the Sikkanese rajas. While such marriages occurred, they appear to have played little role in the calculations of political relations of superordination and subordination. However, it is further worth noting that marriages of people of the Sikkanese royal house did play a role in relationships with other rajadoms on Flores. Thus, for example, in the 1920s a daughter of the raja of Sikka married a son of the raja of Larantuka. The Sikkanese remember this union well, both for its political implications (it finally put to rest the long-standing enmity between the rajas of Sikka and Larantuka) and because by this marriage the raja of Sikka became wife-giver, and thus ritually superior (at least, from the point of view of the Sikkanese) to the ruling house of Larantuka.

In the *Hikayat* there are many mentions of the exchange of ceremonial wealth for political allegiance. In 'The Second Era' of Sikka's history, which was that of the rule of Don Alésu, the *Hikayat* reiterates the means by which the rulers of Sikka secured their authority over the rajadom. The following excerpt illustrates the general principle:

> Don Alésu spoke to the heads of the tribes of Sikka saying: how well it would be if we were to go and visit the countryside and villages since it has been a long time since I visited our people; and we must take the ivory tusks which I brought from Malacca and place them in the largest and busiest territories (*negeri*) so that when people see the tusks they will think of me. His [Alésu's] intention was that if there ever was a rebel, he would see the tusk which is a sign of my [Alésu's] *li'ar dira, rang ngang*, my sharp voice and my powerful manner, a sign of the raja of Sikka. And those who guard and keep the tusks will be entitled Mo'ang Mangung, which means the masts of the prau; this phrase means further standing erect or upright, at one's full length like a tree. His aim was to show the uprightness of his creation and that the raja of Sikka is not submissive to anyone else in the rajadom. Said Don Alésu:

Waké né'i ba'a mangung,	After you have erected the mast of the great ship,
Mangung lepe lau prebeng,	The mast that shelters the door sill, And after raising
'Ore né'i nora lajar, Lajar	the sail, With the sail slapping the mast,
tongka wawa dang,	
Odo ganu serdadu, Gareng	Then I give orders as to troops, I lead as you lead a
ganu marsélu (manyelu),	corps of soldiers, So when speaking, do not
Kiring li'ar lopa leder,	contradict others, And when counting, do not
Gata wang lopa gawang,	exaggerate,
Dena niang lopa biko 'liong,	So that the earth does not bob up and down like an
Tana lopa kiling kolok,	udder, And the land is not askew and does not roll
Dadi mangung wau	like a ship, So the central mast shelters the villages,
'wisung, Lajar gong	And covers the remote hamlets,
wangang,	
Tali lera léma waté.	And the sail's sheet raises the liver [that is, heart].

> N.B. It was usual to give a 'mast' (*mangung*), that is, a tusk at least a fathom in length, to the large villages. The 'sail' (*lajar*) was a *doko*, or a crescent shaped piece of gold, given to small villages. *Tali lera* (the sail's sheet) was a length of chain given to many smaller hamlets.[29]

The text then contrasts Don Alésu's method of alliance formation with that of the previous two rajas:

> In the time of Mo'ang Bata Jawa and Mo'ang Baga Ngang they divided large plates to be offered to the gods, that is: *pigang sisa*.[30]

Thus, perhaps significantly, Bata Jawa and Baga Ngang, the two pre-Catholic proto-rajas, distributed plates to those with whom they contracted alliances, whereas Alésu, the first of the Catholic rajas, distributed to his subalterns ivory tusks and gold, which he had acquired in Malacca and brought back to Sikka.

The narrative continues:

Thus Don Alésu returned from giving the *bala mangung* ('ivory mast'), saying:

A'u pangkor Sikka paing lado, Ata bi'ang pu'ang humang, Uring lau bénu wuli, Wa'ang réta paing lado. Waké né'i mangung, Sorong né'i pangkor Sikka, Pangkor Sikka paing lado, Ata bi'ang pu'ang humang.	I am the hero of Sikka whose hat bears a plume, The person who is the source of war, Around my neck I wear beads and shells, My head wears a plumed hat, I have installed the central mast, And promoted soldiers of Sikka to office, Those heroes of Sikka whose hats are plumed, The men who excel in war.

The praise for the raja when he grants the 'ivory mast':

Ina lau krus pu'ang, Diat beli nora pu'ang, Ama lau gereja wang, Dokang beli nora kating,	The mother who stands below the cross, Has given the strongest foundation, The father who stands before the door of the church, Has bestowed authority,
Baké ba'a nora mangung, Bikong 'lo'a lopa 'liong. Oré beli ba'a nora lajar, Kiling ba'a 'lo'a lopa kolok,	And has raised up the ship's mast, So the ship will not pitch and roll, And has hoisted the sail, So it does not droop and flutter,
Mangung lau laru walu, Lajar lusi réta wata pitu.	Eight masts below, Seven sails above.

The reply of the people who receive the 'ivory mast':

Belirang Amat, 'Ulit gung mako lékong, Naha amat geru mela.	Like the volcano Belirang Amat, Your skin is thick and old but not scorched by the sulphur, Only you can swallow it.

In this way Don Alésu da Silva visited all of the territories in the western part of Flores, including Keo, Torung, Lambo, Toto, Mbei and Kota Jogo, and returned by sea along the north coast landing at Kero Kelisi and then straight on to Bebeng (Wuring). At each landing he delegated a deputy to summon the inhabitants or went ashore and visited them himself.[31]

The elephant tusks which the rulers of Sikka distributed to the leaders of local communities were called *bala mangung* (SS ivory mast). Over time, the *bala mangung* and the villages in which the rajas placed them came to mark the territorial limits of the authority of the raja of Sikka. Kondi cites the raja of

Sikka's dispute with the raja of Larantuka over rights to tax the people of Téru to the east of Maumere and comments:

> the former rajas from the time of Raja Don Alésu had put the ivory in Téru because, wherever the ivories of Sikka were, there also was the authority of the raja. Usually the rajas of Sikka placed ivory called *bala mangung* in a large *negeri*. The person who kept it was titled Mo'ang Mangung, and the *negeri* and its surrounding area were allies with Sikka (there was also ivory which was kept by *tana pu'ang*, which were called *bala tana pu'ang*).[32]

Furthermore, according to the *Hikayat*:

> The goods [the elephant tusks and other gifts from the raja of Sikka] were kept in a place (a district, a village) as a sign that they were allies with or federated with Sikka. So [in the case of Téru and the dispute between the rajas of Sikka and Larantuka over taxation], it was better to call the people from Téru (Koja Mota) who kept the ivory, so that they could explain in more detail from where the ivory came.[33]

These gifts from the raja to local headmen established the sovereignty of the raja, but the expectation was that the local people of the *negeri* kept the 'histories' of the gifts and Kondi continues:

> Obviously their ancestors would have told them the story about it over and over.[34]

Conclusion: Precedence and Hierarchy in the Sikkanese Culture Complex

Despite similarities between Sikka and Tana Wai Brama, among the differences between them is this. As the home village of the rajadom, Sikka Natar began as a confederation of immigrant groups, but incorporated new groups by territorial expansion in its later history. Sikka's development can thus be conceived as extensional. In contrast, the development of the society of Tana Wai Brama can be described as intentional. Wai Brama never expanded its territory, but incorporated new groups by assimilation as they arrived in the domain.

To the extent that this is so, Figure 1 and Map 1 provide, in graphic form, the clues we need to understand the most fundamental difference between Sikka and Tana Wai Brama. The mythic histories of Tana Wai Brama tell the story of how a limited number of origin groups came from outside and moved inward into the domain. Since its foundation, people from clans other than the five core clans of Tana Wai Brama have taken up residence in the domain, but not in large numbers and not in sufficient numbers to require a change in the representation of society as made up of five groups. In contrast, Sikka expanded territorially, incorporating as it expanded communities of diverse identities. In principle there might have been no end of that expansion (in practice Kerajaan Sikka ended at the frontiers where its territory bordered that of neighbouring rajadoms or was limited by the Dutch). It may be that an overlay of hierarchical order is a necessary condition of an extensional polity, but, whether this is generally true or not, it was the solution to the problem of government devised by the rajas of Sikka.

Map 1. Schematic representation of the expansion of the Sikkanese polity

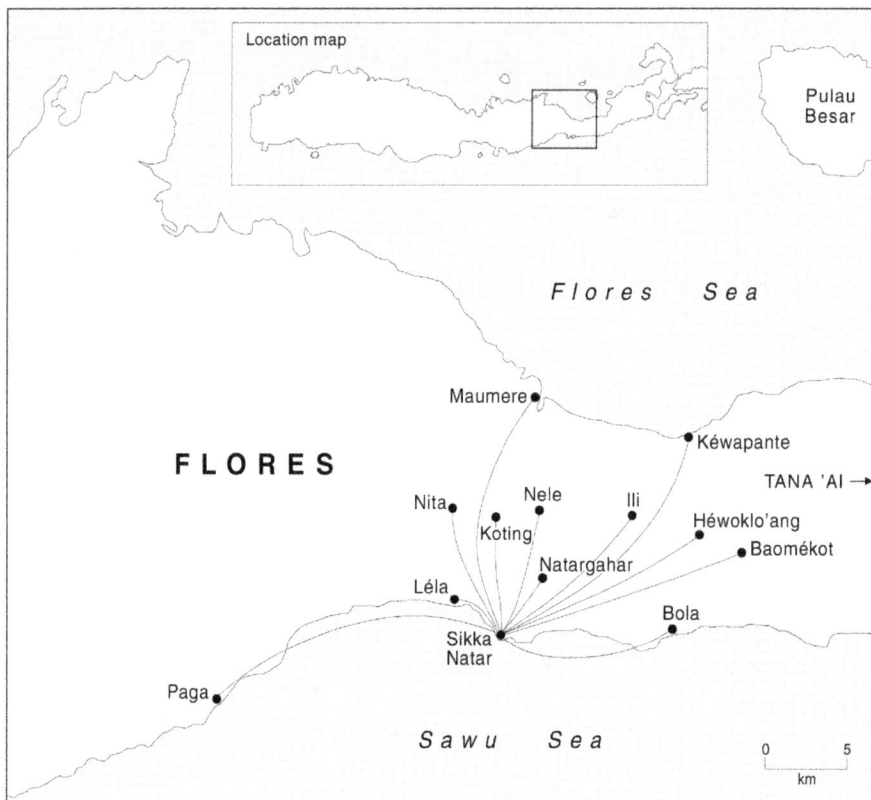

But there is more to be learned from the comparison of precedence in Tana Wai Brama and Sikka than the ways in which, in each case, it accords with a particular and distinctive modulation of territorial space. It may be that precedence-based social systems conceive and structure time and history in ways different from hierarchy-based social systems.

In both Tana Wai Brama and Sikka, contemporary states of affairs are constantly discussed, explained and manipulated in terms of the past. And, in this respect, Tana Wai Brama and Sikka are remarkably similar despite apparent differences. In addition, the pasts of both societies include beginnings with the coming together of immigrants over time. Both societies recognize a group of people who were first immigrants, and who were thus founder groups, but neither society recognizes any group as descendants solely of autochthonous people. This means that, in their histories as they are conceived by contemporary people and represented (whether orally in the narration of myth or in writing), the descendants of the founding ancestors, those who today claim social, ceremonial or political pre-eminence, must make their claims not in terms of some special relationship to place, location, land or territory, but in terms of temporal precedence which, to a degree, is shared by the descendants of the founding ancestors of all the constituent groups of society. Claims to precedence (and hence pre-eminence with respect to some aspect of social life) are claims to position on a scale of relative positions, each of which is gauged by reference to the single value of temporal priority.

Precedence thus differs from hierarchy which, as Dumont (1980:241–243) has argued, is founded in a logic whereby a classificatory unity encompasses categorical difference. The peoples of Sikka conceive of the constituent groups of their societies neither as opposed to one another nor as one encompassing another, but in terms of the accretion of elements in time, each related to the others as complementary parts of wholes. In Sikka, such tropes as the broken plate are transformations of the complementary relationships that obtain between, for example, wife-givers and wife-takers and between feminine and masculine categories in a system of dual classification that permeates Sikkanese thought. The same is true of Tana Wai Brama, whose people emphasize in both discourse and action the complementarity of the clans that constitute the domain, the houses that constitute a clan and (as in Sikka) the wholes that result from the bringing together of male and female (Lewis 1996c).

Nevertheless, Sikka contrasts with Tana Wai Brama in a number of respects, all of which, I would argue, spring from its peculiar history as a polity and a petty state. Firstly, the incorporation of alien *negeri* into the rajadom had as a practical result the need to maintain a distinction between ruler and ruled. The raja was the ruler; the people of the communities of the larger region of Sikka were the ruled. But even this apparent opposition was mitigated by the *mo'ang pulu*, the 'ten lords', who were drawn from the nobility of Sikka Natar (that is, from the oldest houses of Sikka) but who lived in the *kapitanschappen*, the administrative districts into which the rajadom came to be divided during the period of Dutch rule after the 1860s. Thus, the apparent opposition between ruler and ruled was in fact a hierarchy of four classes which cross-cut local identities: the people of the royal house, the people of the Sikkanese nobility, the free commoners and indentured retainers. Indeed, while all were under the political authority of the *ratu*, each *negeri* had its own headman, its own *tana pu'ang* (source of the earth) and its own *ngasung riwung* (SS 'hundreds and thousands', that is, 'common people', 'society').

In Tana Wai Brama the asymmetry of affinal alliance, the precedence of complementary origin groups in the composition of society and the dynamics of social and ceremonial exchange produce a fluid social system in which, through generations, the descendants of ancestors change status as the dynamics of the social system necessarily reallocate them among clans and among houses within clans (see Lewis 1988a). In Sikka what once may have been an analogous system acquired the added dimension of social statuses which were (and to a degree are still today) represented as ascribed and inflexible.[35]

Tana Wai Brama provides us with an excellent example of a society in which we find precedence in its clearest manifestation. Sikka provides us with another, perhaps more profound, example of a society which at once manifests both precedence and hierarchy. This tells us that the two principles of order, at least as they are found in Florenese societies, are by no means incompatible and suggests that they can be transforms of one another.

In precedence, one sequence of events in the past provides a model for — or the proper interpretation and order of — events in the future, but in restricted realms. Precedence thus involves a reduction in scale from the 'real time' of history to bounded 'ritual time' and 'social time'. This allows (1) the preservation of the past as a template for future action and (2) the free occurrence of future random events, the order of which defines future precedence relations. Precedence as process converts chaos into future order and acts as a governor, a kind of feedback loop, which promotes a degree of homeostasis in the social system. By precedence, some in the community become guardians of *hadat* ('traditions') while others are free to challenge the old ways; some may become rulers and others subjects of rule without losing all freedom of action.

Thus, precedence is about both structure and action. But more than a structure, precedence is a temporal template for how things should go (and how things that go should be interpreted) in the future. The result is an observable similarity, a common pattern between occurrences of delimited events. Precedence leads to the ritualization of events; an original sequence of random events becomes orderly by the acquisition of meaningful sequentiality. In other words, in precedence, the future and the past are in a relationship of complementarity. Hierarchy, in the Sikkanese case, accords with a history that is extensional and open-ended and, thus, progressive.

Tana Wai Brama and the Rajadom of Sikka are cases in which we find both processes of social differentiation and integration. In both, people of disparate origins entered into confederations and became integrated, their unification giving rise to societies. Integration and unification nevertheless allowed the groups to preserve their original identities in terms of precedence: we are not you because our ancestors arrived after (or before) yours. These cases from a single district of Flores thus also illustrate how a single and formally simple principle of order and organization can, through time and the contingencies of history, produce social differentiation, in one instance, a proliferation of houses within clans and, in the other, a system of social classification that ordered authority and the exercise of power in an expanding polity.

This essay owes much to Professor J.D.M. Platenkamp of the Westfälische Wilhelms-Universität Münster who, while convincing me to share a bottle of Scotch whisky in Leiden one night in late 1993 or early 1994, could not convince me that what I meant by precedence was logically a transform of what Dumont meant by hierarchy. For my part, I do not remember whether I convinced him of my reasons for thinking that eastern Indonesian societies are fundamentally different from Indian societies, for by the time the argument progressed to that point, the bottle was just about empty. My thanks to Professor Richard K. Reed and to Trinity University, San Antonio, Texas, which, in 2008, provided me with a congenial academic home in which to revise the essay.

References

Butterworth, D.J.

2008 Lessons of the ancestors: ritual, education, and the ecology of mind in an Indonesian community. Unpublished PhD thesis. Melbourne: Department of Anthropology, The University of Melbourne.

Dam, H. ten

1950 *Nita dan sekitarnya.* Bogor: Balai Perguruan Tinggi R.I., Fakultet Pertanian.

Dumont, Louis

1980 *Homo hierarchicus: an essay on the caste system.* Revised edition. Chicago: The University of Chicago Press.

Fox, James J.

1995 Origin structures and systems of precedence in the comparative study of Austronesian societies. In P.J.K. Li, Cheng-hwa Tsang, Ying-kuei Huang, Dah-an Ho and Chiu-yu Tseng (eds), *Austronesian studies relating to Taiwan,* pp.27–57. Taipei: Symposium Series of the Institute of History & Philology: Academia Sinica 3.

Lewis, E.D.

1988a *People of the source: the social and ceremonial order of Tana Wai Brama on Flores.* Verhandelingen van het Koninklijk Instituut voor Taal-, Land- en Volkenkunde 135. Dordrecht, Holland/Providence, USA: Foris Publications.

1988b A quest for the source. The ontogenesis of a creation myth of the Ata Tana 'Ai. In James J. Fox (ed.), *To speak in pairs: essays on the ritual languages of eastern Indonesia* (Cambridge Studies in Oral and Literate Culture, No. 15), pp.246–281. Cambridge: Cambridge University Press.

1989 Idioms of kinship in the cosmological thought of the Ata Tana 'Ai. *Mankind* 19(3):170–180.

1996a Origin structures and precedence in the social orders of Tana 'Ai and Sikka. In James J. Fox and Clifford Sather (eds), *Origins, ancestry and alliance: explorations in Austronesian ethnography*, pp.154–174. Canberra: Department of Anthropology, Research School of Pacific and Asian Studies, The Australian National University. Comparative Austronesian Series, ANU E Press: http://epress.anu.edu.au/.

1996b Myth, history and precedence in the chronicles of the Rajadom of Sikka. Paper presented to the conference on 'Hierarchization in the Austronesian world: processes of social differentiation', International Institute of Asian Studies, Leiden, The Netherlands (April 1996).

1996c The paradox of difference: essays on kinship and gender relations in Tana Wai Brama. Unpublished manuscript.

1998a The tyranny of the text: oral tradition and the power of writing in Sikka and Tana 'Ai, Flores. *Bijdragen tot de Taal-, Land- en Volkenkunde* 154(3):457–477.

1998b Don Alésu's quest: the mythohistorical foundation of the Rajadom of Sikka. *History and Anthropology* 11(1):39–74.

1999 The encyclopædic impulse: accounts of the origin of the Rajadom of Sikka by two Sikkanese authors. *Bijdragen tot de Taal-, Land- en Volkenkunde* 155(3):543–578.

forthcoming. *The stranger-kings of Sikka*. Leiden: KITLV Press.

Lewis, E.D., Timothy Asch and Patsy Asch

1993 *A celebration of origins*. 16mm film. Watertown, Massachusetts: Documentary Educational Resource, Inc.

Lewis, E.D. and Oscar Pareira Mandalangi

2008 *Hikayat Kerajaan Sikka*. Maumere, Flores: Penerbit Ledalero.

Metzner, J.K

1982 Agriculture and population pressure in Sikka, Isle of Flores: a contribution to the study of the stability of agricultural systems in the wet and dry tropics. Development Studies Centre Monograph No. 28. Canberra, Australia, and Miami, Florida, USA: The Australian National University.

Pareira, M. Mandalangi and E. Douglas Lewis

1998 *Kamus sara Sikka bahasa Indonesia*. Ende, Flores, Indonesia: Penerbit Nusa Indah.

ENDNOTES

[1] See Butterworth (2008) on the distinctiveness of the Krowé communities of central Sikka.

[2] Lewis and Mandalangi (2008); see also Lewis (1998a, 1998b, 1999, and forthcoming).

[3] See Lewis (1999) and Lewis (forthcoming, Chapter III).

[4] See Lewis (1998a, 1998b and forthcoming) for accounts of the provenance of Boer's and Kondi's manuscripts and how they came to my attention. An edition of Boer's and Kondi's longest manuscripts that integrates the authors' works into a single narrative is now in press under the title *Hikayat Kerajaan Sikka* (Lewis and Mandalangi 2008). Lewis (forthcoming) includes an English translation of an abridgment of the *Hikayat* with ethnographic notes and analyses of the text.

[5] BI for Bahasa Indonesia, M for Malay, SS for Sara Sikka, D for Dutch, P for Portuguese, L for Lio.

[6] The phrase *Hindia belakang* is a translation into Malay of the Dutch geographical term *achter Indië* ('beyond India'), which designates East and South-East Asia.

[7] Lewis forthcoming, Chapter X, 'Don Alésu's Journey to Malacca'.

[8] Indeed, Boer's and Kondi's narratives of Don Alésu and Augustinyu da Gama, while much more detailed, are essentially the same as those which I recorded as highly elided oral renditions in Sikka Natar in the late 1970s.

[9] The last *controleur* of Maumere, Mr W. Coté, immigrated to Australia after the war and settled in Melbourne.

[10] I will be most grateful to anyone who can tell me that the name Worilla appears in a history of Malacca, western Indonesia, or Malaysia. The name appears neither in the *Malay Annals* nor in other historiographic sources I have examined.

[11] See Lewis (1996a:162) for a chart showing the genealogical relationships of the 18 rajas of Sikka, but note a typographical error in that work: whereas the name Baga Ngang appears twice in the published version (generations 11 through 13), Bata Jawa's son was Mo'ang Igor and Igor's son was Baga Ngang. See also Lewis (forthcoming) Chapter II, 'Structure and Themes of the *Hikayat Kerajaan Sikka*', for variants of the genealogy of the da Silva dynasty.

[12] 'The First Period' thus accounts for the creation of diarchies in the local *negeri*, in which authority was divided between a ritual leader and a secular leader; see Lewis (forthcoming), Chapter IV, 'Diarchy in the Eastern Lesser Sunda Islands and Sikka', for a critique of the concept of diarchy in the ethnology of the eastern Lesser Sunda Islands.

[13] Lewis (forthcoming), Chapter VII, 'The Autochthons'; Lewis and Mandalangi (2008:7–10), Bab I, 1.1 'Orang Asli'.

[14] The exact location of Mekeng Detung, which is important in the mythic histories of both Sikka and Tana Wai Brama, is something of a puzzle. Both the *Hikayat* and my Sikkanese informants place Mekeng Detung near Ili Bekor, which is one of a series of peaks in a range of mountains arrayed along the east-west spine of the island in central Sikka south-east of Maumere and some three kilometres from the south coast of the island and nine kilometres from the north coast. This range of peaks includes (from west to east): Ili Néwa (752 m.), Ili Gai (909 m.), Ili Bekor, Ili Tolawair (944 m.), and Ili Jele (956 m.) Of these mountains, Bekor is the most frequently mentioned in the *Hikayat* and is closely associated with Mekeng Detung. Metzner identifies the contemporary villages of Natarloar and Tadat, which are very near one another and are located about four kilometres to the north-east of Ili Bekor, as Mekeng Detung (Metzner 1982:282). However, four kilometres is a considerable distance in a region only 12 kilometres across from north to south. I have no direct evidence which confirms Tadat and Natarloar as Mekeng Detung, either from contemporary Ata Sikka or from the *Hikayat*, which mentions neither place. Boer's notes refer to Mekeng Detung both as a specific place and as a region encompassing a number of villages in central Sikka. It is perhaps significant that, in Sara Sikka, the name of Ili Bekor means 'to arise, to rise, to emerge, to come out, to well up, to come out of'. In the mythic histories of Tana Wai Brama, the founders of the domain are said to have *bubuk bekor* (SS), to have 'bubbled up (as water at a spring) and emerged (from the earth)' at Mekeng Detung, the same place cited in the *Hikayat* as that where the Ata Sikka first settled.

[15] In some Sikkanese texts, Woloarung appears as Wolo Laru or Wolo Larung.

[16] See Lewis (1988a, 1996a, 1996b). Lewis, Asch and Asch (1993) depicts the ways in which precedence informs the performance of ritual in Tana Wai Brama.

[17] Lewis (forthcoming), Chapter VIII, 'The Life of Mo'ang Bata Jawa'. The word *pu'u* (SS) means 'centre', 'middle', 'in the middle' and, in folk etymology, is linked to the word *pu'a*, 'trunk (of a tree)'.

[18] Lewis (forthcoming), Chapter IX, 'The Life of Mo'ang Baga Ngang'.

[19] Lewis (forthcoming), Chapter XIX, 'The Life of Mo'ang Baga Ngang'. Ili Egong, also known as Ili Mapi, is an active volcano and, at 1700 metres, the highest peak in Kabupaten Sikka. To the east of Egong is Tana 'Ai, which was brought into the Rajadom of Sikka only late in its history. Manggarai is the far western region of Flores.

[20] In Wai Brama, inexpensive and shallow white ceramic bowls that serve in quotidian and ceremonial meals are stored in stacks in loosely plaited, cylindrical lontar leaf baskets called *kloda*. *Kloda*, and baskets generally, are tropes for the way in which the *tana* (domain) contains its constituent social groups (see Lewis 1989). Stacks of plates are also referred to as *pigang natar ha*, 'stack' or 'nest of plates'. The word *natar* also means 'village', hence *pigang natar ha* is also a 'village of plates'.

[21] The complete name in ritual language of clan Liwu in Tana Wai Brama, the last clan in the order of precedence of the domain's clans, is Liwu Pigan Bitak, 'Liwu of the Shattered Plate(s)'. The origin myth of clan Liwu and the myth that details the clan's incorporation into the society of Tana Wai Brama includes among its episodes the breaking of a stack (*natar*) of many plates (see Lewis 1988a:123–125). People of Liwu are found in many parts of east central Flores apart from Tana Wai Brama, and it is tempting to see Liwu's myth of the shattered plates as an expression of the diaspora of the clan's members in mythic times, one 'sherd' of which became part of the domain of Wai Brama. In the introductory chapter of the *Hikayat*, which details the origins of the various peoples of Sikka (Lewis forthcoming, Appendix 2), it is said that an ancestral figure named Késo Kuit originated at Mekeng Detung and formed the clan of Liwu at Kringa, a domain in the northern realm of Tana 'Ai, and at Hikong, a village in Kringa (Lewis forthcoming, Appendix 2). In the *ngeng ngérang*, the mythic histories of Tana Wai Brama, Késo Kuit was a companion of Hading Dai Dor and Uher La'i Atan, the brothers who founded Tana Wai Brama.

[22] See, for example, ten Dam (1950), for an account of Nita written during the later years of Boer's and Kondi's literary careers.

[23] In both Sara Sikka and Bahasa Indonesia *raja* means 'ruler' and in Sara Sikka *sina* means 'China, Chinese', which is extended to mean any person or thing from the west or north-west in South-East Asia.

[24] Lewis (forthcoming), Chapter XII, 'The Second Period: The Middle rajas'.

[25] Lewis and Mandalangi (2008:194–196), Section 7.6, 'Mengenai Nita'.

[26] Lewis and Mandalangi (2008:262–266), Section 9.2, 'Nong Méak alias Josef da Silva Menjadi Wakil Raja Sikka'.

[27] In the *Hikayat*'s narrative, da Gama arrived in Sikka from Malacca before Alésu's return, but Alésu was responsible for da Gama's dispatch to Flores by Malacca's raja Worilla.

[28] *Ling* (SS) means 'hour (the striking of a clock)' and '(tinkling) sound'; *wéling* means 'value' or 'price'. The Ata Sikka translate the phrase *ling wéling* and the synonym *bélis* into Bahasa Indonesia as '*emas kawin*', meaning in the Sikkanese context, 'bridewealth'.

[29] Lewis (forthcoming), Chapter X, 'Gifts of Ivory Masts and Sails'.

[30] Lewis and Mandalangi (2008:122–127), Section 4.4., 'Don Alésu Menghadiakan dengan *Mangung Lajar*'.

[31] Lewis (forthcoming), Chapter X, 'Gifts of Ivory Masts and Sails'.

[32] Lewis and Mandalangi (2008:217–220), Section 8.1, 'Raja Larantuka Meminta Bea; Masalah Gading di Nita'.

[33] Lewis and Mandalangi (2008:217–220), Section 8.1, 'Raja Larantuka Meminta Bea; Masalah Gading di Nita'.

[34] Lewis and Mandalangi (2008:217–220), Section 8.1, 'Raja Larantuka Meminta Bea; Masalah Gading di Nita'.

[35] In fact, this was not entirely the case: a Sikkanese house (including the royal house) in danger of depopulation could keep its daughters and acquire men by arranging marriages without bridewealth. In such marriages, rather than leaving her natal group, a woman remained in her paternal house and her husband changed house affiliation, joining his wife's father's house. Thus commoners occasionally

became nobles and nobles occasionally became members of the royal house. Retainers were also occasionally 'adopted' by their patrons the term in Sikka Natar is *masuk keluarga* (BI enter the family) – thereby acquiring the status of free commoners and even nobility. (According to my Sikkanese informants, 'slavery' was abolished after World War Two and all of the *maha* of Sikka Natar were adopted *en masse* into the households of their patrons, an event which seems to have caused little disruption in Sikka Natar.)

7. Precedence, Contestation, and the Deployment of Sacred Authority in a Florenese Village

David Butterworth

Introduction

'There will be no road through the middle of our village!'[1]

Thus declared the 'source of the domain' (*tana pu'an*) of Romanduru village in the central highlands of Sikka Regency in April 2006, and to this day the proposed road has not been built. In this paper I elucidate the legitimacy of the authority of the *tana pu'an* in this matter by identifying the order of precedence that differentiates the status of the clans of Romanduru. In doing so I describe various strategies used to contest this order of precedence and argue that the contestation in fact strengthened the authority of the *tana pu'an*..

Since Lewis (1988:81) first translated the Tana 'Ai term *oda* as 'precedence', the concept has been central to our understanding of the Sikkanese speaking peoples. Lewis (1996a, 1996b) has subsequently provided us with studies of precedence in two of the three Sikkanese speaking societies, namely the people of Sikka and of Tana 'Ai. The significance of the third community, who are conventionally named the people of Krowé[2] and of which Romanduru village is a part, is hinted at by their central position in the geographical and cultural continuum that stretches from the lowland Sikka in the west of the Regency, through the highland Ata Krowé in the centre, to the Ata Tana 'Ai in the far east (see Map 1). Lewis (this volume) notes that while precedence maintains its primacy in Tana 'Ai social organization, among the Ata Sikka precedence was augmented, and in some cases displaced, by an hierarchical form of social stratification as this society became a rajadom. I have argued elsewhere (Butterworth 2008) that contemporary Krowé society exhibits a social organization and cosmology that is in many ways similar to what we know of the non-rajadom and non-Catholic aspects of Ata Sikka society,[3] and correspondingly is notably different from the Ata Tana 'Ai. In this socio-historical context the significance of the Krowé for comparative studies of precedence becomes immediately apparent. The Krowé have lived a different history to the Ata Sikka; a history that has kept them at the margins of the hierarchical rajadom and has only admitted Catholicism to any significant degree in the last 70 years. Importantly, the people of Krowé have conserved the social consequence of precedence to a much greater extent than the Ata Sikka.

Map 1. Map of Sikka Regency

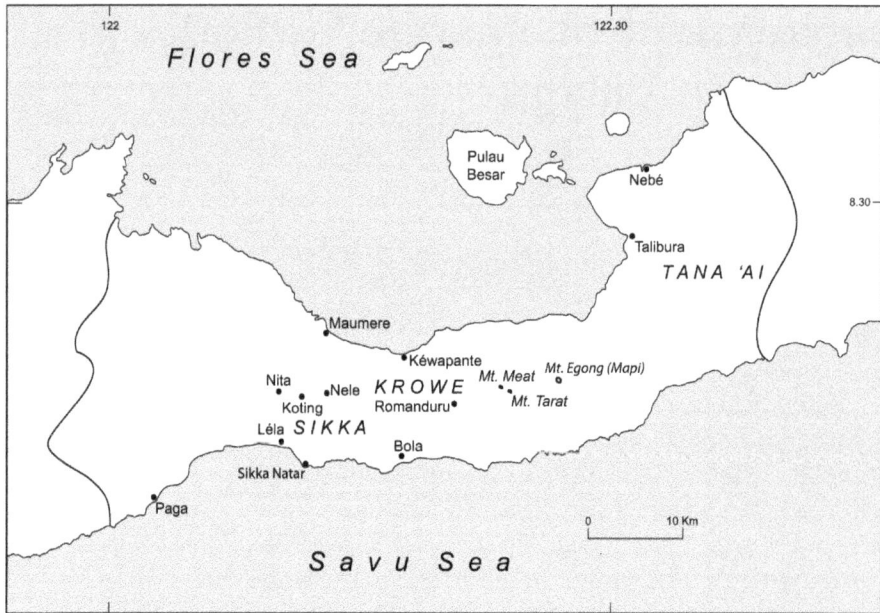

The relevance of precedence as a principle of social organization in Romanduru, and in the neighbouring Krowé villages, is evidenced by the continuing importance of the position of *tana pu'an* (source of the domain). In simple terms, the *tana pu'an* is a position of special social and spiritual responsibility that is accorded to the clan (and is personified by the clan headperson) which first settled in a particular domain (*tana*). The *tana pu'an* is the linchpin of Krowé orders of precedence that join clans within and between particular domains, and its persistence is noteworthy on two counts. First, some 25 years ago in a study of agriculture and population pressure in Sikka Regency, Joachim Metzner (1982:86) asserted that '... the institution of the *tana pu'ang* and the council of elders dealing with land issues (*du'a mo'ang watu pitu*) have ... disappeared in most of Central Sikka'.[4] My research indicates that, at least in Romanduru and the surrounding villages, the *tana pu'an* institution has not disappeared and, moreover, 'land councils' of elders still function, albeit in an informal capacity when compared to the formal authority of secular government apparatus. This brings us to the second point of significance of the *tana pu'an*. Although the authority of the *tana pu'an* is derived from and sanctified by the indigenous religious cosmology, this authority is nonetheless meaningful in ostensibly secular contexts. That is, on certain occasions, especially with regards to issues of land use, land tenure and natural resource exploitation, the sacred authority of the *tana pu'an* can effect secular change (or, as it may be, prevent change). For the Krowé, whose lifeworld articulates a complex mixture of indigenous, Catholic and Muslim influences, the sacred is rarely divorced from seemingly secular events, and precedence is a form of social organization that unites these sacred and secular spheres.

The case study I present to illuminate Romanduru's order of precedence and the authority of the *tana pu'an* is an event that outwardly reflects an antagonism between tradition and modernity. In short, some inhabitants of Romanduru advocated that a new road be constructed through the centre of the village to improve transport for those living some distance from the sole access road located at the top of the village (see Figure 1). Other inhabitants disapproved of the proposal because the road would require the destruction of much of the natural rock formations (which hold religious significance) and the relocation of some of the ritual altars that constitute Romanduru's centre. While this is a small-scale and highly localized dispute, its substance is representative of a wider tension between the value of sacred sites and the imperatives of economic development. However, as I untangle the motivations behind the Romanduru road project and the factors that have led to its denial, I will emphasize that a rubric of 'tradition versus modernity' does not entirely explain this controversial event. That is, what we find in the rejection of the Romanduru roadworks is not simply a triumph of traditional values over a modern infrastructure development, but an intricate social play of authority and contestation that is an expression of inter-personal and inter-clan relationships of precedence.

Precedence is a part of Romanduru tradition because it is produced in the complex of cosmology and sociality that is known by the villagers to have been the indigenous practice of their ancestors. At the same time, precedence is a part of contemporary thought and practice and it warrants recognition as a fundamental part of Romanduru inhabitants' current lifeworld (including their ways of creating and resolving disputes). In this way, precedence is a type of social organization that connects tradition and modernity in the Krowé communities, and cannot be considered simply as a throwback to an earlier mode of living. With this debate in mind, the objectives of this paper are twofold. First, I will describe the order of precedence of the Romanduru clans and explain the authority of the *tana pu'an* based on this order. Second, I will show that the proposal and rejection of the Romanduru roadworks can only be fully understood when precedence is posited as a theory of contemporary social action.

Figure 1. The village of Romanduru taken from the grounds of Santa Maria Senior Secondary School. Note the rock formations and ritual altars in the village centre which would be affected by the proposed road

The Social and Cosmological Bases of Precedence in Romanduru

According to the Krowé logic of precedence, the relative proximity of a domain's clans to the indigenous godhead is indexed to the clans' sequenced arrival and settlement in the domain. The earlier a clan settles in a domain, the closer it is to the deity, and the more responsible it is to the deity for the well-being of the domain. There are several social and cosmological aspects of Krowé life that must be explained in order to understand this operation of precedence. We must first define 'domain' and 'clan' and discern the relationship between the two. We must then explain how the connection between clan and domain is configured as a connection between the founding clan and the deity.

The village of Romanduru stands on the western slopes of Mt Méat in the central mountains of Sikka Regency in the eastern Indonesian Province of Nusa Tenggara Timur (NTT). In 2006 the population of Sikka was 282,795, of whom at least three quarters speak the dialects of the Sikkanese language.[5] At this time Romanduru consisted of 53 households which were home to 224 people, and the surrounding villages have similar numbers. In this densely populated area Romanduru and its neighbouring villages dot the sharp ridges and saddles that extend down from the mountain peaks.[6] The first point essential to our understanding of Krowé precedence is that in this region the traditional 'origin villages' (*natar gun*) and clans (*suku* or *kuat wungun*) are inseparable because such villages are constituted by clan wards (*'wisung wangar*).[7] Wards are small adjoining parcels of land on which clans have their central houses (*'wisung wangar lepo woga*). In villages constituted by such wards' houses are built within metres of each other, water is gathered from the same spring, and men, women and children of different clans share their daily lives. The clan ritual altars (*wu'a mahé*) also stand side-by-side in the middle of the village, and on special occasions (such as the *lodo hu'er* mortuary ritual) all are jointly offered sacrifices. These wards and altars are the nexus of village and clan identification. That is, through these sacred plots of land and assemblies of stones different clans join as one village.

All origin villages are located in their own domain called a *tana*, and each has a source, or founder, called the *tana pu'an* (source of the domain). In fact, the village and domain are essentially the same entity, and are unified in local idiom as *natar tana* (village domain). Domains in Krowé are demarcated by borders (*duen geté hoat mosang*) signposted by certain physical landmarks such as trees and valleys, in ritual activity located at the borders, and in the memories of community members. The *tana pu'an* is the clan that was the first to settle in the area, establish a *'wisung wangar* ward and erect a *wu'a mahé* altar. There are in fact two types of *tana pu'an* in Krowé domains; the *tana pu'an hoak héwér* (the source of the domain who has pinned his headdress to the tree) is the foremost source of the domain, and he may delegate authority over segments of his land to the *tana pu'an luli hodan* (the source of the domain poured out from the bowl). However, in the relatively small domain of Romanduru only the former type of *tana pu'an* was operational at the time of my fieldwork. The villages are formed around the source clan by the subsequent inclusion of other clans who also establish a *'wisung wangar* clan ward and erect a *wu'a mahé* ritual altar.

In ritual language the members of the same clan are called *ue lu'ur liwun, wari lodar lélén*. This nomenclature is significant and worth noting. *Ue* (or *wue*) refers to 'elder sibling' and *wari* 'younger sibling'. The terms *lu'ur* and *lodar* are synonyms that can be glossed as 'successive', 'lined up in a row', or 'straight', while *liwun* and *lélén* mean 'together' or 'in union'. The phrase 'elder and younger siblings lined up together' gives only some indication of the complex meaning contained in the original couplet. For example, and as will become more apparent below, the meaning of *ue* and *wari* extend beyond strict sibling relationships and encompass broader social relationships. Furthermore, the close *lu'ur* relationship, denoting people of the same clan, can be contrasted with *dolor* relationships which denotes people who are related but of different clans (see Lewis 1988:191 for the Tana 'Ai form of *lu'ur dolor* relationships). Within a clan, which are large corporations, social and ritual life revolves around the smaller nuclear family units, known locally as an *orin* or *lepo woga* (both of which mean house). This arrangement is typical of the 'house' communities found in eastern Indonesia, in which houses double as physical edifices and units of kinship, linked via the cosmological principles embedded in the house's construction and pattern of social relations (see Cunningham 1964; Fox 1993). A house essentially consists of an *ina* (mother), *ama* (father), and *mé* (children) who are *nara* (brother) and *winé* (sister). Social houses are created through marriage, dissolved when the couple dies, and remain unnamed except insofar as the names of the family members are used. The house of a clan's head-person, however, is always called the *lepo geté* (great house). In distinction to the broader clan, people of the same house often refer to themselves as *ue wari lepo woga* (elder and younger siblings of the house).

The number of clans residing in Krowé villages varies.[8] The village of Romanduru, for instance, has the highest density of clans of the villages in which I worked, they being clans Buang Baling (*tana pu'an*), Mana, Klukut Mude La'u, Wodon, Lio Lepo Gai, Lio Watu Bao, Keitimu Lamen, Keitimu Wain, Wewe Niur, and Ili Newa. I have counted 35 clans in the region, however most people were not concerned with establishing an accurate count. In ritual language the phrase *kuat wungung*[9] is used to designate a clan, whereas in everyday language it is called a *suku*. The phrase *ata kuat* is also frequently used, meaning 'people of the clan'; thus *ata kuat buang baling* refers to the 'people of the clan buang baling'.

Clans, moreover, extend their field of influence outside the clan wards of villages because clan 'houses' (*lepo woga*) are also located in other villages, either having established *'wisung wangar* in other villages in the distant past or settled in the new villages that have sprung up as the population has increased. Alliances are thus established by relationships between clans within a *natar tana* (village and domain) and, by extension, between villages which share the same member clans. In other words, alliances *between* villages are crystallized by the alliances of multi-local clans *within* villages. However, it is important to note that the structure of precedence of clans only operates within domains, not between domains. Thus, a clan which is the *tana pu'an* of one domain can be subject to the authority of another *tana pu'an* clan in a neighbouring domain. Whereas the social stratification evident *within* domains and villages is based on the different origins of clans, the relationship *between* domains and villages is a function of the multi-locality of clans. In other words, precedence relationships within villages bind clans together, and the multi-locality of clans bind villages together.

Having defined Krowé clans and domains and outlined their relationship in sociological terms, I will now examine the sanctity of this relationship that underwrites the spiritual authority of the *tana pu'an*. To do this I will look at three other elements of Krowé society in which precedence is expressed, namely;

marriage, ritual and cosmogony. Precedence in Krowé society is largely premised on mythic origins that are at once human, spiritual and geographical. The minimal requirements for this system are the community's knowledge of the sacred connection between the deity and the domain, and their knowledge of sequence of the arrival of clans in the domain. However, in the local exegeses of origins there is a disjuncture in the narratives that treat the creation of the universe by the deity and the arrival of clans in the various villages and domains. Both events have a distinct corpus of mythology which do not make mention of each other, and each mythic history at first seems to represent a discrete conceptual domain. And yet, both events are related, as indeed they are related to the institution of marriage. In different aspects of Krowé social and spiritual life (such as marriage, ritual and cosmogony) precedence is structured by asymmetric dyadic sets that *only* find their full value through their systematic connection within a totality. Thus, while the precedence of the clans of a domain is structured by the political value attributed to the dyad 'first//subsequent', and is ostensibly free of spiritual value, the full value of this precedence order is only articulated in the community, and known to the ethnographer, when it is brought into relation with other orders of precedence.

When two clans contract a marriage they enter into an exchange relationship in which the wife-giving clan is known as *ina ama* (mother and father) and the wife-taking clan is known as *me pu* (children and nephews/nieces). This itself constitutes a discrete order of precedence that is configured for the length of the exchange cycle of bridewealth and counter-prestations (usually the lifetime of the couple and sometimes beyond) in which the 'mother and father' clan is differentiated from, and cast as prior to, 'children and nephews/nieces'. In this case, precedence is accorded to the genitor, or life-giver, in favour to the progeny, or life-taker, on the basis of an order that indexes the bride and her clan as the source of life and the bridegroom and his clan as the offspring (see Fox 1996 for a discussion of the categorical validity of genitor and progeny instead wife-giver and wife-taker).

Although the 'marriage' order of precedence operates differently to the 'domain' order of precedence I focus on in this paper, its structure is useful in helping us appreciate the multiplicity of asymmetric values that simultaneously constitute Krowé orders of precedence. Since the precedence of the clans in a Krowé domain is determined by the sequenced arrival of those clans, the dyadic set of 'first//subsequent' represents the status differentiation of clans that was set in motion in the ancestral past and is reproduced in contemporary inter-clan relationships within a particular domain. With marriage, the dyadic set of 'genitor//progeny' represents the differentiation of wife-giver and wife-taker clans that is articulated when a women leaves her natal clan, enters her husband's clan, and gives birth to children for her new clan. The historical movement from first to subsequent is at once analogous to the movement of the wife between clans and the parting of mother and child during birth. The equivalence of these two dyadic sets, and the orders of precedence they represent, becomes even more evident when we delve deeper into the Krowé indigenous cosmology.

The Krowé cosmogonic myths and ancestral journeys of clans are narrated in a formulaic register of 'ritual language' that is composed in semantically parallel couplets. Ritual language, and the ideas it communicates, is part of a religious and ritual system which is called *adat* by the local community. *Adat* is an Indonesian word of Arabic origin used throughout the archipelago in reference to traditional and customary cosmologies and practices. However, the communities of Sikka Regency also use the term to refer *specifically* to their indigenous cosmology. In a community with no general native ethnonym, and, furthermore, no single native term for liturgy or ritual speech, it is not surprising that a foreign word stands instead of a native umbrella term for the indigenous religion. Here it is important to note that Krowé *adat* exists alongside Catholicism and the majority of the community practise both religions. For example, marriages are commonly conducted first according to *adat* and subsequently according to Catholicism. In the formidably syncretistic lives of the Krowé, Catholicism and *adat* are not contradictory, rather, they are regarded as complementary truths that have different genealogies and emphases.

The Krowé *adat* cosmogonic myths that I have collected and analysed depict the segmentation of an original, primordial unity and describe a relationship of obligation between humans and spiritual beings that provides the rationale for sacrificial ritual (see Traube 1986:13; Lewis 1988:45; McKinnon 1991:16 and Forth 1998:217 for similar cosmogonic themes in other eastern Indonesian societies). These sacrificial rituals, which are the most visible aspect of Krowé *adat*, are carried out at household altars (*ulu higun*) as *piong tewok* rites and at clan altars (*'ai tali* and *wu'a mahé*) as *tung piong* rites. All Krowé ritual activity, from the simplest to the most elaborate ceremonies, are based on sacrifice and involve offerings to the deity and ancestor spirits of rice, egg, tobacco, betel pepper and areca nut, fish tail and, depending on the event, offerings of raw and cooked chicken, dog and pig. Large public rituals, which are held on occasions of marriages, funerals, the implementation protection charms, and the building of new houses, roads, and public buildings, also involve complex arrays of other formulaic activities, such as material exchanges. Other occasions for ritual include return from or commencement of travel, study or work, times of illness and recovery, and requests for good fortune in any number of endeavours.

According to the Krowé cosmogonic myths, the primeval unity of all things is broken by the separation of the earth from the sky, the deity from humans, humans from animals, males from females, and good from bad. The consequence of separation and individuality is a mutual obligation between the human and spiritual realms in which the deity (called *ina nian tana wawa, ama lero wulan*

reta [mother of the earth and land below, father of the sun and moon above])
provides the materials necessary for human life, and in return humans provide
the deity with sacrificial offerings. The rituals of sacrifice fulfill obligations
because they 'reconstruct the source' (*wake pu'an*) and reunite the primevally
separated entities. During the 'heat' of ritual, humans, ancestors (*nitu noan*), the
deity, and even the sacrificed animals, are joined together in a potent field of
communication not otherwise experienced in normal life. Seen in this way, *adat*
rituals not only benefit the human participants (for whom the ritual settles
cosmological debts, sanctions social transformations such as marriage, and
generally ensures good harvests, health and fortune) but also benefit the deity
and ancestors. Like children returning home to their parents, reconstructing the
source in ritual momentarily gives back to the deity and ancestor spirits their
progeny, who become increasingly distant as over time they irrevocably move
away from their source.

Krowé ritual practice and cosmogonic myths tell us that the deity is
synonymous with the source of all things. In ritual, participants make
supplications to the deity for the purpose of reconstructing the source and joining
together all the beings and objects involved in ritual. Unhindered by temporal,
geographical or cosmological distance, humans make the requests and the spiritual
realm provide the assistance that allow life to continue smoothly. In effect, the
cosmogonic myths speak of the segmentation of an original unity (which was
constituted by the deity in its purest form) into the diversity of the world as we
know it, and this segmentation is reversed by ritual as the original unity of the
deity is momentarily re-formed. Thus, the dyadic sets that represent the
precedence of clans with regard to marriage and domain relationships can be
construed in terms of another dyadic set that represents the dynamics of ritual
and cosmogony. I identify this as a structure of source//product, and in local
idiom is represented variously as *ai pu'an//tali ubut* (tree trunk//vine tip),
pu'an//tawa (source//growth) and *wu'un//matan* (bamboo node//bamboo sprout).
The primeval source that is reproduced in ritual and defined as the deity is both
the temporal first and the reproductive genitor. All things were created from
the primeval source, and so too do the 'subsequent' clans follow the *tana pu'an*
clan and the progeny of children and nephews (*me pu*) issue from their mothers
and fathers (*ina ama*).

Precedence in Krowé operates in several, inter-related spheres. Cosmogony,
ritual, marriage and domain clan relationships all exhibit a structure of
precedence. By identifying the source//product structure in cosmogony and
ritual it is not my intention to suggest that marriage and domain clan relationship's
are thus determined. Instead, I wish to illustrate that although particular dyadic
representations of precedence are privileged (or, at least, more noticeable to the
ethnographer) in the symbolism and practice of each sphere, all are nonetheless
connected in a unitary system. The connection is semantic, such that the

privileged idioms of, for instance, first//subsequent, genitor//progeny, source//product are all imagined as a movement from an origin point outwards through time and space. The connection is also maintained in the practical relationships between the different spheres of precedence as they are enacted. For example, marriages are rituals that make contracts between clans, clans live in domains and the existence of both is explained in mythic histories, and cosmogonic histories contain themes that are enacted in marriage ritual. Thus, in local imaginations fed by, and which feed into, the symbolic and practical activities of marriage, ritual, myth, clan and domain, the 'first' is semantically and practically linked with the concepts of 'genitor' and 'source', and 'subsequent' is equated with 'progeny' and 'product'.

In sum, in Krowé the first clan that settles on a domain becomes the source of that domain with reference to the subsequently arriving clans. The physical land and biological life that constitutes the domain itself has a source in the form of the deity. The human and spiritual sources of the domain are thus linked in a special relationship. This is not to say the *tana pu'an* clan is the deity, rather that this founder clan is *closest* to the deity in another order of precedence that proceeds from source of the universe (deity), to source of the domain (*tana pu'an*), to delegated *tana pu'an luli hodan* positions, to other clans of the domain, and, if we extend the sequence, to individuals not affiliated to a clan of the domain. With the position of *tana pu'an* comes the responsibility for the well-being of the land and success of harvests in the domain because, being closer to the deity, the *tana pu'an* is able to make more effective entreaties to the deity. In return for this responsibility the source clan receives tribute called *wawi peping ara piong* (the pig's jaw and rice offering) from the other clans. The *tana pu'an* is primarily a spiritual position based on a close relationship, via the particular *tana* (domain), with the deity.

The Order of Precedence of Romanduru Clans

One of the tenants of the theory of precedence is that there can be several co-operating values in any one order of precedence. In the previous section I argued that the order of precedence among the clans living in a Krowé domain is fully articulated when the privileged dyadic set of first//subsequent is augmented by the values of other, related orders of precedence. Thus, the temporal first also contains the values of source and genitor. In this way the founding clan of a domain, as source and genitor, is brought into a relationship with the deity, and thereby assumes certain responsibilities over the domain and the people within it. In this section I will focus on the specific order of precedence among clans in Romanduru as it is expressed in the mythic history of the *tana pu'an* clan of Romanduru, Buang Baling. Through this analysis I will introduce another dyadic set that further valorizes of the order of clan precedence within domains. The mythic history represents the distinction between first clan and subsequent clans in terms of a distinction between elder and younger. The asymmetric relationship between the clans of a domain are therefore valorized in a way that in part duplicates the relationships of elder and younger siblings which, as I emphasized earlier, constitute individual clans.

The Buang Baling clan history presented below sourced from the notebooks of Mo'ang Elias Esi, a native of Koting. As a young man in the late 1960s Esi travelled throughout the Krowé region recording clan histories and other *adat* knowledge. This particular narrative was recorded from a Buang Baling chanter named Mo'an Raga Dobo Piring from the village of Dobo. During my fieldwork I did not witness clan histories recounted with the depth and breadth of description, or the remarkable poetics, of this narrative (which in its totality contains 698 lines of strictly parallel verse). Nonetheless, the fundamentals of clan histories are still widely known and spoken by members of Romanduru clans.

Clan histories are part of a genre of ritual speech called *kleteng latar* (bridging speech). Literally, *kleteng* refers to a bridge made of wood and vine ropes spanning a creek or river. This metaphor evokes the primary function of ritual language as a method for enabling clear and effective communication, be it between the human and spirit realms, or simply between humans. More specifically, *kleteng latar* defines ritual language that explicates ethics, law or history. In the later case, it is used interchangeably with *ngeng ngerang* (dispersal of generations) and is commonly used in an argumentative and entertaining manner in which two people recite their clan histories in tandem while testing each others knowledge. Histories are also often chanted immediately before or upon death to ease the transition of the deceased's soul (*maen*) to the afterlife (*nitu natar noan klo'ang*). It is said that reciting the names and travels of the deceased's clans' early ancestors, provides necessary guidance for the soul as it seeks to join its fellows.

I will present a selection of the Buang Baling narrative that explicitly deals with the question of precedence. Before proceeding, it is important to note that Krowé clan histories are examples of what Fox (1997) has called a 'topogeny'. In reference to the Atoin Meto of Timor, McWilliam explains that a topogeny is an

> ideology of affiliation through fathers to sons [which] tends not to be expressed genealogically in the record of particular generations of named ancestors, but rather spatially across the landscape by associating the group's name with specific places and named localities (1997:103).

For the Krowé, membership to clans is immediately reckoned through patrilineal descent, however the historical corporate stability of clans is not reckoned by unbroken genealogies stretching back into the distant past. Clans are defined both *contemporarily* by the *lives* of one's grandfathers, grandsons and those in between, and *historically* by the *journeys* of one's earliest ancestors. Moreover, the journeys link clan ancestors to particular physical features and tracts of land. This link is of most consequence when clans end their journeys and found a village and domain.

The Buang Baling history begins with the departure of Du'a Wio Bota[10] (female) and Mo'an Supung Balen Sina (male) from the island of Bali after a natural disaster which is described as '*kasi nian mutu o bitak, bitak nang ganu pigang, blua nang ganu kleto*' (Oh my land was destroyed, it cracked like a fallen plate, like the worms turn the earth). Throughout the narrative the Buang Baling ancestors visit various locales and meet numerous travellers from other clans. I recount a selection that begins towards the end of the narrative, when Du'a Wio Bota have already journeyed along the south coast of Sikka Regency and upwards into the central mountains (like most Krowé clan histories, the male counterparts of the leading female ancestors disappear from the narrative quite early). The story begins at a place called Klo'ang Gunit, a temporary settlement of Du'a Wio Bota near the as yet undiscovered Romanduru. Du'a Wio Bota pause in search of water:

	a'u Wio a'u Bota	I am Wio I am Bota
580	*teri puput ling kiok*	sitting to fan the flames
	ora dota degang kletak	swinging my hammer and striking
582	*ulit eh ra'i wair*	my skin is dirty and needing water
	boir sa mara wair	my throat is dry and thirsty for water
584	*po ita wair nora pu'an*	we look for a water spring
	a'u huk du uku aka	I think and deliberate
586	*nera du pokang peler*	I meditate and consider
	a'u huk poi e uwung	I think deep in my heart
588	*nera poi e nain*	I consider with my life's breath
	ana tupat kokor	a basket made from plaited coconut leaves
590	*sisi ora awu luk*	filled with fine ash
	pete e ahu i'ur	tied to the dog's tail
592	*ahu Jawa ahu Mola*	the dogs named Jawa and Mola
	ahu ia bano dete	the dog leads the way
594	*awu ia luk lurus*	the ash is fine

Du'a Wio Bota then follow the trail of the ash as the dogs run in search of water. The narrative takes the listener (or reader) on a tour of the streams and spring waters that surround the village of Romanduru:

wae e ripa ba'u	heading down to the right
596 *ripa wair puat rano dadin*	to the spring waters forming a pond
wair ia meting poi marat poi	the water there has dried up
598 *ahu ia bano dete*	the dogs lead the way
ripa lawang ba'it henan blanun	to Lawang Ba'it Henan Blanun
600 *loret loret ripa ba'u*	descending further down to the right
ripa wair herit bere seng	to the spring of Herit Bere Seng
602 *ia du meting poi marak poi*	there it is also dry
ledu leder lau ang	in single file down they go
604 *era ni'a era kliat*	standing looking, standing considering
ahu ia poa wi'in poma wi'in	the dogs splash and play in the water
606 *a'u ata higi mitan*	I am a wise person with coloured teeth[11]

The discovery of a rich waterhole confirms the wisdom of Du'a Wio Bota and, indeed, expresses the sympathetic relationship that they have for this locale. The Buang Baling ancestors excavate the spring so that the water 'flows free and pure', and then walk upslope to survey the site of the future settlement:

di ni'a lau a ita	now I look down, seeing
608 *teking ora kebung rebu*	carrying a branch of sugar palm[12] wood
'o'i wawa wa'u ali	shovelling and digging downwards
610 *ali 'ata golo wair*	digging and discovering much water
lema reta loki klasar	ascending to the rocky outcrop[13]
612 *ahu gita beli wair*	the dog sees and gives water
wair wulut liro linok	at *wair wulut liro linok* [14]
614 *ahu i'ur jewa jaong*	the dogs' tails wag and splash the water
wai dahi rawong	the water flows free and pure
616 *a'u Wio a'u Bota*	I am Wio I am Bota
hu'i ripa wa'un ta'u	bathe and collect water there
618 *popo ripa wa'un te*	wash and dry there
ban buno ripa napun blatan	the cool water flows through the valley
620 *ripa napun tepak blikon blawan*	at the stream sloping this way and that

Having found a spring around which to establish a village the two women are joined by Du'a Saru and Du'a Watu, ancestors of two other clans. Du'a Watu married Mo'an Blua to form clan Klukut Mudé La'u, and Du'a Saru married Mo'an Bela to form clan Mana. In the following instalment the structure of precedence is introduced. As the pair from clan Buang Baling meet the newcomers they invite (*pahar*) them to stay and build a village together (line 664, 665, 670). In this final section of ritual speech the narrator switches between speaking in the first person of both Du'a Wio Bota and Du'a Saru Watu. Thus:

654	*a'u Saru a'u Watu*	I am Saru I am Watu
	a'u hu'i wali ang ta'u	I bathe and collect water there
656	*popo wali ang te*	I wash and dry there
	a'u lair ra'intan golo ue	I know who my elder siblings are
658	*wuen* [15] *Wio wuen bota*	Elder Wio elder Bota
	wuen lau nian ngeng	they came down inhabiting the land
660	*a'u tangar regang golo*	I meet and respect them
	wuen lau tana ngerang	elders who came down dispersing on the land
662	*wuen lau tana ngeng*	elders who came down giving descendents
	wuen Wio wuen Bota	elder Wio elder Bota
664	*'au pahar wi meti pita*	eagerly you invite us to stay
	pahar Saru wai Watu	inviting the wives Saru and Watu
666	*idet wi doé mala*	pulled in and held in hand
	nane Laju du'a Plu'e	with Du'a Laju Plu'e
668	*warin lau tana ngerang*	younger siblings dispersed on the land
	uen Wio wuen Bota	elder Wio elder Bota
670	*pahar wi meti pita*	an invitation made eagerly
	libu wi'it liar liwun	together our voices are one
672	*kula wi'it ganu wulan*	conferring with each other like the moonlight
	ita ro'a le'u duru e	we clear the *duru* trees
674	*tena song sugo tion*	making the correct measurements of our houses
	kara wi'it ganu lero	deliberating with each other like the sunlight
676	*ita sapi le'u klukut*	we clean away the rubbish
	oh tena kadang hereng belan	oh we ensure the foundations are properly set
678	*song na'in sugon tion*	placing the correct measurements
	sugon tion dadi lepo	correct measurements become a house

680	*a'u Wio a'u Bota*	I am Wio I am Bota
	turu weli nora wisung	pointing out a dwelling place
682	*wisung wae lau ba'u*	a dwelling place facing from down there[16]
	lau likong tana klasar	from down at Likong Tana Klasar
684	*lau saru lau watu*	from Saru and Watu
	a'u tutur weli 'au	I speak and give you
686	*nora wangar*	a place to reside
	wangar wae wali main	a dwelling place facing the southern winds[17]
688	*hi'ung wali na glikung*	others glance towards us jealously
	du'a pli'at ba'a ganu liat	our women have already built hearths
690	*leta wi'it let wi'it*	welcoming and encouraging each other
	ta lako dueng geté	going to visit the great borders
692	*pani wi'it gaging wi'it*	of one mind and direction
	bar tana hoat mosan	calling upon the principal boundaries
694	*tana a'u ler mangan*	the land upon which I lean with strength
	dadi ami ruga ba'a ubut tobong	so we have trimmed the tips of the trees
696	*nian ami liting gi'it*	the earth upon which we rest with surety
	ami paket tadan ba'a olan lahin	we have raised *tadan* [18] and marked our place
698	*dena tana ler mangan*	making this our land and strength

In lines 658, 661, 662, 663, 668 and 669 of this passage an 'elder//younger' (*ue wari*) relationship is explicitly formed between Buang Baling (as elder) and clans Klukut Mudé La'u and Mana (as younger). Thus, the terminology of *ue wari*, normally used for members of the same agnatic clan, is applied *within* the village for members of different clans. There is great clarity and forcefulness in the assertion of the brotherhood of the clans — they are, as is stated in line 692, 'of one mind and direction'. The position of the 'elder' *tana pu'an* is by no means autocratic, and by virtue of their co-residence on the same *tana* all the clans are united in a fraternal bond. Furthermore, it is important to remember that, as I stated earlier, this structure of precedence only operates within *tana*, not between *tana*, and a clan who is 'younger brother' to the *tana pu'an* of one territory can be its 'elder brother' in another.

The Buang Baling clan history establishes a structure of precedence that is archetypal for all clans and domains in Krowé. A domain is first discovered and settled by a particular clan, and subsequent arrivals are incorporated into the settlement under the auspices of the first clan. This structure of precedence burdens the source clan (*tana pu'an*) with the honour and responsibility of mediating the relationship between the deity and the people who live upon the domain. Importantly, the precedence-based stratification of clans within Krowé domains operates with a simple division between the first arrival and 'the rest'. The different clan histories do give a general idea of their sequenced arrival. For example, in the history presented above we see that clan Buang Baling was immediately followed by clans Mana and Klukut Mudé La'u and none of the other seven clans had yet arrived. However, unlike in the neighbouring community of Tana 'Ai where the sequential order of clans is recapitulated and contested in the Gren Mahé rites (Lewis 1988), according to my data this extended order does not presently have social or ritual consequences in Krowé. For example, as I noted earlier, the *tana pu'an* is differentiated from other clans in ritual activity with the tribute *wawi peping ara piong* (the pig's jaw and rice offering). In the past, when subsistence agriculture was still practised, this tribute to the source of the domain would occur regularly with harvest, however, nowadays it mostly occurs when public village land is put to use. I have witnessed several instances of this tribute, all as components of rituals that consecrate construction (*laba lepo sorong woga*). The tribute on each occasion was a token amount of money given to the *tana pu'an* on behalf of *all* the other clans of the domain acting in unison.

Strategies of Contestation and the Legitimization of Authority

In this section I relate the strategies deployed by both the *tana pu'an* and the pro-road faction as they argued their respective positions. I wish to emphasize that both factions in this dispute could muster persuasive reasons *for* and *against* the road construction. Indeed, I suggest that the dispute was not primarily about the road, but was a calculated test of the Romanduru order of precedence for which the road was a means, or front, to enact this contestation.

The centre of Romanduru village, where the road in question was proposed to be built, is constituted by a natural rocky outcrop (*loki klasar*), ten ritual altars (*wu'a mahé*) — one for each of the village's clans — and the convergence of the ten clan wards ('*wisung wangar*'), which are rectangular parcels of land located side-by-side in two parallel rows. These aspects of the village are sacred for the inhabitants of Romanduru, all of whom adhere to the indigenous cosmology. The rocky outcrop is known as a gateway to a potent, and dangerous, spiritual domain and is the home of a spiritually empowered python (*naga sawaria*). The ritual altars were erected by each clans' earliest ancestors and are used for the final stage mortuary rites called the *lodo hu'er*. The clan wards are the physical nexus at which humans join together as a community under the auspices of the deity. Thus, each aspect holds an extremely important place in the imaginations and practices of the community, and the destruction, removal or modification of these sacred sites and objects would represent a transgression against the deity.

The authority of the *tana pu'an* over the village and domain of Romanduru is underpinned by the order of precedence which connects the temporal priority of clan Buang Baling with the cosmological priority of the deity. As such, more than any other clan in Romanduru, the people of Buang Baling are responsible for the 'health' of the domain, including the village centre. This, I argue, is the imperative that encouraged the *tana pu'an* reject the proposed road. It is also the imperative that encouraged the contesting faction submit to the authority of the *tana pu'an* in this matter. For, although the *tana pu'an* is most responsible, all members of the community have a stake in the maintenance of good relations with spiritual powers. In fact, some 20 years ago the *wu'a mahé* of one Romanduru clan was repaired using cement and, I was told, shortly afterwards seven different members of this clan, including the clan head, were injured or killed in unusual circumstances. In other words, all the inhabitants of Romanduru, including the pro-road faction, were aware of dangerous occult consequences for disrupting the sacred village centre. The key question now becomes, 'why was a road through the centre of Romanduru village proposed when its rejection was ultimately never in doubt?'

In purely practical terms, the construction of the road would undoubtedly make life easier for many people, including the *tana pu'an*. For those living near the top of the village, close to the sole access road, a new road would facilitate the transportation of crops harvested in gardens located on the ridgeline and valley slopes below the village. At the moment all harvested cocoa, cloves and coconuts are carried by foot and shoulder in bags weighing up to 50 kilograms. Depending on the garden's position, such loads are carried for a number of kilometres, and several harvesting hours are lost per day as a result. It goes without saying that a road allowing motorcycle, or even truck, access to these gardens would greatly increase harvesting efficiency. For those living at the bottom end of the village, closer to the gardens but further from the top access road, a new road would also ease crop transportation, especially as the yields must be delivered personally to the agents in the coastal town of Geliting. Moreover, distance from the top access road means that building materials must be hand carried, at an extra cost, to construction sites for new houses or extensions, and parking and storage of motorcycles must be negotiated with those living close to the access road. It is also notable that electricity cables do not extend to the lower section of the village and, in general, these residents state that the further one is from a road, the further one is from the benefits of modernity.

There are, however, alternative routes that could have been lobbied for. A road could circumnavigate the village centre by being routed behind either row of the parallelly aligned houses. Or, a road could be constructed from an access point on the neighbouring ridge-line and be routed through the valley and connect to the lower houses of Romanduru from the northern side. Each of these alternatives were spoken of by various members of the community and each was readily dismissed because of the need to occupy private land, and thus reduce the arable land of some farmers. Furthermore, these roads would be difficult and expensive to build because of their position along the steeply sloping valley walls. In fact, the economic and logistical challenges of these alternative routes are not insurmountable, and in the most recent news I have received (some two years after the heat of the dispute described here) a road connecting the lower section of Romanduru to the neighbouring ridge-line is under development.

The dispute is characterized by a situation in which a road that would benefit all the village was proposed by some parties to be built through the village centre, even though this location would engender spiritual sanction and other routes are available. The *tana pu'an* was bound to reject this proposal, and had the authority to do so, and yet the proposal was still made. There were no hard boundaries between pro-road and anti-road factions that strictly divided all the village's clans, however it was clear that the *tana pu'an* clan, Buang Baling, were as a whole adamantly against the road. Those contesting the *tana pu'an* were led by members of several other clans, including members of the two clans who settled in Romanduru immediately after Buang Baling, namely Mana and Klukut Mude La'u. Although I did not poll the entire village on what was at the time a very sensitive matter, the general relationship between opinion and clan membership plainly corresponded to the 'source' and 'product' structure of precedence that differentiates the *tana pu'an* clan from all the others.

With this structure of precedence in mind, I wish to argue that the road proposal was made by prominent members of the non-*tana pu'an* clans, not to secure the road, but to contest the authority of the clan Buang Baling as 'source of the domain'. Paradoxically, this contestation helped to re-legitimate Buang Baling's authority. This last point will become clear as we consider the background of the road dispute and the strategies of contestation used.

The clans contesting the authority of the *tana pu'an* did so at a time when clan Buang Baling was in transition. The head of the clan, and thus the personification of the *tana pu'an*, had been ill for several years and died in early 2006. As is normally, though not necessarily, the case, the position of clan headship passed to the deceased's eldest son. This was not an easy transition.

For decades the eldest son had lived away from Romanduru as a transmigration worker. Having lived so long away from home the new *tana pu'an* was not as knowledgeable about local history and cosmology as his father had been. The situation was further complicated by the succession of the former *tana pu'an*, which some in the village considered questionable. While this succession had occurred many years ago, the personal strength of character of the *tana pu'an* had nullified the matter, and people only dared to raise this matter after his death. And so at the time of the road dispute the *tana pu'an* clan of Romanduru was weakened by internal difficulties relating to the transition between clan leaders occasioned by death. Although the authority of the source of the domain is always upheld in the poetics of clan histories, at such a time the clan's ability to *enact* its authority is at its most fragile. In other words, the time was ripe for contestation by other clans and, equally, the integrity of the system as a whole required re-affirmation.

The strategies of contestation employed by the pro-road faction extended beyond a simple contentious proposal. Numerous power-plays were set in motion. I do not doubt that many plays were too subtle for my understanding, and so here I will only relate to the two most public challenges to the authority of the *tana pu'an*. First, an attempt was made to pressure the new *tana pu'an* into conducting incorrect ritual action. The *tana pu'an* was asked by a member of another clan to seek advice from the deity and ancestor spirits regarding the propriety of the road, and potentially sanctify the project, by making a *tung piong* sacrificial offering at clan Buang Baling's *wu'a mahé* ritual altar. There are several types of ritual altar in Krowé, and the *wu'a mahé* has very restricted use in that it is only used to offer sacrifices during the *lodo hu'er* mortuary rites. To have performed a sacrifice in this context would have been devastating for the reputation of the new *tana pu'an*. Second, a provocative *tung piong* sacrifice was performed at the lower edge of the village on a temporary ritual altar (*watu mahang tung piong*). This ritual was performed correctly and was legitimately performed to sanctify the widening of the footpath that connects the lowest houses to the village centre. Although this was a seemingly innocuous event, the footpath would eventually connect to any road routed through the village centre, and the positioning of the temporary ritual altar was precariously close to the village centre. In its suggestive timing and positioning this ritual was construed by many as an attempt to pre-emptively sanctify the village centre in preparation for roadwork without the express permission of the *tana pu'an*.

The important point to be made here is that both 'contestations' were unlikely to be successful. Although the events took place in a tense and exciting atmosphere and were conducted with haste, confusion, emotion and a degree of intoxication, I suspect that all sides were cognizant of the fallibility of these tactics of contestation. Despite his time away from the village, the new *tana pu'an* was more than capable of recognizing the proper use of ritual altars. And the ritual sanctification of the widened footpath was correct enough to justify its ostensible purpose, and its covert intention to sanctify a simple footpath was ambiguous enough to be ignored. The *tana pu'an* was challenged, but he and his clan were only challenged in a way to which they could be expected to ably respond. By responding to these contestations with such authority, the condition of uncertainty that initially prompted the contestation was effectively trumped. The strategic use of ritual to attempt to sanctify road construction and circumvent the authority of the *tana pu'an* , while perhaps sincere in its implementation, was not in fact a powerful challenge to the order of precedence. It is possible that heavier pressure could have been exerted on the *tana pu'an* to substantially weaken his authority within the existing order of precedence, however in my view this degree of contestation was not attempted.

In sum, at the time of the proposed roadworks the authority of the *tana pu'an* was fragile due to problems of succession. The efforts to contest the authority of the *tana pu'an* provided a platform on which the *tana pu'an* was then able to re-assert his and his clan's authority. In other words, only after staving off several challenges to his wavering authority was the recently inducted *tana pu' an* of Romanduru able to preside with *great* authority over the domain's sacred sites. Several questions arise from this conclusion. Were the individuals contesting the *tana pu 'an* wittingly re-legitimating the *tana pu'an*'s weakened authority with the objective of supporting Romanduru's traditional order of precedence? Or, alternatively, were they sincere in their efforts to undermine the *tana pu'an* and unwittingly subject to a structural, homeostatic regulator that automatically restored balance? Further, given that a truly successful contestation of a particular Krowé order of precedence would effectively undermine the cosmological tenants on which the system itself is based, we must ask what benefits can be gained by any contestation at all?

Conclusion

Finding answers to the questions raised above is beyond the scope of the current investigation. Nevertheless such questions are useful for delineating the way forward for studies of precedence in Krowé, and their answers are essential for attaining a more complete understanding of Krowé social life. With this paper I have provided a platform on which to achieve these aims by describing the structure of Krowé precedence and its particular manifestation in the Romanduru domain. I then proceeded to outline a recent event in which the Romanduru structure of precedence was articulated and contested by the 'source' clan, Buang Baling, and a pro-road faction led by members of a number of 'product', or subsequent, clans. With this discussion I have shown that precedence, when used as an analytical concept, is as much a theory of social action as it is a theory of structural status differentiation. Precedence refers to a structure of relations between the clans of a domain based on the sequenced arrival of proto-ancestors chanted in ritual language and which assigns different responsibilities to the different clans. Precedence also refers to embodied co-operative and contested relationships between clans as they contract marriages, offer and receive tributes, and generally conduct village affairs — as was the case when different clan members challenged each other over the road project. And yet, having come this far, when we seek to understand the *outcomes* of a contested order of precedence, we arrive back at another problem defined by seemingly dichotomous notions of structure and agency.

I have demonstrated that the authority of Romanduru's *tana pu'an* was rejuvenated by the challenge of the pro-road faction. However, we do not yet know if the pro-road faction intentionally withheld from launching a sustained attack on the *tana pu'an*, or if their actions were limited by structural determinants. The definition of precedence as both structural and agential is a lesson that can be carried forth into future analyses of the outcomes of contestation, whether they be focused on Krowé, Sikka, or beyond. Vischer (1996) and Fox (1989) have shown that the possibility of contestation is inherent in all structures of precedence, whether that be in ritual performances or in the recursion and reversal of dyadic sets in ritual language. Additionally, I have emphasized in this paper that a practical instance of contestation in Romanduru was at the heart of an event that outwardly reflected a tension between tradition and modernity. Thus, precedence is made legitimate and relevant to a community by their actions as they seek to contest (or preserve in response to contestation) an order of precedence, and such actions can be fundamental to the motivations and behaviour of people in many different spheres of social life. We must now turn our attention to producing more detailed ethnography that reaches into the relationship between structure and agency as it is expressed in the processes and outcomes of contestation. This will not only deepen our understanding of precedence, of which contestation is an integral part, but also broaden our understanding of societies in which the full influence of precedence in contemporary social life has yet to be charted.

References

Arndt, P.

[1993]2002 *Gesellschaftliche Verhältnisse im Sikagebiet (ostl. Mittelflores)*. Ende, Flores: Arnoldus.

Butterworth, D.J.

2008 Lessons of the ancestors: ritual, education and the ecology of mind in an Indonesian community. Unpublished PhD thesis. Melbourne: Department of Anthropology, The University of Melbourne.

Cunningham, C.E.

1964 Order in the Atoni house. *Bijdragen tot de Taal-, Land- en Volkenkunde* 120:34–68.

Forth, G.

1998 *Beneath the volcano: religion, cosmology and spirit classification among the Nage of eastern Indonesia*. Koninklijk Instituut voor Taal-, Land- en Volkenkunde, Verhandelingen 177. Leiden: KITLV Press.

Fox, James J.

1989 Category and complement: binary ideologies and the organization of dualism in eastern Indonesia. In David Maybury-Lewis and Uri Almagor (eds), *The attraction of opposites: thought and society in the dualistic mode*, pp. 33–56. Ann Arbor: The University of Michigan Press.

1996 The transformation of progenitor lines of origin: patterns of precedence in eastern Indonesia. In James J. Fox and Clifford Sather (eds), *Origins, ancestry and alliance: explorations in Austronesian ethnography*, pp.130–153. Canberra: Department of Anthropology, Research School of Pacific and Asian Studies, The Australian National University. Comparative Austronesian Series, ANU E Press: http://epress.anu.edu.au/.

1997 Genealogy and topogeny: towards an ethnography of Rotinese ritual place names. In James J. Fox (ed.), *The poetic power of place: comparative perspectives on Austronesian ideas of locality*, pp.91–102. Canberra: Department of Anthropology, Research School of Pacific and Asian Studies, The Australian National University. Comparative Austronesian Series, ANU E Press: http://epress.anu.edu.au/.

Fox, James J. (ed.)

1993 *Inside Austronesian houses: perspectives on domestic designs for living*. Canberra: Department of Anthropology, Research School of Pacific and Asian Studies, The Australian National University. Comparative Austronesian Series, ANU E Press: http://epress.anu.edu.au/.

Lewis, E.D.

1988 *People of the source: the social and ceremonial order of the Tana Wai Brama on Flores*. Verhandelingen van het Koninklijk Instituut voor Taal-, Land- en Volkenkunde 135. Dordrecht, Holland/Providence, USA: Foris Publications.

1996a Origin structures and precedence in the social orders of Tana 'Ai and Sikka. In James J. Fox and Clifford Sather (eds), *Origins, ancestry and alliance: explorations in Austronesian ethnography*, pp.154–174. Canberra:

Department of Anthropology, Research School of Pacific and Asian Studies, The Australian National University. Comparative Austronesian Series, ANU E Press: http://epress.anu.edu.au/.

1996b Invocation, sacrifice, and precedence in the Gren Mahé rites of Tana Wai Brama, Flores. In S. Howell (ed.), *For the sake of our future: sacrificing in eastern Indonesia*, pp.112–131. Leiden: CNSW Publications Vol. 42.

McKinnon, Susan

1991 *From a shattered sun: hierarchy, gender, and alliance in the Tanimbar Islands.* Madison: The University of Wisconsin Press.

McWilliam, A.R.

1997 Mapping with metaphor: cultural topographies in west Timor. In James J. Fox (ed.), *The poetic power of place: comparative perspectives on Austronesian ideas of locality*, pp.103–115. Canberra: Department of Anthropology, Research School of Pacific and Asian Studies, The Australian National University. Comparative Austronesian Series, ANU E Press: http://epress.anu.edu.au/.

Metzner, J.K.

1982 Agriculture and population pressure in Sikka, Isle of Flores. a contribution to the study of the stability of agricultural systems in the wet and dry tropics. Development Studies Centre Monograph No. 28. Canberra, Australia, and Miami, Florida, USA: The Australian National University.

Traube, E.G.

1986 *Cosmology and social life: ritual exchange among the Mambai of East Timor.* Chicago: The University of Chicago Press.

Vischer, M.P.

1996 Precedence among the domains of the Three Hearth Stones: contestation of an order of precedence in the Ko'a ceremonial cycle (Palu'é Island, eastern Indonesia). In James J. Fox and Clifford Sather (eds), *Origins, ancestry and alliance: explorations in Austronesian ethnography*, pp.175–198. Canberra: Department of Anthropology, Research School of Pacific and Asian Studies, The Australian National University. Comparative Austronesian Series, ANU E Press: http://epress.anu.edu.au/.

Wurm, S and S. Hattori

1983 *Language atlas of the Pacific area.* Part 2. Canberra: Australian Academy of the Humanities.

ENDNOTES

[1] The ethnographic material used in this paper was collected during fieldwork in Sikka Regency in 2005 and 2006. I would like to thank Candraditya Research Centre for the Study of Religion and Culture for their sponsorship of my research. I would also like to thank Prof. James Fox, Dr E. Douglas Lewis and Dr Peter Dwyer for their comments and assistance.

[2] I have argued elsewhere (Butterworth 2008) that the ethnonym 'Krowé' is an imperfect generalization of the variety of distinctive villages and clans that are found in the central highlands of Sikka Regency. For the purposes of stylistic clarity I will use Krowé in this paper. I ask the reader to be mindful that the term is not widely used locally, and in daily life people most commonly identify with their villages and clans.

[3] I am hesitant to use the prefix 'pre' (that is, pre-rajadom and pre-Catholic) or the term 'indigenous' in this context because the rajadom is largely of indigenous production and many elements of the Ata Sikka indigenous cosmology are still practised alongside Catholicism (for example, bridewealth exchanges).

[4] *Tana pu'ang* is cognate with *tana pu'an*, and is indicative of Ata Sikka, rather than Ata Krowé, usage.

[5] The indigenous language spoken in Krowé villages is a dialect of Sara Sikka, a language that Wurm and Hattori (1983) classify as part of the Flores-Lembata (Lomblen) Subgroup in the Timor Area Group in the Central Malayo-Polynesian Subgroup of the non-Oceanic Austronesian languages. Most people also speak the national language Bahasa Indonesia, which is used in schools, on official occasions such as governmental meetings, and when trading or otherwise engaging with non-Sikkanese speaking people. However, the indigenous language is most frequently spoken, albeit now with a considerable mixture of Indonesian words and phrases. The local language is often revealingly called *bahasa itan*, which is a mixture of Indonesian and Sara Sikka meaning 'our language'.

[6] Kewapante, the sub-district (*kecamatan*) of which Romanduru is part, has one of the highest population densities for a rural area in the entire province (444.39 people p/km²).

[7] Large, recently constituted non-origin villages are called *natar werun* (new village). Small settlements that are located within a *tana* as overflow from the *natar gun* (origin village) are called *klo'ang* (hamlet). These settlements are not constituted by *'wisung wangar*. However, some *natar tana* (such as Klo'ang Popot and Hewot Klo'ang) take the name *klo'ang*. It is possible that in the distant past these villages developed from *klo'ang* into independent *tana*.

[8] Krowé clans are exogamous, named descent groups. Children are born into their parents clan, and when females marry they enter their husband's clan. A male can only change clans in special circumstances, such as when he cannot afford bridewealth and thus enters his wife's clan in a marriage ritual called *lébo kuat* (cook the rice to enter the clan).

[9] Arndt ([1933]2002:101) defines the *kuat wungung* of Sikka and Nita based on totemism, stating that they are 'a group of people who have a special relationship with a particular species of animal or plant and because of this relationship they are unified with each other'. My data supports this definition only insofar as each clan has specific taboo plants or animals which cannot be consumed. However, nowadays such totemic taboos have little practical relevance to the majority of the community, and membership to a descent group is measured more so through descent and marriage.

[10] Du'a Wio Bota are two women named Wio and Bota and Mo'an Supung Balen Sina are two men named Supung and Balen Sina whose names are combined as one, as is stylistically often the case in *ngeng ngerang*.

[11] *Ata higi mitan* literally means 'people with black teeth'. The extended form is *ata higi mitan here meran* which means 'people with black, yellow and red teeth'. This phrase refers to the fact that humans are creatures who smoke tobacco and chew betel and areca quids. By smoking and chewing people are distinct from lesser creatures (for example, pigs are said to have white teeth), and are thus 'wise'.

[12] Sugar palm (BI: *enau*) (L: *arenga pinnata/saccharifera*).

[13] This rocky outcrop is located at the centre of Romanduru village.

[14] *Wair wulut* is the name of the Romanduru drinking water spring.

[15] *Wuen* is cognate with *ue* (elder).

[16] This is the *'wisung wangar* of clan Klukut Mudé La'u, located at the bottom of Romanduru village.

[17] This is the *'wisung wangar* of clan Mana, located on the northern side of the village.

[18] A *tadan* (or *tada*) is a spiritual barrier erected around a village with ritual to protect it from harm.

8. A Tale of Two Villages: Hierarchy and precedence in Keo dual organization (Flores, Indonesia)

Gregory Forth

A recent turn in the social anthropology of Austronesian-speaking communities has involved analysis of local social forms with reference to concepts of 'hierarchy' and 'precedence'. In this context, 'hierarchy' more specifically refers to Dumont's notion of 'hierarchical opposition', or 'hierarchical encompassment' (1979, 1980), and particularly a version applied by students of Dumont to several Indonesian societies (see for example, Barraud 1979, Barnes et al. 1985, Pauwels 1990; see also Platenkamp 1990, Forth 2001). Deriving from ethnographic studies by Australian-based anthropologists (for example, Lewis 1988; Molnar 2000; McWilliam 2002; Reuter 2002), 'precedence', a social principle conferring higher status on groups considered the older or oldest components of a social and territorial unity, has largely been conceived as an alternative to 'hierarchy' (see Fox 1994), understood as a relation in which two or more components are differentially related to a social whole. Concerning local forms of dualistic social organization, a pattern widespread and evidently ancient in Austronesia, the present paper demonstrates how hierarchy and precedence, rather than denoting distinct or theoretically contrary principles of order, can define different aspects of one and the same order. Comprising a history of relations among clans and villages in the western part of the Keo region of south central Flores, in eastern Indonesia, the case further reveals ways in which particular hierarchical relations have been contested with reference to different local interpretations of precedence. As I show, single groups commonly participate in a series of hierarchical part-whole relations entailing varying degrees of dependence. And insofar as orders of precedence, also, necessarily pertain to particular spatial wholes, changing residential arrangements can involve local groups participating in more than one such order.

As demonstrated elsewhere (Forth 2001), Keo society is pervasively dualistic. In one of very few published references to Keo, that great missionary-ethnographer of Flores, Paul Arndt (1954:19), remarked on the prevalence of what I have elsewhere called 'double settlements' in the region. 'Double settlement' refers to an arrangement in which two villages (*nua*) are outwardly identical and located adjacent to one another, or at least sufficiently close together to form a palpable pair. While such settlements are indeed typical of Keo, Arndt misconstrued them in two ways. First, he described the settlements as single villages divided into two intermarrying halves. Actually, these 'halves' are separate villages, as signalled and defined by each possessing its own sacrificial instrument, or *peo* — a living tree, forked post or stone column erected in the centre of each village. Secondly, Arndt claimed that the two parts of such settlements (or a pair of villages) were related through a symmetric exchange of women in marriage. In fact, the connection between component villages of a double settlement is thoroughly asymmetrical, in regard to affinal alliance as in other respects.

In one sense, however, Arndt was correct; for in numerous instances, relations connecting paired villages are further reflected within single villages. In part, this replication, or recursion, is attributable to a common historical process whereby over time what were once paired *nua* have become single *nua*. Yet in this same process, additional issues of inequality have arisen. As a single village normally possesses a single sacrificial instrument (*peo*), when two formerly separate groups merge and combine, hierarchy, partly manifest in an order of ritual precedence, must then be realized in relation to this object. Relevant here is the significance of *peo* as symbols of territorial unity and independence. As the site of collective buffalo sacrificing, the sacrificial instrument is the means whereby component parts of a socio-political whole publicly express and affirm claims to parts of the territory in question and thus membership of groups (clans or villages) that possess and maintain the land, not communally, but in concert (Forth 2001:71–72, 79–81; see also Forth 1989, 1998, on the neighbouring Nage).

Key Features of Keo Social Structure

While processes of combination necessitate a realization of hierarchical relations, how this is done — that is, how unequal status has been construed or constituted — varies from place to place. In order to shed light on this variation (and the competing local views implicated in it), it is useful to concentrate on a single case. To do so effectively, it will be necessary first of all to review other general details of Keo village society.

Most Keo villages (*nua*) comprise two or more clans (*suku*), usually no more than three or four.[1] Where several groups (which may be clans, or formally separate and locally distinct divisions of a clan, or 'houses') share a single *peo*, two are always pre-eminent. At the same time, the two are themselves unequal. The seniormost group, or more precisely its male leader, holds the status of 'trunk rider' (*saka pu'u*) or 'earth breaker' (*ta koe*). It is he who rides on the trunk (that is, the lowermost) end of a new sacrificial post when the object is carried — trunk end first — into the village. As the second designation would suggest, the leader of the seniormost group is also the first to stab the earth when digging the hole in which to plant a new sacrificial instrument. The precedence of the leading group finds further expression in buffalo sacrificing, since the animal provided by the trunk rider (or earth breaker) is always the first to be killed.

In all of these respects the leader of the second group, called the 'tip rider' (*saka lobo*), makes his appearance directly after the trunk rider. In accordance with the local title, he occupies the tip end of a new post (*peo*). Designated as the 'excavator' (*ta kabhe*), this man also scoops up a little of the earth first broken by his more senior partner. Similarly, his buffalo is slaughtered immediately after the animal contributed by the trunk rider (or earth breaker). In collective sacrifices, the buffalo of other groups are then slaughtered, each in a definite sequence decided or affirmed in advance of the ritual.[2]

For the benefit of Indonesianists especially, it should be remarked that the opposition of trunk rider and tip rider does not define or coincide with a contrast of religious and temporal authority. Nevertheless, the two positions — equally religious and equally political — do figure as a major instance of a more general opposition of 'trunk, origin, source' (*pu'u*) and 'tip' (*lobo*) operating as a fundamental principle of Keo social order. Closely bound up with their shared relationship with sacrificial posts, trees, or columns, these positions of dual leadership can be assigned on the basis of agnatic seniority within clans. Where a *peo* is the possession of a single clan (*suku*), the trunk rider will then belong to the seniormost house (*sa'o*) of the clan while the tip rider will be found in the next junior house. Particularly where two previously separate clans have come together in a single village, however, the statuses are usually connected with residential priority, so that the group recognized as having been the first to settle in the village territory, and to have founded the village, is recognized as trunk rider, and thus the principal 'owner' (*moi*) of a shared sacrificial instrument (*peo*).

Especially where segments (or houses) of a single clan divide statuses of trunk rider and tip rider, the two positions are distinguished respectively as *ka'e*, 'senior, elder', and *ari,* 'junior, younger'. The partial coincidence of this binary relation with that of 'trunk (or source, origin)' and 'tip' is in each case consistent with the temporal precedence of the superior term. Just as a botanical trunk is always older than the tip (or branches), so elder sibling always precedes younger. *Ka'e* and *ari*, however, have a far broader application in Keo social classification than in articulating the asymmetric contrast 'trunk' and 'tip'. When compounded as *ka'e ari*, the two terms together denote a reciprocal relationship shared by members of a single clan or of a clan segment occupying a single village; in fact, in its most inclusive sense the compound can refer to any kind of social bond or unity, the parties to which are moreover not necessarily distinguishable as 'senior' and 'junior' (Forth 2001:99–104). In a few instances, the terms are further applied to pairs of distinctly named clans occupying separate villages but recognizing a common origin. Connections between Bale and Bolo, two groups to be discussed presently, provide an instance of this variant of *ka'e ari*.

Besides the opposition of trunk rider and tip rider, residential priority, or temporal precedence, is bound up with another fundamental binary contrast. This is the opposition of 'mother' (*ine*) and 'child' (*ana*). Whereas in regard to sacrificial posts (*peo*) the contrast of 'trunk' (*pu'u*) and 'tip' (*lobo*) is internal to villages, however, the contrast of 'mother' and 'child' is largely external. The main instance of the opposition is the relation of 'land mother' (*ine tana*) and 'defending child' (*ana tuku*).[3] 'Land mother' — or more completely 'mother of the land, father of the stones' (*ine tana, ame watu*) — denotes the ancestor or group considered to have been the first to occupy and divide a territory among a number of 'children' or 'defenders'. By virtue of this division, all 'defending children' receive the right to found their own villages (*nua*) and erect their own *peo*. In the same way, they come to be recognized, or to affirm their status, as members — and prospectively, ancestors — of independent clans. In return the defenders, as their name should suggest, are obliged to assist in protecting the entire territory of the 'mother' against intruders and hence to maintain its boundaries.

As represented in Keo oral history, such transfers of independent rights to land frequently accompanied the marriage of a woman of the land mother clan to a male forbear of a defending group. In this way, the status of 'defending child' (*ana tuku*) is regularly associated with that of 'wife-taker', a status similarly conceived under a filial rubric as *ana weta* ('children of sisters'). How far such affinal connections have been perpetuated by way of further marriages over the generations is variable. Furthermore, obtaining wives from another group has by no means always involved simultaneously obtaining rights to land; hence 'wife-taker' is a rather more inclusive category than is 'defending child'.

In response to direct questioning, Keo usually say that the terms 'mother' and 'child' when applied to two clans always specify them as land mother and defender. Yet observation reveals that the contrast of *ine* and *ana* is sometimes employed in another, looser way. As demonstrated by the case to be discussed, a group may be described as the 'mother' of another purely on the basis of temporal precedence within a shared territory (a village or double settlement). In such instances, the older group, though it may provide the more recent immigrant with wives and even a share of its land, does not — indeed cannot — grant the latter a sacrificial instrument (*peo*) of its own. Granting the right to erect a *peo* to a group that previously did not independently possess a sacrificial instrument is indeed a prerogative of the land mother. On the other hand, where two groups merge to form a single village, the earlier established group usually shares its own sacrificial instrument with the more recent arrival, granting it the right to slaughter, and possibly another ceremonial status (for example, the position of tip rider) as well, while retaining the seniormost position for itself.

Especially in view of the partial coincidence of 'wife-givers' (*moi mame* or *moi ga'e*) and 'land-givers', much of the foregoing will be quite familiar to students of Indonesian societies. But two points are worth stressing. First, while the contrast of 'trunk' and 'tip' and that of 'mother' and 'child' largely pertain to distinct relationships, a certain connection is discernible in an association of wife-givers with the concept of 'trunk', or *pu'u*. That is, in Keo, as in other parts of eastern Indonesia, wife-givers are conceived as the trunk, origin, or source of their wife-taking affines (see for example, Barnes 1974, Fox 1980; Forth 1981:286–290, Forth 2001:125ff; Lewis 1988). Secondly, and consistent with these parallels, instances of all three category pairs — trunk and tip, mother and child, and wife-giver and wife-taker — are linked with images implying a relation of whole and part, and hence a subsumption or conceptual encompassment of a subordinate entity by its superordinate partner.

Without rehearsing all ethnographic particulars, we might for example note that a land mother retains nominal dominion over an entire territory, even though parts are formally ceded to 'defending children' who, as a category, are then identified with the boundary or peripheries of the domain. In formal speech, defenders are thus described as 'those who occupy the edge and reside at the end' (*ndi'i singi, mera sepu*). Noteworthy here is the way in which a whole-part relation is translated into a contrast of centre and periphery. Equally remarkable is the tendency, where two or more clans share a single village, for the oldest and senior group (the 'mother', if not the 'land mother') to be identified with the village as a whole. The clearest expression of this is where the entire village and the oldest clan bear the same name. Thus, in numerous instances, a village named X contains a clan also named X as well as a more junior clan named Y (Forth 2001:84–86, 297–298).

The same part-whole relationship is further evident in the asymmetric affinal connection that is regularly associated with various other non-reciprocal relations. Simply stated, in several ways Keo represent wife-takers as parts of a wife-giving group. To begin with, there is the notion of *poro* or *dhodho* which, although both terms translate directly as 'descent' (or 'to go down'), actually refers to inherited affinal connexion, or 'alliance'. It does so by virtue of an identification of a child (*ana*) with its mother (*ine*), and hence with the female component of a social whole commonly specified as a house (*sa'o*). Thus, just as a woman, upon her marriage, 'descends' from her raised, natal house to proceed to the residence of her husband, so Keo envisage her children as having descended with their mother from the wife-giver's house (Forth 2001:130–133).[4]

As mentioned above, Keo history demonstrates how initially separate groups (clans or villages) have amalgamated, forming together single villages. In the course of time, external dualities (including land mother and defender) have thereby become transformed into internal ones. Permitting, even facilitating, this process is the conceptual encompassment articulating fundamental binary relations. In some instances, amalgamation occurred after the advent of the colonial period, effectively beginning around 1910. In fact, evidence I review below suggests how institutions of colonial (and subsequent national) administration have affected particular hierarchical outcomes. Nevertheless, it is quite clear from other evidence that recent village amalgamations must be understood as continuing manifestations of a process that is much older and is definitely pre-colonial in origin.

Map 1. Map of Western Keo

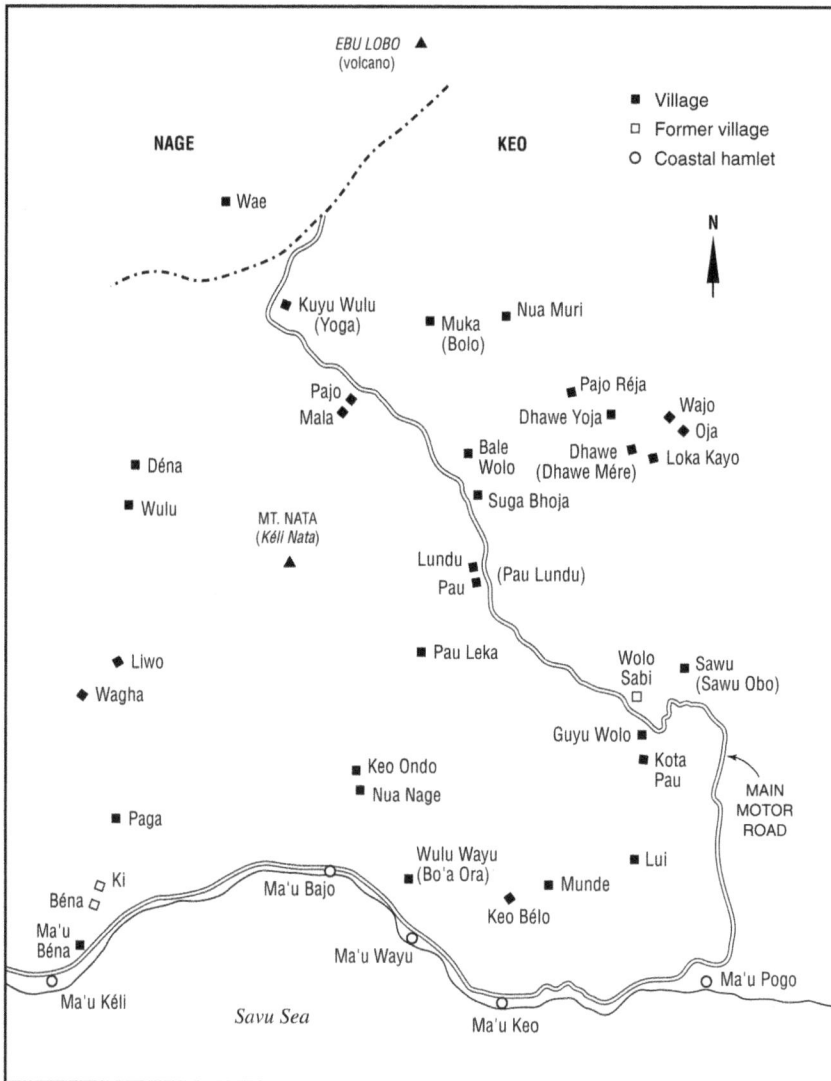

The village of Pajo Wawo (Upper Pajo Mala)

In what follows I show how historical processes of combination have raised questions, leading to local contestations, of hierarchical order internal to a particular village. With reference to the same case, I also demonstrate how arrangements in place at any given time must be understood as merely the most recent outcome of ongoing competition concerning the application, in particular contexts, of basic principles of Keo social organization. Insofar as dualistic social arrangements form the focus of this analysis, dualism must therefore be understood as a tendency and process and not as a static institutional form.

Figure 1. Stylized plan of the double settlement of Upper and Lower Pajo Mala

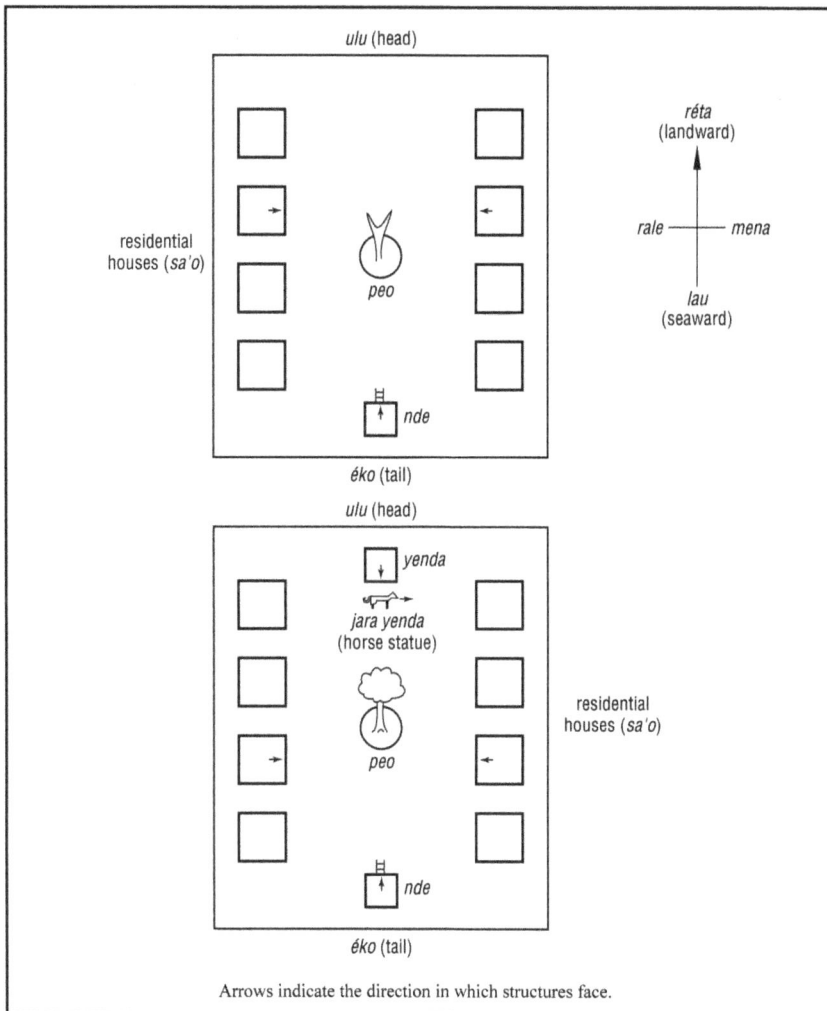

When viewed from the main road that winds above their present sites, the villages of Upper and Lower Pajo Mala might appear the very model of a double settlement (see Figure 1). Possessing a sacrificial instrument (*peo*) in the form of a stone column, the older village, Lower Pajo Mala (Pajo Au), is located immediately seaward of Upper Pajo Mala (Pajo Wawo), whose centre is marked with a forked wooden *peo*. According to the usual local representation, each of the two villages contains three clans. The principal clan in the older village is Pajo Wolo ('Hill Pajo'), a group that appears to have lent its name by antithesis to the whole village and hence to the entire double settlement (Pajo Mala, 'Pajo of the Plain'). It is joined by clans Kayo (or Pajo Kayo) and Bindi Wae.[5] The trio inhabiting Upper Pajo Mala consists of clan Kate plus the Upper and Lower divisions of a group called Bale, each of which is recognized as a separate clan. At the same time, Upper and Lower Bale together are sometimes described as a single 'clan', and in other ways as well the two groups compose a unity combining dualistically with Kate.

Despite appearances, both the manifestly binary combination of Lower and Upper Pajo Mala and their formal symmetry are relatively new, having originated in the colonial period just 80 to 90 years ago. Before this, Lower Pajo Mala — which was then the only village named Pajo Mala — stood alone. At this time, Kate and the two divisions of Bale were resident some distance to the west, in another double settlement named Kate Bale.

The history of Kate Bale and its transformation into Upper Pajo Mala is the main focus of this paper. In what is virtually the only colonial report providing detailed and substantial information on indigenous social organization in the administrative region that came to be known as 'Nage Keo', in 1940 the Dutch official Louis Fontijne described the clan Kate as the earliest known group to inhabit the southern part of the Nage district of Wolo Wea (Forth 2004). From there, the ancestors of Kate several generations previously had been driven out of their original villages of Wolo Kate and Kate Kela by their enemies, the ancestors of Kéli Mado, another Nage domain, located to the south of Wolo Wea. Fleeing from their villages of origin, the Kate people moved further south and westwards, towards the western part of Keo where their present descendants are now found in the village of Upper Pajo Mala.

While Fontijne says no more than this, his report corresponds in all essentials to the history of Kate as told to me by Kate people in the 1990s. After arriving in Keo, the Kate leader, Léwa Dhéma, settled temporarily on land belonging to clan Bindi Wae, one of the present inhabitants of Lower Pajo Mala. Following one version of the Kate genealogy, Léwa Dhéma took a wife from Bale (specifically the clan Upper Bale), who were already settled in the vicinity in a village called Nua Bale ('Bale Village') or One Bale (*one* is 'inside, interior', and can thus mean 'place of'). Other evidence suggests that marriages between Kate and Bale began two generations after Kate's arrival. Whatever the precise details, an early union between a Kate man and a Bale woman initiated an asymmetric affinal alliance between the two groups that has since been perpetuated by at least seven further marriages. Kate genealogies show Léwa Dhéma living eight generations prior to the present Kate leader, a man now in his seventies. If a generation is estimated as 25 to 30 years, the removal of the Kate people to western Keo would therefore appear to have occurred between 200 and 300 years ago.

Connected with Kate becoming a wife-taker of Bale — either as precedent or antecedent — Mepe Lape, the son of Léwa Dhéma, moved with other Kate people to a new site near the village of the Bale people (Nua Bale). Since wife-givers are often also land-givers, it should be stressed that Kate did *not* receive land from Bale. Rather, in addition to plots previously obtained from the clan Bindi Wae, Kate acquired rights to further areas of land within the territory of Lape, the seniormost 'land mother' in the whole of western Keo. At the same time, Kate people describe their ancestors as having obtained land from Lape with the support and mediation of Bale. The land in question had initially been assigned to Pajo Wolo, one of the most important 'defending children' of Lape and the leading clan in Lower Paja Mala. Upon founding its own village, the Bale group also had acquired lands within the domain of Lape. Hence, in regard to territorial rights, Kate and Bale were, and remain, generally of equal standing. After founding a double settlement with Bale, the new village established by Kate was simply named Nua Kate ('Kate Village') and the entire settlement was designated, in a typically binary fashion, as 'Kate Bale'.

Owing to its prior occupation of the older half of Kate Bale, the Bale group (which as noted nowadays comprises two clans) is commonly described as the 'mother' while Kate, the latter arrival, is accordingly the 'child'. Bale is not however considered land mother in relation to Kate. That status is occupied — in relation to Bale as well as Kate — by the clan of Lape, although in certain contexts it is Pajo Wolo, as the principal 'defending child' of Lape in this part of Lape's ancestral territory, that is so designated.[6] As the foregoing reveals, while Bale was older than Kate in Kate Bale, both groups are relatively recent arrivals in western Keo. Bale in fact represents the most recent of several waves of immigration from Ola Bolo ('Place of Bolo'), a settlement located in what is now the eastern part of the Ngadha district. Earlier immigrants from Ola Bolo were a group that retained the name Bolo and which at present resides in the village of Muka (also known as Bolo), some distance landward of Upper Pajo Mala. Like Bale, Bolo too comprises a pair of clans, similarly distinguished as Upper Bolo (the more senior group) and Lower Bolo.[7] In respect of their common geographical origin in Ola Bolo, the two clans of Bale and the two of Bolo together compose a grouping known as 'Bolo Bale'. Within this non-localized dualistic whole, Bale is the junior component and, in ways I describe presently, is still politically and ritually subordinate to Bolo. Indeed, Bolo and Bale continue to operate in certain contexts as a single corporate entity, even to the extent of assigning heirs, when necessary, to houses and estates of the opposite group. Moreover, insofar as Bolo tends to be identified with the whole which is named 'Bolo Bale', it would not be inaccurate to describe Bale as a junior segment of Bolo.[8]

Also relevant in this connection is a period of co-residence with Bolo, after Bale first arrived in western Keo, in an earlier village also named Bolo (or, more completely, Bolo Ndata). Later, the Bolo group founded another village, adjacent to the village of Yoga, thus forming a double settlement known as Bolo Yoga, and about the same time Bale removed some distance landwards to establish its own village of Nua Bale. As noted, in order for a village to be ceremonially complete and independent it must possess a sacrificial instrument (*peo*). By all indications, however, the Bale people, while residing alone in Nua Bale, did not possess a *peo* of their own. Indeed, they appear to have first erected such an object only when they founded Upper Pajo Mala, just 70-odd years ago. Although this settlement is spoken of as Nua Bale, this circumstance thus casts some doubt on its formal status as a *nua*, or 'village'. At the same time, Bale's lack of a sacrificial instrument (*peo*) is quite consistent with the group's continuing subordination to Bolo, a matter to which I return in a moment.

Especially in regard to its sacrificial status, Kate's circumstances upon arriving in western Keo were quite different from Bale's. One version of the clan's genealogy indicates that Kate erected a *peo* in its own separate village of Nua Kate just two generations after settling there. As this would suggest, the paired statuses of trunk rider and tip rider connected with the sacrificial instrument were then both occupied exclusively by men of clan Kate, which by this time had bifurcated to form two separate 'houses', one identified with the trunk rider and the other with the tip rider. Indeed, as trunk and tip riders must always come from separate houses and estates, Kate's erecting and inauguration of a *peo* was likely the occasion of this bifurcation. Reckoning genealogical time in the way specified earlier, the evidence suggests that Kate erected their *peo* sometime in the early or middle part of the nineteenth century.

Since several kinds of sacrificial instruments are in use in the Keo region, it is important to note that the *peo* Kate claim independently to have erected in Nua Kate was a *peo yebu*, a carved forked post of Cassia wood (*yebu, Cassia fistula*). As this is the sort employed throughout the Nage region, Kate's claim to rightful possession of such a post thus agrees with the clan's geographical derivation from southeastern Nage. Although resident in an immediately adjacent settlement, the Bale people never slaughtered buffalo at Kate's post; if ever they did so it was only as invited guests and not as a matter of right. Within their own former village of Nua Bale, in order to affirm their independent ownership of land Bale performed sacrifices without the aid of a *peo* by employing only *yaka* and *ia*, structures after which the two divisions, or clans, of Bale are still regularly named.[9] As subordinates of Bolo, moreover, Bale were obliged to participate in buffalo sacrifices in the village of Bolo.

The evidence of local history thus indicates that, within the double settlement of Kate Bale, the clan Kate enjoyed not only ceremonial independence from Bale but, since only they possessed a *peo*, a kind of superiority as well. Towards the beginning of the twentieth century, however, relations between Kate and Bale underwent a fundamental change. At this time, people of Kate Bale began moving to the site of what is now Upper Pajo Mala. The first to do so were people of Bale, whose previous village (Nua Bale) had suffered serious damage in a landslide sometime after 1910. Kate moved later. Following local estimates, the entire move was completed, and Kate Bale became entirely abandoned, around 1927. Before this time, the site of Upper Pajo Mala had been a hamlet (*bo'a*) containing field houses belonging to people of Lower Pajo Mala and was ceded to Bale and Kate by the leading clan in the lower village, Pajo Wolo.

In accordance with the relative disposition of the former Nua Kate and Nua Bale within the double settlement, upon moving to Upper Pajo Mala the Kate people built their houses towards the seaward end of the settlement, while Bale settled at the landward end. It must be stressed, however, that with this move, what had previously been two villages (*nua*) — Kate and Bale — became a single village. On the other hand, by locating the settlement just above Pajo Mala, which subsequently became Lower Pajo Mala, the new village became part of another dual combination in which Kate and Bale together were subordinated to the earlier established member of the pair — Lower Pajo Mala (Pajo Au).

To understand the subsequent course of events, it must first be noted that the movement of Kate people to Upper Pajo Mala and their amalgamation with Bale was encouraged by local leaders appointed by the colonial administration. Prominent among these was Lowa Bule, the 'major mandur' (*mando mére*) of the colonial subdistrict which included both Kate Bale and Pajo Mala.[10] A man of the clan Bo Bana in the village of Pau Lundu (located several kilometres seaward of Pajo Mala), Lowa Bule was a wife-taker of Bale, more specifically of Lower Bale (Bale Au). Largely in his position as 'mandur', the same man was also influential in the decision, taken not long after 1927, to erect a forked sacrificial post (*peo*) in Upper Pajo Mala. To obtain such a post, goods conceived as a bridewealth must be given to the owner of the land where the symbolically feminine tree is cut. Both Bale and Kate contributed to this bridewealth, with Bale supplying a buffalo, and Kate a pair of gold ornaments and a knife. Kate and Bale thereby both obtained rights in the sacrificial post. For reasons already explained, however, the two groups would necessarily share in the post unequally.

So it was that a forked *peo* of Cassia wood was obtained and erected in Upper Pajo Mala in 1929. But before this could be done, decisions had to be taken as to who would serve as trunk rider and who as tip rider. Citing the fact that only they had possessed a *peo* in the previous settlement of Kate Bale, and moreover a forked post of precisely the same kind as the one to be erected, people of clan Kate claimed that they should occupy both positions. In addition, and by virtue of this possession, the clan was already divided into segments identified with the two ceremonial statuses. In the event, however, and with crucial support from the aforementioned Lowa Bule, the people of Bale successfully claimed that men of their group should be recognized as riders of both the trunk and the tip of the new *peo*. In this arrangement, the division of Bale into Upper and Lower clans came into play, with Upper Bale, the senior group, occupying the position of trunk rider. According to one local formulation, then, what had previously been the *peo* of Kate (in Kate Bale) became the *peo* of Bale. Worth noting in this connection is the fact that the post planted in 1929 — like its replacement, erected in September 1991 — is still referred to as the *peo* of Kate Bale, a name that in fact is still occasionally applied to the modern village of Upper Pajo Mala.

According to another argument, advanced by Kate people when I discussed the matter with them in the 1990s, while Upper Bale acquired the position of trunk rider in 1929, both Lower Bale and Kate were jointly recognized as tip rider. In regard to the shape of the forked post — consisting of a single trunk but two branches — this interpretation has a certain plausibility. Nevertheless, it controverts the consistently dualistic form of ritual organization relating to any *peo*, and for this reason was rejected by others involved in the debate.

Bale's claim to both the trunk and the tip of the sacrificial post erected in 1929 is less explicitly rationalized than the unsuccessful counter-claim of Kate. Even so, it is clear that Bale's earlier occupation of Upper Pajo Mala counted in their favour, as did the fact that they were settled in Nua Bale before Kate people founded Nua Kate. But Bale's right to erect a forked *peo* of Cassia wood, the same sort previously possessed by Kate, is less firmly grounded. Implicitly, it is based on a conception of the *peo* in Kate Bale, more precisely in Nua Kate, as a joint possession of both Bale and Kate, reinforced by a view of Upper Pajo Mala as the successor of the double settlement. According to a more explicit, and quite different, local interpretation, by erecting a forked post Bale were merely following the precedent of their senior relatives, the group called Bolo, who had erected a *peo* of the same kind in the village of Muka sometime before this, probably early in the twentieth century. In fact, in relation to their own *peo*, the Bolo people regard the forked post in Upper Pajo Mala as a 'branch *peo*' (*peo taya*), that is, one that has 'grown out of' and is subsidiary to the *peo* belonging to Bolo.

This connection with Bolo, however, raises another contentious issue, namely, whether Bale, being subordinate to Bolo, was fully justified, in 1929, in erecting a *peo* of any sort. Kate's position on this point goes without saying. But there is yet another twist. Some local sources argue that Bolo itself had no obvious right to employ a forked Cassia wood *peo*, since prior to their removing to Muka, Bolo had possessed a sacrificial instrument of another sort — a living *kesi* tree, a *peo muri* ('living *peo*') planted in the centre of Bolo's section of the former double settlement of Bolo Yoga. Whatever force temporal precedence may have had in advancing Bale's claim to the primary positions of trunk and tip rider, moreover, it appears that what was crucial to its realization was the involvement of an outsider, Lowa Bule, whose influence partly derived from his occupying an administrative position completely foreign to the cultural framework in which decisions regarding the hierarchical positioning of individuals and groups in relation to sacrificial posts are traditionally taken.

If Bale's claim was compromised by its subordination to Bolo, Bolo in turn remains subordinate to clan Yoga (in the context of the former double settlement of Bolo Yoga), which is one of the principal 'defending children' (*ana tuku*) of land mother Lape. Viewed in this way, Bale is as it were three times subordinated. And by the same token, the clan is at least twice subsumed — in Bolo Bale and thence in Bolo Yoga. Kate, on the other hand, has the hypothetical advantage of having come to western Keo out of a socio-political and cultural 'nowhere', successfully maintaining along the way, or at least until its removal to Upper Pajo Mala, a major symbol of independence, a forked *peo*, originating in its country of origin. In this regard, then, Kate need recognize the ceremonial precedence only of the land mother, Lape. And insofar as Kate's *peo* was not in fact granted by Lape, they need recognize the ceremonial precedence of no one at all.

Characteristically, Keo villagers point to physical objects as 'evidence' (usually expressed with the Indonesian term 'bukti') of historical processes and their outcomes in present-day social configurations. While Bale may have been able in 1929 to erect a *peo*, the continuing subordination of Bale to Bolo is visibly manifest in the absence of a ceremonial building called *yenda*, which one might expect to find at the landward extremity of Upper Pajo Mala. Present in all villages with a claim to be truly complete and fully independent in sacrificial matters, the *yenda* is a building adorned with a wooden horse statue (*jara yenda*; see Figure 1) and used to store the skulls and horns of buffalo sacrificed at the *peo*. As a structure thus complementary to a sacrificial post, in parallelistic speech the former is named together with the latter, as *peo yenda*.

As the junior component of Bolo Bale, however, even today the Bale people are obliged to take the heads of buffalo they slaughter in Upper Pajo Mala to the village of Muka. Once reduced to horns and skulls, these are then placed in the *yenda* belonging to Bolo. Kate, on the other hand, is under no such obligation. Horns and skulls of buffalo they slaughter are stored in a similar building called *nde*, which stands at the seaward end of Upper Pajo Mala and replaces another structure of this sort formerly maintained by Kate in Nua Kate. Since trophy horns are normally kept in *yenda*, the *nde* being used for other purposes, this practice of Kate's is somewhat irregular. Yet it makes perfect sense in respect of the relationship between Kate and Bale since the establishment of Upper Pajo Mala, as well as in the context of Bale's continuing dependence upon Bolo.

In 1991, a further revision of these relationships took place. By this time the *peo* erected in 1929 was badly rotted, and it was decided that a replacement had to be found.[11] As always when people need to obtain a new *peo*, all interested parties had to review the question of who should serve as trunk rider and who as tip rider. Without going into detail, it may be sufficient to note that, by this time, the clan Kate had recovered some of the political ground it had lost to Bale in, or sometime before, 1929. When I first discussed the matter with them, Kate people were still claiming that, by rights, it was they who should occupy the position of trunk rider, and that the most Bale could claim was the position of tip rider. Yet they were apparently willing to compromise; and in the event the tip was ridden by Kate and the trunk by Bale (specifically Upper Bale). Thus whereas, previously, Bale had gained control of both principal positions associated with the sacrificial post, now one at least, the junior of the pair, had been assigned to Kate.

Since I have already demonstrated how the presence or absence of physical objects can serve as a visible sign of the status of a settlement and internal relations among its component groups, it should further be noted how the revision of relations between Bale and Kate in 1991 finds expression in the outward form of the new *peo* post, more particularly in certain items ancillary to the wooden structure. Prior to 1991, at the base of the old post and atop the platform of stones that surrounded it, were planted three short upright stone pillars called *ia* (like the object always planted seaward of a *peo*).These represented the three clans that composed Upper Pajo Mala, and that were able to sacrifice at the post as a matter of right, namely, Upper Bale and Lower Bale (the trunk and tip rider respectively) and Kate. After the new *peo* was erected, however, four upright stones were erected around the post. What is more, the new stones were explained not with reference to component clans, but to the ceremonial positions associated with the post. Specifically, two stones represent the trunk and tip riders, thus respectively Upper Bale and the senior segment of Kate, while the other two are identified with Lower Bale and a more junior segment of Kate (specified as occupants of two lesser ceremonial statuses that figure in rites performed when obtaining a new *peo*; see Forth 2001:62 note 9). The stone identified with the trunk rider, Upper Bale, is noticeably larger than the other three; in addition, being located on the landward side (or towards the 'head' of the village) and on what is arguably the right side of the *peo* post, it also occupies a position superior to the other three stones. Nevertheless, whereas Kate previously appeared as a poor third within the triad of clans occupying Upper Pajo Mala, as the new set of stones attests Kate has achieved a kind of numerical parity with Bale, even though the clan remains subordinate to Upper if not to Lower Bale.

Conclusion

Ongoing competition between Bale and Kate reveals the importance of temporal precedence — who arrived in a place first — in determining hierarchical relations within dualistic wholes in western Keo. Bale's main claim to a superordinate position in relation to Kate rested largely, and reasonably securely, on its having been the older component of the double settlement named Kate Bale, and indeed the first to arrive in the village of Upper Pajo Mala as well. Yet simple chronological priority is not always sufficient to ensure precedence in a fuller sense. In Keo, precedence rests on establishing a part-whole relation in which the superordinate member of a pair or series is first (or original) in relation to a clearly defined whole. In this regard, Bale suffers from two weaknesses. First, when joined by Kate to form Kate Bale, Bale was not the principal group within the wider territory in which Kate was subsequently included. Indeed, the lands that made up the domain of Kate Bale derived from other sources and from other groups exercising prior claims. Secondly, Bale appears to have been unable to claim precedence in relation to the whole of Kate Bale owing, at least in part, to its continuing subordination to — indeed, its encompassment by — yet another group, namely Bolo. As shown with reference to the structure called *yenda*, ceremonial incompleteness in Keo can signal a group's standing as a subordinate part of a whole external to the village. 'Wholeness' might therefore be described as a precondition for superordinate status or, equating hierarchy with encompassment (as does Dumont 1979), identification with another kind of 'whole'.

In Keo society, hierarchy, understood as a part-whole relation wherein a greater part conceptually subsumes a lesser, normally coincides with precedence, conceived in the first instance as chronological priority. Yet, as in the case just reviewed, the two values can sometimes figure as competing principles in determining relationships that can be conceived in terms of either hierarchy or precedence. In both Kate Bale and Upper Pajo Mala, Bale was first (and in this respect could claim precedence). Yet in relation to neighbouring groups, Kate has always been less encompassed than Bale, and thus less subordinated.

Bale's incompleteness and subordination to Bolo bears on another feature of Keo traditional order highlighted by the present case. Often, localized dualities can only be understood in relation to long-standing connections with groups outside of villages or double settlements, or what, as the grouping called 'Bolo

Bale' exemplifies, may be described as non-localized dualities. In other words, a group (usually specifiable as a 'clan') can participate in a number of dualisms of varying contextual relevance which are nevertheless potentially connected one with another. At a conceptual level, this connection corresponds to the overlap, or partial coincidence, of such widespread Austronesian category pairs as 'mother/child' (*ine/ana*), 'trunk/tip' (*pu'u/lobo*), 'elder/younger' (*ka'e/ari*), and 'wife-giver/wife-taker' (*moi mame/ana weta*). At the same time, how relations between actual social groups — often reflecting processes of combination rather than bifurcation — are at any given time interpreted in reference to these contrasts may reflect political forces and processes that are relatively independent of this conceptual order, and are based upon other values.

References

Arndt, Paul SVD

1954 *Gesellschaftliche Verhaltnisse der Ngadha*. Studia Instituti Anthropos Vol. 8. Wien-Mödling: Verlag der Missionsdruckerei St. Gabriel.

Barnes, R.H.

1974 *Kédang: a study of the collective thought of an eastern Indonesian people*. Oxford: Clarendon Press.

Barnes, R.H, Daniel de Coppet, and R.J. Parkin (eds)

1985 *Contexts and levels: anthropological essays on hierarchy* (JASO Occasional Papers No. 4). Oxford: *JASO* (*Journal of the Anthropological Society of Oxford*).

Barraud, Cécile

1979 *Tanebar-Evav: une société des maisons tournée vers le large*. Cambridge: Cambridge University Press/Paris: Editions de la Maison des Sciences de l'Homme.

Dumont, Louis

1979 The anthropological community and ideology. *Social Science Information* (Sage: London and Beverly Hills) 18(6):785–817.

1980 *Homo hierarchicus: the caste system and its implications*. Complete revised English edition. Chicago: The University of Chicago Press.

Forth, Gregory

1981 *Rindi: an ethnographic study of a traditional domain in eastern Sumba*. Koninklijk Instituut voor Taal-, Land- en Volkenkunde, Verhandelingen 93. The Hague: Martinus Nijhoff.

1989 The pa sése festival of the Nage of Bo'a Wae (central Flores). In C. Barraud and J. Platenkamp (eds), *Ritual and socio-cosmic order in eastern Indonesian societies. Part I, Nusa Tenggara Timur. Bijdragen tot de Taal-, Land- en Volkenkunde* 145(4):502-519.

1998 *Beneath the volcano: religion, cosmology and spirit classification among the Nage of eastern Indonesia*. Koninklijk Instituut voor Taal-, Land- en Volkenkunde, Verhandelingen 177. Leiden: KITLV Press.

2001 *Dualism and hierarchy: processes of binary combination in Keo society*. Oxford: Oxford University Press.

2004 *Guardians of the land in Kelimado: Louis Fontijne's study of a colonial district in eastern Indonesia*. Edited and translated by Gregory Forth with the assistance of Han F. Vermeulen. Leiden: KITLV Press.

Fox, James J.

1994 Reflections on 'hierarchy' and 'precedence'. In M. Jolly and M. Mosko (eds), *Transformations of hierarchy: structure, history, and horizon in the Austronesian world*. *History and Anthropology* (Special Issue) 7:87–108.

Fox, James J. (ed.)

1980 *The flow of life: essays on eastern Indonesia*. Cambridge, MA: Harvard University Press.

Lewis, E.D.

1988 *People of the source: the social and ceremonial order of Tana Wai Brama on Flores*. Verhandelingen van het Koninklijk Instituut voor Taal-, Land- en Volkenkunde 135. Dordrecht, Holland/Providence, USA: Foris Publications.

McWilliam, A.R.

2002 *Paths of origin, gates of life: a study of place and precedence in southwest Timor*. Verhandelingen van het Koninklijk Instituut voor Taal-, Land- en Volkenkunde 202. Leiden: KITLV Press.

Molnar, Andrea K.

2000 *Grandchildren of the Ga'e ancestors: social organization and cosmology among the Hoga Sara of Flores*. Koninklijk Instituut voor Taal-, Land- en Volkenkunde, Verhandelingen 185. Leiden: KITLV Press.

Pauwels, Simonne

1990 From Hursu Ribun's 'Three hearth stones'. In C. Barraud and J. Platenkamp (eds), *Ritual and socio-cosmic order in eastern Indonesian societies, Part II, Maluku. Bijdragen tot de Taal-, Land- en Volkenkunde* 146(1):21–34.

Platenkamp J.D.M.

1990 The severance of the origin: a ritual of the Tobelo of North Halmahera. In C. Barraud and J. Platenkamp (eds), *Ritual and socio-cosmic order in eastern Indonesian societies. Part II, Maluku. Bijdragen tot de Taal-, Land-en Volkenkunde* 146(1):74–92.

Reuter, T.A.

2002 *The house of our ancestors: precedence and dualism in highland Balinese society.* Koninklijk Instituut voor Taal-, Land- en Volkenkunde, Verhandelingen 198. Leiden: KITLV Press.

ENDNOTES

[1] Derived from Malay, *suku* is the term Keo most often use for 'clan', even when speaking their own language. Reputedly older terms (which at present have more currency in other parts of central Flores) are *woe* and *'ili woe*. Affiliation to clans is normally patrilineal, with the majority of men paying bridewealth to the wife's clan and thereby securing the incorporation of children to their own clan.

[2] This description is necessarily condensed. Trunk rider and tip rider refer specifically to functionaries connected with forked posts of Cassia wood. Earth breaker and excavator on the other hand are the equivalent positions when a living tree or stone column is employed as a *peo*. However, when a forked *peo* is erected, the trunk rider serves as earth breaker as well. In accordance with the case discussed below, I hereafter speak only of trunk rider and tip rider.

[3] 'Defending child' is mostly a convenient gloss. *Tuku* means to 'shut off, out' and 'to bar, dam (up)', thus conveying the image of a protective barrier. As Austronesianists will recognize, *ana* has a wider range of meanings than 'child', generally conveying ideas of subordination, relative smallness, and membership of a collectivity.

[4] *Ana weta* are thus not just 'children' of 'sisters'; they are in a definite sense also 'children' of the wife-giving group, and belong to it by virtue of their relation to the group's female members who retain a connection to their natal house. In the expression *ana weta*, moreover, *ana* ('child') refers not just to offspring but to 'descendants' of (or through) women (Forth 2001:115–117).

[5] Bindi Wae is itself a dual composition, comprising Bindi and descendants of its wife-taker, a segment of the clan Wae.

[6] The clan of Lape, the foremost ancestor, is actually called Céla, but it is more usually the ancestor, Lape, rather than his clan that is specified as the land mother.

[7] Like Upper Pajo Mala, the village of Muka (Bolo) also includes a third (and in this case decidedly subordinate) group: the clan Suga. In fact, it is quite usual in Keo to find settlements locally represented as comprising two groups but which nevertheless include a third and sometimes a fourth separately named component (Forth 2001:301–303).

[8] Bale men publicly and formally introduce themselves as 'Bolo Bale' when they slaughter buffalo in Muka, the present village of the Bolo people. Keo sometimes refers to Bolo Bale as a 'clan' (*suku*). The usage illustrates the relativity of the concept of *suku*, which as noted is also applied to the two divisions of Bale conceived as a unity. The same relativity characterizes *nua* ('village'), used both for single villages and for double settlements comprising two villages.

[9] *Yaka* denotes a bamboo lattice erected seaward of a sacrificial post, column, or tree. It is through the *yaka* that the tethers of sacrificial buffalo are placed. *Ia* refers to a vertical stone or stake erected on the landward side of a *peo*, to which the ends of the tethers are tied. Upper Bale (Bale Yape Wawo) is thus alternatively known as Bale Yape Ia, and Upper Bale (Bale Yape Au) as Bale Yape Yaka.

[10] 'Mandur' is usually translated as 'foreman'. In central Flores, 'major mandur' referred to a native official assigned to execute the orders of the native headman of a sub-district.

[11] Whereas *peo* of Cassia wood can last up to a century or longer, this post had deteriorated considerably by the 1980s, just 50 years after it was cut. Villagers attributed this lack of durability to the tree having been too young and too small, a circumstance which suggests that the 1929 *peo*, perhaps connected with the controversy surrounding its installation, was obtained in haste.

9. Hierarchy, Precedence and Values: Scopes for social action in Ngadhaland, Central Flores

Olaf H. Smedal

While anthropologists have been alerted to the regimented and thwarted research which a strict adherence to regionally developed 'gatekeeping concepts' (Appadurai 1986) may effect, it is neither necessarily more productive nor less hazardous to export/import such concepts across regions. As a case in point, James Fox has remarked (1989:51–53, 1994) that there are inherent difficulties in applying Dumont's concept of hierarchy (1980) to societies of eastern Indonesia. These do not have the encompassing religious coherence that Dumont has attributed to India; for this reason, hierarchy cannot be described as a single principle nor identified with a specific opposition, such as pure and impure. In Eastern Indonesia there are a variety of contending oppositions that are of considerable importance to the definition of hierarchy and it is not one opposition but the interplay among various oppositions that gives rank to elements of a whole in the relation to the whole (Fox 1989:51).

The validity of this general assessment of eastern Indonesian societies depends perhaps as much on the theoretical bent and analytical perseverance of the investigator as it does on the nature of the 'contending oppositions' themselves. But be that as it may, attempts to conflate hierarchy and stratification, to link the one to the other, or to insist that one generates the other (see several articles in the Transformations of hierarchy volume of History and Anthropology [Jolly and Mosko 1994]) — despite Dumont's expressed formulations to the contrary (for example, 1980:65–66), is perhaps counter-productive. Anthropologists have long been accustomed to the possibility that not only indigenous terms but analytical ones as well can turn out on inspection to be polythetically constituted (Needham 1975). We have been warned that failure to recognize this may cause confusion and, correspondingly, pointless theoretical dispute. Will an insistence on pushing 'stratification' into 'hierarchy' lead to sharper models, or will it muddle them?

My own position on this issue is agnostic. But if my tentative skepticism is not misplaced, then we may be well advised to simply accept Dumont's definition of the concept and the accompanying strictures — but with a proviso: to regard his definition as nomological — not essential. That way we can at least avoid a dialogue of the deaf. Thus I shall not use this particular term in the following, except when its meaning is unambiguously Dumontian, explicitly discussed, or when I quote or paraphrase other authors.

Since my argument, such as it is, is principally informed by data derived from field research among the Ngadha ethno-linguistic group, central Flores, I begin with a rough sketch of Ngadha social organization.[1]

Those who are familiar with (especially eastern) Indonesian societies will not be astonished to learn that Ngadha evince a pervasive concern with scalar, seriated classification. Houses are placed in ranked classes, plots and tracts of land are divided into ordered categories, and persons are ascribed to social strata. Asking what these classifications are basically about, I shall elaborate the programmatic answers I offer now as I go along.

With respect to Houses[2] and lands the classification is most abstractly to do with what one could label seniority, or authority; 'an ordering on a gradient of stepped differences from low to high' as Adams (1974:328) puts it with regard to Sumba intellectual order — the most apt word for the concept I wish to convey is perhaps 'precedence', as Lewis (1988) has used it. And the primary idiom employed, implicitly or explicitly, in this discourse of gradient order or degrees of precedence is that of 'origin'. The closer the classified entity (House, land) is to the origin (conception, inception) — of which it is in a sense merely a later version, pale copy, or weak reflection — the grander, loftier, mightier, more important, and more valued it is held to be.

Central to understanding Ngadha social organization are first of all the categories *sa'o* ('House') and *woé* ('House coalition network'), into which every Ngadha person is born. Every person is, accordingly, referred to as the 'child' (*ana*) of such and such House and *woé*. Whereas 'House' is an accurate translation of the Ngadha *sa'o*, the (provisional) gloss 'House coalition network' for *woé* is mine — other ethnographers (Bader 1953; Arndt 1954) have used instead 'clan' or other terms which misleadingly evoke 'descent' as the sole principle for recruitment.[3] Second is a principle of social stratification. Ngadha are divided into three strata: nobles or aristocrats, commoners, and (former) slaves, between which marriage is strictly regulated. With a view to the overall context of the discussion that follows, it should be pointed out that there is no record of any central institutions of political or religious power in Ngadhaland prior to the moderately successful installation of 'rajas' following the establishment of Dutch military control in the early twentieth century.

Houses

As seems to be the case in a great number of eastern Indonesian societies Ngadha Houses are simultaneously dwellings, corporate estates, ancestral abodes, ritual centres and repositories of heirloom sacra. They are also frequently partners in exchanges predicated on marriage. In short, Ngadha Houses are — if any such thing exists — prototypical Houses in the Lévi-Straussian (1982) definition of that term. As Fox formulated it in 1980, 'house' 'is a fundamental cultural category used in eastern Indonesia to designate a particular kind of social unit'; its characteristics including an idea of localization or origin, a strictly stipulated physical structure, elder/younger hierarchical relations — yet not necessarily gender-specific, and a notion of a 'flow of life' (usually women) between the houses (Fox 1980:11–12). I must leave out the ethnographic details which show that in contrast to comparable units elsewhere in eastern Indonesia the Ngadha House is not 'a primary descent group' (Fox 1988:xii), but want to stress that traditional, strictly stipulated architecture is practised in Ngadhaland with remarkable vigour.

A visitor to a traditional Ngadha village (*nua*) will notice that at least two Houses look slightly different from the others. One will have a tiny model of a house, called *ana ié*, at the centre of the ridge of its roof, the other a human-like figurine, called *ata*, at the corresponding place. These Houses are the two initial ones of any one *woé*. As far as I know every Ngadha *woé* will have minimally these two Houses. The one with the little house on it is called *sa'o* (or *saka*) *pu'u*, the other *sa'o* (or *saka*) *lobo*.[4] These designations indicate the place allotted a male elder of the House in question when a new *ngadhu* or 'two-pronged sacrificial pole' is carried into the village. This is a rare event; a *ngadhu* may stand for a century or more and the political act of instituting a new *woé* is not a frequent one. The more senior of these two Houses — and positions — is *pu'u*. When the *ngadhu* — placed horizontally atop a huge bamboo scaffold — is carried from the place where it has been carved into the village, a war-clad, prominent male affiliate of the *sa'o pu'u* stands on the trunk/root part of it (which enters the village first) while an affiliate of the *sa'o lobo* stands atop its tip end.

Having pointed out that 'at least' two Houses look different from the others, I must emphasize that many villages include Houses of more than one *woé*. Where this is the case there may be a corresponding number of *sa'o pu'u* and *sa'o lobo* pairs — and indeed also of pairs or more accurately couples of *ngadhu* (a sacrificial pillar, the manifestly 'male' representation of the *woé* founding ancestor) and *bhaga* (a miniature house, the manifestly 'female' representation of the *woé* founding ancestress) at the centre of the village plaza. Thus a visitor to a Ngadha village will normally know at a glance the number of *woé* its residents are affiliated to — it suffices to count the number of Houses with a little house on the ridge purlin, or the number of Houses with a figurine, or the number of *ngadhu*, or the number of *bhaga*. It must be pointed out, however, that this 'normal' situation does not always prevail. Firstly, for certain (chiefly economic) reasons any one House, *ngadhu*, and/or *bhaga* in a village is possibly yet to be put up; secondly, a village may include 'cadet' Houses of *woé* centred elsewhere. I shall comment further upon the *ngadhu/bhaga* 'emblematic couple' shortly, but should point out here that they, together with certain House and *woé* heirlooms, belong to an unnamed Ngadha category of inalienable sacra. These are physical objects possessing to a degree certain attributes commonly ascribed to sentient beings; they are frequently conceptually gendered, they can feel abandoned, and experience hunger — especially for the blood of a sacrificial animal.

Decisions affecting the *woé* in its entirety are ultimately the responsibility of its 'trunk House' (*sa'o pu'u*), the rightful residents (office-holders, stewards) of which are said to have 'full rights' (*ha benu*). Marginally second in prominence is the 'tip House' (*sa'o lobo*). Accordingly, *woé* land is divided into trunk (House) and tip (House) land. While decisions on land use can be made with relative autonomy by any named House that possesses at least one symbolic 'House digging stick' (*su'a sa'o*), no *woé* land can be sold without the explicit approval of the trunk House.[5]

I shall discuss aspects of 'marriage' and related topics below, but should make clear at this point that the *woé* division into trunk and tip sides is never invoked with respect to past, current, or contemplated marriages; there are no moieties in Ngadha social organization.

Less prominent than the trunk and tip Houses are the *wua gha'o* and, subordinated to these again, *kaka*. These are all named cadet Houses and are collectively referred to as *sa'o mézé, lésa mézé* (great Houses), *sa'o ngaza* (named Houses) or *lanu*. The term *wua gha'o* exploits a fundamental Ngadha idea — one that will not surprise anyone familiar with ethnographies of eastern Indonesia — that human relationships are mostly asymmetrical: *wua* means 'fruit', 'child'; *gha'o*, equivalent to the Bahasa Indonesia (BI) term *géndong*, means 'carry on the small of the back or the hip, supported by the waist and one arm, often with the help of a cloth sling' (Echols and Shadily 1990:184). The relationship between a *sa'o mézé* and its *wua gha'o* is thus metaphorically expressed as one between parent and child. The meaning of *kaka* is less specific, but among its many possible glosses are 'member', 'belong to', 'support', 'protect' and 'assist' (Arndt 1961:230). Ngadha men and women often explain to the investigator that just as large upright stones need smaller ones next to them in order not to fall over, men depend on women, and trunk Houses need the support of *wua gha'o* and *kaka*. Another conventional indigenous synecdoche for the structure of the House coalition network (*woé*) is the *ngadhu* itself. As a sacrificial pillar at which *woé* affiliates kill water buffaloes in ritual it is the emblem for the *woé* in its entirety, although this emblem is ineffective without the *bhaga* complementing it. The *ngadhu*'s trunk and tip stand for the trunk and tip Houses or, to put it in an equally valid way, the labels 'trunk House' and 'tip House' themselves refer directly back to the high-profile ritual when senior males of each House ride atop either end of the *ngadhu*, as just mentioned. The *ngadhu*'s branches —

and the branches of its roots — represent the two sets of *wua gha'o* and *kaka* Houses.[6]

I have already mentioned that the *ngadhu/bhaga* couple are replicated in yet another set of miniatures: the *ata/ana ié* atop the two founding Houses of the *woé*. It is worth noting that the 'male' trunk House is adorned with the minuscule House model while the 'female' tip House features the figurine.

I should also reiterate that every House 'belongs' to one of the two sides: to the tip side or the trunk side. The entire *woé* is as it were split down, or along, the middle. Importantly, only when the one side is completely extinct can affiliates from the other move in to become permanent dwellers of those Houses. The main point is that every House (and person and plot of land) belongs to either the trunk or the tip side, and that each House relates to any other of its side in an order of precedence.

By the same token, the size of a traditional House — its physical proportions — must also correspond to its position in this scheme of precedence. Largest of any *woé* House is *sa'o pu'u*, the second largest is *sa'o lobo*. And Houses of each consecutive level (*wua gha'o*, *kaka*) must be, if only barely, smaller than the one preceding it. Moreover, socio-symbolic spatial categories, elements of construction, and a multitude of evocative carvings embossed on the House, are all salient to the many meanings of the House (cf. Smedal 2000).

With demographic growth further diversification takes place, viz. the building of subsidiary, unnamed Houses — invariably outside the traditional village compound (*loka nua*) — referred to as *baru*.[7] Finally, the inhabitants of most *lanu* and *baru* build also a field house (*kéka*) or two where they spend a great deal of time 'guarding the maize' as crops mature and tempt monkeys and wild pigs.

Notably, the number of named Houses in any one village is not fixed once and for all. But the expenses associated with the requisite ceremonies for turning an unnamed *baru* into a named *lanu/sa'o*, even when people aspire to do so, render such transformation all but impossible at present. An important reason why a great measure of organizational stability obtains in Ngadha villages, therefore, is that while politico-ritual relative autonomy is always attainable its cost is great.

Further establishment of Houses may occur when — for diverse reasons — people from elsewhere come to live on and work the *woé* territory. These may found their own *woé* or, over time, be incorporated into one already existing, with their own named Houses. Hence a *woé* need not consist only of people that are either consanguineally or affinally related. Conversely, just as Houses may be incorporated from the outside (a practice reminiscent of adoption) they may of their own accord break loose and establish their own *woé*, complete with *ngadhu* and *bhaga*, although, as just noted, this is economically prohibitive.

Land

It would take me too far afield to detail how Ngadha in various ways link land with collectives: *woé* and Houses, but a few comments are in order. Very summarily, there are three categories of *woé* land: the nominally primordial 'base rock and solid earth' land; secondly 'land softened by digging sticks' — this refers to territory over which *Houses* have all but total control; and thirdly 'rows of maize and lines of sugarcane' land — plots over which *households* have usufruct rights. Furthermore, while private ownership to land is recognized, it is so only to a limited extent. It has almost always come into being as a result of individual, not collective, effort (or transgression). Such land may be inherited — as private property — by male and female offspring alike, and can subsequently be put up for sale. But with succeeding generations the distinction between private and collective will blur. What was once 'private' becomes first joint, then collective — absorbed into the House estate, though not into that of the *woé* — yet the names of tracts of land and the narratives of how the plots were acquired are preserved in House lore.

Still, there is no mistaking the profound conceptual difference between the two. *Woé* land is in principle (if not, for historical reasons, in practice) the *sine qua non* for the *woé* itself. Stories relate how the *woé* came to reside in and move between specific localities, and how the land came to be *woé* land in the first place. These narratives are by definition tied to the establishment of the trunk and tip Houses.

People

Having discussed so far Houses and land, I turn now to the principle by which people are classified. What is at play when a Ngadha says that someone is 'noble', 'commoner', 'slave'? Ngadha themselves (and not only nobles) answer that rank is ultimately to do with morals and responsibility. Whoever is classified as 'noble' is obliged to think before speaking, is expected to consider the many sides of an issue, to be generous, and to have regard also for the needs and interests of others. Most Ngadha people, who have probably never heard the phrase *noblesse oblige* would recognize its sense immediately. In Ngadhaland it translates into an expectation among nobles and commoners alike that nobles — particularly and most conspicuously the men — assume positions of sometimes severe but usually benign authority and responsibility in community affairs. At the level of personal behaviour standards the nobles — men as well as women but women especially — are subject to a plethora of prescriptions and proscriptions. These moral regulations are rigorously sanctioned by fellow nobles, often near kin. Whoever transgresses is scolded, ridiculed, or deranked. And in Ngadhaland the only direction social mobility can take — along this traditional axis — is downwards. Above all, therefore, the symbolic capital of Ngadha nobles is *moral* capital.

Commoners, on the other hand, are the ordinary folk whose behaviour is less severely scrutinized, whom the nobles 'protect' and who in turn 'support' the nobles. Again, an image commonly employed is of a large, upright stone toppling over unless propped up by smaller ones on either side. The (former) slaves are not actually integral to these fundamental categories of two classes of freemen. In part descended from captives taken in past wars, in part from commoners (and no doubt nobles, too) who once plummeted into debt bondage, they are unaccounted for in myth and legend. But if the division between nobles and commoners is fundamental it is so partly because it is not primordially *given* — it *took place* in myth. It explains how things have become what they now are, not how they were to begin with. It is the Ngadha parallel to the Fall, but instead of ascribing the Change to the violation of God's command not to eat the fruit of the Tree of Knowledge it ascribes it to the brother's sexual knowledge of his sister; a transgression of something social, not divine (see Smedal 2009).

In concluding this brief outline of Ngadha social organization I should state how relationships are structured. Unlike other eastern Indonesian ethno-linguistic groups on record, the Ngadha are known to reckon kinship cognatically and have been described as practising no form of affinal alliance (Barnes 1980). Hence, also in contrast to other eastern Indonesian groups, Ngadha do not conceptually contrast between 'wife-givers' and 'wife-takers'; marriage within the *woé* and within the House is permitted — cross cousins and parallel cousins are terminologically lumped together and may all marry (Smedal 2002). Exchanges in connection with marriage between Houses ('bridewealth') are decisive in determining post-marital residence and, consequently, any one person's House affiliation. Yet these interdependent exchanges and practices (uxorilocality/matrilateral affiliation, and virilocality/patrilateral affiliation) exhibit extremely clear, predictable and geographically localisable patterns, effectively generating zones where 'choice' is ruled out in practical, economic terms — though not in principle.

A concern with origins, therefore, and a drive for morally acceptable behaviour: these would appear to be two sources of gravitational pull for Ngadha representations. But ultimately the latter is eclipsed by the former. For however admirable one's behaviour may be it is ephemeral and therefore worth little compared with the ultimate authority that derives from origins. Acts can affirm and attest to claims of bonds with origins but they cannot replace them, or, at least not directly. Certain acts, moving now from the domain of morals to the neighbouring and sometimes overlapping one of politics, are carried out precisely in an attempt to replace certain bonds and tales of origins with others;

transforming and projecting along the way present feats into former ones. Successful ascendance to politico-ritual leadership in non-literate societies, as Howell (1991), for example, has demonstrated for the northern Lio further east on Flores, depends on the acceptance of such reformulations of the past. It is, I think worth stressing, that the operative word here is 'acceptance'.

Asymmetry: hierarchy? stratification? power? exploitation?

I begin this section by emphasizing the important difference between those social systems where holders of spiritual or secular power live, as it were, for free (or at least nearly so), and those where this is not the case — that is, the contrast between those social systems where the livelihood of political or religious leaders is provided by others, and those where political and ritual office does not entail exemption from regular, productive labour (see Sahlins 1974). Ngadha nobles, who constitute a social stratum or segment — not a class in the Marxian sense — can hardly be said to receive tribute in any substantial sense. And specialists, noble or not, can only claim such 'tribute' that might just as accurately be termed 'payment' for services rendered. Examples of such payments would include the fees male wood carvers charge for their work on Houses, and the remunerations female weavers ask for pieces of indigo cloth. While this is the gist of the matter, a modifying remark is in order.

Houses and *woé* are usually land-holding corporations and often lease land to non-affiliates. Importantly, these corporations are no less land-holding units in the event that its inhabitants/stewards/care-takers are commoners. Moreover, Ngadha land rent — as far as swidden agriculture and horticulture are concerned — is negligible. Regardless of the size of the plot in question (commonly between half a hectare and a hectare) the household renting land is obliged to present — once a year — a measure of hulled rice (approximately three kilograms), a fowl, and one or two bottles of palm gin to the relevant House (now in its role as landlord, *mori tana* 'lord of the land'). In the unlikely event that all three items were purchased they would represent a modest monetary value: in 1993 less than US$3. Landowners and tenants alike describe this as a token payment. Still, in addition to this rent in 'pure form', landless peasants are required to participate in the pooling of resources when on occasion a landholding *woé* House is rebuilt. Minimally each household must bring a medium-sized pig for the festive inauguration of the House when sometimes a couple of hundred people are fed, but tenants may also be asked to contribute food for the builders while they are at work, or to assist in the construction of the House.[8]

Usurpation — routinely attributed as endemic among those 'at the top' — is difficult to identify among the Ngadha. Indeed, and at the risk of appearing the naïve observer, I would hazard the assertion that usurpation or exploitation cannot be ascribed to the 'system'. To the degree that such traits can be observed at all, they are attributable rather to specific persons in specific positions vis-à-vis specific others. To take just one example: intelligent, hard-working men who are able to set aside some of their earnings can turn into ruthless moneylenders; the standard yearly rate of interest being 100 per cent. Thus I am neither suggesting that interpersonal conflict is absent, nor that relations between more inclusive social units (Houses, *woé*, allied *woé* or federated villages) are inherently harmonic. But the roots of politico-economic conflict in Ngadhaland are not, I submit, buried in the system of social stratification. As I have tried to explicate, there is no political, economic or ritual power inhering in nobility as such, nor is it possible to achieve noble status through social action, hence there is no vying for such status nor can there be. Another way of putting this is to say that there is no ready channel through which moral capital can be converted to economic capital or vice versa.

While it may make sense with respect to certain social formations elsewhere in the Austronesian world to say that ascribed rank is no less than achieved rank a claim, a political resource which actors deploy and which must be backed by achievement, and, more sweepingly, that a given social order (including, presumably, its value system) is always a contested one (Jolly 1994:384; Otto 1994), the general applicability of such statements is questionable. There is no lack of contestable claims in Ngadha social life (to plots of land, for example, to items of bridewealth, or to House affiliation), but claims to nobility are not among them. I have already tried to show why there is little *reason* to 'claim' noble rank, for example. When I presently explain how rank is produced and reproduced it will become clear, I hope, that such claims are either legitimate and accepted or illegitimate and absurd.

But before I do I want to add a brief comment on the expression 'contestable' just employed because an unreflected, common sense use of it may blur a distinction in meaning which I think is important to be clear about. The distinction I have in mind is parallel to that between 'contesting' and 'competing'. It is true that in everyday language these two terms are nearly synonymous. Yet there is a vast difference between contesting a value and competing *in terms of it*. In the second case the objective is to seek acceptance for a claim phrased in *established* terms. In the first case the objective is to replace one value with another by seeking acceptance for a claim phrased in terms *alternative* to those currently acknowledged. The importance of the difference lies in that only the former effort, when successful, alters the value system — and potentially the social order as well. The second, in contrast, confirms them. So, when Ngadha speakers 'contest' a land claim by referring to their seniority or precedence with respect to origins, they are more accurately *competing* for land in terms of a recognized value — origin proximity — which thereby becomes all the more entrenched.

The production and reproduction of ranked persons

In many Ngadha traditional domains there are few if any aristocrats left. This is so partly because there is no mechanism by which a commoner can be promoted to noble status but several by which a noble can be relegated to commoner status, and partly because all over Ngadhaland one encounters a version of a principle of preferential hypergamy which affects a surplus of marriageable women at the top with the consequence that very few women give birth to nobles.

The general rule in Ngadhaland is that a noble man may marry a noble woman, a commoner man may marry a commoner woman, and a noble man may marry a commoner woman. Hence, if a man and a woman of these reciprocal strata engage in sexual play, and if neither of them is already betrothed or married, no *rule* may be invoked to prevent their subsequent marriage — although other factors (such as genealogical proximity, relative age, or relative generational position) are relevant. But if a commoner man has sex with a noble woman the union constitutes a major breach of *adat* and is referred to as 'making a misstep' (*la'a sala*), a term which also denotes sexual acts between persons closely related (consanguineally or otherwise); 'incestuous' relationships. Formerly transgressors of the rule were executed, if caught. For the past seventy or eighty years, however, this execution of the couple has been performed symbolically. Besides, a major ritual must be carried out for the social person of the woman to be restored, since she is no longer noble; she is, temporarily, *persona non grata*. I cannot describe, let alone analyse this chilling ritual here. For the present it must suffice to say that the female transgressor simply has no place in the village social fabric until the ritual, which includes the ritual killing of a dog and two water buffaloes, has been carried out. Indeed, until then she is forbidden to enter the village plaza and any of the Houses delineating it. Afterwards, however, the couple are free to marry.

Ngadha considerations on the topic of sex between nobles and commoners are comparable to those between nobles and (former) slaves. Thus, no sanctions apply if the noble is male. In the converse case the woman suddenly fallen from nobility is banished from the House, the *woé*, and the village she was born into, and is barred from returning until the ritual of symbolic execution has been carried out. Afterwards the transgressing woman belongs to the rank of her sexual partner for, be he commoner or slave, she has become 'like him'.

Commoner women, likewise, should not have sex with (former) slaves. Whoever does, 'becomes' of their partner's status. An important distinction between noble and commoner transgressors, however, is that only the former are referred to as having, or having committed, *la'a sala*. The upshot of it is that a Ngadha woman should only marry — indeed should only have sex with — a man of her own or a higher rank.

Below I present the consequences of the Ngadha version of the principle of preferential hypergamy in tabular form, especially with a view to the frequent outcomes of sexual and marital unions, namely children — or, more precisely, for the rank of these children.

In Table 9.1, illegitimate combinations are marked by parentheses. These same combinations lead to a change, invariably negative, in the woman's rank — namely to that of her partner or 'husband' (whose rank is never affected on account of his sexual-marital liaisons) — and are marked with a division sign ('÷').[9]

Table 1. Parentage, filiation and social stratification

Father	Mother	Child
noble	noble	noble
noble	commoner	commoner
noble	slave	slave
(commoner)	(noble) ÷	commoner
commoner	commoner	commoner
commoner	slave	slave
(slave)	(noble) ÷	slave
(slave)	(commoner) ÷	slave
slave	slave	slave

Of the nine conceivable combinations, six are permitted, three prohibited. Two of the latter concern noble women — who have only one legitimate option: to marry a noble man. A noble woman known to have had sex with a man of commoner or slave extraction is promptly and irreversibly demoted to the rank of her partner, whether or not the union produced a child.[10] Such strict limitation in the options for potential partners is conversely the case for men of slave status; they can only legitimately have sex with or marry women of their own rank. A noble man, in contrast, may have sex with, or marry, women of any rank. Similar multiple options are legitimately available also for women of slave status.

Of the six unions considered legitimate it will be seen that only one can result in a noble child, two in a commoner child, and three in a slave child. It is evident also that only one union among all nine would generate a noble child. And of the three illegitimate unions resulting in a woman's loss of rank, two would produce a slave child. In other words, only legitimate unions can produce noble children, two legitimate and one illegitimate can produce commoner children, while three legitimate and two illegitimate ones can yield slave children. I formulate the tabular information in this manner deliberately, because I wish to bring out clearly a central Ngadha perception — voiced by commoners and nobles alike — that nobles, and with regard to sexual behaviour, noble women, lead morally more exacting lives than do other people. If they err they pay dearly, for there is no mechanism or practice by which their status, once having changed, can change back again. The formulations also accentuate the mental association in Ngadha freemen's minds between slave status and contaminating disgrace. It is to be expected, therefore, that the moral pressure exerted upon noble women by their near kin to marry noble men and no one else, in order to secure noble offspring (and to avoid public humiliation), is considerable. Nor is it surprising that given the absence of a prohibition on noble men to marry women of lower rank and the fact that such unions are unexceptional, it is too often the case that there is no suitable noble man around to marry. In many villages old, single, noble women live alone; the only remaining noble of their House they are referred to with humorous pity as 'waiting maidens'.[11]

It should be made clear, finally, that even if a noble man has had sex with or even children by a commoner or (former) slave woman, though has not 'married' her, he can still marry a noble woman and sire noble children by her. A noble man's status, therefore, cannot be altered on account of his amorous exploits.

But although it is only the women who, on account of sexual liaisons with men of lower rank, can fall from grace, be banished, become a person of lower rank, and henceforth give birth only to persons of lower rank, noble men can or could be demoted, too, but not on grounds of inter-rank sexual transgression. The consequence of breaking one or another of the plethora of rules (often in the form of *piré* 'taboos') traditionally applying to the behaviour of nobles was that the transgressor immediately lost rank. This is apparently no longer so, but most of the rules and taboos are still known and one's behaviour is judged according to them. One is that a noble male, in mixed-rank company, should never walk behind commoners, another that any noble person should never take shelter under a commoner's house or field hut (although to spend time *in* it is all right). A third instance often quoted to me concerns the noble who, while walking across the village plaza, slips and falls into the mud. This is just the sort of thing a noble must not do and, worse, the fall is probably observed by all who happen to sit on their verandah. Now, according to Ngadha a water buffalo, insofar as it ever makes a sound, utters a nasal *hoa*. What the (presumably noble) mirthful onlookers say when they see the noble prostrate in the mud is precisely that; '*hoa*'. Or they just raise their chin, baring their throat, as a buffalo is made to do at sacrifice. What everyone understands is that unless the hapless noble immediately fetches a buffalo and kills it he is no longer considered noble.

Thus the path of the noble 'is very narrow, scarcely as wide as a reed (*wako*) leaf', as Arndt puts it (1929:842). One important difference between men's and women's transgressions, however, is that men are often able to rectify theirs by sacrificing a buffalo; by taking action. Women are not similarly blessed (Arndt 1960:180).[12]

What I have not discussed explicitly is politico-economic power or influence. If political clout does not inhere in or emanate from high rank as such, as I have tried to argue, then whence does it derive? The answer is that it is cultivated in a discursive field where personal knowledge, experience, prowess and achievement are all-important, and where the difference between nobles and commoners is of no matter.

Men (not women) of authority are generally referred to as *mosa laki* — an achieved status in Ngadhaland, although certain categories of *mosa laki* may have inherited the basis for that status, especially land. Among an indeterminable number of *mosa laki* types are the following seven:

1. *mosa kaba laki wéa*
    a *mosa laki* who is rich in livestock and gold (chains)
2. *mosa tana laki watu* OR *mosa watu laki tana*
    a *mosa laki* who owns a large plot of land
3. *mosa nua laki bo'a*
    a *mosa laki* within the village (not the greatest of *mosa laki*; a 'local hero')
4. *mosa wiwi laki lema*
    a *mosa laki* with exceptional oratorical skills
5. *mosa toa laki wela*
    a *mosa laki* who frequently practices ritual killing of water buffaloes and pigs
6. *mosa pedu laki rona* OR *mosa péu laki rona* OR
    mosa wiu laki pi'u OR *mosa pedu laki pada*
    a *mosa laki* who always gives good advice to others
7. *mosa po laki péra*
    a *mosa laki* able to instruct others

Now all these labels are equally applicable to males of noble and commoner rank — not to slaves, who are excluded by definition from fields of *adat* discourse, just as are children and the mentally infirm. There are other labels, some of them mocking or ironic, which designate puny, pretentious, ineffectual, incapable or sexually irresponsible '*mosa laki*'. And these labels, too, are as freely applied to nobles as they are to commoners.

Interestingly, the advent of Indonesian nation state institutions have altered the state of affairs I have just described. But while persons of slave extraction are sometimes employed in regency-level bureaucracies and are known to have run successfully for office in urban areas, partly because as Indonesian citizens they are as entitled to higher education as anyone else and they can thus acquire relevant qualifications, they have failed so far to make an impression in village-level politics. This is not surprising since the requisite expertise at this political level can be attained only by those who know village life intimately, which comprises details on historical, genealogical, personal, and, above all, *adat* matters.

Final remarks

In rounding off I shall make a couple of remarks only tenuously related to the Ngadha material, hoping to stimulate debate.

1. We can take it as axiomatic, I think, that no social system is totally stable, and as equally axiomatic that social scientists are interested in how social systems are maintained while they change — in continuities as well as in discontinuities. Now it appears that some analysts take it as axiomatic, too, that the threat to social stability comes from 'below', from the sub-altern. On the basis of the slim evidence I have been able to introduce here I want to propose instead that the threat to Ngadha social stratification does not come from below but from the top.

It is indeed difficult to see what interest the sub-alterns, at least the commoners (descendants of former slaves are another matter, but they constitute a very small minority) have in toppling 'the system'. The nobles do not usurp the commoners; the commoners are not exploited by the nobles. Furthermore, recall the moral standards which apply to aristocrats and which would render the life of a commoner-turned-noble — an impossible aspiration anyway, as I have explained — much more onerous than it already is. Commoner landlords and House stewards have the same social responsibilities and prerogatives as do the noble ditto, and noble peasants till the soil, harvest their crops, and raise their pigs just the way commoner peasants do. But the nobles lead lives which are under constant scrutiny.

And this is the point: Because many cannot live up to those standards, because greed may turn gamblers into paupers, because infatuations can cross social divides, because only noble women can produce noble children, because, in short, that 'reed leaf' is so very narrow, it is the actions of the nobles themselves which threaten 'the system'.

2. In my view there is a regrettable, if predictable trend in some current anthropological theorizing to bracket what might be labelled the 'structural' constraints on action and zoom in on person-centred action itself. If an exaggeration may be permitted, it is as if in an effort to 'countermand hierarchy' (Jolly 1994:385ff.), one simultaneously fails to note what is currently taken-for-granted and what-goes-without saying in any one community, society or culture.

Now there is a troublesome side to this renewed concern for individually attributable action insofar as it tends to be accompanied by a reluctance to explicate the socio-cultural horizon within which it can be effective — indeed *make sense* at all (Smedal 1992). And I wonder if the current emphasis on individuals and action and choice and instability to the (relative) exclusion of collectivities and structure and rules and stability is as anti-ethnocentric as some rhetoric would have it. It may well be that anthropologists have overplayed the differences between Us and the Exotic Other. It may well be, too, that individual ploys, stratagems and tactics in small(er)-scale societies have been underplayed, and precolonial societies have of course waxed and waned in a variety of dimensions. But it seems to me that the accelerating change many people in certain areas of the world experience, most aptly indexed perhaps by massively funded cybertechnological and biomedical innovation, is very unevenly distributed. It is also, and this is not a coincidence, observed in its purest form — continually ramifying, being recalibrated and propelled forward — in societies or ideological climates where individual choice and action have been accorded great value (Dumont 1986). In brief, I sense that the pendulum of intellectual fashion has been driven to its present extreme less by an effort to understand what is difficult to accept than by an inclination to phrase it in terms that match the turmoils of our own. It is 'we' who, probably more than anybody before us (or beside us), cannot choose not to choose, and it is 'we' who must do so among a steadily proliferating set of alternatives between which differences become as steadily difficult to discern.

Obviously, people everywhere act and choose, clearly they apprehend and 'construct' their vision of the world. But I think it cannot be stressed enough, first that this construction is not carried out in a social vacuum, but that it is subjected to structural constraints; secondly, that the structuring structures, the cognitive structures, are themselves socially structured, because they have social origins; thirdly, the construction of social reality is not only an individual enterprise, but may also become a collective enterprise (Bourdieu 1990:131). This is as true for the observed as it is for the observers.

References

Adams, Marie Jeanne

1974 Symbols of the organized community in East Sumba, Indonesia. *Bijdragen tot de Taal-, Land- en Volkenkunde* 130:324–347.

Appadurai, Arjun

1986 Theory in anthropology: center and periphery. *Comparative Studies in Society and History* 28(2):356–361.

Arndt, Paul SVD

1929 Die Religion der Ngada [Part I]. *Anthropos* 24:817–861.

1954 *Gesellschaftliche Verhältnisse der Ngadha.* Studia Instituti Anthropos Vol. 8. Wien-Mödling: Verlag der Missionsdruckerei St. Gabriel.

1960 Opfer und Opferfeiern der Ngadha. *Asian Folklore Studies* 19:175–250. Tokyo: Folklore Studies [Asian Folklore Studies], Society of the Divine Word.

1961 *Wörterbuch der Ngadhasprache*. Fribourg, Switzerland: Pertjetakan Arnoldus, Endeh/Posieux. [Studia Instituti Anthropos 15.]

Bader, Hermann SVD

1953 *Die Reifefeiern bei den Ngadha (Mittelflores, Indonesien)*. Mödling bei Wien: St.-Gabriel-Verlag. [St.-Gabrieler Studien 14.]

Barnes, R.H.

1980 Marriage, exchange and the meaning of corporations in eastern Indonesia. In J.L. Comaroff (ed.), *The meaning of marriage payments*, pp.93–124. London: Academic Press.

Bourdieu, Pierre

1990 *In other words: essays towards a reflexive sociology*. Trans. Matthew Adamson. Cambridge: Polity Press.

Dumont, Louis

1980 *Homo hierarchicus: the caste system and its implications*. (2nd edn). Chicago: The University of Chicago Press.

1986 *Essays on individualism: modern ideology in anthropological perspective*. Chicago: The University of Chicago Press.

Echols, John M. and Hassan Shadily

1990 *Kamus Indonesia-Inggris: an Indonesian-English dictionary*. Jakarta: Gramedia. 3rd edn. revised and edited by John U. Wolff and James T. Collins, in co-operation with Hassan Shadily.

Erb, Maribeth

1987 When rocks were young and earth was soft: ritual and mythology in Northeastern Manggarai. Unpublished PhD thesis. Stony brook, New York: State University of New York at StonyBrook.

Fox, James J.

1980 Introduction. In James J. Fox (ed.), *The flow of life: essays on eastern Indonesia*, pp.1–18. Cambridge, MA: Harvard University Press.

1988 Foreword. In E.D. Lewis, *People of the source: the social and ceremonial order of Tana Wai Brama on Flores*, pp.xi–xiv. Verhandelingen van het Koninklijk Instituut voor Taal-, Land- en Volkenkunde 135. Dordrecht, Holland/Providence, USA: Foris Publications.

1989 Category and complement: binary ideologies and the organization of dualism in eastern Indonesia. In David Maybury-Lewis and Uri Almagor (eds), *The attraction of opposites: thought and society in the dualistic mode*, pp.33–56. Ann Arbor: University of Michigan Press.

1994 Reflections on 'hierarchy' and 'precedence'. In M. Jolly and M. Mosko (eds), *Transformations of hierarchy: structure, history and horizon in the Austronesian world. History and Anthropology* (Special Issue) 7:87–108.

Howell, Signe

1991 Access to the ancestors: re-constructions of the past in non-literate society. In Reidar Grønhaug, Gunnar Haaland and Georg Henriksen (eds), *The ecology of choice and symbol: essays in honour of Fredrik Barth*, pp.225–243. Bergen: Alma Mater.

Jolly, Margaret

1994 Epilogue: hierarchical horizons. In M. Jolly and M. Mosko (eds), *Transformations of hierarchy: structure, history and horizon in the Austronesian world. History and Anthropology* (Special Issue) 7:377–409.

Jolly, Margaret and M. Mosko (eds)

1994 *Transformations of hierarchy: structure, history and horizon in the Austronesian world. History and Anthropology* (Special Issue) 7.

Lévi-Strauss, Claude

1982 *The way of the masks*. Trans. Sylvia Modelski. Seattle: University of Washington Press.

Lewis, E.D.

1988 *People of the source: the social and ceremonial order of Tana Wai Brama on Flores*. Verhandelingen van het Koninklijk Instituut voor Taal-, Land- en Volkenkunde 135. Dordrecht, Holland/Providence, USA: Foris Publications.

McKinnon, Susan

1991 *From a shattered sun: hierarchy, gender, and alliance in the Tanimbar Islands*. Madison: The University of Wisconsin Press.

Needham, Rodney

1975 Polythetic classification: convergence and consequences. *Man* (ns) 10:349–369.

Nooteboom, C.

1939 Versieringen van Manggaraische huizen. *Tijdschrift voor Indische Taal-, Land- en Volkenkunde* 79:221–238.

Otto, Ton

1994 Feasting and fighting: rank and power in pre-colonial Baluan. In M. Jolly and M. Mosko (eds), *Transformations of hierarchy: structure, history and horizon in the Austronesian world. History and Anthropology* (Special Issue) 7:223–239.

Sahlins, Marshall D.

1974 *Stone age economics.* London: Tavistock Publications.

Smedal, Olaf H.

1992 Social anthropology, radical alterity, and culture. *Canberra Anthropology* 15(1):58–74.

2000 Sociality on display: the aesthetics of Ngadha houses. *RES: Anthropology and Aesthetics* 37:106–126.

2002 Ngadha relationship terms in context: description, analysis, and implications. *Asian Journal of Social Science* 30(3):493–524.

2009 On the value of the beast, or the limit of money: notes on the meaning of marriage prestations among the Ngadha, Central Flores (Indonesia). In K.M. Rio and O.H. Smedal (eds), *Hierarchy: persistence and transformation in social formations*, pp.269–297. Oxford and New York: Berghahn Books.

ENDNOTES

[1] Field research 1990–91 and 1993 totalling some 14 months was financed by the Norwegian Research Council for Science and the Humanities and by the Institute for Comparative Research in Human Culture, Oslo, and was conducted under the auspices of Lembaga Ilmu Pengetahuan Indonesia and Universitas Nusa Cendana, Kupang, Timor. The Department and Museum of Anthropology, University of Oslo, provided a six-month grant which enabled me to think through some of the material reported here. The first draft of this text was presented in Leiden in April 1996. I am grateful to Michael Vischer and the International Institute for Asian Studies for inviting and hosting me, to the Department of Social Sciences, University of Tromsø for financing my trip to Leiden, and to the Department of Social Anthropology, University of Bergen, for providing the opportunity to finalize the article.

[2] The term 'House' (with capital 'H') designates a social unit.

[3] Arndt offers a long list of meanings of *woé* of which several have potential relevance here: first of all 'sib', 'family', 'clan', and *Rangstufe* ('level of social stratification' or 'place in hierarchy'); but also 'friend' (gender neutral), 'troupe', 'gathering', 'people'; 'to embrace', 'to bind', 'to draw in', 'to tie together' (1954:204; 1961:57). Realizing that 'House coalition network' hardly evokes the semantic range — nor of course the poetic potential — of the Ngadha term, I still search for a better English gloss.

[4] *Saka* 'to ride'; *pu'u* 'trunk', 'stem', 'origin'; *lobo* 'top', 'tip'. The correct and complete designations of the two 'apex' Houses is as follows: *sa'o pu'u saka pu'u* and *sa'o pu'u saka lobo*. Thus there are two *sa'o pu'u* for each *woé*. But houses are not usually referred to in this way; people always speak of the first as *sa'o pu'u* and of the second as *saka lobo*.

[5] I cannot deal here with the subtle symbolic significances of the *su'a sa'o*.

[6] Unlike the neighbouring Keo 'clan' *péo* (see Forth, this volume), Ngadha *ngadhu/ bhaga* couples are exclusive to each *woé*.

[7] A word not, I think, cognate with the BI word *baru* 'new'; in (northeastern) Manggarai, immediately west of Ngadhaland, houses are referred to as *mbaru* (Nooteboom 1939:231). Erb remarks that until such a house has been ritually inaugurated it is called not *mbaru* but 'garden house' or simply 'forest' (1987:212).

[8] In none of the villages where I did fieldwork is irrigated rice cultivation practised to any extent and none of the irrigated plots are worked by tenants. But I was informed that whenever someone rents such plots sharecropping is common; the landowner is likely to demand between one- and two-thirds of the produce, euphemistically referred to as *fara* 'do together'. Insofar as this information is reliable the two modes of 'land rent' are of decidedly different orders of magnitude, as people themselves stressed.

[9] My remarks on this topic can be usefully compared with McKinnon's discussion of rank and its permutations in Tanimbar (1991:259–276), and my 'Table 1' with her 'Figure 11.1' (1991:262). It is clear that the principles in Tanimbar and in Ngadhaland have much in common; the main contrast appears to be the extreme severity with which Ngadha treat illegitimate unions.

[10] According to Arndt it sometimes happened that all affiliates of the woman's House were demoted — or demoted themselves voluntarily (1954:24–25).

[11] Since *Homo hierarchicus* hovers in the background already I wish to juxtapose Ngadha hypergamy as described above and Dumont's discussion of the phenomenon as it occurs, admittedly with greater complexity, in India (1980:112–125). Among several arresting differences I note three. The first is that hypergamy in India usually takes place *within* a greater endogamous caste or subcaste group. The permitted status difference between the spouses, in other words, is one of degree rather than categorical. Secondly, in India the status discrepancy is usually neutralized normatively. The rule there is that the father's status, not the mother's, is transmitted to the couple's children who are, as it were, promoted. This feature inevitably produces motivations. Thirdly, according to Brahmanical ideology, marriage entails the 'gift of a maiden' and, for the gift to be meritoriously pure, no counter-prestation can be demanded, or even accepted.

Dumont comments, with respect to the Indian material, that the distinction between obligatory hypergamy and optional (or preferential, the most appropriate term with respect to the material at hand) hypergamy 'does not in fact have much interest' (1980:117) — a statement it is impossible to disagree with, referring as it does to a situation where every clan is differently ranked from any other, and one must marry outside the clan. However, had he discussed the Ngadha version of the principle — which may as well be called 'hypogamy prohibition' — he would, I think, have had to reconsider that statement, because the Ngadha permit, as I have mentioned, and even encourage, *woé* ('clan') and House ('clan segment') endogamy.

[12] Arndt (1954:335–343 and 1960:242–250) provides further details on the prescriptions and proscriptions on nobles' behaviour.

10. Hierarchy and Precedence in Keiese Origin Myths

Timo Kaartinen

There are two senses in which localized origin is socially significant to people living in the East Indonesian islands of Kei. Each Keiese village society consists of heterogeneous elements which trace their ancestry to places outside their present environment. Traditions of ancestral migration and contact with other island communities indicate a claim to chiefly offices and status, but they occur among common people as well. Apart from the stories of migration, however, there are myths of origin which only concern the origins of the local society itself. In present-day Kei, the origin myths are generally known but rarely subject to public performance. The main difference between the two genres is that whereas traditions of migration focus on the differentiating effects of external relations for the local society, origin myths represent a synthetic perspective on such relationships. Without explicitly stating its implications for the present society, each origin myth in fact indicates a particular order of precedence.

The logic by which precedence is constructed and contested in mythical discourse can only be found out by comparing different myths. I will do this with reference to case material from Kei Besar, an eastern Indonesian island. My purpose is to examine what category relationships define myths of origin as a genre, and how they feature in the social constitution of place as a durable social reality.

I am concerned here with the significance of 'local origin' for validating people's relationships to places and each other. With reference to case material from Kei Besar, an island in eastern Indonesia, I will examine what category relationships define myths of origin as a genre, and how they feature in the social constitution of place as a durable social reality. My general argument is that hierarchy in the communities I have studied is most apparent in the topological definitions of society, whereas the manner in which currently living people trace their relationship to cultural landmarks constitutes a discourse of precedence.

Hierarchy and precedence resemble each other most in their formal criteria of definition. Both involve asymmetric and complementary symbolic oppositions which are applied to social and cosmic relationships. There have been several different approaches at analysing these oppositions in the Pacific and Austronesian context. The theory of hierarchy implies that they are first of all classifications of exchange relationships which constitute the whole of society

(Barraud 1979; Barraud et al. 1994). Precedence is a privileged relationship to a cosmological origin or source which is constructed from similar symbolic resources as hierarchy and does not presuppose the existence of society as a whole. Instead, the emphasis of an approach which focuses on precedence is on the numerous metaphoric expressions which in Austronesian languages suggest at once organic growth and the process of coming into existence (Fox 1988, 1994).

Generally the two concepts point to different problems and approaches. An exception, however, is the study of cosmology and myth. In origin myths, one finds temporal structures characteristic of precedence, but also the idea that the source hierarchically encompasses all of presently existing society. In the cosmogonic myths of many Pacific societies, social and cosmic relationships appear as a hierarchical unfolding in which the source or beginning is type and the outcome or issue is token of the same, ontologically basic categories (Sahlins 1985:14; Valeri 1985; Siikala 1991:54).

I will not attempt a comprehensive review of these concepts and approaches, but explore them in the hope of finding out elements in them that best apply to the problems I am trying to address in studying historical traditions and genres in the Kei Islands. My focus in this paper will be on myths of origin called *tum*, probably the best documented folkloric genre in the Kei Islands. A number of these myths were published by Hein Geurtjens (1924), a Dutch Catholic missionary who collected them between 1900–1920, during the first years of actual colonial presence in Kei. Through Geurtjens' book, the myths were also an influential source for F.A.E. van Wouden's (1968) perspective about society and cosmos in eastern Indonesia.

Tum in Keiese means 'basis' or 'origin' and has a connotation of organic growth, as is indicated by its cognate words from many other Austronesian languages (Fox 1988:14). The name of the genre indicates that the stories are regarded as fundamental to the existence of society. The problem is, *what* society? *How* can we account for the effects of the myth in constituting it? If we begin to look at myth as a reflection of observable social life, we end up reducing its meaning to particular contexts and fail to account for the structuring power of its symbolism either in terms of hierarchy or precedence.

This problem, however, does not have to arise if myth is regarded as an integral part of social life. Jukka Siikala suggests that in order to take myths 'seriously' one must consider both their 'internal' and 'external' continuity. The internal continuity or 'plot' of the text, and the external continuity of such texts as a socially significant tradition together define myth as historical, which in turn justifies the study of myth in order to say something about society in general (Siikala 1991:4).

In my examination of *tum*, I will begin from their general, social context and suggest where in terms of social relationships and institutions these myths could be 'located' in Keiese society. I will then compare two particular myths and show that they represent opposed perspectives on society and the world. The hierarchical implications of these myths likewise have a definite place in society. 'Society as a whole' in this case is topological. Certain places are the foci of ontologically fundamental relationships to people who live in the social milieu defined by them. The final problem is how these milieux and relationships are related to the general context of social life: is it justified to speak about categorical encompassment as more than a contextual phenomenon?

People of the Mountain, People of the Cape

Kei, located some 500 km from Ambon in Southeast Maluku, is divided into two groups of islands. Small Kei, the western part of the group, consists of flat coral islands, while Great Kei, the eastern part, is dominated by one long island, essentially one mountain range which rises from the sea. The village of Banda Eli where I stayed during my fieldwork in 1994–96 lies in the northern part of Great Kei. Unlike the surrounding villages which tend to be divided into Islamic, Protestant and Catholic sections, Banda Eli is wholly Islamic. Its inhabitants also speak a different language from Keiese, and a majority of them claim ancestry in the Banda Islands at the time before the original Bandanese found refuge from Dutch colonization in Kei.

Despite their linguistic and ethnic difference from the Keiese, people of Banda Eli are very much part of Keiese society. Pure Bandanese ancestry is regarded as a criterion of chiefly status in the village, whereas the commoners are said to have at least some Keiese ancestors. The position of chiefs is explained largely in the same manner as in the surrounding Keiese villages. When the village was founded, chiefs established a privileged relationship to land through various kinds of alliance with previous land-owners, and later gave protection to other settlers who became their dependants. Past connections with the Keiese are, in other words, fundamental to their authority. Even though predominantly immigrant chiefs constantly make reference to origins outside the Kei Islands, their precedence within the local community depends on their connection to the autochthonous past.

I say precedence because there is by no means any consensus about chiefly authority and the chiefs' relationship to autochthonous Keiese society. Banda Eli is founded on land identified with several 'villages of origin,' each with its own stories and landmarks. The idea of these villages and of autochthonous society in Kei generally is in radical contrast with the present idea of society. Autochthonous Keiese are said to have lived in an undifferentiated community, either dwelling in a single big house or in a cave, with no institution of marriage and no knowledge of cooking (Geurtjens 1924:241, 277). Social differentiation and marriage were brought to them by immigrants who also became the rulers and chiefly class of the islands (Geurtjens 1921:179). A prominent symbol of the deified principle of 'law' brought by the immigrants is *hawear*, a sign of prohibition made of white coconut leaf. The leaf indicates that the entity — a woman, a garden, or a piece of land — which it protects is inviolable; in Keiese eyes, it signifies the value of that entity.

Representations of Keiese society as a whole have often focused on the division between people of different status, known as *mel-mel* ('chiefs'), *ren-ren* ('commoners'), and *iri-iri* ('slaves') (Geurtjens 1921:179; Klerks 1939). However, the categories of *ren-ren* and *iri-iri* can only be understood in their respective relationship to *mel-mel* (Barraud 1979:120). The opposition of chiefs and commoners is associated with the dualism of autochthonous and immigrant people through topological metaphors such as *mel tum lair, ren wuar tel*: '*mel* originate from the cape, *ren* from three mountains'. Commoners are also associated with immobility, chiefs with mobility and action. The Keiese words for cape and mountain occur in local place names which define the community as something composed of autochthonous and immigrant elements, but do not identify these components with any social groups.

The status of 'slaves', on the other hand, is related to ideas about morality and personal value. The ancestors of slaves are said to have trespassed against the moral order, known as the law of *Larwul Ngabal*. This law was brought to Kei by the ancestors of the chiefly class and is under the guardianship of local rulers (*rat*) whose domains in Kei consist of up to a dozen villages each. The influence of state administration and trade have strengthened the position of chiefly groups over the last one hundred years and sustained an interpretation of status by which kings and chiefs are all identified with *mel-mel* who then rule all different levels of community, segmented into individual domains (*ratschap*), villages, hamlets, and clans.

It is possible to argue that the two relationships of *mel-mel* to other people and the two levels of community ruled by ordinary chiefs and the kings constitute levels in a comprehensive social ideology. What easily remains understated in such a model, however, is the capacity of local communities to reproduce these levels in other institutions and in more limited social settings. In northern Great Kei, ritual exchanges between local and external forces are not confined within a single village, but take place within the framework of dyadic alliances between Houses of different villages. Such alliances which may be conceptualized in several ways are often strikingly intimate in nature. The parties barter foodstuffs and make gardens together. They participate in each others' healing rituals and family feasts. The Keiese concept of *rahantaran* ('stopover house') which applies to many such relationships in Banda Eli suggests that people in one House issue from the other House. They may have been concretely recruited from the 'donor' House, but in other cases their birth is said to have been the result of its fertility magic.

Rahantaran is not the only relationship between Houses which is of relevance here. There are many stories in which immigrant Bandanese help a Keiese family in a war against another Keiese party and receive land in reward. Other alliances result from the settlement of a feud which results from an elopement between the subordinate people of two Houses. I will not attempt a systematic analysis of these relationships here, but want to point out their significance as a context for cosmological ideas. Each House has a network of relationships with other Houses in distant parts of Kei, and by virtue of these relationships they become part of intense disputes and fights which arise from the symbolic connection between land rights and honour. In each case, general categories which define personal value and origin become salient as people, to use an indigenous phrase, 'become aware' of durable social attachments.

Alliances and networks of this kind extend so widely in space that it would be difficult to call them constituting elements of society if people were not constantly reminded of them by well-known landmarks. Tuburlai, a cove in the northern end of Banda Eli, is known as the place where *Larwul Ngabal*, the immigrant principle of justice, 'first landed' in the vicinity, and was received by people who lived on top of a steep cliff next to the cove.

Such places are often recognized as *pomali* or 'taboo' by people who live near them. On the other hand, not everyone in the respective communities participates in rituals which focus on the sites. A single village may have several cosmological sources, each with a mythological account of its own. Ritual exchanges between immigrant and autochthonous parties which take place in these places maintain the sense of myth as part of social reality; the sites, in turn, would not remain potent if people were not reminded of their importance by myths (Siikala 1991:3).

Ideas of Autochthonous World

The two myths I will examine below were collected in an atmosphere of rivalry between persons who both aspired to headmanship in a village north of Banda Eli. They were in fact close relatives, but belonged to Houses with entirely different kinds of claims to land and people in their village. The occasion which prompted the telling of the myth in each case was talk about the relationship between a chiefly and a commoner House. This is a synopsis of the first myth:

> When the world began, an old man and woman were living alone at the shore. The man set a fish-trap and repeatedly caught two *nabi laut*, pieces of driftwood which he eventually brought back to his house. When the old couple went to their garden in the morning, the logs changed into two little boys who cooked food for the man and the woman. The man and the woman caught them and decided to bring them up as their

children. When the boys were grown up, the elder of them asked the old man to make a bow and arrows. He got them and shot an arrow at the mountain. A flower was planted at the house: it would wither if he died. He followed the arrow and found a princess (*putri*) who lived in a fortress in the interior of the island. He married the princess and stayed in her house for a week. Then he shot another arrow towards the cave of a *suangi*, a demon living in the cave of Fotun Kub. Another flower was planted at the princess's house to show if he was dead or alive. Despite the warnings of the princess, the boy went on to retrieve the arrow and was devoured by the demon. The flowers withered.

Thus the younger brother who had stayed in the village knew that his elder brother was in trouble. He went to look for him and shot another arrow towards the mountain. By following the arrow, he first found the princess, then the demon. He killed the demon and rescued his brother from its belly. They returned to the princess who was the elder brother's wife. The land and the slaves of the princess were divided between the two brothers: the younger went and ruled over the land and sea to the west of the mountain; the elder ruled over the land and sea to the east (the land which includes part of Banda Eli). The elder brother's grandson finally descended to the shore and was integrated into a coastal village by means of exchange of land with a House already living at the coast.

The old couple who live at the seashore represent the autochthonous people, but they are clearly incapable of reproducing themselves. Miraculously they get two 'sons' who drift into their midst and only become human after they have been brought into the house. A related motif in other Keiese myths is the transformation of a sea-snail or frog into a nobleman after it has been cooked by an old woman (for example, Geurtjens 1924:215, 257, 263). Each motif exemplifies a Keiese cosmological pattern: before the immigrant male has been incorporated in society, he lacks the capacity to move autonomously and approaches the island and the woman in it like flotsam (Barraud 1990:206).

Active agency is consistently represented by the two male heroes, but such agency only appears after they have been brought up by the old couple. Thus the boys are not incorporated into island society by marriage, but by receiving food; even their maleness can be seen as a local product. The fertile aspect of autochthony is represented as a princess who lives on the mountain. When the heroes are ready to face her, they do so in a very masculine way, by penetrating it with arrows. It is here that the myth introduces the categories of elder and younger brother and constructs a relationship between east and west coast in terms of their precedence. The elder goes first, stays with the princess and has intercourse with her for a week, but later gets eaten by the demon. The younger brother goes after him, abstains from sex with the princess, succeeds in killing the demon, and rescues his brother. The stage is set for a diarchic arrangement which reflects the two aspects of the 'stranger king' (Sahlins 1985:91). But instead of playing out this opposition, the brothers part: the younger becomes chief of the western and the elder of the eastern side of the island.

In this way, Keiese myths speak about relationships between places rather than identifiable people. In the context in which I was told this story, it only points to hierarchical relations which focus on a single chiefly House, and never mentions its rivals. The second myth describes the relations of the rival House to subordinate people and land:

> A man called Terngun lived at the coast. One day a gust of wind knocked over the coconut milk which his daughter had prepared to wash her hair. The hero decided to declare war against the northern wind. On his way to the village of the wind, he encountered a water-fowl, a sea-cucumber, and an octopus who joined in and helped him. The war was a test of whether the wind could knock over the hero's boat. With the help of the sea-animals, the hero managed to stay immobile in the water and then proceeded to destroy the village of his adversary. Defeated, the northern wind gave the hero two golden objects which he brought back to his village.

The second myth is in direct contrast with the first in that the male hero is a warrior from the beginning and moves outwards rather than inwards relative to the island. His adversary, the male outsider, is not recognized as a human being but as a tempest. However, the incoming wind causes uncontrolled movement by spilling the coconut milk which significantly resembles the uncontrolled, inward movement of the two drifting logs in the first myth.

The motif of the wind which symbolically rapes the girl and that of the contest against the wind are also found in other Keiese myths, with similar consequences for the plot (Geurtjens 1924:269). The hero takes revenge from the outsider by winning a contest in which he has to control his movement and stay immobile in the sea.

The contrast between the two myths concerns (1) the initial value of male agency, and (2) the domain in which this agency operates. In the first myth, the male hero loses his battle after encountering the autochthonous female; however, the order of seniority and the order of events in the narrative indicate that fertility is established as the encompassing value in this encounter. In the second myth, the hero who goes to fight out at sea brings home valuable metal objects as ransom. Had he not been given them, it can be expected that he would have brought back the dead enemy instead. The valuables represent the outcome of heroic male action and a replacement of the powers of autonomous reproduction inherent in the girl. Each myth thus celebrates a different aspect of the autochtonous society: its fertility and its capacity to interact with outsiders. A crucial difference between the myths is suggested by the different condition (dead versus alive) in which the outsider is incorporated into society. In the first myth, male heroics are encompassed by autochthonous fertility; in the second myth, fertility is just a starting point in the interaction between the self and the other which eventually transforms the notion of value within society itself.

As Barraud (1990:207) suggests, the inversion of movement in the two stories coincides with an inversion of values. Valuable human beings arrive from the sea in the first myth and establish society as a complementarity between the masculine and feminine. Seen against the background of the Keiese institution of bridal payments, the valuable things which are brought in from the sea in the second myth enable autochthonous society to maintain its reproductive autonomy by introducing exchange within its own boundaries.

Ethnography of other Maluku societies contains various instances of cosmology and mythology in which two antagonistic perspectives can ultimately be seen to complement and implicate each other. One example are 'myths of life and image', two kinds of accounts of the origin of the state, in Halmahera (Platenkamp 1988). In Kei, an active, violent attitude directed towards the outside world is opposed to an attitude of ritually controlled, pacific interaction between society and external forces (Barraud 1979:65). A comparable opposition between cosmological perspectives is associated with the classification of local societies into groups called *siwa* and *lima* in the Central Maluku. Here *lima*, the division of society in 'five', is associated with the idea of transformative male action and control of the external world as superior value, while societies called *siwa* ('nine') value fertility and the complementary relationship between male agency and female powers (Valeri 1989:133).

Cosmology in Society

Comparison of the myths I have outlined with other Keiese myths and to similar cases elsewhere in Maluku suggests that Keiese cosmological thought does involve 'levels of value'. Each conceptualization of how the community relates to the external world is confronted by an opposite hierarchical evaluation, making the two perspectives inseparable (ibid.:137). Transposed to presently existing society, however, the common reference of the myths is far more difficult to see. Each of the stories makes reference to an entirely different set of people and places known by name, but does not have anything to say about the elements of society or the landscape which are the subject of the other myth. The relationships they *do* address concern individual Houses, not presently existing communities in their entirety.

The application of hierarchy in this case would presuppose that certain cultural values which are perceived as universal are instantiated in concrete social relationships which not only constitute a discursive or performative context for those values but are 'decisively oriented' by them (Dumont 1980:37). I have suggested previously that, rather than looking at presently existing divisions between villages and other entities, one should be looking for such context in alliances between Houses which mediate each others' relationship with autochthonous and foreign powers.

The profound significance of such an alliance became clear to me through events which occurred towards the end of my fieldwork. A man was gravely ill, and his family summoned a woman from another House to help find the cause of his sickness. The woman's House stood in a peculiar relationship of alliance to the House of the sick man: when its male line had become extinct after a feud generations ago, new men had been recruited to it from the allied House. The relationship between these Houses thus follows a general pattern of complementarity between the autochthonous and the immigrant: while autochthonous people depend on the immigrants for men in order to reproduce themselves, the immigrants need autochthonous people to mediate their relationship to local spirits (cf. Barraud 1990:205).

The affliction of the man was construed as a potential effect of a marriage between persons from different generations. This rule is an essential part of what people in northern Great Kei include in the concept of autochthonous 'law' which was later replaced by a new law known as *Larwul Ngabal* brought by immigrants. Autochthonous society is still present in the form of spirits known as the 'disappeared' which punish immoral conduct through possession, illness or death. Geurtjens (1924:ii) tells that origin myths used to be told only at night because in the daytime they might summon the spirits who might take some of the living with them. Their punishment is said to be more violent and 'severe' than that dictated by *Larwul Ngabal*. In order to escape the punishment of the 'disappeared', the entire family of the afflicted person has to make an offering at the site where *Larwul Ngabal* first landed on the island.

The offering to the autochthonous spirits thus repeats a founding event of society, the arrival of the immigrants whose law replaces the old one. In general terms, the singular image of *Larwul Ngabal*, compared to the plurality of autochthonous spirits, indicates that the local society is encompassed by external principles. In this context, however, the 'doing of justice' clearly consists of tribute by external powers to the autochthonous ones. The ritual offering (an old coin) is said to replace the body of the person who would otherwise have to be offered as a human sacrifice. Such replacement, Barraud et al. (1994:15) argue, implies the subordination of one party to another, in this case, of immigrants to the autochthonous party.

The guardian of *Larwul Ngabal* is a ruler called *rat* whose domain covers a dozen villages in northern Great Kei. In an abstract sense, this domain represents an encompassing socio-political level in Keiese conceptualizations of society (Barraud 1979:62). At least in northern Great Kei, however, the relationship of local communities with the domain can be constructed in several ways. The first myth cited above defines the eastern shore as the domain of the 'elder brother' and the western shore as the domain of the 'younger brother'. Relative to this, the ruler's path represents a categorical inversion, since he first settled at a village on the western coast before moving to his current seat on the eastern coast. In the second myth, the external world provides local society with valuables which replace the dead enemy. The ruler, in turn, is said to have settled in Great Kei because his sister, an immigrant woman, married an autochthonous man.

In this way, Fox (1994:99) argues, precedence allows people to change the relative emphasis of such oppositions as elder/younger or male/female, and sometimes reverse their order of value and trace their relationship to the mythical source or origin in multiple ways. Precedence so conceived does not conflict with the existence of a hierarchy of values; my point is, however, that the institutional order oriented by it is open to various overlapping definitions.

The Seriousness of Myth

The structures of precedence associated with the contemporary social order of villages and domains indicate that the category relationships which emerge in the myth are also broadly used in the discourses which order Keiese society as a whole. Origin myths called *tum*, however, are clearly not charters of this order. As we have seen, mythical categories are applicable to Keiese society in general, but often have a specific connection to a place. Two theoretical perspectives open up from these observations: myths can be seen either as shared cultural resources, or as discursive knowledge with conditions of truth and validity defined by the spatial and social context.

The first approach appears better founded in light of the fact that the connection of the myth to a particular landmark or place is not an essential feature of the genre as a whole. Commentaries which Geurtjens (1924) added to the myths he collected often suggest that the plausibility of mythical events in indigenous eyes derives from the familiar circumstances in which they take place. This would support the view that the 'root paradigms' of a culture, assumptions about what motivates action for various kinds of agents (men, women, chiefs, witches, exchange partners, and so on) and ideas about the risks and supernatural forces which affect people in different milieux (forest, village, sea, and so on) are reflected in and reinforced by textual models (Turner 1981:150).

Unfortunately, such perspective leaves unanswered the question which arises from what is specific and theoretically interesting in the symbolic resources and patterns of the myths. If origin myths are in some sense the 'basis' or 'origin' of some aspects of present-day society, as their generic name indicates, what is this society, and how do myths constitute it? The consideration of the social context of myths has already suggested that the answer might be found by looking more closely at the connection of certain myths to a place. In his collection of forty Keiese stories, Geurtjens (1924) sets aside what he calls 'patriotic' stories, while others are just stories. Stories of the former kind are held to be true by particular communities, but included in the same genre as ordinary tales. Fox (1979:16–19) describes a similar difference between ordinary tales and 'true tales' in Roti: the truth of the story ultimately depends on whether or not it refers to the royal genealogy of the domain where it is told. The domains and places to which the stories are connected might be seen as discursive spaces in which a specific sense of reality and truth determines the constitutive power or 'seriousness' of the myth.

The idea of myth as 'discourse' implies that speaking about the past is constrained by conventions and norms which reflect and constitute order. Lamont Lindstrom (1990:25) has applied such an approach to the Polynesian Tanna culture by defining it in terms of procedures and controls which regulate the distribution of knowledge. These procedures make certain kinds of knowledge 'serious' by 'divor[cing] it from the local everyday background' and organizing it into 'doctrines' and 'disciplines' (ibid.:28, 30).

The difficulty of treating Keiese origin myths as discourse in this sense is that there are no well-defined conditions of truth, seriousness and textual authority which would correspond to Lindstrom's description. Keiese *tum* do not constitute an object of firm belief, nor is their truth a matter of doctrine or coherent theory. Neither do they constitute society as an *ordered* whole. After watching Keiese people who made arguments about land rights by narrating *tum*, Geurtjens (1924:iii) observed with amazement that nobody ever contradicted the facts in another person's story. Instead, he would just tell another story which, on the surface, bore no relationship to the previous one. Instead of making truth claims, as discourse does, in a generalizing cognitive framework, mythical thought 'comes to rest in the immediate experience' (Cassirer 1953:32), drawing the limits of things and providing internal organization for human activity as a precondition for any discursive awareness of foundational events.

Myths speak to each other at the level of Keiese cosmological notions, but each of them affirms a singular event or place as the origin of society. These events and places do not define presently existing communities, but ancient ones. Likewise, the alliances through which individual Houses are connected across village and status boundaries thus have little to do with society as an organized whole. They arise from sociality which alternates between a recognition and non-recognition of the external world. This sociality differs from present-day social order in that it requires the periodic restoration of society in its autochthonous undifferentiated state (cf. Spyer 1996:31). The possibility of such non-recognition of the external world is conceivable in the smallest societies, even those seemingly too small to sustain autonomous social life, as Valeri (1994:202) argues in reference to the way in which the Huaulu of Seram seek to encompass the complexities of their historical environment.

People of different status have a different relationship to autochthony. The status of chiefs or *mel-mel* is defined by their immigrant origin to the extent that by admitting marriages between their ancestors and autochthonous Keiese, they would forfeit their superior status. For this reason, chiefly narrators make a difference between the origin of the Houses which they occupy and their personal origin outside Kei. In their accounts, the autochthonous founders of a land-owning house have become extinct, and new people have been recruited from an immigrant chiefly house sometimes several times over. Not a trace of *personal* relationship is acknowledged to remain between the founders of a House and its present occupants. Commoners, by contrast, are often able to work out an unbroken genealogical chain between mythical origins and the present.

Interestingly, genealogical accounts going back to the beginning of the world are always about 14 generations long. The uniformity of this time-frame is in itself remarkable: it demonstrates that there is a broader, genealogical discourse about the personal origin of different people outside Kei, and about their value and honour as persons. Unlike mythical accounts about the origin of places and Houses, genealogical accounts can be debated and contested. The character of these two genres as discourses of value in society therefore depends on the way in which they establish a connection between the ancestral past and the present.

Narrative has different ways and modes of creating such connectedness between different chronotopes which, as defined by Mikhail Bakhtin, exist both in texts and in the consciousness of people who read or listen to them (1981:84). As the name of the genre suggests, the primary chronotope of *tum* is the understanding of mythical events as precedents. In terms of the 'internal' continuity of the myth, this means that later events repeat (and sometimes invert) the pattern of earlier ones. Through ritual, past and present are connected through space rather than through time (Valeri 1990:72). 'Externally' myths extend their meaning to the present through such institutions as local House alliances, the ruler and his domain, or daily interaction between chiefs and commoners in the village context. Mythological schemes alone do not constitute these institutions and contexts as a hierarchical order. However, an interest in creating such orders is evident whenever a society affirms its own totality against external, differentiating facts, pitting its myths against other myths with no more than implicit recognition of its constant dialogue with social others.

References

Bakhtin, Mikhail

1981 *The dialogic imagination*. Austin: University of Texas Press.

Barraud, Cécile

1979 *Tanêbar-Evav: une société de maisons tournée vers le large*. Cambridge: Cambridge University Press/Paris: Editions de la Maison des Sciences de l'Homme.

1990 Wife-givers as ancestors and ultimate values in the Kei Islands. *Bijdragen tot de Taal-, Land- en Volkenkunde* 190(2–3):193–225.

Barraud, C., D. de Coppet, A. Iteanu and R. Jamous

1994 *Of relations and the dead: four societies viewed from the angle of their exchanges*. Oxford: Berg Publishers.

Cassirer, Ernst

1953 *Language and myth*. New York: Dover Publications

Dumont, Louis

1980 *Homo hierarchicus: the caste system and its implications*. (2nd edn) Chicago: The University of Chicago Press.

Fox, James J.

1979 Standing in time and place: the structure of Rotinese historical narratives. In A. Reid and D. Marr (eds), *Perceptions of the past in Southeast Asia*, pp.10–25. Singapore: Heinemann Educational Books (Asia) Ltd.

1988 Origin, descent and precedence in the study of Austronesian societies. Public lecture in connection with De Wisselleerstoel Indonesische Studiën, 17 March 1988, Leiden.

1994 Reflections on 'hierarchy' and 'precedence'. In M. Jolly and M. Mosko (eds), *Transformations of hierarchy: structure, history and horizon in the Austronesian world. History and Anthropology* (Special Issue) 7:87–108.

Geurtjens, H.

1921 *Uit een vreemde wereld of het leven en streven der inlanders op de Kei-Eilanden*. 's-Hertogenbosch: Teulings.

1924 *Keieesche Legenden*. Verhandelingen van het Koninklijk Bataviaasch Genootschap van Kunsten en Wetenschappen 65(1). Weltevreden: A. Emmink and The Hague: M. Nijhoff.

Klerks, Jos

1939 Gegevens over Keieesche huwelijksadat. *Bijdragen tot de Taal-, Land- en Volkenkunde* 98(3):285–323.

Lindstrom, Lamont

1990 *Knowledge and power in a South Pacific society*. Washington DC: Smithsonian Institution Press.

Platenkamp, Jos

1988 Myths of life and image in Northern Halmahera. In D. Moyer and H. Claessen (eds), *Time past, time present, time future*, pp.148–167. Verhandelingen van het Koninklijk Instituut voor Taal-, Land- en Volkenkunde 131. Dordrecht: Foris Publications.

Sahlins, Marshall

1985 *Islands of history*. Chicago: University of Chicago Press.

Siikala, Jukka

1991 *Akatokamanava: myth, history, and society in the Southern Cook Islands*. Auckland: The Polynesian Society in association with the Finnish Anthropological Society, Helsinki.

Spyer, Patricia

1996 Diversity with a difference: *adat* and the New Order in Aru (Eastern Indonesia). *Cultural Anthropology* 11(1):25–50.

Turner, Victor

1981 Social dramas and stories about them. In W.J.T. Mitchell (ed.), *On narrative*, pp.137–164. Chicago: University of Chicago Press.

Valeri, Valerio

1985 *Kingship and sacrifice: ritual and society in ancient Hawaii*. Chicago: University of Chicago Press.

1989 Reciprocal centers: the Siwa-Lima system in Central Moluccas. In David Maybury-Lewis and Uri Almagor (eds), *The attraction of opposites: thought and society in the dualistic mode*, pp.117–141. Ann Arbor: The University of Michigan Press.

1990 Diarchy and history in Hawaii and Tonga. In Jukka Siikala (ed.), *Culture and history in the Pacific*, pp.45–79. Transactions 27. Helsinki: Finnish Anthropological Society.

1994 'Our ancestors spoke little': knowledge and social forms in Huaulu. In Leontine Visser (ed.), *Halmahera and beyond: social science research in the Moluccas*, pp.195–212. Leiden: Koninklijk Instituut voor Taal-, Land- en Volkenkunde Press.

Wouden, F.A.E., van

1968 *Types of social structure in eastern Indonesia.* Koninklijk Instituut voor de Taal-, Land- en Volkenkunde, Translation Series 11. Transl. Rodney Needham [Preface by G.W. Locher]. The Hague: Martinus Nijhoff.

11. Contestations: Dynamics of precedence in an eastern Indonesian domain

Michael P. Vischer

This paper serves as a companion text to the film 'Contestations', which is available online at http://epress.anu.edu.au/precedence_citation.html.

Introduction

This contribution is concerned with a fundamental issue in the study of human societies: the process by which unequal or asymmetric relations are established, asserted and contested. A second and underlying concern is the development of a comparative method in anthropology, which goes beyond the regional mutually interpretative stance that, in the best of cases, still stands for comparison. In the case of precedence, particular processes of social differentiation involving asymmetric relations can be compared that have been identified as being characteristic to the societies of eastern Indonesia and, by extension, also to the societies of the wider Austronesian world.[1]

This paper investigates one specific case of precedence, the domain of Ko'a on the eastern Indonesian island of Palu'é. The analysis is directed at particular events which occurred in the context of the opening of the ceremonial cycle of the domain of Ko'a. Such cycles were earlier identified as constituting the main order of the domain and the principal arena in which positions of precedence are contested and asserted (Vischer 1996b).[2]

These cycles are carried out only once in a decade and ideally extend over a period of five years. However, periods of intense activity are confined to the opening of a cycle, where water buffalo are purchased on the neighbouring island of Flores and where preliminary sacrifices are held to make amends for transgressions against ancestral law.[3] Five years later, at the closure of a cycle during its second period of intense activity, the main sacrifice is carried out that ensures the future welfare of the domain.[4]

These events are exemplary in that they are interlinked in a manner highly characteristic of such processes. Furthermore, all of them are connected to earlier events and situations that are traced in the analysis. The language of Ko'a provides a term for this form of tracing which is used mainly in legal context. The term *susu* refers to the establishment of the history of a given issue, and in practice the more extensive a *susu* is the stronger the case that can be made in customary courts. This *susu* process is reflected in the current analysis. The analysis thus maintains a strong diachronic perspective as it moves between the level of events and individual actors and the medial level of abstraction of precedence as an analytic concept.

Ko'a Precedence: The First Settlers' Model

The Ko'a case is exemplary of systems of precedence of eastern Indonesia. In Ko'a, as well as elsewhere in the Austronesian world, precedence is characteristically predicated upon a notion of multiple origins of society. The different groups of the domain maintain different narratives of origin according to which they settled in the domain at different times. There are two different Ko'a origin groups that subscribe to the same myth of origin and creation of the domain, which they have appropriated as the myth of origin of their own group by inserting the names of their own original ancestral pair at its beginning. In this myth, the voyage of the first ancestors is recounted as they travelled from the westernmost rim of the earth to the island. According to the myth, these ancestors brought with them a stone and some earth which, when they had reached the present location of Palu'é, grew to the size of the island as it is now. The myth has the form of a chant consisting of hundreds of paired place-names delineating the path taken by the first ancestors, from the distant point of origin all the way to the domain. In many ways the myth provides a blueprint for the ideology of the first-settling origin groups of the domain, whereby every one of its individual couplets represents a point of access to a different facet of ancestral knowledge. On the basis of literal precedence in the sequence of settlement in the domain, the two Ko'a origin groups that have appropriated the myth of origin and creation, claim ceremonial and political leadership. At two separate centres these origin groups periodically sponsor and conduct the ceremonial cycles of the domain, during which this myth of origin and creation is re-enacted. A successfully conducted cycle then ensures the continuity and welfare of the domain. Although in cosmological terms they both constitute separate centres of the Ko'a universe, in all ceremonial matters one centre always takes precedence over the other. Subsequently settling groups were integrated into the domain by means of marriage alliance. First settlers allocated agricultural land and gave wives to subsequent settlers, which made the latter contextually subordinate to the former. Unlike, for instance, in the case of precedence among the Ata Tana 'Ai of Flores (compare Lewis 1988), where subsequently settling groups constitute a sequential order, *oda*, the sequence of settlement of the later settling groups of Ko'a is not differentiated, with the exception of one group that holds an intermediary position as traditional wife-givers to the first settlers. This, in a nutshell, is the first settlers' model of Ko'a precedence.

Figure 1. The ceremonial courtyards of Ko'a

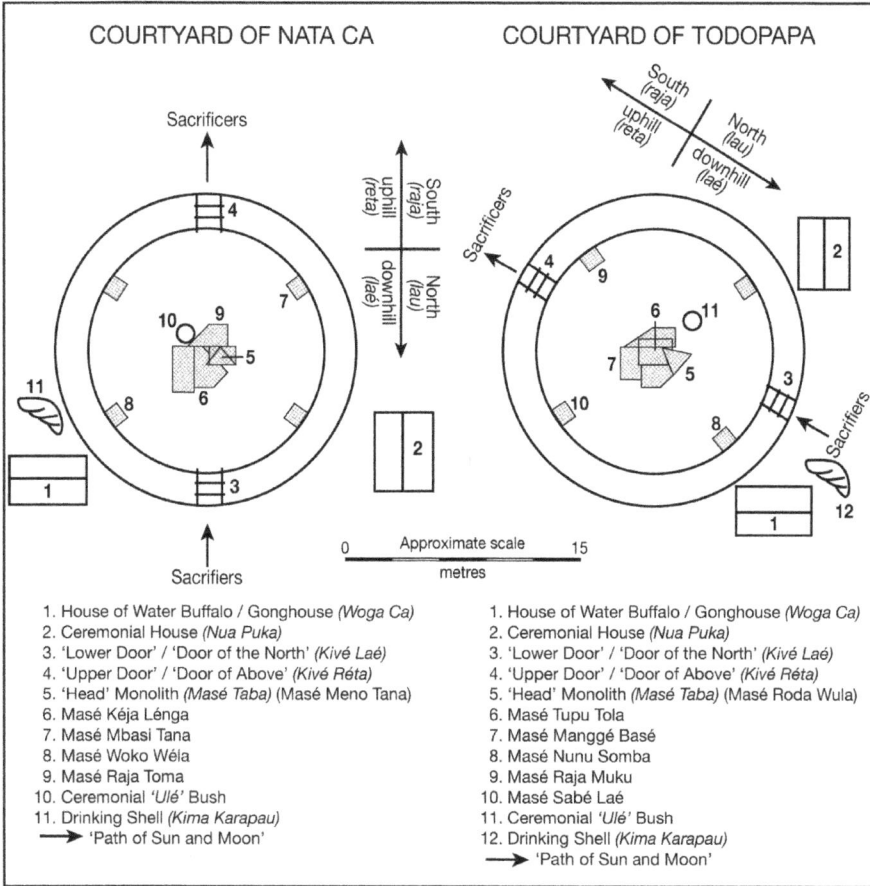

COURTYARD OF NATA CA   COURTYARD OF TODOPAPA

1. House of Water Buffalo / Gonghouse *(Woga Ca)*
2. Ceremonial House *(Nua Puka)*
3. 'Lower Door' / 'Door of the North' *(Kivé Laé)*
4. 'Upper Door' / 'Door of Above' *(Kivé Réta)*
5. 'Head' Monolith *(Masé Taba)* (Masé Meno Tana)
6. Masé Kéja Lénga
7. Masé Mbasi Tana
8. Masé Woko Wéla
9. Masé Raja Toma
10. Ceremonial 'Ulé' Bush
11. Drinking Shell *(Kima Karapau)*
→ 'Path of Sun and Moon'

1. House of Water Buffalo / Gonghouse *(Woga Ca)*
2. Ceremonial House *(Nua Puka)*
3. 'Lower Door' / 'Door of the North' *(Kivé Laé)*
4. 'Upper Door' / 'Door of Above' *(Kivé Réta)*
5. 'Head' Monolith *(Masé Taba)* (Masé Roda Wula)
6. Masé Tupu Tola
7. Masé Manggé Basé
8. Masé Nunu Somba
9. Masé Raja Muku
10. Masé Sabé Laé
11. Ceremonial 'Ulé' Bush
12. Drinking Shell *(Kima Karapau)*
→ 'Path of Sun and Moon'

There are two ceremonial centres of the domain, which represent exclusive points of connection with the multi-layered universe. Each of these centres in turn is divided into a lower and an upper half. The houses located at the upper half are associated with the sacrifice of water buffalo and those located at the lower half are associated with the ceremonial purchase of the sacrificial animals. At one centre, all of the ceremonial offices are held by one and the same origin group, whereas at the second centre, these offices are held by two different origin groups. With respect to the localized spirits of the domain, the sacrifiers at the upper half attend to the lower half of the domain and the sacrificers or purchasers to its upper half.

Figure 2. The Ko'a village grounds: principal houses and ceremonial courtyards

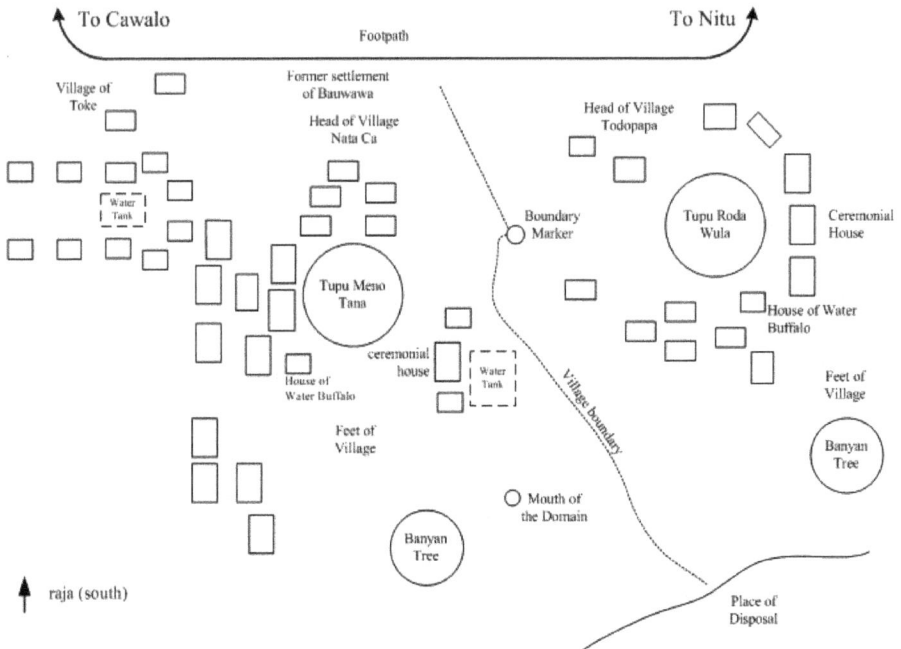

The dwellings of houses of subsequently settling origin groups are arranged in lines in secondary positions behind and along the side of the centres, whereas the dwellings of houses of first-settler status are located in a primary position surrounding the centre. The settlement pattern thus is to some degree an expression of the Ko'a order of precedence.

The Ko'a social order seemed fixed and rigid in the way it was presented to the ethnographer as a first settler's model. The position of the two first-settling origin groups could not be altered in any way. Junior houses of a given origin group seemed to have no option to attain a position of seniority, and within a given house a younger sibling could never become the superordinate first-born son. Although there had been a few vague indications that this order may have looked different in the past, hardly any information could be obtained regarding such changes. There clearly had been changes at the second ceremonial centre of the domain. A few generations ago, the group that used to hold the position of sacrificers or purchasers of water buffalo at the second centre was ousted by its sacrificers because of incest. The group in question relocated to the first ceremonial centre and no longer assumed first settler status. As a replacement a house of an origin group that did not hold first settler status but an intermediary position was installed as purchaser at the second ceremonial centre. Other than that no changes in the Ko'a order of precedence were ever mentioned.

The ethnographer's understanding of Ko'a precedence changed significantly, once he had participated in his first Ko'a water buffalo sacrificing cycle (1984–1987). There he witnessed contestations and assertions of positions of precedence not only between the two centres of the domain, but at virtually every socio-cosmic level: At the level of the house, between junior and senior members and at the level of origin groups, between junior and senior houses of the same origin group. There were contestations and assertions of positions of precedence between the two origin groups claiming first-settler status and even between the allied domains of the island. The cycle revealed itself to me as a total social phenomenon in the Maussian sense, involving all levels of Ko'a society. It constituted the main arena in which positions within the order of precedence of the domain were contested, and the holders of those in turn were continuously engaged in asserting their position.[5]

The opening of the Ko'a sacrificing cycle of 1994

I should have known that Opa, the main priest-leader of the domain, had a hidden agenda when he invited me to return to Ko'a to film the opening of the last water buffalo sacrificing cycle. It was in early 1994; I had just completed the study of the major corpus of texts connected with that cycle. In fact, I was hoping to conclude my fieldwork on Palu'é and if anything, this offer seemed to be a clever way to lure me back to the domain. When I returned six months later on the date we had agreed upon, everybody in Ko'a was worried. The main priest-leader's daughter, a young unmarried woman called Mia Poké, had not returned yet from Malaysia, where she had been spending most of the year cooking for her labour migrant brother Sundu. At that time Mia Poké was virtually the only person eligible to take on the office of ceremonial virgin for this cycle. This officiant is regarded to be the spouse of the main sacrificial water buffalo. At various stages of the cycle she goes into seclusion and following the sacrifice the same stringent mortuary restrictions apply to her as they do to any woman who has lost her spouse. In principle any unmarried woman of a house of first-settler status that is engaged in the purchase of water buffalo can be selected for this office, on the condition that a major part of the bridewealth for her mother has already been paid. However, at that time there was no other candidate. So without Mia Poké's presence the cycle could not be opened.

It was the beginning of the rainy season and the seas were turning rough, and with every day that the voyage was delayed the trip would become more dangerous. As the main priest-leader's younger brother by way of adoption, the task fell to me to get Mia Poké back from Malaysia.[6] It took several weeks to trace them in Malaysia and another couple of weeks to convince Mia Poké and her brother Sundu to come back. No doubt the prospects of being greeted in Flores by a camera crew as they alighted from the boat helped convince them to come. When they finally had arrived, they did not join me on the boat back to Palu'é but stayed on for a few more days in the district capital of Maumere on Flores as they said, to do some shopping, seemingly oblivious to the fact that all of Ko'a was anxiously waiting for them.

A few days later, the Ko'a priest-leader's firstborn son Sundu and his sister Mia Poké entered the village. Only minutes after their arrival we witnessed the first scene of contestation to the Ko'a order of precedence.[7] Sundu walked straight up to the grave site of his recently deceased foster mother, a woman called Moré. There he dropped to the ground and began to cry. Two classificatory grandmothers hugged and comforted him while another one could be seen sitting on the porch of the priest-leader's house next to the grave site. She lamented that, although he had not been ill when he was informed that his foster mother was dying, he had not come home. Then Sundu's father, the main Ko'a priest-leader arrived and took his son, whom he had not seen for many years, into his arms and they wept together. The father then moved towards the porch where his daughter Mia Poké was sitting. As they embraced, both were crying.

Meanwhile, inside the priest-leader's house several of Sundu's classificatory mothers were opening a small basket containing the fingernails and hair locks of the three last generations of deceased members of that house. These are the named ancestors that a given house can draw on for support in its daily undertakings. The women were looking for the relics of the recently deceased Moré. Lisé, a classificatory brother of the main priest-leader Opa joined in the search and began to unwrap a small parcel containing Moré's fingernails. The women asked him not to open it. As he grabbed the parcel they begged him not to take it outside. He insisted, saying that he was taking it outside to show it to the priest-leader's son Sundu. Weeping himself now, he handed the parcel to Sundu. Walking together to the front part of the house they held on to each other and Sundu exclaimed in tears that his foster mother Moré was truly dead. The key to understanding this emotionally charged scene is to be found in the troubled relationship between Lisé and his classificatory brother Opa, the main Ko'a priest-leader.

Figure 3. Kinship diagram of Opa and Lisé (abbreviated)

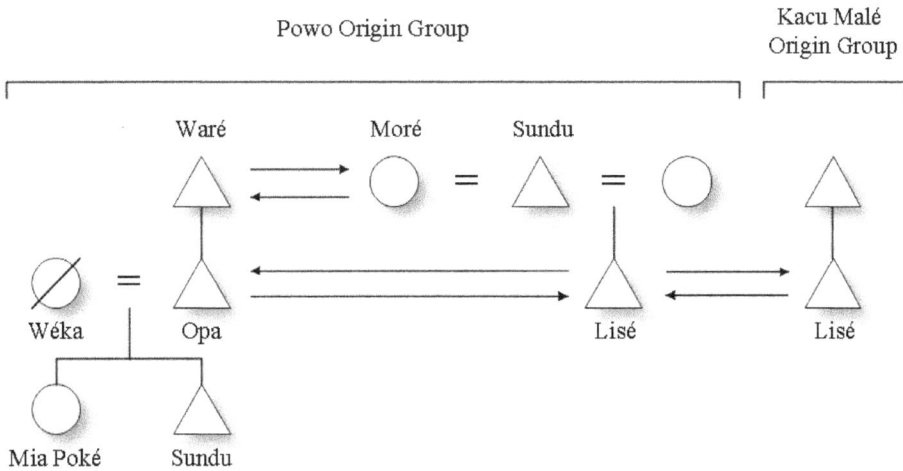

The troubled relationship between Lisé and Opa has some of its origins in the common practice of child transfer. Children often choose to eat and sleep in another house of the same origin group, and that is considered to be quite normal. If a child ends up spending extended amounts of time in a particular house it will after a while be considered to be a member of that house. In the case of Opa and Lisé there was something of a switch-over going on. As a young child Opa apparently spent a lot of time in the house of Lisé's father Sundu, who used to be the local government representative in Ko'a and Lisé in turn spent a lot of time in the house of Opa's father Waré, who held the position of main priest-leader. So when they still were young, at times Opa would be considered to be Sundu's son and Lisé would be considered to be Waré's son. This situation was further complicated by the fact that Lisé had chosen not just one, but two alternative houses in which to spend his time, and the second house was a house of a different origin group. Eventually Lisé gained rights to land use in that origin group, and when Opa's father Waré died, he also laid claim to a specific lot of land held by Waré's house. Opa contested that claim in court but the court solomonically divided Waré's lot in two, awarding one half to Opa and the other half to Lisé.

Moré, the woman Sundu and Lisé had been crying for, followed a similar pattern. Initially she was considered to be Sundu's wife, because Sundu had paid a considerable amount of bridewealth, but at times she also stayed in Waré's house. Since she could not bear any children, this did not give rise to any conflicts. Being barren, she was not really regarded as the spouse of either. When Opa's first wife died, it was Moré who took care of the two children, Mia Poké and Sundu. Because in her youth she had been instructed by a renowned ritual specialist, Moré also handled some of the ritual affairs connected with the ceremonial centre, albeit only on behalf of the main priest-leader.

Opa and Moré never got on well and apparently before her death they had been fighting about Moré's scheming to find an appropriate spouse for Sundu. Moré was hoping for an alliance between Sundu and one of the houses of her own natal origin group, an alliance that would be very much in line with Ko'a presciptive alliance.

In seeking to broker a marriage for Sundu, Moré was aiming at re-instating her natal origin group as the traditional wife-giver to the first-settling groups of the domain. Such marriages had become rare and for a number of reasons her natal origin group was becoming more and more insignificant. In the past, Moré's natal origin group had held much more of a prominent position in the order of precedence of the domain. As the traditional wife-givers to the priest-leaders, they were in particular contexts even superordinate to them. According to their own origin myth, they had brought the technologies of fire, metal and weaving to Ko'a and for that they had received the special right to act as custodians of the ceremonial house of the main ceremonial centre of the domain. This is also the house the ceremonial virgin inhabits during periods of seclusion. However, the custodians of the ceremonial house were dying out, and in the absence of successors, custodianship would fall back to the first settlers and so would the prestige that went with this custodianship. A marriage of her natal origin group with the priest-leader's son, who would be the next main priest-leader of Ko'a, would counteract this impending loss.

For several reasons Opa felt that such an alliance would not be desirable. In this intrigue, Sundu sided with his father Opa, whereas his sister Mia Poké sided with Moré. Much of this dispute took place in the absence of Sundu, who for a number of years had migrated to Malaysia to work in a timber camp. During all that time, Mia Poké was being instructed in ritual matters by Moré. When Moré died and Opa refused to pay for the mortuary costs, his daughter Mia Poké apparently left Ko'a in anger to go, as they say, 'to cook for her brother' in Malaysia. Opa felt that since Moré had been Sundu's spouse and since Lisé had inherited Sundu's land holdings, it was up to Lisé and not him to provide pigs for Moré's funeral.[8] So that was one of the reasons why Mia Poké had not wanted to return to Ko'a to take up her office as the ceremonial virgin for the new cycle.

252

She saw an opportunity to contest her father's position and did just that, thereby effectively preventing the domain from opening a new ceremonial cycle and endangering the welfare of all of its members.

Seen in this context, my somewhat flattering invitation to come to Ko'a and film the cycle appears to have been part of Opa's strategy to get his daughter back. I was the one in the family, so to speak, who had connections in the outside world and who could perhaps effect her return. Given that I had committed myself fully to the project, he knew very well that I would be trying my best to get her to come home. Perhaps he also hoped that Mia Poké would be intrigued by the possibility to be filmed in her identity as a ceremonial virgin. Opa's ruse had worked. Interestingly, no one in Ko'a seemed to wonder if perhaps one of the reasons why Mia Poké did not want to return was that she did not want to become a ceremonial virgin in the first place.

One event that occurred during the opening phase of the cycle does provide an indication of Mia Poké's ambivalent disposition with regard to her office as *kombi* virgin. During the cycle, which ideally extends over a period of five years, she is regarded as the spouse of the sacrificial water buffalo and is, therefore, not eligible for marriage. Once the main sacrifice at the end of the cycle has been carried out, she is still not free to get married, but is subject to the same mortuary restrictions generally applied after the loss of a spouse. Even after these restrictions have been lifted, the bond to the water buffalo remains intact. Should anyone wish to marry her, special payments in addition to the negotiated bridewealth must be made to buy her loose from this bond. This arrangement acts as a deterrent to potential suitors and effectively precludes any opportunities for marriage the young woman might have. At the opening and at the closing stages of the cycle, the *kombi* virgin goes into seclusion in the small ceremonial house adjoining the centre her water buffalo is affiliated with. There, she is attended to by a female member of that house. Particularly during the purchasing voyage, she must remain absolutely still, to the point that her attendant must feed her when she is hungry and scratch her back when she is itching. As the old lady attending to her during that part of the cycle pointed out before the purchasing parties departed, whatever movement Mia Poké might make has a detrimental effect on the boats as they are out at sea. In the event, the boats unexpectedly met with stormy weather soon after they had left the island. Sudden gusts of wind tore up the sails of her father's boat and the boats of both purchasing parties were dispersed. As the winds hit, those on board anxiously called out for Mia Poké to remain still, fearful that the adverse conditions were being prompted by movements the *kombi* virgin was making in her seclusion back home. All boats eventually did reach Flores safely, but the weather remained stormy for six days and nights and prevented them from returning to Palu'é. During the return trip there was more bad weather, but miraculously none of the small vessels capsized in the rough seas, even though they were loaded well beyond their capacity. Finally, at the end of the trip, as the boats prepared to unload the animals at the Ko'a beach, one of the boats did capsize. (This event will be discussed in detail below.) One of several lines of explanation offered for this incident was that the *kombi* virgin had not remained completely still in her ritual seclusion. Eventually other lines of explanation for the incident were favoured, but upon returning to the villages there was talk that Mia Poké had not stayed in seclusion during all of the seven days of the purchasing voyage and that she had been seen playing around with her friends, while her father's party was out at sea. Clearly Mia Poké had some resistance against the restrictions imposed upon her by her office.

In order to understand Opa's refusal to pay for the mortuary costs of Moré as an act of assertion of his primary position within the Ko'a order of precedence and in order to appreciate Lisé's tearful display as an instance of contestation, we must turn to yet a further set of events of the past. Here Lisé exploited this grey zone created by his moving back and forth between Sundu and Waré's house during his childhood. According to *hada*, the ancestral corpus of rules and regulations, the first-born son of the most senior house of the first-settling origin group is eligible for the office of main priest-leader. Lisé was indeed a few years older than Opa and yet he was not the main priest-leader of Ko'a.

Apparently, three cycles ago, that is roughly thirty years earlier, Lisé had made an unsuccessful bid for priest-leadership. Working in concert with a man called Lopo, the priest-leader of the second ceremonial centre of the domain, he had gained support from the main priest-leader of the domain of Cawalo, a traditional ally of Ko'a. The main priest-leader of that domain was a staunch opponent of Opa's, who would have liked to have seen Lisé, who had a much weaker and more malleable personality, in the position of main Ko'a priest-leader (see Vischer 1996b). At the time, the people of Ko'a enthusiastically followed Lisé and his allies to purchase water buffalo on Flores, thereby showing their approval for this new main priest-leader of their domain. Lisé's sacrificial animal, however, did not survive. This was generally interpreted as a sign that the Supreme Being and the ancestors of his origin group did not agree with Lisé's bid for priest-leadership. The event is hardly ever mentioned in Ko'a, perhaps because there is a certain sense of embarrassment for having so easily shifted loyalties from one priest-leader to the next, only to have to embrace again the one they had rejected previously. The supernatural sanction, of course, also strengthened Opa's position considerably. Ever since then, Opa has used every opportunity to humble Lisé publicly, as he did by refusing to contribute to the mortuary payments for Moré. In refusing, he was pointing to the fact that Lisé was to be considered Sundu's son and, therefore, fully responsible for the mortuary payments for Sundu's deceased wife. Opa, however, seemed to want things both ways. On the one hand he rejected responsibility for Moré, but on the other hand he kept her fingernails and hair locks stored together with those of his own ancestors in his house. Lisé's crying as he clutches these relics seems to be saying: 'Behold the injustice that has been done to me. I have been badly cheated. I paid for Moré's funeral, but look, it is he and not I who gets to keep her relics (in order to be able to draw upon her support as an ancestor of his own house)'.

Here we can identify one of the important strategies in the processes of assertion and contestation. If customary regulations, such as those pertaining to mortuary issues have been breached and no supernatural sanction has ensued, this indicates the action has been approved by the ancestors and the Supreme Being. Such a breach of custom actually strengthens the position of the offender.[9]

One such instance, where Lisé's actions nearly resulted in humiliation and subsequent loss of status, took place at the very end of the water buffalo purchasing voyage. In the unloading of the sacrificial animals at the Ko'a harbour, the order of precedence between the two ceremonial centres of the domain must be maintained strictly. The sacrificial animal for Opa's centre is always to be unloaded first, followed by that of Lopo's, the second priest-leader of the domain. Upon unloading, the tether of the sacrificial animal must be passed to a member of a particular origin group that holds rights over the harbor of Ko'a. That origin group then guides the water buffalo along a particular path up the mountain to the boundaries of the village where the tether is passed on to the main priest-leader. He then takes the animal up to the boundary of the second ceremonial centre, where he hands it over to that priest-leader, in line with the order of precedence between the two centres. Any mistakes in the unloading or in the sequencing of the tether can result in the death of the water buffalo. It is during this first stage, following the unloading, that the water buffalo that Lisé had brought back twenty years earlier had died. On this most recent occasion Opa delegated the unloading to Lisé.[10]

In the event, Lisé unloaded first the main sacrificial animal of the cycle, the 'water buffalo of the domain' *(karapau tana)* affiliated with the main ceremonial centre. This is the animal that is to be raised in Ko'a and sacrificed, ideally after a period of five years, at the conclusion of the ceremonial cycle. Following the 'water buffalo of the domain', Lisé unloaded two more animals affiliated with his centre. These animals are referred to as '<water buffalo> to sacrifice and throw away' *(pati kao)*, in allusion to the fact that following their sacrifice at the opening of the cycle their carcasses are left on the ground to be scavenged by outsiders. In the cycle in question there were a number of such animals which were to be sacrificed as atonements for transgressions against ancestral prescriptions. The specifics regarding these animals will be discussed further below. Just as Lisé was unloading them, the boat carrying the main sacrificial animal of the second centre capsized. Fortunately for Lisé, the animal, which was trapped in its cage, survived the ordeal. Had the animal died, a new purchasing voyage would have had to be initiated to replace the 'water buffalo of the domain' of the second ceremonial centre.

At the time, several explanations for the capsizing were offered in Ko'a. Some of the participants at both centres speculated that the incident took place because Lisé had unloaded both, the main sacrificial animal of his centre as well as those dedicated to the preliminary sacrifices in one go, rather than allowing the second ceremonial centre to unload its own main sacrificial animal right after the main sacrificial animal of the first centre, and only then unloading the other animals. Such a sequence would have been more in line with the order of precedence of the domain, where any ceremonial activity always must be initiated by the first centre, after which the second centre is permitted to commence the same activity. As it is commonly put in Ko'a, the first centre always must 'go forth' (*nolo*), whereas the second centre always must 'follow' (*tetu*). Breaches generally involve significant supernatural sanction and can also entail legal consequences. Had the animal died and had this line of argumentation prevailed, it is more than likely that Lisé would have had to be the sole sponsor of a new purchasing voyage, an undertaking that doubtlessly would have put him deeply into debt. Furthermore, the public ridicule possibly would have reduced his status for good. As it turned out, on that particular occasion Lisé was fortunate and his blunder did not have immediate consequences.[11]

Incest and Precedence

During the previous Ko'a ceremonial cycle of 1985–1988, Lisé had not been quite that fortunate. At the beginning of that cycle, soon after the main sacrificial animals had been ceremonially installed in the domain, the water buffalo of the domain, which was affiliated with the main ceremonial centre, suddenly died. At the time divination revealed that the animal had died because Lisé had committed incest with a classificatory sister residing in an allied domain. Not only was he obliged to sponsor a new purchasing voyage to replace the main sacrificial animal but he was forced to purchase a second animal, which was to be sacrificed for his transgression (see Vischer 1996b).

The incident indicates that the accusation of incest, particularly between members of first settling houses, may be another strategy that can be resorted to in the contestation or assertion of positions of precedence. At any point in time there is a number of marriages in the domain that, strictly speaking, could be considered to be 'wrong marriages' (*vai cala*), either because the alliance was contracted across generations or between classificatory siblings. However, only rarely are such cases contested, unless an occasion arises, where a particular advantage can be gained, as had been the case with Lisé's transgression.

In this light, the reason given for the ousting of the origin group responsible for the purchase of water buffalo at the second ceremonial centre of the domain acquires new significance. A number of generations ago, this origin group had been accused of incest and was driven away from its centre. At the time, the two halves of this centre were traditional partners in marriage alliance. It is, however, not clear which group held the position of wife-taker and which that of wife-giver. More likely than not, the direction of alliance was periodically inverted (see Vischer 1992). According to the scanty information available, the members of the ousted group were about to move to a different domain, when the priest-leaders of the main Ko'a centre invited them to settle in their part of the domain, albeit without retaining their first settler status.

In doing so they became members of the category of subsequent settlers commonly referred to as 'women of eight' (*vai valu*), a term, which also denotes widows and orphans, the rationale here being that all the members of the domain go into mourning at the death of one of its priest-leaders. The complete ritual speech couplet, which refers to those members of a domain that do not hold first settler status, is 'women of eight // children of *halo*' (*vai valu // hana halo*). The first composite term of this couplet refers to the Ko'a notion of gestation, where female children are born eight months after conception, whereas the period of gestation for male children is nine months. Subsequently settling groups in the domain are thus conceptually female. According to Ko'a classificatory thought they are, therefore, subordinate to the conceptually male first settlers. The second half of the couplet refers to a related contrast, where subsequent settlers are classified as 'child people' (*hata hanané*), as opposed to first settlers who are classified as 'father people' (*hata hamané*). The term *halo* is a reference to a myth of origin subscribed to by a number of different origin groups on the island, which points to a region in neighbouring Lio on Flores as a place of outside origin. This clearly identifies them as subsequent settlers.

The two houses that subsequently stepped into the vacant positions at the lower half of the centre do not maintain alliance relations with the upper half of that centre, as had been the case with their predecessors. Rather, they sought alliances with the origin group in charge of the main ceremonial centre of the domain. This relationship is in line with the traditional position of their original origin group, which in this process of replacement they had split off from, as wife-givers to the first settlers of the domain.

During the most recent Ko'a cycle, another case of incest between first settlers was sanctioned. This case was far from arbitrary, in that it involved two siblings who had been born from the same parents. About fifteen years ago, Cawa, a man now in his late thirties had left Ko'a to seek work in the Malayan state of Sabah. More than a decade later, his young unmarried sister Wéka went to join him there to assist in his household. As it was explained to me in Ko'a, when he had left home Wéka had been still a little girl, so the two never had known each other as adults. In Sabah they had sexual relations and eventually they conceived a severely handicapped child. Although initially they tried to hide this fact from other Ko'a migrants, the news eventually got back to Palu'é.

Unless incest has occurred between members of first settling houses, the sanctions called for by ancestral law are relatively light. Sleeping mats on which the transgression has occurred are burned and a pig from the house in question is killed on its door step. Instead of allocating individual cuts to particular related houses, as is usually the case, the cuts are thrown across the roof to the back of the house, where they are gathered up by human scavengers.

Incest between first settlers is altogether a different matter. Because of the close affinity constructed between members of first settling groups and the domain itself, incest between these can cause earthquakes, volcanic eruptions and tidal waves (see Vischer 2001). In pre-colonial times the culprits would have been sacrificed at the top of the volcano in order to avert such natural disasters, whereas nowadays water buffalo are employed as a replacement.

In Opa's speech to the people of the domain, which immediately preceded the sacrifice of the incest buffalo on the volcano, the main Ko'a priest-leader couched the issue in terms of morality and responsibility.[12] He began by making allusion to the mythical foundations of incest sanctions and mentioned the story of Noni and her brother Karé who 'swam together' (that is, had sexual intercourse) in the lake inside the volcano, as a result of which the 'mountain descended and the sea rose up' (that is, natural disaster ensued).[13] He pointed out that in the case of Cawa and Wéka, their father Rugu and his brother Sundu had to pay for the sacrificial animal, in order 'to keep the mountain up and the sea down' (that is, to avert natural disaster) and that this should be a warning to anyone whose children were working in Malaysia, lest their children 'play with the wrong drums and gongs' (that is, have incestuous sexual relations). Implicit in this last statement was the notion that henceforth incest among members of houses that were not of first settler status would be fined in the same way as first settlers. Understandably, this new regulation was not welcomed by the members of the domain.

A third water buffalo was sacrificed for transgressions against ancestral prescriptions two days after the incest sacrifice. This sacrifice, which took place at the main ceremonial courtyard of the domain, is referred to as '<the water buffalo of> the arm span of the earth' *(repa tana)*. Its designation refers to the notion that for any deep cavities, such as excavations occurring during construction activities (ideally, cavities that exceed a depth of one arm span), a water buffalo must be sacrificed. At every cycle one such animal is sponsored by all Ko'a houses, rather than only by its first settlers, since all members of the domain have in one way or another been involved in construction activities during the years following the closure of the previous ceremonial cycle.

The underlying cosmological notions for this sacrifice are linked to the conception of the island as a living body, beneath the surface of which blood flows, as it does through the human body (see Vischer 2001). The embodied domain weakens at every instance that cavities are inflicted upon it, eventually resulting in loss of fertility. Only blood sacrifice can heal these 'wounds' and restore the integrity of the incorporated entity. A sick body is conceptualized as being hot. The sacrifice of animals is aimed at removing this heat and at reattaining a state of beneficial coolness. Thus, to heal the wounds of the domain a water buffalo must be sacrificed at the opening of each new ceremonial cycle. Ko'a first settler ideology constructs a close affinity between the blood flowing beneath the surface of the domain, the blood of its first settlers and the blood of the sacrificial water buffalo. In the 'repa tana' sacrifice, the blood of the animal shed at the ceremonial centre is viewed as a substitute for the blood of its main priest-leader. This came out clearly at the end of the speech given by the main priest-leader at his ceremonial centre, immediately preceding the sacrifice.[14] In his address he first made allusion to the incest sacrifice and repeated his earlier admonitions, because some of the members of his domain, as well as many members of allied and neighbouring domains present on that occasion, had not been able to attend the sacrifice at the top of the volcano. He also asked those who had come from outside mainly in order to scavenge, to be patient and to enjoy themselves and socialize before they cut up the carcass, the reason being, that by allowing the blood to penetrate fully into the ground the efficaciousness of the sacrifice is increased. The central statement of his speech dealt with the reasons for this sacrifice: that the embodied domain had been harmed through the collective actions of its people and that it was everybody's responsibility to conduct this water buffalo sacrifice, rather than for him to sacrifice himself. He said: "I do not agree to sacrifice myself, I do not consent to give up my body. I replace my body; my cuts fall to the ground. I replace my blood; my blood pours down." Implicit in this statement was again the strong identification of the priest-leader with the domain. If the domain is not healed through sacrifice, then its priest-leader in turn can become ill and may even die (see Vischer 2001).

The repa tana sacrifice and the sanctions for incest among the first settlers both highlight clearly the privileged cosmological position of members of first settling origin groups in the domain. As such they can be understood as periodically recurring assertions of precedence. However, one might argue that the extension of the costly sanctions for incest among first settlers to all members of the domain announced in Opa's speech at the top of the volcano ultimately would undermine this special position, because such an extension implicitly accords the same cosmological ramifications to the actions of subsequent settlers as it does to first settlers. This is perhaps why to date this new regulation has never actually been applied.

Origin, Place and Precedence

On the day following the sacrifice at the top of the volcano, the very same people who had been fined for this case of first settler incest were called upon to provide yet another water buffalo, this time to make amends for a different type of transgression. The sacrifice was held at a place called Powo, a location, which is of central importance to the identity and status of Opa's origin group as first settlers. Powo is the original place of settlement of this group. The place, which according to the Ko'a myth of creation, grew out of the stone and soil the first settlers had brought along with them on their mythical voyage from the western rim of the universe. As such it is virtually an icon of their precedence in the domain. Powo was abandoned many generations ago, when the various origin groups of the domain moved from their separate and dispersed places of original settlement to form the two current main Ko'a villages, Nata Ca and Todopapa.

In everyday speech, the abandoned place of original settlement is simply referred to as Powo and the group that subscribes to this place as its place of origin, as Hata Powo, People of Powo. The full name of this origin group, which is used only in formal contexts, consists of a string of place names denoting a patch of sacral forest surrounding the ceremonial centre of the abandoned first settlement. The trees of this forest are the home of a particular supernatural being that can be addressed only by the Powo priest-leader. This being has pendulous breasts which, during a drought, are slung across her shoulders. Through cracking open a coconut on one of the monoliths of the abandoned centre, her breasts can be made to fall off her shoulders. This immediately results in heavy rainfall throughout the domain. Because of this supernatural presence linked to the provision of rain, which is of the highest importance in a predominantly agriculturalist society, it is prohibited to cut down any trees inside the sacral forest of Powo. Any disturbance could cause this being to flee, leaving the main priest-leader without the means to influence the fecundity of the domain.

Powo has been a place of contention for some time. Ownership and rights to usufruct are shared by all of the houses of the Powo origin group. In the past, members of those Powo houses associated with the upper half of the main Ko'a ceremonial centre and thus with the act of sacrificing water buffalo, have attempted on several occasions to clear the Powo forest. Powo is located at only a short distance from the Ko'a settlements, and because the land has never been used for agricultural purposes, its soil is a lot more fertile than that of most other parts of the domain. Partly for those reasons, some of the sacrificing houses of Powo dearly wish to turn the forest into agricultural land.[15] Misfortune occurring in the sacrificing houses following any attempts in clearing have to date acted as deterrents to further clearing. However, to the Ko'a main priest-leader, such attempts to clear Powo are viewed as a direct challenge to his position. They undermine one of his crucial functions as priest-leader, to provide the domain with rain in times of need.

In a speech at Powo addressed to the members of the domain and to the crowd of visitors from all over the island, the main Ko'a priest-leader explicated the reasons for this sacrifice which was about to take place.[16] He began by invoking the paired formal term for fire making sticks (*poco no'o laci*), which according to ancestral law stands for the unlawful burning off of land. He mentioned that twice in the past Powo had been burned down accidentally by the same people, while they were clearing gardens surrounding the forest. He went on to state that the offence had been perpetrated by the very same houses which had only just been fined for incest. Properly speaking, he said, they should be liable to sacrifice two animals at Powo in addition to the one already sacrificed on the volcano. However, because they were related through marriage, the fine would amount to just two animals: 'one for above (the volcano) and one for below (Powo)'. Finally he threatened to fence off the sacral forest, an action which would close an important path leading to gardens located above the Powo forest. Although it is generally not permitted to close or relocate any of the paths in the domain, he insists that his origin group had already resorted to such measures in the past. This last statement was received critically by the people of Ko'a and there was some resentment about this assertion of precedence, because of the disruption of everyday agricultural activities such a measure would entail.

Figure 4. Kinship diagram of Opa/Wéka and Rugu/Sundu (abbreviated)

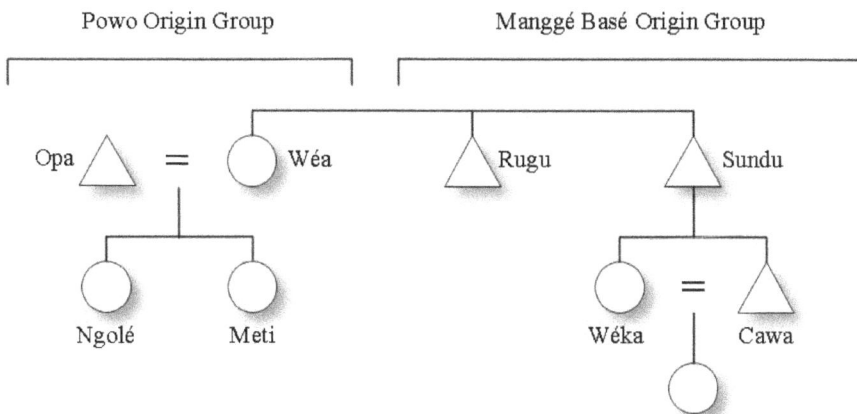

The relatedness Opa was referring to in his speech pertains to his second marriage to a woman called Wéa, a sister of Rugu, the very same man who had been fined for the incestuous relationship in which his brother's children had engaged in Malaysia. Opa had had two daughters with Wéa, both of whom were in their early teens. Being unmarried and of first settler status, they would have been appropriate candidates for the office of *kombi* virgin. However, because Opa had never made any significant instalments of bridewealth to their mother's natal house, they were not eligible for that office.

Generally, defaulting on bridewealth instalments eventually entails supernatural sanctions for the wife-taking house. Opa and his wife-givers could, therefore, well have interpreted the accidental burning of the Powo forest as such an instance. The possibility was, however, never publicly voiced. Although Rugu's house was also of first settler status and a member the sacrificing houses of the second Ko'a ceremonial centre, it had a junior position within that origin group and even though wife-givers are in some contexts superordinate to wife-takers, Rugu did not stand up to his wife-taker and demand that bridewealth be paid. In this instance, the amount of bridewealth owed to him by Opa was actually reduced by the fact that it had been Opa who had paid for the two animals that had been sacrificed on behalf of Rugu's house. Rugu himself would have been hard pressed to provide the necessary funds for these sacrifices and, therefore, had to agree to reduce the amount of bridewealth owed to him, by accepting the two animals in lieu of the ivory tusks, golden ear pendants and large pigs customarily given to wife-giving houses. Having accepted these, it was not likely he would be receiving any further instalment of bridewealth in the near future. In this particular case, Opa managed to turn a potentially threatening situation into a distinct advantage. By staging these highly visible sacrifices that emphasized the privileged cosmological position of his group and the primacy and sacredness of its place of origin, he asserted very effectively its position of precedence in the domain, while at the same time reducing the amount of bridewealth he owed to his brother-in-law.

Apart from this underlying issue of bridewealth, there is yet another aspect to the two buffaloes sacrificed for the transgressions of Opa's wife-givers. In both instances, immediately preceding the sacrifice, the tether of the sacrificial animal was passed through the cracked bamboo wall of Opa's house and placed on his house altar to inform his ancestors and the Supreme Being of the impending sacrifice.[17] Strictly speaking, the priest-leader of the second Ko'a ceremonial centre or the senior house of the sacrificers of that centre should have been doing this at their own house altar, since the offences had been committed by members of the sacrificing origin group affiliated with that centre. At least with respect to the incest sacrifice, the responsibility clearly was with the second centre. It is not altogether clear why this matter was handled in this way. The pragmatic reason given by Opa was that it had been he who had purchased those animals and brought them in from Flores. The implication is that neither the sacrificers nor the priest-leader of the other centre had made any moves to atone for their transgressions, leaving it up to him to avert the supernatural sanctions that threatened the whole of the domain. In a way his responsible, but also somewhat self-righteous, action amounted to an assertion of his precedence over the second Ko'a centre. There is, however, also a cosmological angle to this issue. According to Ko'a ideas about the afterlife, the deceased members of the domain reside inside of the volcano. There they lead a life which is very similar to that of the living, except that the dead experience neither pain nor hunger. The placement of the tether of a sacrificial animal on the house altar enables the deceased members of that house to conduct their own ceremonial cycles and tend to their social network among the dead by exchanging various categories of goods. Ancestors who are successful in these undertakings in turn can give strong support to the living members of their house in their dealings in the world of the living.

Ritual, Precedence and Marriage Alliance

Another line of argumentation that was raised with regard to the near disaster that occurred during the unloading of the sacrificial animals at the end of their voyage from Flores, one taken by members of the main ceremonial cycle, involved a further facet of the notion of maintaining the order of precedence between the two centres, where virtually every ritual activity is commenced first at the main ceremonial centre and then only followed by the second centre. This refers to an incident that took place at the beginning of the purchasing voyage, during the crossing over to Flores.[18] The small fleet comprised of boats of both centres was dispersed due to bad weather shortly after departure from Ko'a. Those boats affiliated with the main Ko'a centre sought safety for the night in a cove along the Flores north coast. On the following morning, upon arriving at its final destination, the main purchasing party found that the boats of the second party had arrived there before them. Although there was no direct evidence indicating that this had been intentional, the inversion of the proper sequence of arrival did constitute a considerable breach in the order of precedence between the two centres. The capsizing of the boat carrying the main sacrificial animal of the second centre, therefore, was to be interpreted as a warning by the Ko'a Supreme Being to maintain the order of precedence between the two centres.

On a personal level Opa did not get on well with Lopo, the priest-leader of the second Ko'a centre. To Opa, Lopo was ignorant in ritual matters and, unlike himself he had no privileged connection with the Supreme Being. He was an outsider whose ancestors had been placed in their current position as a result of the case of incest. For virtually every ceremonial activity at his centre, he depended on the instructions of Pali, an old lady, who was a prominent member of its sacrificers. Furthermore, Opa was well aware of the fact that Lopo in the past had been giving Lisé support in his ambitions to become main Ko'a priest-leader. Lopo had even married a sister of Lisé, which in particular contexts placed him in a subordinate position with regard to Opa's origin group. Generally, first settling origin groups are not supposed to be linked by marriage alliance, partly for that very reason.

After the controversial incidents of the purchasing voyage, Opa used the first opportunity that presented itself to assert his position. Once the sacrificial animals have been brought to the domain, the priest-leader of each centre calls the collective ancestors and the Supreme Being to his respective centre in a ritual referred to as *kao pollo*, which translates as to 'divide and to throw away'. During this ritual the pervasive dual socio-cosmic order of the domain is explained, hence the appellation 'to divide', and a commitment is made in the presence of the Supreme Being about the date of the final sacrifice. This division of the domain applies not only to its two ceremonial centres, but also to the internal division of each centre into an upper and lower half. (see Diagram No.1).

In a playful rice throwing battle between the upper and lower halves of each centre, the Supreme Being and the localized collective ancestors of the domain are invited to attend. These ancestral spirits are closely associated with particular named locations, referred to as 'the names of the domain' (*tana ngarané*). Female officiants of the upper and lower half of each centre call out the names of the localized ancestral spirits, whereby the officiant at the upper half of each centre calls upon the 'names of the domain' of the lower half of the domain and that of the lower half of each centre calls upon those of the upper half of the domain, in line with their respective spheres of influence.

In that context Opa not only asserted his own position, but strongly contested the position of the priest-leader of the second centre.[19] Immediately after having concluded the *kao pollo* ritual at his centre, he climbed onto the mound of the second ceremonial centre and stated that there really was only one Ko'a priest-leader ('there is really only one mother, there is really only one father'). After which he, rather than the priest-leader of that centre, proceeded to conduct the *kao pollo* ritual. Such a move effectively amounted to a usurpation of the position of the second priest-leader of the domain and clearly called for a strong response from Lopo.

Once the *kao pollo* has been carried out, the stage is set for a different type of event. Due to the ancestral presence and the presence of the Supreme Being in the Ko'a villages, every act and every word acquires a heightened valency. Every night both centres become the stage for a particular type of dancing and chanting *(togo tio pata,* literally, to dance and chant). The chants follow prescribed structures. They are largely metaphoric and employ a vocabulary, which is mostly different from everyday speech. These chants provide an important channel to air grievances publicly, or to taunt and tease adversaries. Preceding the 1970s, such dances were also frequently held outside the context of the cycle. The local government eventually forbade them because they were perceived as a source of discord within the community. Chanting and dancing of this type is now reserved exclusively for the ceremonial cycle and confined to the two centres of the domain. Words chanted on those occasions and in the presence of the ancestors and the Supreme Being acquire a quasi-legal character. A given chant is repeated over and over again, until there is an acceptable reply. The chants generally are deliberately opaque and allusions to a particular event or an offence in question mostly are veiled, thus designed to incite replies from more than one party.

During the night following the incident of the *kao pollo* ritual, such a chant was being rehearsed at Lopo's centre.[20] The chant was uncharacteristically direct, in that it did not leave any doubt about the issue in question, nor about the persons to whom it is addressed. In this chant, the prominent Ko'a chanter and poet Woko made allusion to his unsuccessful voyage to Malaysia to seek out Opa's children Mia Poké and Sundu. This he chanted on his own account, in line with his own position as wife-taker to Opa's origin group. Woko also chanted on behalf of Lopo, the second Ko'a priest-leader who had married Toci, one of Lisé's sisters. This part of his chant dealt with issues of bridewealth between the two Ko'a groups of first settler status. Essentially it accuses the wife-givers of failing to reciprocate in exchange. The chant goes as follows:

I ask Meno Tana [Opa's centre] to reciprocate.
The [marriage] path is bent,
the child goes in circles,
the child goes in circles,
come quickly and reciprocate.
I was to go north [to Malaysia],
to find Opa's daughter Poké,
or was I to go to the north [to Opa's centre],
where Lopo's [wife] Toci came from ?
The gifts you carried were not enough.
Malaysia is so large you can look for ever,
I went over there to look for Opa's children.
Opa was tired of waving and calling
for the male (his son) to come back from the north.
I went all the way from here to the north,
to call back the male from Powo Wawo [Opa's origin place].
I am calling for the male [the priest-leader],
to come across to Manggé Basé [Lopo's] centre,
to see for himself.
We have seen one side of the moon,
now we need to see the other.
I ask for your gift at your offering place [Opa's centre].
Ndasa's husband [one of Opa's brothers] is north as well.
Oh, the drums follow the ankle bells,

oh, Opa's drums have no voice,
oh the drums of Taku Tolé have no voice.

Marriage alliance on Palu'é is effected through the exchange of gendered goods. The wife-taking house, together with the other houses of its origin group, makes prestations of conceptually male goods to the wife-giving house. These consist of large pigs, golden ear pendants, ivory tusks and money. The wife-giving house and the constituent houses of its origin group reciprocate with conceptually female goods consisting of textiles, harvest goods, furniture, ivory arm rings and a particular type of ancestral beads that can also be substituted by land. The amount of goods to be exchanged is negotiated and so is the time schedule of instalments. At every instalment the resources of the two origin groups involved are pooled, and the goods received are redistributed among the participating houses. Instalments usually take place over an extended period of time and can go beyond the life span of the couple in question, thereby extending obligations between wife-givers and wife-takers to the following generation. The very end of these exchanges is marked by a partial inversion. Once the wife-taking house has made its last major prestation, the wife-giving house reciprocates not only with conceptually female goods, but also with a large-sized male pig. This final prestation is referred to as 'to bring across the fish' (*mboro ika*), thereby obfuscating the categorical inversion.

In the marriage alliance between the houses of Lisé and Lopo, Lisé over the years had already received his share of bridewealth. The final prestation of a large sized pig and a set of golden ear pendants, therefore, was made to Opa's house, as the senior house of the wife-giving origin group. At the time, Opa accepted these goods from Lopo, thereby implying that he would reciprocate with the *mboro ika* pig. However, when the time came to reciprocate, he refused to do so, on the grounds that Lopo's prestations had been insufficient. On an everyday basis, his refusal caused a lot of tension between the origin groups involved, but because Lopo as a wife-taker was subordinate to his wife-giver, specifically in the context of alliance related exchange, he was not in the position to exert any significant pressure on Opa.

Issues of reciprocity in exchange are a frequent topic of the type of chanting that takes place during the cycle. Often they lead to one party making amends on the very morning following the chanting. The chant created by the poet Woko on behalf of Lopo was, therefore, not unusual. What was somewhat unusual was the directness in which this chant was formulated. In this particular case, the chant was formulated in such a transparent and direct fashion, in contravention of the highly valued stylistic conventions of opaqueness, that Opa felt he had been publicly affronted by his wife-taker. During the opening phase of the ceremonial cycle, the members of Lopo's centre chanted this chant on several occasions at Opa's centre, without receiving a satisfactory reply.

Opa did eventually reply to this chant.[21] His chant simply stated what he had already said on previous occasions, that Lopo's prestations had been insufficient and that he, therefore, did not feel bound to reciprocate. Unlike Woko's blunt and direct chant Opa's chant maintained a certain degree of opaqueness by using metaphors as well as semantic inversion, allowing for multiple interpretations, rather than just one evident interpretation.

> Male male male,
> widows and orphans.
> I, the priest-leader, speak to you widows and orphans,
> I, the priest-leader, speak to you the people of Ko'a.
> Together we made the right sacrifice up at the volcano,
> it lies there visible to [the ancestors inside] the volcano.
> Up at the volcano my blood pours down,
> I am outside, my soul is watching.
> No sooner was I offered, that my soul flew away.
> My soul has disappeared, have you seen it anywhere?

At one level of interpretation, the chant deals with the incest sacrifice conducted at the volcano and by extension also with the other preliminary sacrifices. In all cases, Opa felt the carcasses had been scavenged too soon after the sacrifices for the blood to penetrate fully into the ground, thereby diminishing the efficacy of the ceremony. He chanted that his soul, *lobo*, was displaced through the scavenging. At another level of interpretation, the term can also be understood as word play on the name of Lopo (the letter p in the name is implosive, whereas the letter b in the term for soul it is not), the second Ko'a priest-leader. In such an interpretation, the chant alludes to the issue of outstanding bridewealth and to Lopo's insufficient prestations. Whatever the case may be, Lopo did not create a further chant to reply to Opa's chant and he also did not continue to chant the chant Woko had created on his behalf. The Ko'a poets and specialists of chanting, therefore, concluded that Lopo had accepted the chant.

Popular Resistance and Priest-Leadership

Interestingly, at the very same time at which Opa was chanting this chant, bridewealth negotiations were being conducted between some Ko'a houses and some houses of a neighbouring domain right next to Opa's centre.[22] Such negotiations are often major social events, involving large numbers of guests. Usually they are not held in conjunction with the ceremonial activities of the water buffalo sacrificing cycle, because all houses of the domain are supposed to use their resources for catering to the guests attending the dances, rather than for other purposes. This intention is rather more pronounced at the end of the cycle. Once the final sacrifice is under way, no large scale undertakings involving exchange, such as the construction of houses or boats, may be undertaken, until the pole onto which the skull of the sacrificed animal has been fastened has decayed and fallen over. This process may take several years, the end of which is ritually marked by the priest-leader. The negotiations in question were being conducted by houses not holding first settler status, and the very fact that they were conducted at that point in time and at that particular place is suggestive of resistance among the 'child people' of the domain against the continuous assertions and contestations of positions of precedence among its 'father people'.

In the course of the opening phase of the cycle, there had been a number of issues to which the people of Ko'a objected. The extension of sanctions for incest among first settlers to include all members of the domain had not been well received, since it involved bringing in sacrificial water buffaloes from Flores at a cost that few houses could afford, rather than the customary slaughtering of a pig. Given that accusations of incest among first settlers were handled in a somewhat arbitrary manner, the new sanctions were perceived as a serious economic threat. Those who were not engaged in labour migration to Malaysia and who by that very fact were not affluent, would be liable to be held to account for the doings of the absent members of their house, as had been the case with Rugu and Sundu, the father and father's brother of the siblings who had conceived a child in Sabah.

Another measure to which the people of Ko'a objected was the closing of a path leading up the mountain, which Opa had announced as a measure to protect his place of origin against uncontrolled burning. This path was important to all those, whose gardens lay in the upper half of the domain. Though there was an alternative route that followed the bottom of an erosive gully, this represented a significant detour, which was highly inconvenient, since on Palu'é all goods must be carried.

A third point of contention was the unresolved issue of bridewealth exchange in the marriage alliance between Lopo and Lisé's sister. This marriage alliance between the two houses of first settler status not only concerned their respective origin groups, as is usually the case, but it affected virtually the whole of the domain. Just about every house of the domain was involved in this exchange, either on the side of the wife-givers, or then on that of the wife-takers, simply by virtue of having supported one or the other side with goods of the appropriate category. Any dissonance in the conclusion of the extended process of bridewealth exchange between the two first settling groups of the domain was, therefore, a source of discontent to all members of the domain.

Only few days after the poet Woko had chanted his chant on behalf of Lopo, he created a new chant while he was engaged in the tapping of a lontar palm tree, this time on behalf of the people of Ko'a.[23] His new chant was welcomed in Ko'a because it expressed the general feeling about the politics of marriage alliance between the priest-leaders of the two centres. Through Woko's voice, the people of Ko'a appeared to be contesting not only Opa's precedence, but that of both priest-leaders of the domain. In his chant he reminded the priest-leaders of their dependence on the people of the domain. The chant mainly addressed the issue of bridewealth, but its implications went well beyond that. Although it stated that the priest-leaders needed their people as partners in marriage alliance, the implication was that without the people of Ko'a there could be no priest-leaders, no water buffalo sacrificing cycles and ultimately no domain. As it is put in the idiom of the father child relationship between first settlers and subsequent settlers, 'a father needs <his> children, <as much as> children need a father'. As Woko was chanting, he was overheard by other men tapping in the vicinity, and the news about the chant travelled across the island even before Woko had returned home from tapping. His chant will be repeated perhaps for years, until the priest-leaders of Ko'a create a reply that the people of Ko'a accept.

Oh, let's chant!
You have been fooling all of us with your marriage alliance.
I descend on the offering place [Opa's ceremonial centre],
I fly to the offering place.
The people rush to the offering place,
the male [priest-leader]
and the widows and orphans.
The male needs the women of eight [the people],
in future who can the priest-leaders find to marry?
I have said it before,
the return gift [to Lopo] is still missing.
Oh Nata Ca [Opa's settlement],
we wish to see your gift,
how can we follow you?
This is what I have come to ask you at your centre.
At least Ratu Cavané [the ethnographer] got Poké
[Opa's daughter] back.
She had been stalling and delaying [in Malaysia].
Oh, where did you put Toci [Lopo's wife]?
I will say it again and again
at your place of offering,
until I can no longer say it.

Holding a primary position within an order of precedence does not necessarily convey priest-leadership, as the case of Lisé amply demonstrated. Although priest-leadership on Palu'é is ascribed, in that generally only the first-born son of the senior first settling house is eligible for priest-leadership, much depends on the personal abilities such an individual brings to the office, and on the amount of approval and recognition that can be generated among the members of the domain and its allies, whether such a person actually can take up priest-leadership and whether that person can retain that office over time. One of the important functions of a priest-leader is to adjudicate on customary matters and, therefore, a candidate must be knowledgeable about customary law (*huku pata*) and even handed in his dealings with people. Extensive knowledge of *hada*, the ancestral corpus of knowledge, is another precondition for priest-leadership, particularly in the realms of the rituals of the centre, ritual speech, bridewealth negotiation, mythology and the history of the domain and its houses. Such knowledge is usually transmitted over many years from a priest-leader to the first-born son. A priest-leader approaching old age will begin to delegate matters connected with his office to that son, in order for the son to gain experience and also in order for him to gain gradually acceptance and authority in the domain. A son who does not have the abilities necessary for the office may be overlooked in favour of a different member of that house and failing that, even in favour of a member of a different house of the first settling origin group in question. This is probably what happened several decades ago in the case of Lisé, after the former main Ko'a priest-leader had died.

Approval by the priest-leaders of the allied domains is another important factor in securing priest-leadership. This used to be a lot more important in the past, when every closure of a ceremonial cycle was followed by disputes over boundaries shared with non allied domains. Such disputes more often than not escalated into warfare, and there the support from allied domains was absolutely crucial. Currently alliances between domains mainly have a bearing on the quality of a ceremonial cycle and the prestige with which a given domain emerges from its cycle. If the allies have attended the nightly dances over the months preceding the final sacrifice and if they have been catered to appropriately, then a hosting domain may assume a position of precedence with respect to its allies, a relationship which is expressed in terms of gender classification. A hosting domain thus can change its status from female to superordinate male and exercise influence on matters pertaining to the alliance, in line with its position of precedence among its allies (see Vischer 1996b).

It appears that priest-leadership can even be acquired, regardless of the status of the house of the holder, as in the case of Lopo's house that replaced the ousted former priest-leader and his origin group. Although Lopo's house at this point has not yet established firmly its position as a first settling house, partly because the transition occurred rather recently during Lopo's father's father's time, but certainly because of the lack of knowledge in customary matters displayed by Lopo, it may be only a matter of time for the links to his former origin group to be forgotten and for his house to create mythological connections or a historical narrative that more solidly establishes its identity as first settlers.

Priest-leadership and even first settler status also can be forfeited, as had been the case with the ousted sacrificers of the second ceremonial centre in Ko'a. In the Palu'é domain of Tua Nggéo there is currently only one priest-leader. The second ceremonial centre of that domain has been in disuse for several decades and its custodians no longer exercise priest-leadership. The reason given for this by the current main priest-leader is that the former priest-leader of the second Tua Nggéo centre had become 'embarassed' (méa). Although this is not further elaborated upon, the implications are that the former priest-leader was not up to the task and neither was any other male member of his house or origin group. This is where a chant such as the one created by Woko over time may effect a change in the order of precedence of the domain. If, for one reason or another, the flow of approval of the members of a domain and its allies ceases, then a priest-leader becomes highly vulnerable and eventually he may even lose his position. When three cycles ago Lisé made a bid for Ko'a priest-leadership by sponsoring a ceremonial cycle and purchasing sacrificial water buffalo, he could only do so because Opa had lost the approval of the members of his domain and that of its allies. However, approval alone is insufficient for priest-leadership. Lisé failed not simply because his sacrificial water buffalo did not survive. He failed because, in spite of being structurally in the right position, he lacked one absolutely crucial element of priest-leadership.

A significant part of Palu'é priest-leadership is achieved. A given priest-leader who is successful in ensuring the welfare of the domain is believed to have a privileged relationship with the collective ancestral spirits and with the Supreme Being. Of such a person it is said that 'he has <a special relationship with> the Sun and the Moon' (that is, a special relationship with a particular aspect of the Supreme Being) and he is feared, respected and loved for this very reason. If a priest-leader is not successful, it is said that 'the sun and the moon are not with him'. Eventually such a priest-leader will lose the support of the members of the domain to conduct a ceremonial cycle. In illness, a healer sorcerer or a medical practitioner, rather than the priest-leader will be contacted. Periods of ritual restrictions on agriculture will no longer be respected and legal issues will be put directly to the district courts, rather than being dealt with by him in the first instance. At the time of Lisé's bid, Opa was able to resume priest-leadership in Ko'a because the premature death of the sacrificial animal had indicated to the members of the domain that Lisé did not have a privileged relationship with the supernatural, that is, that 'the Sun and the Moon were not with him'. Opa, on the other hand, may not always have had the approval of the members of his domain, but time and again he had proven that he had a very special relationship with the 'Sun and Moon' (see Vischer 1992). The benefits of having someone in charge in the domain who had these particular qualities, in that instance apparently outweighed the fact that every now and then that person made unpopular decisions that affected all of the domain.

Concluding Remarks

With regard to the ethnography of the domain of Ko'a, it has been demonstrated here that precedence as an analytic concept can bring together a whole range of diverse realms (such as issues involving ritual, cosmology, mythology and sacrifice, issues of incest, labour migration, child transfer or adoption, issues of succession, mortuary prescriptions, issues of ceremonial maturity and eligibility, marriage alliance, issues of reciprocity and exchange, leadership, political rhetoric as well as poetics) that in another mode of analysis perhaps would not be easily recognized as interconnected.

The application of the analytic concept of precedence to key events taking place in the context of the Ko'a ceremonial cycle and the tracing of their individual histories has provided insights into processes of social differentiation, involving the establishment, assertion and contestation of unequal or asymmetric relations, which are characteristic to Austronesian societies and which another mode of analysis would probably not have arrived at. This establishes the practical value of this analytic concept for the comparative study of Austronesian social life.

References

Fox, James J.

1995 Origin structures and systems of precedence in the comparative study of Austronesian societies. In P.J.K. Li, Cheng-hwa Tsang, Ying-kuei Huang, Dah-an Ho and Chiu-yu Tseng (eds), *Austronesian studies relating to Taiwan*, pp.27–57. Taipei: Symposium Series of the Institute of History & Philology: Academia Sinica 3.

Kelly, R.

1993 *Constructing inequality: the fabrication of a hierarchy of virtue among the Etoro*. Ann Arbor: The University of Michigan Press.

Lewis, E.D.

1988 *People of the source: the social and ceremonial order of Tana Wai Brama on Flores*. Verhandelingen van het Koninklijk Instituut voor Taal-, Land- en Volkenkunde 135. Dordrecht, Holland/Providence, USA: Foris Publications.

Platenkamp, J.

1988 *Tobelo: ideas and values of a North Moluccan society*. Leiden: University of Leiden.

Vischer, M.P.

1992 Children of the black patola stone: origin structures in a domain on Palu'é Island (Eastern Indonesia). Unpublished PhD thesis. Canberra: Department of Anthropology, The Australian National University.

1996a Contestations: dynamics of precedence in an eastern Indonesian domain. 55 mins videorecording (P. Asch, ed.) Canberra: The Australian National University/Leiden: International Institute for Asian Studies.

1996b Precedence among the domains of the Three Hearth Stones: contestation of an order of precedence in the Ko'a ceremonial cycle (Palu'é Island, eastern Indonesia). In James J. Fox and Clifford Sather (eds), *Origins, ancestry and alliance: explorations in Austronesian ethnography*, pp.175–198. Canberra: Department of Anthropology, Research School of Pacific and Asian Studies, The Australian National University. Comparative Austronesian Series, ANU E Press: http://epress.anu.edu.au/.

1996c Early Austronesian social structure in the light of the Ko'a social order. In P. van der Velde (ed)*Yearbook of the International Institute for Asian Studies 1995*. Leiden: International Institute of Asian Studies.

2001 Substitution, expiation and the idiom of blood. *Journal of the Finnish Anthropological Society* 3:30–44.

ENDNOTES

[1] The parameters of comparison have been defined linguistically. For our present purposes they are confined to the world of speakers of the Central Malayo-Polynesian Subgroup (CMP) of the Austronesian language family (that is, the two dozen or more languages of Flores, Sumba and Timor in the eastern part of Indonesia). The contention is, however, that what is being said about CMP speakers with regard to precedence also holds true to varying degrees for that family as a whole. As was to be expected, research into groups located in Austronesian border areas has revealed a considerable cultural overlap on both both sides. See for instance Platenkamp 1988. These findings do not diminish the value of this informed comparative approach. They do, however, raise questions as to what exactly the characteristic features of Austronesian societies might be, an issue, which clearly requires further research.

[2] The case under investigation was documented extensively by videographic means in late 1994 and early 1995. Some of this footage subsequently was edited by the ethnographic filmmaker Patsy Asch at the Ethnographic Film Unit of the Department of Anthropology at the Research School of Pacific and Asian Studies (The Australian National University) and made into a social anthropological film for teaching about the analytic concept of precedence. The film 'Contestations' (Vischer 1996a) depicts a series of contestations and assertions of the order of precedence of the domain of Ko'a, which took place in the context the opening phase of its water buffalo sacrificing cycle.

[3] The tentative analysis made in 'Contestations' was to a large degree confirmed in the feedback sessions. The participants agreed that in terms of precedence the film not only showed all of the crucial events of the opening of the cycle, but that they had been represented appropriately. As it turned out, the extensive discussions triggered by the images mainly added depth to the analysis, rather than suggesting significantly different interpretations from those already offered in 'Contestations'.

[4] The film 'Contestations' deals with the opening phase of the cycle, as does this contribution. A sequel dealing with the closing phase of the cycle is in post production.

[5] I presented the first results of my analysis in a paper I gave in 1990 at a conference on Austronesian hierarchy hosted by the Department of Anthropology at the Research School of Pacific Studies of The

Australian National University (Vischer 1996b). The paper was essentially an event oriented analysis with a particular focus on precedence relations between allied domains. In my doctoral thesis I then went on to describe the constituent elements of precedence in Ko'a, which I collectively referred to as origin structures (Vischer 1992), in an extension of the term as it had been introduced by Fox (Fox 1995). In a paper published in the 1995 Yearbook of the International Institute of Asian Studies (IIAS) in Leiden (Vischer 1996c) I traced some of the origins of precedence studies and indicated their position in social anthropological theory.

[6] In ritual speech, the subordinate position of the younger brother is aptly described as: 'the elder brother receives the guests // the younger brother prepares the lontar palm leaves for smoking'.

[7] See Contestations: 0.11.28 – 0.14.30. References to the film 'Contestations' (Vischer, 1996a) indicate hours, minutes and seconds.

[8] In disputes over inheritance the Flores district courts use the criterion of who has paid for the mortuary costs to decide who will be awarded rights.

[9] Here precedence may link up with the moral hierarchy or hierarchy of virtue proposed by Kelly (1993) for the Etoro of Papua New Guinea.

[10] See 'Contestations', 0.31.00 - 0.31.20.

[11] Interestingly, many of those present on the beach and certainly some of the people on the capsizing boat must have been aware of the fact that actually it had been my second camera operator who had capsized the boat by positioning himself wrongly, as he was trying to film the unloading. This more obvious line of argumentation was taken up by none of the parties, because the collective focus at that time clearly was on issues of precedence rather than elsewhere.

[12] See 'Contestations': 0.34.05 - 0.35.57.

[13] According to some reports, there used to be a lake inside the Palu'é volcano, similar to the three famous volcanic lakes of Kélimutu on Flores. Volcanic activity appears to have been the cause of its disappearance.

[14] See 'Contestations': 0.00.25 - 0.02.41.

[15] Another aspect of this has to do with the latent antagonism between sacrifiers and sacrificers of that centre. This antagonism is most prominent during the closing phase of the ceremonial cycle. At the closure of the cycle, when sacrifiers and sacrificers ready themselves for the final sacrifice of the 'water buffalo of the domain', the antagonism is expressed in rules of avoidance. At that moment, sacrificers are said to be conceptually hot and dangerous, in line with their ritual office, whereas sacrifiers are supposed to be conceptually cool and beneficial, as is the animal they are offering to the Supreme Being.

[16] See 'Contestations': 0.38.31 - 0.39.10.

[17] See 'Contestations' 0.33.05 - 0.33.42.

[18] See 'Contestations': 0.26.00.

[19] See, 'Contestations': 0.39.37 - 0.42.05.

[20] See 'Contestations': 0.42.36 - 0.44.40.

[21] See 'Contestations':0.46.20 - 0.46.40, 0.47.49 - 0.48.30.

[22] See 'Contestations': 0.46.38 - 0.47.30.

[23] See 'Contestations': 0.48.31 - 0.51.23.

Contributors

ACCIAIOLI, GREG

Greg Acciaioli lectures in Anthropology and Sociology and at the University of Western Australia. He currently researches the intersections of the indigenous people's movement with conservation issues in Indonesia. Most recently, he has co-edited *Biodiversity and human livelihoods in protected areas: case studies from the Malay archipelago*, Cambridge: Cambridge University Press, 2008. Email: *gregory.acciaioli@uwa.edu.au*

BUTTERWORTH, DAVID

David Butterworth received his PhD in anthropology from the University of Melbourne in 2008. His fieldwork in eastern Indonesia focuses on education, ritual, and comparative cosmology. He is currently a Research Assistant with the Resource Management in Asia Pacific Program in the Research School of Pacific and Asian Studies at The Australian National University. Email: *david.butterworth@anu.edu.au*

FORTH, GREGORY

Gregory Forth is Professor and Associate Chair in the Department of Anthropology at the University of Alberta. Based on research conducted on the Indonesian islands of Sumba and Flores, his publications include *Dualism and hierarchy: processes of binary combination in Keo society* (Oxford UP, 2001) and *Guardians of the land in Kelimado* (KITLV Press, 2004). His latest book is entitled *Images of the Wildman in southeast Asia* (Routledge, 2008). Email: *gforth@ualberta.ca*

FOX, JAMES J.

James J. Fox is Emeritus Professor of Anthropology at The Australian National University. His current affiliation is with the Resource Management in Asia Pacific Program in the Research School of Pacific and Asian Studies. He has edited several volumes in the Comparative Austronesian Series. Email: *james.fox@anu.edu.au*

KAARTINEN, TIMO

Timo Kaartinen is University Lecturer and Docent of social anthropology at the University of Helsinki. His PhD dissertation, accepted at the University of Chicago in 2001, was concerned with the motif of long-distance travel in the narratives and rituals of a local society in the Eastern Indonesian islands of Maluku. He is preparing new fieldwork in Indonesia with a focus on a diaspora organized around specific linguistic, historical and temporal awareness. He is co-editor of *Beyond the horizon: essays on myth, history, travel and society*, Finnish Literature Society, 2008. Email: *timo.kaartinen@helsinki.fi*

LEWIS, E.D.

E.D. Lewis holds degrees from Rice and Brown Universities in the USA and The Australian National University. He began fieldwork on Flores in 1977 and has written extensively on the people of Tana 'Ai and Sikka. He is Senior Lecturer in Anthropology at The University of Melbourne. His most recent publications include *Hikayat Kerajaan Sikka* (with Oscar P. Mandalangi) published by Penerbit Ledalero (2008) in Indonesia. *The stranger-kings of Sikka*, Leiden: KITLV Press, is expected to appear in 2009. Email: *edlewis@unimelb.edu.au*

McWILLIAM, ANDREW

Andrew McWilliam is a Fellow in the Department of Anthropology at the Research School of Pacific and Asian Studies, The Australian National University. He has published widely on the ethnography of Timor including the volume, *Paths of origin, gates of life: a study of place and precedence in southwest Timor*, Leiden: KITLV Press, 2002. Email: *andrew.mcwilliam@anu.edu.au*

REUTER, THOMAS A.

Thomas Reuter obtained his PhD in Anthropology from the Research School of Pacific and Asian Studies, The Australian National University, in 1997. He is currently a Senior Research Fellow at Monash University in the School of Social and Political Inquiry. Research for this project was facilitated by grants and fellowships from the Australian Research Council. Research in Bali and more recently in Java has focused prominently on the anthropology of religion, ritual status systems and the cultural politics of representation. Email: *thomas.reuter@arts.monash.edu.au*

SMEDAL, OLAF H.

Olaf H. Smedal obtained his PhD at the University of Oslo and is Associate Professor in Social Anthropology at the University of Bergen. He has conducted long-term fieldwork in Indonesia since the beginning of the 1980s: first among the Lom on Bangka Island, then among the Ngadha in Flores in eastern Indonesia.

Most recently, he has co-edited *Hierarchy: persistence and transformation in social formations*, Oxford and New York: Berghahn Books, 2009. Email: *olaf.smedal@sosantr.uib.no*

VISCHER, MICHAEL P.

Michael P. Vischer holds a PhD in Social Anthropology from The Australian National University. He has been conducting ethnographic field research in Eastern Nusa Tenggara at regular intervals since 1979. He is a private scholar and a practitioner of Chinese medicine living in Basel, Switzerland. Email: *mpvischer@yahoo.com*

www.ingramcontent.com/pod-product-compliance
Lightning Source LLC
Chambersburg PA
CBHW061243270326

41928CB00041B/3394